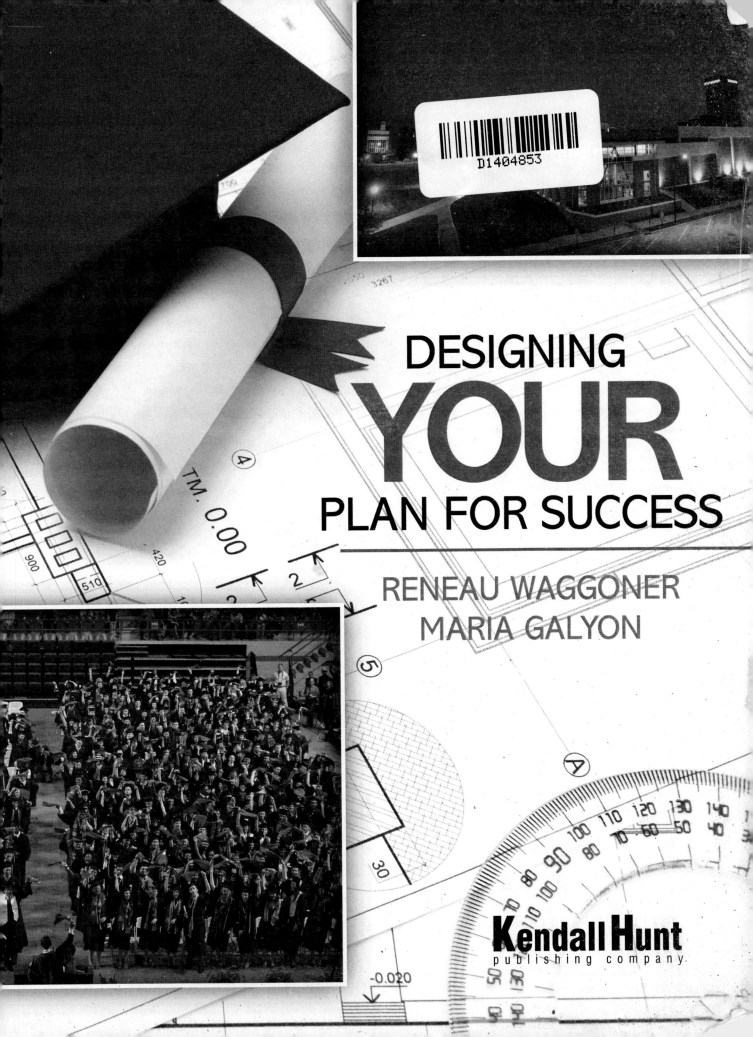

DESIGNING
YOUR
PLAN FOR SUCCESS

RENEAU WAGGONER
MARIA GALYON

Kendall Hunt
publishing company

D1404853

Chapter 1:

This chapter contains adapted material from: "Life-skills for College: A Curriculum for Lifelong Learning" from *Life Skills for College: A Curriculum for Life* by Earl J. Ginter and Ann Shanks Glauser, copyright © 2002 by Earl J. Ginter and Ann Shanks Glauser; "Understanding Motivation" from *College & Career Success*, second edition by Marsha Fralick, copyright © 2003 by Kendall Hunt Publishing Company; "Touching All the Bases" from *Thriving in College and Beyond: Research-Based Strategies for Academic Success and Personal Development* by Cuseo et al. Copyright © 2008 by Kendall Hunt Publishing Company. Reprinted by permission; and "Achieving Your Personal Best" and "Understanding the Way You Learn" from *The Community College: A New Beginning*, third edition by Linda S. Aguilar, Sandra J. Hopper, & Therese M. Kuzlik, copyright © 2001 by Kendall Hunt Publishing Company.

Chapter 2:

This chapter contains adapted material from: "Thinking Critically & Creatively" from *College and Career Success*, second edition by Marsha Fralick, copyright © 2003 by Kendall Hunt Publishing Company; "Learning Strategies for Academic Success" from *Your Utah State Experience: Strategies for Success*, eighth edition by Noelle A. Call and LaVell E. Saunders, copyright © 2002 by Academic Support Services, Utah State University; "Critical Thinking: Developing Critical Skills for the Twenty-First Century" from *Life Skills for College: A Curriculum for Life* by Earl J. Ginter and Ann Shanks Glauser, copyright © 2002 by Earl J. Ginter and Ann Shanks Glauser; "Researching" from *Get What You Want Out of College* by Elizabeth Boucher and John Pigg, copyright © 2003 by Elizabeth Boucher and John Pigg; "Using the Internet as a Research Tool" and "Developing Critical Thinking Skills" from *The University Mind: Essential Skills for Academic Success* by The California University Regents, © 1998 by Kendall Hunt Publishing Company; and "The Lab Partner" from *First Time Around: Case Studies of the Freshman Year Experience* by Michael Welsh, copyright © 1999 by Kendall Hunt Publishing Company.

Credits continued on page 419 and is an extension of the copyright information.

Cover images courtesy Western Kentucky University. Background image © Shutterstock, Inc.

Kendall Hunt
publishing company

www.kendallhunt.com
Send all inquiries to:
4050 Westmark Drive
Dubuque, IA 52004-1840

Copyright © 2014 by Kendall Hunt Publishing Company

ISBN 978-1-4652-4958-6

Printed in the United States of America

Table of Contents

DURING (D)

AFTER (A)

DURING

AFTER (A)

BEFORE (B)

DURING (D)

AFTER (A)

BEFORE (B)

DURING (D)

AFTER (A)

DURING (D)

AFTER (A)

BEFORE (B)

DURING (D)

AFTER (A)

BEFORE (B)

DURING (D)

AFTER (A)

Acknowledgements

We would like to thank Andrew Cullen, Tom Meacham, Craig Biggs, Stacey Biggs, Angela Gray, Dan Kesterson, Maureen Gibson; and our team at Kendall Hunt – Lara Sanders, Lara McCombie and Linda Chapman. We also want to thank our families for their unfailing love and support. Extra special thanks to Carlous Yates for this opportunity; for his support and contributions to this project; and most of all, for his commitment to students and their success.

Introduction to College – Where Am I?

INTRODUCTION TO COURSE

What's it all about? It's all about YOU! YOU becoming self-aware and using your self discoveries to make adjustments and changes; YOU evolving from a passive learner to an active learner and critical thinker; YOU learning *and* applying the strategies and skills both in and out of the classroom; and YOU adjusting to college life by learning about its structure, its mission, and its services.

This is both a challenge and a fact. YOU are challenged to learn new ways of thinking and new ways of behaving that will ensure your success. And the fact is, this course is all about success, YOUR success. Your success in academics, in your chosen career field, and in your personal life. Picture yourself as a success! Imagine a photo of YOU with a cap and gown as you graduate with your degree; picture yourself in a suit as YOU go on an interview; picture yourself in front of your new home or your new car; see yourself in your own

[Insert a picture of YOU here]

personal vision of success. We do. But the fact is, we (your instructors and the professional staff) can't make you succeed. YOU have to make the commitment to work hard, complete all assignments, network, take advantage of the services available, and get involved in campus and community activities.

And finally, this is a dare! Dare to dream, dare to realize your potential, dare to make your dreams come true. We dare YOU!

WHAT DOES BEING "SUCCESSFUL" MEAN TO YOU?*

"Achieving a desired outcome is how *success is commo*nly defined. The word *success* derives from the Latin root *successus,* meaning to follow or come after" (as in the word *succession).* Thus, by definition, success involves an order or sequence of actions that lead to a desired outcome. The process starts with identifying an end (goal) and then finding a means (sequence of steps) to reach that goal (achieving success). Goal setting is the first step in the process of becoming successful because it gives you something specific to strive for and ensures that you start off in the right direction. Studies consistently show that setting goals is a more effective self-motivational strategy than simply telling yourself that you should try hard and do your best (Boekaerts, Pintrich, & Zeidner, 2000; Locke & Latham, 1990).

By setting goals, you show initiative—you initiate the process of gaining control of your future and taking charge of your life. When you take initiative, you demonstrate what psychologists call an *internal* locus of control; you believe that the locus (location or source) of control for events in your life is inside of you, rather than being *external,* or outside of you and beyond your control—for instance, determined by such factors as innate ability, luck, chance, or fate (Rotter, 1966; Carlson Buskist, Heth, & Schmaltz, 2007). They believe that success is influenced more by attitude, effort, commitment, and preparation than by natural ability or inborn intelligence (Jernigan, 2004).

> *"I'm a great believer in luck, and I find the harder 1 work the more I have of it"*
>
> —Thomas Jefferson, third president of the United States

Research has revealed that individuals with a strong internal locus of control display the following characteristics:

1. Greater independence and self-direction (Van Overwalle, Mervielde, & De Schuyer, 1995);
2. More accurate self-assessment (Hashaw, Hammond, & Rogers, 1990);
3. Higher levels of learning and achievement (Wilhite, 1990); and
4. Better physical health (Maddi, 2002; Seligman, 1991).

> *"The future is literally in our hands to mold as we like. But we cannot wait until tomorrow. Tomorrow is now."*
>
> —Eleanor Roosevelt, UN diplomat and humanitarian

An internal locus also contributes to the development of another positive trait that psychologists call *self-efficacy*—the belief that you have power to produce a positive effect on the outcomes of your life (Bandura, 1994). People with low to them rather than taking charge and making things happen for them. College students with a strong sense of self-efficacy believe they're in control of their educational success and can take control of their future regardless of their past or current circumstances.

"What lies behind us and what lies in front of us are small matters compared to what lies within us"

—Ralph Waldo Emerson, 19th-century American essayist and lecturer

People with a strong sense of self-efficacy initiate action, exert effort, and sustain that effort until they reach their goals. If they encounter setbacks or bad breaks along the way, they don't give up or give in; they persevere or push on (Bandura, 1986; 1997). They don't have a false sense of entitlement—that they're entitled to or owed anything; they believe success is something that's earned and the harder they work at it, the more likely they'll get it.

Students with a strong sense of *academic* self-efficacy have been found to:

1. Put considerable effort into their studies;
2. Use active-learning strategies;
3. Capitalize on campus resources; and
4. Persist in the face of obstacles (Multon, Brown, & Lent, 1991; Zimmerman, 1995; 2000);

* From *Thriving in College and Beyond: Research-Based Strategies for Academic Success and Personal Development* by Jospeh B. Cuseo, Aaron Thompson, Michele Campagna, and Viki S. Fecas. Copyright © 2013 by Kendall Hunt Publishing Company. Reprinted by permission.

"Nothing ever comes to one that is worth having, except as a result of hard work."

—Booker T. Washington, born-in-slavery Black educator, author, and advisor to Republican presidents.

HOW DO I GO ABOUT IT?

You understand now that it's all about you and you've accepted our dare. But how do you go about it? We know that many of you work, have kids, plan to transfer, have been out of school for a while, may be the first person in your family to go to college, and the list goes on. You enter from various points: straight out of high school, completed GED, lost your job, etc. These challenges often make it difficult the first semester of college, which is why this course, and the strategies you will learn, are all the more helpful to you.

But to be honest, there is only *one strategy* that is the key to your success. By following this one strategy, you will be successful academically, professionally, and personally. So what is this strategy? The strategy is **BDA**, which is short for **Before (B), During (D), and After (A).**

BEFORE (B)

There are several tasks to be accomplished before you even get started. The Before (B) section of the strategy focuses on *preparation, self-awareness,* and *planning*.

Preparation

You must be ready for the expectations and requirements of college, which include . . .

- **Purchasing all required course materials**
- **Completing all assigned tasks** (readings, homework, research papers, projects, etc.) before class
- **Checking your e-mail, Blackboard, and Student Self-Service (PeopleSoft) daily**
- **Anticipating the lecture** (preview, review, ask questions—all before you get to class!)

Self-Awareness

You have to know yourself and where you are in order to improve and become a better person. You can accomplish this by . . .

- **Telling the truth**—about your habits, actions, preferences
- **Completing assessments**—about your personality, how you learn best, what your career interests are, etc.
- **Being accountable**—taking responsibility for your actions; adjusting your behavior for the setting you are in—there are certain ways you interact with friends/family in an informal setting (home, family events) and another, more formal and business-like, way that you behave in an academic/professional setting (college, classroom, work).

Planning

You have to know what you want (your goal) and then figure out how to get it (your plan), which includes . . .

- **Conducting research** (on you, on the topic/subject at hand, on success strategies, etc.)
- **Developing a plan** (how will you balance work, school, fun, and other responsibilities)
- **Using a planner** (to keep track of your assignments, to prioritize your activities, and to track whether you have completed them and what changes you need to make)

DURING (D)

There are also things you should be doing while you are in the process of becoming a better student, better professional, and better person. The During (D) section of the strategy focuses on one thing—*action*.

Action

- **Writing things down** (taking notes as you read and during a lecture; commitments and tasks in your planner; making mind maps)
- **Learning and practicing supplemental strategies** (additional tips and "tools of the trade")
- **Being an active learner** (watching for clues from professors, developing your own tools, thinking critically about what you read and hear)
- **Communicating effectively** (using instructor's office hours, expressing your ideas in a professional manner—without anger or using obscenities)
- **Self-Evaluation**—While you are in the process, think about your thinking and analyze your behavior. Are you utilizing the strategies you have just learned?

AFTER (A)

The work doesn't stop there. After you complete the process, there are additional tasks to be completed. The After (A) section of the strategy focuses on **review** and **revision**.

Review

- **The strategies you have learned and practiced** (that help you evolve into a more active learner)
- **The things you wrote down** (reading notes, notes from lecture, commitments and tasks in your planner)
- **Your study plan** (Did I complete my first review within 24 hours? Did I schedule additional daily reviews in my planner? Am I covering the right materials? Am I eliminating distractions?)

Revision

- **Make any corrections and fill in any blanks** (on your notes and tests, in your planner)

Self-Modification

- **Analyze what worked and didn't work** (Did I spend enough time on review? Did I try to cram? Am I reading critically or just skimming? Am I writing things down, taking notes, using my planner?)
- **Make any needed changes to what you are currently doing . . . or not doing** (the amount of time and types of materials you are studying, how you are using your time)

What is the next step? Start the process all over again. Is it really that simple? Yes and no. Yes, in that this really is all it takes. No, if you are not used to it. At first, it will seem difficult or that it takes too much time. Just know that it is worth it in the end and you will actually save yourself a lot of time, frustration, and potential setbacks. You should also know that this textbook is designed to help you make the most of your learning and is divided into sections by the BDA strategy, which will help you focus your study and assist you in the learning process. Finally, please know that you have support from faculty, staff, and support services, all of which are here to help you. With that in mind, it's time to begin. Go ahead and turn the page. Let's get started.

WHERE AM I?

Where am I? What is this place? and other questions are often asked about the educational institution known as college. What is college?

According to the Oxford English Dictionary the word *college* refers to "a society of scholars . . . formed for the purpose of study or instruction." The words "a society of scholars" imply that both students and professors are actively engaged in the learning process. In a real sense a college is a dynamic city of learning for all its inhabitants. In the United States of America the first center for higher learning was Harvard, and it is widely recognized for its excellence since its inception in 1636.

While a college's unique history, traditions, and achievements certainly can contribute to why a student completes and sends an application packet, is it possible there are other concerns that play a larger role in the student's decision? If you were to ask other students why they are attending this or some other college, you would hear them offer numerous reasons. Taking a closer look at their reasons would most likely reveal a common theme. They are here to "get a better job." A college certainly helps one prepare for a career, but a college also offers many other opportunities. A college can help you to develop the skills you need for life-long learning.

Colleges are environments where students soon discover, compared to earlier learning environments such as high school, they will not only be required to work hard but more importantly must be self-motivated to do well. Well-established colleges tend be competitive academic environments because the academic potential of students rises over time, which has a direct impact on the difficulty level of the college. Established colleges most often select the academically strongest students from the pool of applicants. In such competitive environments, made up of essentially "good students," many beginning students will experience a drop in their performance because they are competing according to a new set of standards. In some cases the same effort that may have resulted in an A in high school now results in a C or lower.

BEFORE (B)

Before you begin college, there are several tasks (tasks related to *preparation, self-awareness,* and *planning*) that need to be completed and information that you need to know, such as:

- **Understanding how college is different than high school and other forms of education.**
- **Understanding the value of a college education**
- **Knowing what you want from college**
- **Choosing a college**
- **Becoming a student**

HOW IS COLLEGE DIFFERENT FROM HIGH SCHOOL AND OTHER FORMS OF EDUCATION?

College is entirely different from high school and adult literacy programs, different in structure, administration, focus, and academic rigor. The primary differences between high school and college are indicated on the following chart:

HOW IS COLLEGE DIFFERENT FROM HIGH SCHOOL?

Personal Freedom in High School	Personal Freedom in College
• High school is *mandatory* and *free* (unless you choose other options).	• College is *voluntary* and *expensive*.
• Your time is usually structured by others.	• You manage your own time.
• You need permission to participate in extracurricular activities.	• You must decide whether to participate in extracurricular activities. (*Hint:* Choose wisely in the first semester and then add later.)
• You need money for special purchases or events.	• You need money to meet basic necessities.
• You can count on parents and teachers to remind you of your responsibilities and to guide you in setting priorities.	• You will be faced with a large number of moral and ethical decisions you have not had to face previously. *You* must balance your responsibilities and set priorities.
• Guiding principle: You will usually be told what your responsibilities are and corrected if your behavior is out of line.	• Guiding principle: You're old enough to take responsibility for what you do and don't do, as well as for the consequences of your decisions.

High School Classes	College Classes
• Each day you proceed from one class directly to another.	• You often have hours between classes; class times vary throughout the day and evening.
• You spend 6 hours each day—30 hours a week—in class.	• You spend 12 to 16 hours each week in class.
• The school year is 36 weeks long; some classes extend over both semesters and some do not.	• The academic year is divided into two separate 15-week semesters, plus a week after each semester for exams.
• Most of your classes are arranged for you.	• You arrange your own schedule in consultation with your academic advisor. Schedules tend to look lighter than they really are.
• Teachers carefully monitor class attendance.	• Professors may not formally take roll, but they are still likely to know whether or not you attended.
• Classes generally have no more than 35 students.	• Classes may number 100 students or more.
• You are provided with textbooks at little or no expense.	• You need to budget substantial funds for text books, which will usually cost more than $200 each semester.
• You are not responsible for knowing what it takes to graduate.	• Graduation requirements are complex, and differ for different majors and sometimes different years. You are expected to know those that apply to you.

High School Teachers	College Professors
• Teachers check your completed homework.	• Professors may not always check completed homework, but they will assume you can perform the same tasks on tests.
• Teachers remind you of your incomplete work.	• Professors may not remind you of incomplete work.
• Teachers approach you if they believe you need assistance.	• Professors are usually open and helpful, but most expect you to initiate contact if you need assistance.
• Teachers are often available for conversation before, during, or after class.	• Professors expect and want you to attend their scheduled office hours.
• Teachers have been trained in teaching methods to assist in imparting knowledge to students.	• Professors have been trained as experts in their particular areas of research.
• Teachers provide you with information you missed when you were absent.	• Professors expect you to get from classmates any notes from classes you missed.
• Teachers present material to help you understand the material in the textbook.	• Professors may not follow the textbook. Instead, to amplify the text, they may give illustrations, provide background information, or discuss research about the topic you are studying. Or, they may expect *you* to relate the classes to the textbook readings.
• Teachers often write information on the board to be copied in your notes.	• Professors may lecture nonstop, expecting you to identify the important points in your notes. When professors write on the board, it may be to amplify the lecture, not to summarize it. Good notes are a must.
• Teachers impart knowledge and facts, sometimes drawing direct connections and leading you through the thinking process.	• Professors expect you to think about and synthesize seemingly unrelated topics.
• Teachers often take time to remind you of assignments and due dates.	• Professors expect you to read, save, and consult the course syllabus (outline); the syllabus spells out exactly what is expected of you, when it is due, and how you will be graded.

(continued)

Studying in High School	Studying in College
• You may study outside of class as little as 0 to 2 hours a week, and this may be mostly last-minute test preparation.	• You need to study at least 2 to 3 hours outside of class for each hour in class.
• You often need to read or hear presentations only once to learn all you need to learn about them.	• You need to review class notes and text material regularly.
• You are expected to read short assignments that are then discussed, and often re-taught, in class.	• You are assigned substantial amounts of reading and writing which may not be directly addressed in class.
• Guiding principle: You will usually be told in class what you needed to learn from assigned readings.	• Guiding principle: It's up to you to read and understand the assigned material; lectures and assignments proceed from the assumption that you've already done so.

Tests in High School	Tests in College
• Testing is frequent and covers small amounts of material.	• Testing is usually infrequent and may be cumulative, covering large amounts of material. You, not the professor, need to organize the material to prepare for the test. A particular course may have only 2 or 3 tests in a semester.
• Makeup tests are often available.	• Makeup tests are seldom an option; if they are, you need to request them.
• Teachers frequently rearrange test dates to avoid conflict with school events.	• Professors in different courses usually schedule tests without regard to the demands of other courses or outside activities.
• Teachers frequently conduct review sessions, point out the most important concepts.	• Professors rarely offer review sessions, and when they do, they expect you to be an active participant, one who comes prepared with questions.
• Mastery is usually seen as the ability to reproduce what you were taught in the form in which it was presented to you, or to solve the kinds of problems you were shown how to solve.	• Mastery is often seen as the ability to apply what you've learned to new situations or to solve new kinds of problems.

Grades in High School	Grades in College
• Grades are given for most assigned work.	• Grades may not be provided for all assigned work.
• Consistently good homework grades may help raise your overall grade when test grades are low.	• Grades on tests and major papers usually provide most of the course grade.
• Extra credit projects are often available to help you raise your grade.	• Extra credit projects cannot, generally speaking, be used to raise a grade in a college course.
• Initial test grades, especially when they are low, may not have an adverse effect on your final grade.	• Watch out for your *first* tests. These are usually "wake-up calls" to let you know what is expected—but they also may account for a substantial part of your course grade. You may be shocked when you get your grades. If you receive notice of low grades on either an Early-Term or a Mid-Semester Progress Report, see your academic adviser or visit the Learning Center.
• You may graduate as long as you have passed all required courses with a grade of D or higher.	• You may graduate only if your average in classes meets the departmental standard—typically 2.0 or C.
• Guiding principle: "Effort counts." Courses are usually structured to reward a "good-faith effort."	• Guiding principle: "Results count." Though "good faith effort" is important in regard to the professor's willingness to help you *achieve* good results, it will not *substitute* for results in the grading process.

Other forms of education may have unique differences in addition to the ones listed above. For example, work-related training could have more one-on-one interaction with the instructor/trainer but could also be more intense and fast-paced. In online classes, the student/instructor interaction and feedback may be less frequent. Whether you are coming to college as a first-generation college student (you are the first person in your family to attend college), recent high school graduate, GED recipient, or returning after being out in the workforce, you must be prepared to adapt to these differences in order to be successful in your classes.

WHAT IS THE VALUE OF A COLLEGE EDUCATION?

Many college students say that getting a satisfying job that pays well and achieving financial security are important reasons for attending college. By going to college you can get a job that pays more per hour. You can work fewer hours to earn a living and have more time for leisure activities. You can spend your time at work doing something that you like to do. A report issued by the Census Bureau in 2011 listed the following education and income statistics for all races and both genders throughout the United States. Lifetime income assumes that a person works forty years before retirement.

Notice that income rises with the educational level. A person with a bachelor's degree earns almost twice as much as a high school graduate. Of course these are average figures across the nation. Some individuals earn higher or lower salaries. People have assumed that you would certainly be rich if you were a millionaire. College won't make you an instant millionaire, but over a lifetime you earn over a million and a half dollars by having an associate's degree. People fantasize about winning the lottery. The reality is that the probability of winning the lottery is very low. In the long run, you have a better chance of improving your financial status by going to college. You will learn more about this in Chapter 11.

Money is only one of the values of going to college. Can you think of other reasons to attend college? Here are some less tangible reasons . . .

- **College helps you to develop your potential.**
- **College opens the door to many satisfying careers.**
- **College prepares you to be an informed citizen and fully participate in the democratic process.**
- **College increases your understanding and widens your view of the world.**
- **College allows you to participate in a conversation with the great minds of all times and places. For example, reading the work of Plato is like having a conversation with that famous philosopher. You can continue great conversations with your faculty and fellow students.**
- **College helps to increase your confidence, self-esteem, and self-respect.**

WHAT DO I WANT FROM COLLEGE?

Succeeding in college requires time and effort. You will have to give up some of your time spent on leisure activities and working. You will give up some time spent with your friends and families. Making sacrifices and working hard is easier if you know what you want to achieve through your efforts. One of the first steps in motivating yourself to be successful in college is to have a clear and specific understanding of your reasons for attending college. Are you attending college as a way to obtain a satisfying career? Is financial security one of your goals? Will you feel more satisfied if you are living up to your potential? What are your hopes and dreams, and how will college help you to achieve your goals?

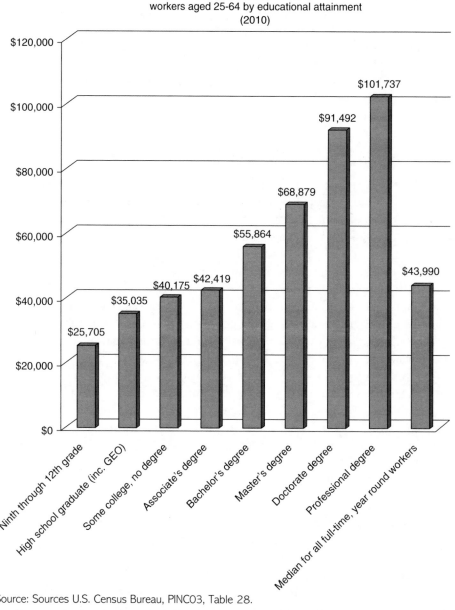

Median earnings for full-time, year-round
workers aged 25-64 by educational attainment
(2010)

Source: Sources U.S. Census Bureau, PINC03, Table 28.
http//www.censusBowthes/www/epstables/032011/new03_028html

In addition, the Census Bureau released a report, Education and Synthetic Work-Life Earnings Estimates (pdf), in September, 2011 providing projected lifetime earnings for males and females by both educational attainment and race/ethnicity. This represents an effort to show the long-term consequences of such education differences. As the graph below demonstrates, the overall trend for all groups is that income goes up as educational attainment increases, though the nature of the benefit varies by both gender and race/ethnicity.

When you are having difficulties or doubts about your ability to finish your college education, remember your hopes and dreams and your plans for the future. It is a good idea to write these ideas down, think about them, and revise them from time to time.

CHOOSING A COLLEGE

The reasons that students enter an institution of higher learning are as diverse as the typical student body of said institution. For instance, students enroll in college to get away from their parents, to find a mate, to find themselves, to delay entering the workforce, to get a job promotion, to change careers, to increase their salary at their present job (you get the picture). Regardless of the reasons for enrolling in college, there are some important aspects that every student should research.

First Things to Think about When Choosing Higher Education

The first decision that anyone who is considering a college degree must make is what type of school they would like to attend. There are actually many different factors in this decision.

—First, *what degree would you like to earn?* Undergraduate degrees include one to two year certificate programs, two to three year associate's degree programs, and three to six year bachelor's degree programs. These can all take longer if you attend part-time. Also available are five to ten year combined bachelor's-graduate programs, often in professional fields like medicine, architecture, engineering, and law.

Certificate programs are often in technical or vocational fields, and can certify you to practice a trade like cosmetology or auto repair. **Associate's degrees**, sometimes referred to as 2-year degrees, can be associates of science, associates of applied science (vocational), associates of the arts, or one of many other more specific types, often prepare you for entry-level work in fields like medical assisting, paralegal work, and child care. They can also provide an opportunity for students to bolster their academic performance before transferring to a bachelor's program or for students looking to save money by spending part of their college career at a less expensive institution. While associate's degrees may be referred to as 2-year degrees they are actually earned when the required number of credits for the degree are earned. Most associate's degrees are approximately 60 credit hours. Both certificate programs and associate's degrees are often earned at a community and/or technical college.

Bachelor's degrees can be bachelor's of science, bachelor's of arts, bachelor's of music, bachelor's of fine arts, and many other more specific degrees. Bachelor's degrees are sometimes referred to as 4-year degrees but like the associate's, the length of time it takes to get the degree depends on how long it takes to earn the required number of credits for the degree. Most bachelor's degrees are approximately 120 credit hours. They prepare you for further graduate or professional study in your field or for many kinds of employment, such as teaching, business, registered nursing, or advertising.

—Second, *what would you like to study?* Different schools have different curricular strengths. Some schools specialize in the arts, others in technology. Some larger schools have programs in fields like nursing or paralegal studies that are very separate from the rest of the institution. If you would like a broad general education, in addition to your focus, you would choose a different school than if you wanted intensive study in just one field.

—Third, *what features are you looking for?* Will you need a school with student housing and meal plans or do you need support services for day students? Would you like to participate in athletics or do you need academic support services? Can you attend full time in the day or do you need evening or weekend programs?

—Fourth, *what geographical area are you looking for?* Do you need a school that is close to home or do you want to get away? Think about this carefully. Going to school across the country may seem like a good idea, but coming home on breaks will be difficult and costly. You may get homesick and miss your family and friends. And the culture shock that comes with a move from, say, a rural town in the south to a big northern city may be too much. On the other hand, don't cross your dream school off of your list just because it is far away. It may prove to be the right place for you.

Also important is whether the area you desire is urban or rural. Urban schools often have access to more recreation and cultural activities, but they may lack the grassy campus and community feeling of rural schools. And small-town schools may have surprising and fun resources!

—Fifth, ***consider the size and academic reputation of the school.*** If you enjoy anonymity or want to study something obscure, you'll probably want a large university. However, if you don't enjoy competition or if you are lacking in self-confidence, you might benefit from the personal attention at a small liberal-arts college. Some people want highly ranked competitive colleges. Others enjoy the nurturing aspects of a noncompetitive college or need someplace that will accept them with low high school grades.

Researching the **accreditation** of your chosen college is important. A college or university's accreditation ensures the integrity of the school and that credits earned at the institution will transfer to other institutions. Most public state institutions are credentialed and make it relatively easy for students to transfer credits. For example, most state institutions in Kentucky are accredited by the Southern Association of Colleges and Schools (SACS). If an institution is not accredited by this, or one of the other five regional accrediting agencies in the United States, most likely the credits will not transfer to other institutions—as is the case for many **proprietary (for-profit)** institutions. Be sure you research this so you are confident in the institution you have chosen.

And don't forget to think about things like the gender balance at your school, the percentage of students from your racial or ethnic background, how diverse it is (culturally, racially, ethnically, religiously, and in terms of age, disability, and socio-economic status), the kind and amount of financial aid awarded, and whether you will find a religious or cultural community you are comfortable with.

BECOMING A STUDENT

Following the selection of a college, there are other factors to consider and other processes to complete:

- **Admissions**
- **Assessment**
- **Orientation**
- **Academic Advising**
- **Registration**
- **Housing**
- **Tuition and Fees**

While completing these processes, you will be exposed to a whole new language filled with college terminology relating to policies and procedures, functions of the administrative offices, and the college environment in general. Faculty and staff will use these terms and expect you to know what they mean.

Admissions

Once you have selected your school, you must complete the process by which you are accepted into the college, collectively called the admissions process coordinated by the **Admissions Office**. You are required to submit an application and pay a fee to process this application. You are also required to submit a copy of your college entrance exam, such as the **ACT** (American College Test) and/or **SAT** (Scholastic Aptitude Test). Most colleges have a minimum score you must obtain on the entrance exam in order to be accepted into their school. In this case, they are considered to have a **selective admissions** policy. If the college does not require a minimum score on the ACT or SAT and accepts students with high school diplomas and/or **GED** (General Education Development diploma), they are said to have an **open admissions** policy. Even if the college has an open admissions policy, they may still require an entrance or an **assessment** exam that measures your skills in critical areas such as reading, writing, and math. The results of these types of measurements determine your current skill level and knowledge base of the particular subject area, as well as the courses you may enroll in. These courses are often mandatory based on the college's placement policy. If your skills are deficient in any of the areas, you may be required to take **transitional/developmental courses** (also called remedial courses) that improve your skills in the deficient area. On the other hand, if you feel you have mastered the content of an area, such as math, language, or computers, because you participated in advanced placement courses in high school or professional development opportunities at your job, you can take a **CLEP** (College-Level Examination Program) exam and receive credit for what you already know.

As a student of your college, you will need to obtain a copy of the **college catalog**, the college publication which outlines admissions information, tuition and fees, academic information (calendar, policies, regulations, standards, classification), college degree requirements, **course descriptions** (outlines of what will be taught in the course that are classified by a number and title), and services available to students.

Assessment

The general function of Assessment was outlined in the previous section. Some institutions administer testing to determine the academic skill level of students who have not taken the ACT or SAT and received a score determined by the institution for admission or for eligibility to take certain classes. Assessment Offices may also administer English as Second Language (ESL) testing, proctored exams for online classes, and testing for certain programs or certifications.

Orientation

Most colleges and universities provide some type of orientation program for their new students. It may be required or it may be voluntary. Participating in whatever kind of orientation your school has is always a good idea. This is your opportunity to learn about the environment where you will be spending the next years. Every attempt will be made to inform you of the services and facilities that your college offers, but if there is some service not mentioned, ask questions. It is still your responsibility to seek out help.

Academic Advising

Full-time students at most colleges/universities are usually assigned an academic advisor. **Academic advisors** may be full- or part-time faculty, administrators, or other staff that provide assistance with deciding on a major, selecting courses, teaching study skills, or a number of other services for students.

The advisor will assist with course selection that fulfills the college degree requirements and transfer information either in his or her office or the **Advising Center**. Advisors are there to assist you in your selection process, but don't expect them to do your "homework" for you. For example, familiarize yourself with the college catalog (available on-line), the curriculum guide for your program/major, and the Academic Program Plan (APP) before meeting with your academic advisor.

When you meet with him/her, bring along your placement test results, and/or ACT or SAT scores, the schedule of classes for the semester, an advisor summary listing all previous courses taken at your institution, and/or transcripts from other colleges and universities. By having everything you need, you will make the best use of your time with your advisor.

Whether you have declared a major or are undecided, you are expected to have reviewed the college catalog which explains the **core curriculum**.

Most colleges and universities have some kind of core curriculum. This means that all students are required to take the same group of courses. The purpose of these courses is to provide you with a well rounded education, not just to prepare you for an occupation.

General education courses that form the core curriculum typically include humanities (theater, art, music, etc.); English; math (college algebra); physical education; communications (basic public speaking or interpersonal communication); social sciences (sociology, psychology, anthropology, etc.); natural sciences (chemistry, physics, biology, etc.), and history. The advisor will also review whether or not your major offers an **elective**, which is any course of interest to you that is not specified for your major.

The advisor will assist you with schedule planning. In planning your schedule, consider your **course load** (the amount of credit hours you are taking). Labs and physical education courses are generally 1 or 2 credit hours; other courses are generally 3 or 4 credit hours. In order to figure out how much time you should invest in college, take the number of credit hours you have or will register for and multiply that amount by two (2) for outside study; then add the 2 together. For instance, if you are taking 12 credit hours, you should allot 24 hours (number of credit hours times 2) per week outside of class for study, research, review, and completing assignments. Therefore, you will have invested 36 hours per week in college. This is important to note when planning work schedules and considering your family and personal commitments.

Registration

Following advising, you must be officially enrolled into the courses you have selected by completing the registration process. Most colleges now use an online registration process. Registering requires you to know the prefix and course number for each class you are registering for. This information is generally obtained from your advisor and by referring to the academic information provided on your college's website. **Course numbers** are assigned to indicate the level of difficulty for a class. Generally 100 level courses are taken first and may be some of your general education classes and/or prerequisites to 200+ level courses.

Just as there are policies and procedures for registering for a class, there are also those for dropping/adding courses and for withdrawing from a course. The **drop/add** process allows you to be taken out of a course (drop) and select a new course (add) and generally takes place from the beginning of the registration process to a few days during the first week of school. Once the semester is underway, if for some reason you cannot complete the course, you may **withdraw** from a course with or without the instructor's signature depending on the guidelines set forth on the **academic calendar**. The academic calendar highlights the important dates in the academic year such as registration, first and last days to drop classes (and the percentage of refund you are entitled to for the course), holidays, vacations, and mid-term and final exams.

Once you are enrolled and begin taking courses, the official record of the courses you take and the grades you make in them form a **transcript**. This transcript is required when transferring to other schools and in the hiring process for a position in your field. The grades you make in the courses tally into your **GPA** (grade point average).

Calculating Your Grade Point Average

Grades are one way you can track your academic progress or how you are doing on the road to reaching your academic and career goals. Grades are used to evaluate your success in school at the end of each semester. Students who intend to transfer or graduate need to be concerned about their Grade Point Average (GPA). Your grade point average is determined by the number of credits you attempt during a term. Each grade is assigned a value and is worth a certain number of quality points. Most colleges use a 4.0 grading system, although some colleges have a 5.0 grading system.

A = 4 points	**A = 5 points**
B = 3 points	**B = 4 points**
C = 2 points	**C = 3 points**
D = 1 point	**D = 2 points**
E/F = 0 points	**E = 1 point**
	F = 0 points

At most colleges, the traditional letter grading system is used (A, B, C, D, and E/F). Different schools have different rules about computing grade point averages (GPA) with marks of W (withdrawals). Also, any developmental/transitional level class grades are generally not used in calculating GPA.

Knowing how to calculate and keeping up with your GPA is important for a variety of reasons. Many programs require a certain GPA for admission. Scholarships usually require maintaining a certain GPA in order to keep receiving funds. Financial Aid sources also look at your GPA when considering future funding. Also, your GPA helps you see how you are doing overall on your road to reaching your goals.

To calculate GPA, complete the following steps:

1. **Check for any developmental courses** (course number 0 – 99). These courses are listed on the transcript, used in determining your full-time student status, and included in financial aid, but are not used in calculating the GPA. Cross these courses off when calculating GPA.
2. **Determine point equivalent** (A = 4, B = 3, C = 2, D = 1, E/F = 0).
3. **Determine quality points** by multiplying the point equivalent by the number of credit hours.
4. **Add 2 columns: the total number of credit hours you attempted (in 100 level or above courses) and the total quality points.**
5. **Calculate GPA by dividing the total quality points by the total number of credit hours attempted that count towards GPA (excludes developmental courses).**

To calculate your GPA, you have a ratio of total quality points earned divided by semester hours attempted. Total quality points are the product of the point equivalent for the grade earned (A = 4, B = 3, C = 2, D = 1, E/F = 0) multiplied by the credit hours of the class. For example:

Course	Grade	Point Equivalent		Credit Hours		Total Quality Points
ENG 101	B	3	×	3	=	9
PSY 110	C	2	×	3	=	6
BIO 112	B	3	×	4	=	12
MAT 150	A	4	×	3	=	12
TOTALS				13		39

$$\text{GPA} = \frac{\text{Total Quality Points}}{\text{Total Credit Hours}} = \frac{39}{13} = 3.0$$

In order to request a copy of your transcript, contact your school's Registrar's Office which also serves to evaluate your work from other colleges/universities and often determines whether or not you meet the qualifications for graduation.

Another aspect of being enrolled in college is determining your classification. Your classification depends on how many credit hours you have completed. For example, you remain a **freshman** until you have completed 30 credit hours; a **sophomore** until you have completed 60 credit hours; a **junior** until you have completed 90 credit hours; and a **senior** after you have completed 90 hours.

Housing

Depending on your institution, you may be required to live in a residence hall during your freshman year in an effort to acclimatize you to your new world; establish friends; and become involved in your new community.

The housing process is coordinated by the **Office of Residential Housing** (or Housing Office) and involves applying for a residence hall and submitting any applicable fees. You will typically be asked to rank your preferences for the residence hall and sometimes the roommate.

If your institution does have residence halls, it is important to establish a roommate contract in the very beginning. Simply talk with your roommate and discuss your views on quiet time, visitors, use of other's personal items, etc. Following this discussion, you will need to come to an agreement about how such issues will be handled. Be willing to compromise.

Some institutions (most community colleges) are commuter campuses and do not provide the option of living in a residence hall.

Tuition and Fees

As soon as you make the decision to attend college, you should begin planning how you will finance your education. Will your parents pay for it? Will you be working? Are you eligible for financial aid or scholarships?

You will be charged tuition for every credit hour in which you enroll. Variable course fees for such things as photocopies, computer time, and lab equipment are charged in addition to tuition. The course fee is usually listed on the schedule. The college may add other fees such as a registration or testing fee, and you will also be charged a student activity fee. This money helps pay for such things as student clubs, entertainment, special speakers, the school newspaper, literary magazine, or other publications that are distributed free to students.

Regardless of the college you attend and regardless of the payment process, you should always pay early or confirm your payment method as early as possible. This protects your classes and student status as well as helps you to avoid standing in long lines.

Financial Aid

The **Financial Aid Office** coordinates the distribution of funds such as loans, grants, scholarships, and work study. Also, a number of other factors determine your financial standing with an institution. The **Bursar's Office** (Business Office) via the **Cashier's Office** coordinates student records of payment, such as tuition, fees, and fines (parking, failure to return library books, etc.) and may place a red flag or hold on your record if

---

HELPFUL HINTS ABOUT FINANCIAL AID

Apply early! There are many sources of financial aid and the deadlines of these sources vary by state and by institution. Therefore, it is to your advantage to apply as early as possible to qualify for as many types of financial aid as possible. You should apply as early as possible for the next academic calendar year.

Apply on-line (http://www.fafsa.ed.gov)! The on-line application process will notify if you have made an error or not filled in a portion of the application as you move through the screens. You can make changes before the final submission. If you apply by mail, the process is much longer (especially if you have to make corrections).

Know your institution's financial aid policies! Generally, after all tuition and fees (i.e. student services, security, and technology) are paid, any remaining monies come to you residually via debit card. Some schools, incorporate book vouchers into your financial aid package. These book vouchers are communicated to the bookstore(s) and you purchase your books from your financial aid (before receiving residually via debit card). This is often limited to a two-week window and if you do not purchase your books during the allotted time frame, you will have to pay for your books and be reimbursed later residually via debit card.

Make sure your financial aid package is complete prior to payment deadlines! These deadlines are posted in the class schedule. Make sure that you have submitted all documentation and signed the necessary paperwork to ensure that you maintain the classes you have registered for. Do not assume that your financial aid package is complete.

Visit the financial aid office! If you are not sure about your award, contact your financial aid office.

---

payment is not met which will prevent your enrollment for subsequent terms and possibly delay your graduation until payment is settled. failure to pay by the payment deadlines will result in **de-enrollment** (commonly referred to as "the **purge**"), removal from the courses you were enrolled in.

Remember: Each institution has its own payment deadlines. These deadlines are often connected to your registration date.

UTILIZING CAMPUS RESOURCES

Successful performance in college, like successful performance in any human endeavor, is influenced by both the individual and the environment. Your environment (college campus) is chock full of specialized resources that are available to you (in print, in person, and online), all of which can strongly support your quest for educational and personal success. Studies show that students who utilize these resources report higher levels of satisfaction with, and get more out of, the college experience (Pascaralla & Terenzini, 1991, 2005).

For example, two researchers who conducted a comprehensive review of over 2,500 research studies reached the following conclusion. "The impact of college is not simply the result of what a college does for or to a student. Rather, the impact is a result of the extent to which an individual student exploits the people, programs, facilities, opportunities, and experiences that the college makes available" (Pascarella & Terenzini, *How College Affects Students,* pp. 610–611).

Described in this section are some of the most valuable campus services that can support and promote your success.

Remember: Involvement with campus services is not only valuable, but it's also free because the cost of these services has already been covered by your college tuition. By investing time and energy in these resources, you are not only increasing your prospects for personal success, you are also maximizing the return on your financial investment in college.

Academic Support Services

Library

A library can be many things to many different people. To a college student, a library can be a place of academic exploration where they study, research, and gather information. It all depends on your **point of view or perspective** when thinking about what a library means to you. The library can be a very intimidating place—but it doesn't have to be if you know how and when to use University Libraries.

New college students arrive on campus with many different **assumptions** regarding the campus library. Some of these **assumptions** include "I can do all of my research on the internet," "I got but high school without ever going to the library, so why should I start using the library now?" The library is too big and I don't know my way around," and "There's just too much in the library for me to know what's relevant to my research." Countless first-year students have arrived on campus with these and many other **assumptions** and concerns about the library, but soon found all of them to be untrue and fixable. You will learn more about the Library and its resources in chapter 2.

Learning Center/Academic Success Center

Also known as the Center for Academic Support or Academic Success, this is the place on campus where you can obtain individual assistance to support and strengthen your academic performance. The one-to-one and group tutoring provided by the Center can help you master difficult course concepts and assignments, and the people working there have been professionally trained to help you learn "how to learn." While your professors may have expert knowledge of the subject matter they teach, learning resource specialists are experts on the process of learning. These specialists can show students how to adjust or modify their learning strategies to meet the demands of the different courses and teaching styles they encounter in college.

Studies show that students who become actively involved with academic support services outside the classroom, such as the Learning Center or Academic Support Center, are more likely to attain higher college grades and complete their college degree. This is particularly true if they began their involvement with these support services during the first year of college (Cuseo, 2003). Also, students who seek and receive assistance from academic-support services show significant improvement in academic self-efficacy—that is, they develop a greater sense of personal control over their academic performance and develop higher self-expectations for future academic success (Smith, Walter, & Hoey, 1992).

Despite the multiple advantages of getting involved with academic support services outside the classroom, these services are typically under-utilized by college students, especially by those students who could gain the most from using them (Knapp &

Karabenick, 1988; Walter & Smith, 1990). This could be due to the fact that some students feel that seeking academic help is an admission that they are not smart, or that they cannot succeed on their own. Do not be one of these students.

Writing Center

Many college campuses offer specialized support that is expressly designed to help students improve their writing skills. Typically referred to as the Writing Center, this is the place where you can receive assistance at any stage of the writing process, whether it be collecting and organizing your ideas in outline form, composing your first draft, or proofreading your final draft. Since writing is an academic skill that you'll use in almost all your courses, improvements in your writing will improve your overall academic performance. Thus, we strongly encourage you to capitalize on this campus resource.

Services for Students with Disabilities

If you have a documented cognitive, physical, mental, or learning disability, you are entitled by law to **reasonable** accommodations because of your disability. Accommodations are based on a student's functional limitations imposed by their disability. Most campuses have an office that coordinates these services. Services might range from enlarging reading material, providing note takers, arranging for sign language interpreters, furnishing desks in classrooms to accommodating wheelchairs and other physical disabilities, or allowing instructors the facilities to give increased time for testing. Equipment such as tape recorders, calculators, magnifiers, automatic page turners, computer software, recorded textbooks, and large print dictionaries may be provided. Sometimes readers and scribes are provided.

Academic Advisement

College students who have developed a clear sense of their educational and career goals are more likely to continue their college education and complete their college degree (Willingham, 1985; Wyckoff, 1999). However, most beginning college students need help with clarifying their educational goals, selecting an academic major, and exploring future careers. For instance, consider the following findings:

- three of every four beginning college students are uncertain or tentative about their career choice (Frost, 1991);
- less than 10 percent of new students feel they know a great deal about their intended college major (Erickson & Strommer, 1991);
- over half of all students who enter college with a declared major change their mind at least once before they graduate (Noel, 1985); and
- only one of three college seniors end up majoring in the same field that they preferred during their first year of college (Cuseo, 2005).

These findings point to the conclusion that the majority of college students do not make final decisions about their major before starting their college experience; instead, they make these decisions during the college experience. It is only natural for you, a first-year student, to feel uncertain about your intended major because you have not yet experienced the variety of subjects and academic programs that make up the college curriculum. In fact, you will encounter fields of study in college that you probably never knew existed in high school.

Remember: Being undecided or unsure about your major and career is nothing to be embarrassed about because the process of long-range academic planning and effective decision-making is challenging and complex. So, connect early and often with an academic advisor to help you work through this challenging process and to help you find a major that best taps your educational interests, talents, and values.

Career Development Center

Research on college students indicates that they are more likely to stay in school and graduate when they have some sense of how their present academic experience relates to their future career goals (Levitz & Noel, 1989). Studies also show that the vast majority of new students are uncertain about what future careers they would like to pursue (Gordon & Steele, 2003). So, if you are uncertain about a career right now, welcome to the club. This uncertainty is entirely normal and understandable because you have not yet had the opportunity for hands-on work experience in the real world of careers. As Vincent Tinto, a nationally known scholar on student success, points out:

> *Among any population of young adults who are just beginning in earnest their search for adult identity, it would be surprising indeed if one found that most were very clear about their long-term goals. The college years are an important growing period in which new social and intellectual experiences are sought as a means of coming to grips with the issue of adult careers. Students enter college with the hope that they will be able to formulate for themselves a meaningful answer to that important question (1993, p. 40).*

The Career Center is the place to go for help in finding a meaningful answer to the important question of how to connect your current college experience with your future career goals. Although it may seem like beginning a career is light years away because you are just beginning college, the process of investigating, planning, and preparing for career success begins in the first year of college. You can start this important process by visiting the Career Center, which is a campus resource that has been explicitly created to help you:

- explore the rapidly changing world of careers,
- understand the often complex relationship between particular academic majors and related careers,
- identify what careers may be most compatible with your personal interests, abilities, or values,
- locate volunteer (service-learning) experiences and internships that will enable you to test your interest in different careers through direct, real-world experience, and
- develop your resume.

Counseling Center

According to a New York Times article by Tamar Lewin entitled "Record Level of Stress Found in College Freshmen" (January 26, 2011), the emotional health of college freshmen has declined to its lowest level in the last 25 years. Brian Van Brunt, the director of counseling at Western Kentucky University, was quoted as saying that "More students are arriving on campus with problems, needing support, and today's economic factors are putting a lot of extra stress on college students, as they look at their loans and wonder if there will be a career waiting for them on the other side." The article went on to say that it is sometimes a student's own self-inflicted pressure that can lead to feeling of depression and stress.

These findings point to the importance of focusing not only on your academics, but also on non-academic aspects of your adjustment to college and your development as a whole person. In fact, studies of successful people indicate that social and emotional intelligence (EQ) are often more important for personal and professional success than intellectual ability (IQ) (Goleman, 1995).

Counseling services can provide you with a valuable source of support during your first year of college, not only for helping you cope with college stressors that may be interfering with your academic success, but also for helping you realize your full potential. Personal counseling can promote self-awareness and self-development in social and emotional areas of your life that are important for mental health, physical wellness, and personal growth.

Remember: College counseling is not just for students who are experiencing emotional problems. It is for all students who want to enrich their overall quality of life.

Health Center

Making the transition to college often involves taking more personal responsibility for your own health and wellness. In addition to making your own decisions about what to eat, when to sleep, and how to manage your own health, your stress level is likely to increase during times of change or transition in your life. Good health habits are one effective way to both cope with college stress and reach peak levels of performance. The Health Center on your campus is the key resource for information on how to manage your health and maintain wellness. It is also the place to go for help with physical illnesses, sexually transmitted infections or diseases, and eating disorders.

DURING (D)

While you are in college, there are certain *actions* which determine your success:

- **Understand the college classroom**
- **Become a successful student**
- **Develop positive self-esteem**
- **Demonstrate a positive attitude**
- **Commit to being persistent**
- **Discover the traits of a successful student**

THE COLLEGE CLASSROOM

Once you have completed the process to become a student, you are now ready to enter the college classroom. One of the strategies for academic success in the classroom is developing a relationship with **faculty**. Learn their titles (Instructor, Professor, Doctor, etc.) and office hours so that you can get to know them. Your instructors will also want to get to know you. Your attendance and classroom behavior influence your relationship. Your instructors cannot get to know you if you are not present and/or if you behave inappropriately.

Instructors will provide you with a **syllabus**, an outline of what is expected of you in that particular course. The syllabus will explain how you will be graded, what materials are required (can be purchased from the **Campus Bookstore**), and often includes exam dates, assignments and their due dates, and attendance policy. You should refer to your syllabus frequently if you have questions about the course. If you have questions that were not covered in class, meet with your instructor during his/her office hours. Notify your professor (by phone or e-mail) if you will not be able to attend class.

The instructor will also remind you to review the **academic standards**, or the rules pertaining to academic conduct and violations processes in instances such as **plagiarism** (stealing the work of another author without citing the author as a reference and presenting it as if it were your own work) and **cheating** (copying the work of another student).

Other strategies for success in the classroom include awareness of expectations, rights and responsibilities of both the instructor(s) and students.

BECOMING A SUCCESSFUL STUDENT

There are students and then there are students. Just because you have completed the enrollment process does not mean that you will be successful in college. Just because you sit in the college classroom and participate in class discussions does not guarantee your success either. Think about the title of this textbook, <u>Designing Your Plan for Success</u>. The title implies that you will have to do some work thinking about and designing your plan to be a successful student. You must practice critical thinking and develop certain characteristics or traits to ensure college success. It is not something that just happens because you have enrolled in college. For example, you can't expect to lose weight or get in shape just because you have joined a health club. It will take work and commitment to reach your goals.

Let's focus on the positive first and think about the characteristics of successful students. Students who get A's and B's often are no more intelligent than anyone else. However, they practice certain behaviors that give them the edge. Most are not complicated or difficult to implement. You would think that everyone could figure it out, but semester after semester, otherwise bright students earn lower grades or fail because they do not put effort into being successful.

How many of these characteristics do you have? How many could you easily adopt? Use the following chart to identify which positive student behaviors are part of your regular routine and which you need to add.

Characteristic	I Do This	I Need To Do This
I arrive on time for all of my classes. Class attendance is a high priority for me.		
I sit in the front or middle of the class where I can easily see and hear and will not be distracted.		
I pay attention in class. I do not disrupt others by talking, nor do I "space out" and miss important information.		
I come prepared for class. I have read the chapter and my homework is done. I bring my book, notepaper, and pens to class so I am ready to listen and take notes.		
I participate in class discussions. I know I will learn more if I am involved, plus I am contributing to the learning process.		
I ask questions in class, especially if I don't understand or if I want to know more.		
I give the instructor and others positive feedback in class. I make eye contact when someone is talking and express appropriate body language.		
I get to know other students in each class. I have at least one other person I can ask for help or with whom I compare notes. I don't feel like a stranger.		
I contact the instructor if I know I must miss class. I get any hand-outs and information that I missed prior to the next class session whenever possible.		

I develop and use my own, personalized learning tools. I mark my textbooks to suit my needs. I have what I need (calculator, pocket dictionary, planner, etc.) to do my assignments.		
I turn in all assignments on time. I don't lose unnecessary points by turning in late or incomplete work.		
I follow the directions. When I'm doing an assignment, I make sure it is what I'm supposed to do.		
I seek help when I need it. I use the support services the college provides (tutoring, counseling, etc.). I don't let pride keep me from getting tutoring. I would rather pass than fail.		

The flip side of success is failure. And just as there is a list of positive traits, there is also a list of characteristics, traits, and/or behaviors that place students at risk of not succeeding in completing the semester, the next semester, and ultimately, their degree. The list includes, but is not limited to, the following:

- **Personal problems**
- **Unmotivated**
- **Inappropriate behavior (bad attitude)**
- **Diversity and/or interaction issues**
- **Late for/misses classes**
- **Late/missing assignments**
- **Does homework in class**
- **Cannot do required work**
- **Tired/sleeps in class**
- **Works too many hours**

It is important to note again that it is not just academic ability that determines student success, but also factors such as self-esteem, positive attitude, and persistence.

SELF-ESTEEM

The terms self-esteem, self-concept, and self-respect may all have slightly different meanings to a language purist, but for the purposes of this chapter, we're going to define them as the way each one of us thinks and feels about him/herself. It includes the positive and the negative thoughts we have about how worthy, capable, and significant we are. In this chapter, we'd like to examine our internal dialog or "self-talk" and its effect on our behavior, and ultimately on our achievement.

Persons with low self-esteem feel, think, and act differently than those with high self-esteem. Their energy levels are usually different. Their levels of optimism (the feeling that things will work out) are different. The ways they approach problems or difficulties are different. Look at Table 1.1 to compare the behaviors, attitudes, and feelings of people with positive and negative self-esteem.

Of course, our self-esteem does not stay the same all the time. Some days we feel confident and ready to face any challenges. Other days we're discouraged and feel like our lives are out of our control. How we feel about our abilities and ourselves on any given day is based on a complex set of experiences and life events. Understanding these root causes and our responses to them can help us learn how to increase our confidence in areas where it may be lacking.

Table 1.1 Comparison of Positive and Negative Self-Esteem

Characteristic	Positive Self-Esteem	Negative Self-Esteem
Behaviors	• Accepts responsibility for his/her own actions—admits mistakes • Accepts self and others • Builds and uses support systems—isn't afraid to ask for help • Uses positive "self-talk" • Sets realistic goals • Identifies priorities • Tries to predict logical consequences of actions • Uses assertive communication skills • Willing to take risks—faces and works through fears	• Blames others or makes excuses for actions or mistakes • Judgmental of self and others • Won't do anything that might make him/her look bad/inferior to others • Uses negative self-talk • Sets no goals or sets unrealistic goals • Acts like a victim • May act superior to others and try to put them down • Fails to understand and/or predict consequences • Uses passive or aggressive communication skills • Hesitates to take risks or try something new—fears failure/disappointment
Attitudes	• Confident of his/her own abilities • Inner-directed • Self-accepting—doesn't have to be perfect • Able to accept criticism and acknowledges limits on abilities or talents • Positive attitude • Tolerant of others	• Lacks confidence in own abilities • Frequently lacking in motivation • Thinks she/he has no control over what happens • Critical of own actions/behaviors • Vastly underestimates or overestimates own talents or abilities • Negative attitude • Demanding of others
Feelings	• Feels satisfied, competent • Feels safe and secure in relationships • Feels worthwhile • Feels appreciated	• Feels unimportant • Feels manipulated or victimized by others • Fears being rejected • Feels inferior to others or unappreciated

Development and Use of Support Systems

Recognizing when we need help and seeking that help is a characteristic associated with self-confidence and success. Many students who run into academic difficulty are examples of the "too little, too late" academic style. They wait until they are impossibly behind or completely fail a course before they ask for help. By the time they actually seek tutoring assistance, they may not have enough time to improve their grade(s). On the other hand, students who have high levels of self-esteem do not feel stupid or inferior just because they don't know everything. They realize that asking for tutoring when needed is much smarter than failing a course and having to take it over. It is a sign that they are taking their education seriously and want to succeed. They seek help early in the semester and schedule regular appointments so they are not caught in the rush of students trying to get in at the last minute. Getting consistent help throughout the semester usually results in improved understanding of the material and better test scores.

Using support systems isn't limited to the academic arena, either. Having healthy support systems is also an important way to combat stress. In the workplace, major corporations have re-discovered the benefits of teamwork and cooperation. Having positive self-esteem is an important attitude that you need to develop now.

Development and Use of Assertive Communication Skills

The self-confident person is able to communicate his/her needs in a way that is honest, direct, and respectful of others. In the college setting, this may involve asking questions, requesting help from others, expressing your opinion, or declining unwelcome invitations/requests. Each time a person speaks up, the better she/he may feel about handling situations that arise. A person with low self-esteem is rarely an assertive communicator. It's more likely that she/he will passively accept whatever happens, feeling that nothing she/he might say or do will make a difference. Sometimes people with low self-esteem try to mask it with aggressive, bullying tactics and communication.

Moral/Ethical Character

In addition to having a healthy sense of self-confidence, develop and commit to a set of moral and ethical values or principles. This will help you become a better person and a more successful student.

Student Code of Conduct

All accredited colleges and universities have a code of conduct that sets standards for acceptable and unacceptable behaviors on campus. This code is usually published in several forms and is made available to students. The code contains items that are practical guidelines to help everyone at the college function in an orderly manner. Complying with college policies, leaving buildings when the campus closes, obeying directives of the campus police/security, and not disrupting the flow of traffic on campus are all examples of following the rules. Other items in the code fall under the category of moral principles. For example, students are prohibited from stealing, cheating, damaging property, sexually harassing others, and engaging in illegal activities on campus. Students who fail to comply with the code of conduct at their college/university face consequences that can range in severity from a reprimand to expulsion.

AVOID SELF-DEFEATING BEHAVIORS

Your college years require you to use many of the same skills that will be critical to your success on the job. Instructors have certain expectations of students, just as your employers will have expectations of you as an employee. Regular attendance, communication skills, initiative, problem solving skills, being prepared and on time, and producing results rather than making excuses are just some of the expectations your instructors will have of you.

Unfortunately, many students act in ways that are guaranteed to sabotage their academic success. We call these actions self-defeating behaviors.

1. **Procrastination**—When students put off doing assignments or studying for tests until the last possible moment, they increase their stress level and often end up with too much to do in the time they have left. The work they do get done is often not their best, resulting in a lower grade. Many instructors deduct points when assignments are turned in late; some won't accept late work at all.
2. **Attendance/Punctuality**—Students who miss class or come late are sending a nonverbal message to the instructor that his/her class is just not a high

priority. These students often miss important information or announcements that may result in doing an assignment incorrectly or not at all. The missed information from the lecture may be on the test. In addition, many times an instructor will use attendance or class participation as a "tie-breaker" if a student's grade is on the borderline. You can't participate when you aren't in class.

3. **Failure to Follow Through**—Many students start a new project, course, or assignment with enthusiasm. They have good intentions and high expectations, but don't deliver in the end. If you are not dependable and don't finish what you start, you may find that success eludes you.

4. **Excuses/Self-Pity**—College instructors are not interested in excuses for why you didn't get your paper done or why you missed the test. Their focus, like that of employers, is on results. If you do have an emergency that prevents you from attending class, it is courteous to inform the instructor why you missed class (see # 2 above) and provide documentation if that is required. It is your responsibility to keep track of what is due and to manage your time and activities in a way that will allow you to complete your course work. Some instructors will not accept assignments that are turned in late nor allow tests to be made up for any reason.

5. **Failure to Anticipate Consequences**—College students often fail to understand the consequences of their actions or inactions. They miss refund dates, financial aid deadlines, course withdrawal deadlines, tuition payment dates, etc. and then are upset by the consequences. It is your responsibility to be aware of the administrative policies that will affect you academically and personally. For example, falling below full-time student status could result in a loss of scholarship money (or possibly having to return money), athletic eligibility, and/or insurance coverage. "Blowing off" the placement test may add extra prerequisite courses to your academic program.

6. **Accepting False Guilt**—A self-defeating behavior that many people practice is feeling guilty about not living up to unrealistic expectations. They feel they should be a perfect parent/child/friend/spouse/student/housekeeper/repair person/whatever. While it is important to set goals and have high expectations for yourself, it is self-defeating if you set your standards impossibly high. Remember, too, not to allow someone else to motivate or manipulate you with guilt.

7. **Working Too Many Hours**—If you work as well as attend college, you fit the "typical" college student profile. The problem comes when students try to be *full-time* employees while they are *full-time* students with *full-time* social or family lives. Most colleges recommend that full-time students work no more than 20 hours per week. Some recommend taking a lighter load or working 0–10 hours per week your first semester. If you must work full time, consider cutting back to part-time student status. Overloading yourself is a sure way to set yourself up for poor grades, frustration, exhaustion, and failure.

8. **Lack of Self-Direction**—Students who feel that others have more control over their lives will often have attitudes, habits, and behaviors that are very self-defeating and act as though they are not responsible for what happens. They say, "The instructor *gave* me that grade" instead of "That is the grade I *earned*." Students who accept responsibility for their choices and behaviors and who feel competent to deal with life on a daily basis don't want to keep perpetuating behaviors that prevent them from being successful.

CHANGE IS POSSIBLE

Did you recognize some of your "favorite" self-defeating behaviors in the list above? You may have others that were not mentioned. Think about your performance so far this semester. Are you achieving all that you expected? If not, what is happening? The important thing is to recognize what you are doing that keeps you from being the kind of person you want to be and achieving the success you want to achieve. There is an old saying: *"If you always do what you've always done, you'll always get what you've always gotten."* What that means is, when you do things the same old way, you're going to get the same old results. The only way to get better results is to change what you're doing that doesn't work.

PERSISTENCE AND SUCCESS

There is an old saying that persistence will get you almost anything eventually. This saying applies to your success in college. The first two to six weeks of college are a critical time in which many students drop out. Realize that college is a new experience and that you will face new challenges and growth experiences. Commit to follow these tips to help you achieve your goals:

- Make plans to persist, especially in the first few weeks. Plan now to work until the end and not give up when things get tough.
- Get to know a college counselor, advisor or mentor you can talk to when you have questions or concerns
- Plan to enroll on time so that you do not have to register late.
- Attend the first class. It is crucial to attend the first class to meet the professor and learn the class requirements and expectations. You may even get dropped from the class if you are not there on the first day.
- Get into the habit of studying right away. Make studying a habit that you start immediately at the beginning of the semester or quarter.

AFTER (A)

Research indicates that one characteristic of successful learners is that they monitor or watch themselves and maintain self-awareness of:

- Whether they're using effective learning strategies (e.g., they are aware of their level of attention or concentration in class);
- Whether they're comprehending what they are attempting to learn (e.g., if they're understanding it at a deep level or merely memorizing it at a surface level); and
- How to regulate or adjust their learning strategies to meet the demands of different academic tasks and subjects (e.g., they read technical material in a science textbook more slowly and stop to test their understanding more often than when they're reading a novel; Pintrich, 1995; Pintrich & Schunk, 2002; Weinstein, 1994; Weinstein & Meyer, 1991).

> **Remember**
> *Successful students are self-aware learners who know their teaming strategies, styles, strengths, and shortcomings.*

"Successful students know a lot about themselves."

—Claim Weinstein and Debra Meyer,
professors of educational psychology at the University of Texas

You* can begin to establish good self-monitoring habits by creating a routine of periodically pausing to reflect on the strategies you're using to learn and "do" college.

For instance, you can ask yourself the following questions:

- Am I listening attentively to what my instructor is saying in class?
- Do I comprehend what I am reading outside of class?
- Am I effectively using campus resources that are designed to support my success?
- Am I interacting with campus professionals who can contribute to my current success and future development?
- Am I interacting and collaborating with peers who can contribute to my learning and increase my level of Involvement in the college experience?
- Am I effectively implementing the success strategies identified in this book?

* From *Thriving in College and Beyond: Research-Based Strategies for Academic Success and Personal Development* by Jospeh B. Cuseo, Aaron Thompson, Michele Campagna, and Viki S. Fecas. Copyright © 2013 by Kendall Hunt Publishing Company. Reprinted by permission.

SUMMARY

This chapter has focused on introducing you to the college experience from its mission and purpose to its structure and organization; from causes of success to causes of failure; and from "where am I?" to "here's where I'm going." Now that you're here, the rest is up to YOU!

SUGGESTED READINGS

Covey, Stephen. *The Seven Habits of Highly Effective People.* New York: Franklin Covey/ Golden Books, 1997. Davis, Sampson, and Hunt, Rameck and George Jenkins. *The Pact.* New York: Riverhead Books, 2003.

WHERE AM I? – WESTERN KENTUCKY UNIVERSITY

Where Am I?

Western Kentucky University

HISTORY AND TRADITIONS

The History of WKU

On March 21, 1906, the Kentucky General Assembly approved legislation to establish two teacher training institutions, or "normal schools," in the state. A locating commission chose *Bowling Green* to be the site of one, and the Western Kentucky State Normal School was created.

The new state-supported school took over the building and student body of the privately owned Southern Normal School. The owner of the Southern Normal School, Henry Hardin Cherry, had been actively involved in the campaign to establish teacher training schools and became WKU's first president. Classes began on January 22, 1907.

On February 4, 1911, the school moved to its present site on "the Hill," approximately 125 feet above downtown Bowling Green and the former home of The Pleasant J. Potter College. Over the next decade, the curriculum focused on teacher training and certification. Students received practical experience at the Training School, and a model one-room Rural School was opened on campus in 1924. In 1922 the state renamed the institution Western Kentucky State Normal School and Teachers College and authorized it to grant four-year degrees. The first such degrees were awarded in 1924.

WKU's campus expanded in 1927 when it merged with Ogden College, a private young men's school located on the east side of the Hill. WKU's name was shortened to Western Kentucky State Teachers College in 1930, and the following year the master of arts degree was first offered. President Cherry died in 1937 and was succeeded by Paul Garrett.

As WKU's mission broadened, its name was shortened in 1948 to Western Kentucky State College. Dr. Garrett died in 1955 and Kelly Thompson became WKU's third president.

Under Dr. Thompson, both Western's curriculum and its campus underwent major reorganization and expansion. In June 1963, Western merged with the Bowling Green College of Commerce, formerly the Bowling Green Business University. Along with the Graduate School, the Bowling Green College of Commerce became a separate college within WKU's structure. In 1965, the Board of Regents approved the formation of three more colleges: the Potter College of Liberal Arts, the College of Education, and the Ogden College of Science and Technology.

On June 16, 1966 Western Kentucky State College became *Western Kentucky University*.

Dr. Thompson was president until 1969. At that time, *Dero Downing* became president and served until 1979. Dr. Downing had taught at WKU prior to becoming president.

John Minton, former associate dean of Graduate Instruction, Graduate Dean, and Administrative Vice-President, was appointed president effective January 31, 1979 when Dr. Downing retired. He served until July 31, 1979, when Donald Zacharias was appointed president. In recognition of his service, the Board of Regents recognized Minton as WKU's fifth president. At the time of Dr. Minton's retirement in 1986, he held the position of Vice President for Student Affairs.

Dr. Zacharias became WKU's sixth president in 1979 and served until August 31, 1985.

More colleges and reorganization followed throughout the years as WKU continued to expand. The Bowling Green Community College was established in 1986.

Kern Alexander was the seventh WKU president. He had ties to the university through his graduate work at WKU. His tenure as president was a transitional period in the University's history, serving from 1986 until 1988 during which *WKU's regional campus in Glasgow* opened.

Thomas Meredith took office as WKU's eighth president on August 31, 1988. He was also tied to the university through his graduate work. Among his accomplishments were the introduction of WKU's first strategic plan, Distinguished Professorship Program and several new masters degree programs. The campus became fully computer-networked, two new residence halls and a *health and activities center* opened, and WKU's *Hall of Distinguished Alumni* and Athletic Hall of Fame were established. Dr. Meredith served as president until May 17, 1997 when he assumed the duties as the Chancellor of the University of Alabama System.

WKU's current president, *Gary A. Ransdell*, was appointed on September 12, 1997.

The *College of Health and Human Services* was established in 2002. It was established to bring together all health and human services programs under one administrative unit. The College consists of seven departments that represent an array of disciplines, and offers degrees at the associate, baccalaureate, masters and doctoral degree levels.

The *Division of Extended Learning and Outreach (DELO)* launched in 2003. DELO is the outreach arm of the university, offering both credit and non-credit classes to students of all ages. The division partners with faculty and departments to offer convenient and flexible learning opportunities to students. The division works with businesses and organizations to provide customized training, plan special events, and develop degree programs that meet specific needs in the community.

An administrative unit since 1994, *University College* was reorganized in 2009 as an academic unit; it now houses those units and programs formerly part of the Bowling

Green Community College, and serves as the administrative home of *WKU's regional campus programs.*

Today, the University's six colleges are:

College of Health & Human Services

College of Education and Behavioral Sciences

Gordon Ford College of Business

Ogden College of Science & Engineering

Potter College of Arts & Letters

University College

WKU has housed the *Carol Martin Gatton Academy of Mathematics and Science in Kentucky* since 2007. The mission is to offer a residential program for bright, highly motivated Kentucky high school students who have demonstrated interest in pursuing careers in science, technology, engineering, and mathematics.

In 2008, the *WKU Board of Regents* approved creation and development of a fully independent *Honors College* at WKU. The purpose of the WKU Honors College is to offer high-achieving young scholars the environment of a small, highly selective college, while providing the resources and benefits of a large public university. This combination of outstanding research opportunities with an intimate and rigorous intellectual environment not only produces nationally recognized scholars and globally engaged leaders it changes lives. Equally as important, the Honors College experience is helping these scholars make their educational and career dreams come true.

Degree offerings have expanded to meet the needs of the region and state and include programs in *electrical, civil and mechanical engineering* and three stand-alone doctoral programs: *educational leadership, nursing practice* and *physical therapy.*

Through the years, WKU students have enjoyed an intimate scholarly environment on a vibrant campus and are encouraged to become involved in community service, applied research and study abroad. These are among the reasons why WKU is becoming the University of choice in the Commonwealth and A Leading American University with International Reach.

A century of growth has made WKU a respected center of learning and a place where students can succeed on a global level.

The Spirit of WKU

One might describe the "Spirit of WKU" as more than just school spirit. Alumni, students, faculty and staff may describe it as an almost tangible feeling—a deep love and passionate pride for the rich history and tradition of Western Kentucky University, our campus, facilities and community.

WKU President, Dr. Gary A. Ransdell describes it as "an absolute passion, a rich adrenaline created by the WKU experience which drives those in the WKU family to cherish the experience during which memories of a lifetime are shaped and nurtured."

Many prospective students have noticed this feeling upon their first visit to our beautiful hilltop home. Many have stated the Spirit was the defining factor in choosing WKU as their collegiate home. From athletics to administration and everywhere in between, the Spirit of WKU thrives in the hearts of all who have been fortunate enough to experience it firsthand.

We invite you to visit the WKU campus to see if the Spirit lives within you as well!

Alma Mater

WKU's alma mater, "College Heights," was originally written by 16-year-old school-girl Mary Frances Bradley as a poem to be entered in a contest on the campus in 1924.

Miss Bradley combined her poignant words with a beautiful melody composed by her father, Ben J. Bradley, an accomplished songwriter and musician from nearby Franklin, KY.

On March 12, 1925, "College Heights" was first performed at chapel assembly in Van Meter Auditorium by Miss Bradley and, thus an alma mater was born.

The music was subsequently published and then copyrighted by WKU in 1930. On the music is the notation that the song is dedicated to WKU's first president, Dr. Henry Hardin Cherry.

"College Heights"

College Heights, on hilltop fair,

With beauty all thine own,

Lovely jewel far more rare

Than graces any throne!

College Heights, we hail thee;

We shall never fail thee

Falter never, live forever,

Hail! Hail! Hail!

College Heights with living soul

And purpose strong and true,

Service ever is thy goal

Thy spirit ever new.

College Heights, we hail thee;

We shall never fail thee

Falter never, live forever,

Hail! Hail! Hail!

College Heights thy noble life,

Shall e'er our pattern be,

Teaching us through joy and strife

To love humanity.

College Heights we hail thee,

We shall never fail thee,

Falter never, live forever,

Hail! Hail! Hail!

Western Creed

Western Kentucky University is a community dedicated to learning where ideas are offered, examined, and discussed.

As a member of this community, I have both a personal and shared responsibility to participate actively in university life by:

Practicing Personal and Academic Integrity

Seeking unity by respecting the dignity of all persons

Celebrating and embracing diversity

Encouraging freedom of expression

Acting in accordance with basic principles of citizenship

Preserving and appreciating the natural beauty of the campus

Enriching all aspects of life through the educational process and by

Embracing the ideals expressed on the university seal: "Life More Life" and "The Spirit Makes the Master," by pursuing personal growth and a life of excellence.

WKU Fight Song

"Stand Up and Cheer"

Stand up and cheer

Stand up and cheer

For dear old Western

For today we raise

The red and white

Above the rest

Rah-rah-rah

Our boys are fighting

And we're bound to win the fray

We've got the team

We've got the steam

For this is dear old Western's day.

Reprinted by permission of Western Kentucky University.

Legendary WKU Basketball Coach E.A. Diddle

In 42 seasons (1922–64) as the head basketball coach at Western Kentucky, Edgar Allen Diddle's teams claimed 32 conference championships; played in 11 postseason tournaments; won 20+ games eighteen different times (including one stretch of ten years in a row); became the first team from the South to participate in the Olympic Trials; and they won an amazing 759 games! When he stepped down in 1964 Diddle had won more games than any coach in NCAA history and today he still ranks fifth on the all-time list. At the time of his death in 1970 over 100 of Diddle's former players were coaching in the high school, college, or professional ranks—an incredible example of the influence that he had on his beloved players. Visitors of the Basketball Hall of Fame in Springfield, Mass., can view a display honoring Mr. Diddle, which includes one of the coach's legendary Red Towels, which he developed into a Western tradition.

Diddle was one of the first proponents of the fast-break style of basketball and the tremendous success of his early teams helped to popularize and spread this style of play all across the country. Many years later he stated, "We play the fast break because it makes people come to our gymnasium, they like to see scoring. We give them what they like. I see it as entertainment." Even in warm-up drills Diddle's team entertained the crowd using red and white basketballs and by taking every opportunity to dunk the ball . . . something that wasn't widely accepted among the country's more straight-laced coaches in those days.

Most people who knew the coach will tell you that his greatest strength was undoubtedly his amazing ability to motivate his players to perform well beyond their own expectations. Dero Downing, a former Diddle player who later became the second of the coach's team members to become president of WKU, once told of a scolding that he received from the coach, "What makes you think you're such a good basketball player? I found you up there at Horse Cave, just milking a little Jersey cow, and you're not much better now than you were then, and all you know is what I've taught you." Recalling the incident, Downing stated, "Then, when you felt the lowest, like you weren't worth killing, he'd pat you on the rear—and you felt like you could beat the world."

Diddle's other great attribute was his ability to spot unpolished talent and develop that player into an integral part of the team. Coach described it in this manner, "There is nothing that gives me more of a thrill than taking some country kid who is flat-footed, walks like he is following a plow, doesn't know much about basketball, except that the ball is round, and making something out of him." Diddle was a master recruiter, perhaps as fine as college basketball has ever seen. Despite Western's small size, when compared to the larger state universities around the country, Diddle had the ability to cast a spell over a player and his family and convince them in all honesty that Western was the only place for them. One feature that the coach always looked for in potential recruits was big hands and big feet. "I look for tall boys, up over 6'3", with big hands and big feet. If they haven't got big feet, they'll fall down," he would always say. "I want the nervous kind, the kind with temperament and brains, like a race horse." As unorthodox as it all may sound it's kind of hard to argue with the results. However, perhaps the most important thing that he looked for in a player can be carried over to the modern game, and into any sport for that matter. Here is how the coach put it: "A pretty good athlete who is a competitor will beat a talented boy who has a faint heart every time. The thing I always looked for first in a boy was his fire. We can develop his talents, but only God can give him his fire."

Edgar Allen Diddle was born on a small farm near Gradyville in Adair Co., Ky. on March 12, 1895. Growing up as one of five boys Diddle developed into a fine athlete and played all sports at nearby Columbia High School. In 1915 Diddle entered Centre College at Danville, Ky. where he continued to play basketball and football, even earning the nickname of "Mule," for his great physical strength on the football field. In 1918 he joined a naval aviation program and spent most of the year in Europe. Returning to Centre the following year he finished up his career there in 1920 and by the following winter had landed his first head coaching job at Monticello High School where he took his first team all the way to the state finals. The next year saw Diddle assume the head coaching position at Greenville High School. In his second year there his 1922 team posted a 26–2 record and participated in a regional tournament in Bowling Green after a flood, or fate, prevented the team from traveling to their scheduled site of Owensboro. Once in Bowling Green Diddle so impressed everyone with his coaching ability that Western officials extended an offer to him to become the athletics director and head coach of all sports at Western. He eventually accepted, and on Sept. 7, 1922, for the salary of $150 per month, $100 less than he was offered to stay at Greenville, E.A. Diddle began his legendary career with Western Kentucky University.

Diddle was initially in charge of coaching football, baseball, and women's basketball in addition to his men's basketball position, and early on success didn't come easy as Diddle gradually built the program up into the powerhouse it would eventually become. On February 9, 1931, Western played its first game in their new gymnasium, dubbed the "New Red Barn." Officially seating 4,500 spectators the new building became a magical place for Western basketball and a place that to this day inspires fond memories from everyone who was fortunate enough to attend games there. Luckily, it was built right before Diddle and his teams began their march to national prominence. For ten years, from the 1933–34 season through the 1942–43 season, Western's teams posted at least 20 wins per season including becoming the first NCAA school ever to record a 30-win season in 1937–38. They also won or shared the KIAC or SIAA conference championship every year in between. During the 32 years that the Red Barn housed Western basketball it was a regular sell-out, but the coach never turned anyone away whenever possible. He would always instruct the doormen not to let anyone stand outside in the cold if they could possibly be crammed into the gym. Diddle would say, "Anybody who comes 100 miles to see us play is our guest and we'll get him into that gym if we have to use a shoehorn to get him in, and he doesn't have to have a ticket either."

Still, it wasn't until 1941–42 that Western finally made a splash nationally. At that time the NIT was the major tournament rather than the NCAA, and it was considered an honor to be invited to Madison Square Garden to participate. Kelly Thompson, one of Diddle's former football players, who was then the school's publicity man and who would later became president of Western, convinced Ned Irish, the official in charge of the NIT, to invite Western's great '41–'42 team to the Garden. Once there, both the New York media and the public fell in love with Coach Diddle and his exciting team. They especially loved his antics on the sidelines, as the coach would throw and wave his red towel vigorously throughout the game. Unfortunately, the Toppers fell short of the championship. After defeating CCNY in the first game 49-46 and then Creighton 49–36 in the second round, Western lost a 12 point halftime lead to West Virginia in the title game and fell two points shy of the national championship, 47-45. However, Diddle and the Hilltoppers became such crowd favorites that they were to be invited back many times in the future.

Diddle's teams continued their tremendous success over the next two decades as they continued to dominate their conferences and participate in the NIT. However, fate always seemed to intervene and prevent the Toppers from obtaining the elusive national championship that Coach Diddle longed for. And unfortunately the hectic pace began to take its toll on the coach's health. In 1952 he suffered a severe heart attack and was sidelined for most of the '52–53 season. Luckily, Diddle's long-time assistant Ted Hornback, was there to pick up the slack. Hornback, whose brilliant tactical mind meshed wonderfully with Diddle's fire and motivational skills, was probably as fine an x's and o's coach as there was in college basketball at the time, and much of Western's athletic success can be attributed to his brilliant coaching. At one time he even accepted the head coaching job at Vanderbilt but after a short stint in Nashville he felt compelled to return to the "Hill" and Coach Diddle.

As the 1950's turned into the 1960's it was becoming obvious that Diddle was wearing down as his health continued to worsen. However, before his eventual retirement after the '63–64 season, he set the table for the future greatness of Hilltopper basketball as Western became one of the first schools in the South to recruit and sign black athletes for their basketball program. And what a job the coach did. The great class of '63 included future first-team All-American Clem Haskins from nearby Campbellsville and Dwight Smith from Princeton, Ky., two of the greatest players ever to play college ball in the state of Kentucky.

The retirement of Mr. Diddle in 1964 set the stage for a new era of basketball at Western but the Diddle influence was still as prevalent as ever. Longtime assistant Ted Hornback became the athletics director and all three of the new coaches were former Hilltoppers: Head coach John Oldham, and assistants Gene Rhodes and Wallace "Buck" Sydnor. That's not even taking into account former player Kelly Thompson, who was then the president of Western, and who at one time many years earlier had decided to drop out of school before Diddle led him to a downtown bank and acquired a $25 loan for him, enabling Thompson to remain at Western. Just a few years later Thompson would step down from the president's post only to be replaced by another of Diddle's former players, Dero Downing.

Retirement never stopped the old coach from cheering on his beloved Toppers however. In 1963, Western's new gymnasium was completed and it was rightfully named E.A. Diddle Arena. And was he ever proud of that gym! Naturally, the coach became a fixture at the arena and he could usually be found out in front of the stands leading cheers with his Red Towel flying. During a heated game against Dayton in 1968, Diddle decided to climb on top of a press table and lead cheers in front of the student section. However, a Dayton sportswriter, who obviously didn't know who he was speaking to, told Diddle that he couldn't climb on top of the table. To which Diddle snapped, "What do you mean I can't get on top of this table? This is my damn gym!" It was indeed his gym . . . his team . . . his school . . . and his town. On January 1, 1970, Western's finest son and Kentucky's greatest coach passed away. In a game based on numbers Diddle was one of the greatest ever . . . in the game of life he was a true champion.

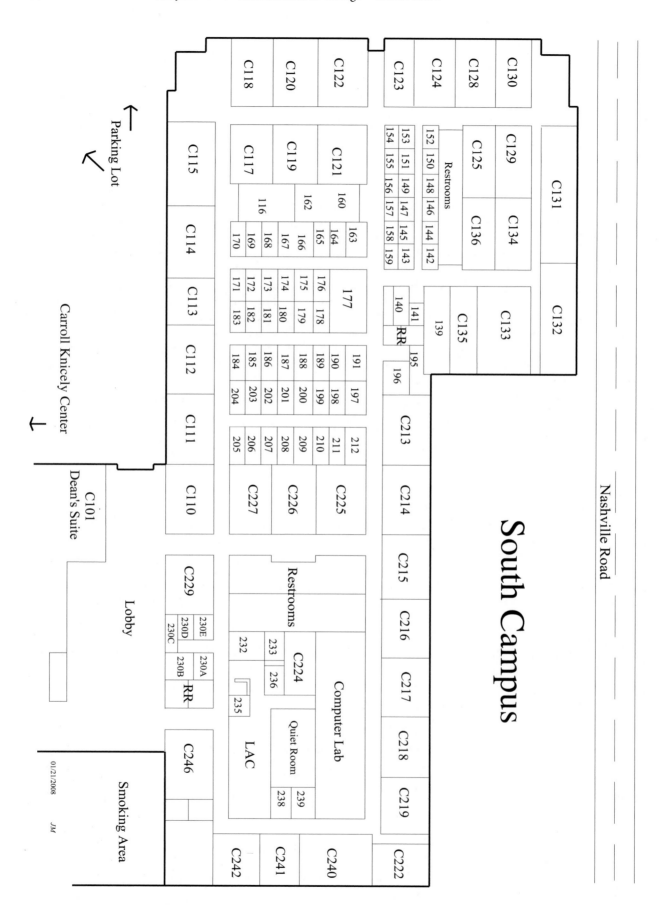

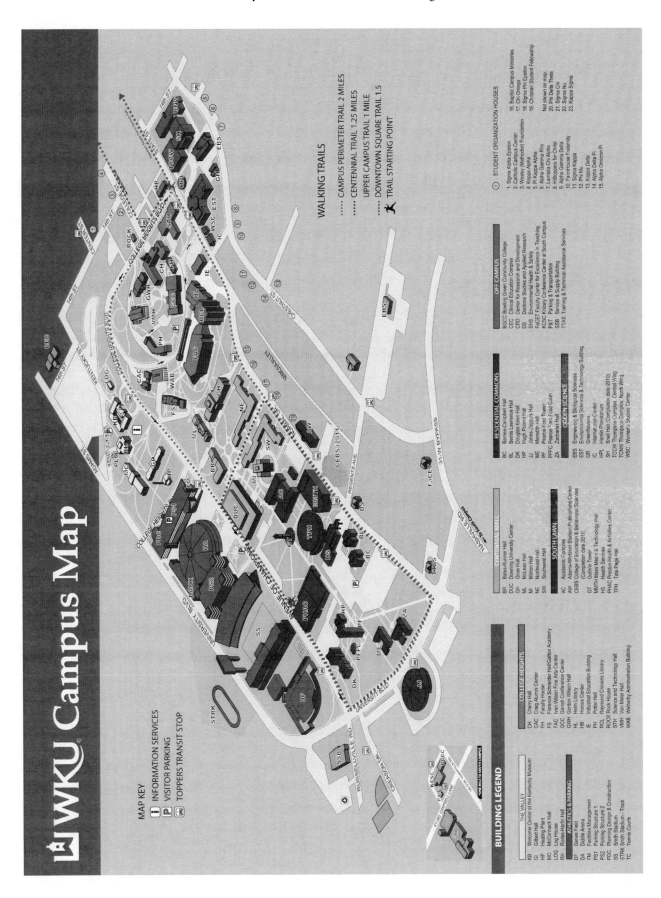

CAMPUS RESOURCES

Alice Rowe Learning Assistance Center (FREE TUTORING)

Room C234 207-780-5636
The primary goal of the LAC is to provide students with the resources they need to become successful, independent learners.

WKU Store at South Campus

You can go online to reserve your textbooks, check textbook prices, and see items available at the bookstore. Information you will need to reserve your books can be found on your class schedule, so please have this available when reserving books online or purchasing books on campus at the bookstore.

To reserve/purchase books online, please visit the following link: http://www.bookstore.wku.edu/

Parking and Transportation

A commuter parking permit is required to park in the South Campus lot. No parking is allowed by students in the Carroll Knicely Visitor Parking area. Also, behind the South Campus there is a Campbell Lane Parking area which is available for use. This lot requires either the Campbell Lane Park & Ride Permit or any other parking permit issued at Western Kentucky University.

Please visit the Parking and Transportation website for purchase prices on permits. Parking permits can be purchased online through Parking and Transportation at the following link: https://wkuparking.t2systems.com/cmn/auth.aspx

Please remember, if you order the permit online by a date specified on the Parking and Transportation website, the permit can be mailed to you. However, permits purchased for the spring and after the priority deadline for the fall will have to be picked up at the Parking and Transportation office located between the Campbell Lane Lot and South Campus, next to the Hattie L. Preston Intramural Sports Complex.

Shuttle services are available at South Campus, which will allow for transportation to classes on Main Campus or various other locations.

Disability Services

Alice Rowe Learning Assistance Center	(270) 780-2536
South Campus	(270) 780-2550
Career Services	(270) 745-3095
Counseling Services	(270) 745-3159
Disability Services	(270) 745-5004
Financial Aid	(270) 745-2755
IT Help Desk	(270) 745-7000
Health Services	(270) 745-5641
Parking/Transportation	(270) 745-2361
Preston Center	(270) 745-5217
South Campus Bookstore	(270) 780-2525
WKU Police	(270) 745-2548

In compliance with the Americans with Disabilities Act, it is the student's responsibility to contact their instructor concerning any special accommodations. **If you need any special assistance and have filled out all the paperwork through Western Kentucky University's Office of Student Disability Services, please see your instructor so they can accommodate your needs. If you need to contact the Office of Student Disability Services please call (270) 745-5004.** Please do not request accommodations without the proper ADA paperwork.

For other campus resources and information, refer to the WKU website at www.wku.edu

Financial Aid Checklist

- Apply for 4-digit FAFSA PIN at www.fafsa.ed.gov. Parents of dependent students will also need a PIN.
- File the FAFSA at www.fafsa.ed.gov, using the appropriate year 1040 tax form. **You are not finished until you click "Submit My FAFSA Now"** *and* **see an EFC number**. The priority deadline is as soon after January 1 as possible, for the next school year, but you may file after that date. Info hotline 1-800-433-3243.
- You will receive a Student Aid Report (SAR) within 2 weeks, which indicates whether you must do Verification. You can make corrections at www.fafsa.ed.gov.
- Within 2–4 weeks, the FAFSA Processing Center will forward your information to WKU. At that point, students are placed into one of two groups:
  A. We will notify via email the approximately 33 percent of students selected to complete Verification. If you are in this group, you will need to submit a Verification Worksheet, available at http://www.wku.edu/Info/FinAid/faforms.htm, along with signed copies of the 1040s you used to complete the FAFSA. The verification process typically takes 4–8 weeks.
  OR
  B. The remaining 66 percent of students not selected do not have to complete this step.
- Your Financial Aid package may include Pell grants, CAP grants, Stafford loans, KEES estimates, Parent PLUS loans, etc. and is largely dependent on your EFC. We will send a message to your WKU email account when you have been awarded.
- You can view this offer and choose to accept or decline the aid in your TopNet account. Select "Financial Aid," "Award," then "Accept Award." It is very important to check "Account Summary by Term" near the start of the semester. This screen shows your WKU bill and payment credits. A positive bottom line number indicates the amount of money you currently owe to WKU, while $0 or a negative balance indicates the bill is paid. If you believe there is an error, please contact us.
- **If this is your first time taking out a Stafford student loan,** please visit www.studentloans.gov and complete the Entrance Counseling Session and the Master Promissory Note. You will need your FAFSA PIN to sign.

Please be aware that it is your responsibility to respond to letters and emails regarding your financial aid. Simply completing the FAFSA does not guarantee financial assistance, but it is the first step in the process. We look forward to working with you!

—WKU Student Financial Assistance, (270) 745-2755

Outreach Counselor: Whitney Hall, extended campus locations and dates at whitney.hall@wku.edu.

STUDENTS' RIGHTS AND RESPONSIBILITIES—OFFICE OF JUDICIAL AFFAIRS

Office of Judicial Affairs

Mission

The mission of the Office of Judicial Affairs is to maintain a campus community conducive to a positive learning environment. The judicial system is an educational tool to initiate student development, learning, and responsibility. In support of the WKU Mission, the Office of Judicial Affairs strives to prepare students to be productive, engaged, and socially responsible citizen leaders of a global society.

The Office will address unacceptable behavior in a manner that informs students and guides them toward modified behavior. The Office will ensure fairness and due process while administering the concepts outlined in the WKU Student Handbook.

General Philosophy

Students are citizens and members of the University academic community. A citizen's rights and liberties under the Constitution must always be applied in light of the special characteristics of the environment in which the rights are to be exercised. Central to the special characteristics of the environment of a state-supported university campus is the special authority of University officials designated by the Board of Regents to control, preserve, and manage University property and affairs and to maintain order and discipline.

Therefore, the WKU Student Code of Conduct was established to ensure that disruptions to the University community are handled in an educational, fair, and dignified manner. The University expects students, parents, and the greater community to respect its rules and procedures governing the WKU community and will resist any unwarranted attempts to influence University policies and procedures.

The University demands high standards of personal conduct and encourages each student to maintain integrity through self-discipline. The University adopts rules and regulations that are necessary for the orderly, harmonious, and beneficial functioning of the University community. Accordingly, each student must respect the rights of others and should abide by the spirit as well as the letter of regulations of the University and laws of the community, state, and nation.

The Office of Judicial Affairs adheres to the Ethical Principles and Standards outlined by the Association for Student Conduct Administration. These Ethical Principles and Standards provide the basis for behavioral expectations within our academic community.

Western Creed

Western Kentucky University is a community dedicated to learning where ideas are offered, examined, and discussed.

As a member of this community, I have both a personal and shared responsibility to participate actively in university life by:

- Practicing personal and academic integrity
- Seeking unity by respecting the dignity of all persons
- Celebrating and embracing diversity
- Encouraging freedom of expression

- Acting in accordance with basic principles of citizenship
- Preserving and appreciating the natural beauty of the campus
- Enriching all aspects of life through the educational process
- Embracing the ideals expressed on the University seal, "Life More Life" and "The Spirit Makes the Master," by pursuing personal growth and a life of excellence.

STUDENT RIGHTS AND RESPONSIBILITIES

Rights

The right of respect for personal feelings, freedom from indignity, and to expect an education of the highest quality.

The right to speak on University property, provided that his/her behavior does not infringe on the rights of others as further defined in the University policy on time, place, and manner of meetings, assemblies, and demonstrations.

The right of freedom to hear and participate in dialogue and to examine diverse views and ideas.

The right to participate in all areas and activities of the University, free from any form of discrimination, including harassment, on the basis of race, color, national or ethnic origin, religion, sex, disability, age, sexual orientation, or veteran status in accordance with applicable federal and state laws.

The right to engage, either individually or in association with others, in off-campus activities, exercising rights as a citizen. When so engaged, in a context in which the participant is identified as a student, there exists a responsibility to make clear that the student does not represent the University.

The right of due process in the disciplinary procedure in accordance with rules of procedures prescribed in the Code of Student Conduct.

Responsibilities

The responsibility of assuming the consequences of one's own actions.

The responsibility to ensure that no student organization, constitution, or other organizational document includes discriminatory clauses pertaining to race, creed, religion, color, sex, national origin, disability, or sexual orientation.

The responsibility to respect the rights and property of others, including other students, the faculty, and the administration.

The responsibility to recognize that student actions reflect upon the individuals involved and upon the entire University community.

The responsibility for knowledge of and observance of established University policies presented in official University publications.

CODE OF CONDUCT:

The Student Code of Conduct educates students about appropriate behavior and fosters a community in which academic success can occur. The following regulations apply to ALL WKU students, including those at the satellite campuses:

1. **Dishonesty.** Dishonesty, such as cheating, plagiarism, misrepresenting of oneself or an organization, knowingly furnishing false information to the University, or omitting relevant or necessary information to gain a benefit, to injure, or to defraud, is prohibited.

2. **Drugs.** Use, possession, production, manufacture, sale, possession with intent to sell, trafficking, or distribution of narcotics, dangerous drugs, or controlled substances, as defined in KRS Chapter 218A, including marijuana, and drug-related activities, including those involving drug paraphernalia, anabolic steroids, and non-prescription drugs except as expressly permitted by law, are prohibited. The manufacture or distribution or attempted manufacture or distribution of narcotics, dangerous drugs, or controlled substances on or off University property is prohibited. **a.** Any student with a violation of the Drug Policy while enrolled at the institution may be removed from student housing and/or suspended from the University. Any student who is found to be manufacturing or distributing drugs on or off campus may be suspended or expelled from the University.

3. **Alcohol.** Western Kentucky University complies with the alcohol regulations of the Commonwealth of Kentucky. Violation of any federal, state, and local laws governing the use and possession of alcoholic beverages, including off-campus, is prohibited. Examples may include but are not limited to driving under the influence (DUI), being assessed as intoxicated in public (AI or PI), and underage consumption. The University prohibits the possession, furnishing, or use of alcoholic beverages (including wine and beer) by student residents of campus housing and/or guests of students in residence halls. The University prohibits the use of rapid consumption devices or drinking games including, but not limited to, kegs, bongs, funnels, and beer pong. Any student found in violation of the Alcohol Policy three times in any one-year period may be suspended from the University for a minimum of one semester.

4. **Sexual Misconduct.** Non-consensual sexual contact, including but not limited to sexual assault or abuse, rape, acquaintance rape, or sodomy (please refer to the Sexual Offense Policy), is prohibited.

5. **Weapons.** Possession or use of firearms, explosives (including fireworks), dangerous chemicals, or other dangerous weapons, or the brandishing of any weapon or any other object in a menacing or threatening manner on institutionally owned or controlled property, is prohibited. A weapon may be defined as an object, instrument, device, or substance designed to inflict a wound, cause injury, or incapacitate. Weapons may include, but are not limited to all firearms, pellet guns, stun guns, paintball guns, air guns, slingshots, martial arts devices, switchblade knives, and clubs. Weapons will be confiscated and placed in the possession of University Police for proper disposal.

6. **Identification.** Refusal to provide proper identification upon request is a violation of the Code of Conduct. Students are expected to carry their valid student identification at all times and to present it upon request by University officials including, but not limited to, University Police, faculty, residence life staff, and other staff of the institution. The University may confiscate any ID card that has been misused, duplicated, or altered. Cards may be retained temporarily while their validity is checked. A student may possess only one ID card. Use of the ID card by any person other than the person to whom it was issued or use of the card under false pretenses is a violation of the Code of Conduct.

7. **Theft.** Theft and possession of stolen property are prohibited. Such property may include, but is not limited to, parking decals and personal or university property. Theft of property having substantial value may result in serious disciplinary action for a first offense.

8. **Hazing.** Hazing refers to practices that are a part of initiation into an affiliation with any organization. Hazing is considered a serious violation of the Student Code of Conduct and is prohibited in all forms. This Code of Conduct is based

on fair and equal treatment with consideration and respect for all students and applies to organizations and individuals alike. Any person receiving bodily injury by hazing or mistreatment shall have a right to sue, civilly, the person or persons guilty.

Western Kentucky University defines hazing as any action, physical abuse, or creation of a situation that recklessly or intentionally endangers the mental or physical health of a participant by any person. A participant is defined as a university student or any pledge. A person is defined as a university student, member, alumnus, affiliate alumnus, guest of any campus organization, or other individuals.

Physical Abuse:

- Forced or coerced use or consumption of liquor, drugs, or any other vile substance.
- Calisthenics (push-ups, sit-ups, jogging, runs, etc.)
- Paddling
- Line-ups

Mental Abuse:

Harassment is defined as exacting degrading and disagreeable work, ridicule, or abusive and humiliating conduct which tends to bring the reputation of the organization or University into disrepute. Any action that intentionally prevents students from fully participating in the academic process is also considered hazing.

- Theft of any property
- Sleep deprivation
- Forced nudity
- Personal servitude
- Forcing a violation of University policies and federal, state, or local laws

9. **Harassment.** Physical abuse, threatening comments, or intimidation of any person on University owned or controlled property or at University sponsored or supervised functions, or conduct which threatens or endangers the health or safety of any member of the University community or any other person or persons, is prohibited. Such conduct includes, but is not limited to, stalking, cyber stalking, harassment, and retaliation as a result of complaints or alleged misconduct.

10. **Unruly Conduct.** Disorderly or lewd conduct, any words or acts that result in physical altercation, fighting, and indecent or obscene conduct or expression that causes physical injury or threatens oneself or others, or interferes with any individual's rightful act, are prohibited. This responsibility also applies at events sponsored and supervised by recognized student organizations, on or off campus.

11. **Demonstration of Physical Harm.** Any student who demonstrates intent to seriously harm himself/herself or otherwise poses a danger causing psychological or physical harm to self is violating the Code of Conduct.

12. **Disrupting the Academic and/or Judicial Process.** Interference or disruptive activity that impedes, impairs, or obstructs teaching, research, administration, or judicial process, failing to comply with the sanctions imposed under the Student Code of Conduct, or other University missions, processes, functions, or other

authorized activities, including its public service function of other authorized activities on University premises, or inhibits full exercise of rights by others, is prohibited.

13. **Class Attendance and Classroom Conduct.** Regular classroom attendance is expected of all students. Although roll may not be taken, grades are based on the performance of assigned work, and this may include class participation and attendance. A professor has the authority to determine acceptable classroom conduct for his or her students as long as those decisions do not infringe on the student's rights. Disruptive classroom behavior may also be considered unruly conduct (see item 10).

14. **Technology Use Ethics.** Any violation of the Technology Ethics Policy as created by the Department of Information and Technology is considered a violation of the Student Code of Conduct.

15. **Shared Responsibility for Violations.** Enticing, inciting others, abetting, conspiring, being an accessory, or passively witnessing/participating in any act prohibited by the Student Code of Conduct is prohibited.

16. **Requests or Orders.** Refusal to comply with directions, requests, or orders by University officials or law enforcement, or failing to identify oneself when requested to do so, is a violation of the Student Code of Conduct. Upon the request of the student questioned, the authorized university official must show identification and state the source of his/her authority. Among those officials who may request a student's ID card are staff members from Residence Life, Downing University Center, WKU Food Services, Faculty and Staff, and the Book Store, as well as any staff member within the Division of Student Affairs.

17. **Misuse of Property.** Unauthorized entry or use of institutional facilities and property; unauthorized possession or duplication of University keys, parking decals, or access cards; tampering with fire equipment; or propping open of exterior residence hall doors or any door to any institutionally owned or controlled property is prohibited. Students may not use University property for any activity prohibited by federal, state, or local laws.

18. **Destruction of Property.** Any act of vandalism or malicious or unwarranted damage or destruction to any institutionally owned or controlled property is prohibited.

19. **Recreational Mobility.** Skateboards, skates, and bicycles may be used on sidewalks for safe transportation purposes only. When using sidewalks, remember pedestrians have the right of way. They may not be used inside buildings or within 50 feet of building entrances. Motorized scooters, mopeds, motorcycles, and similarly motorized vehicles are not to be used on sidewalks or in pedestrian traffic areas. Motorcycles, scooters, mopeds, and other motorized vehicles must park in parking lots in designated cycle parking areas. Registration with the WKU Parking and Transportation Services department is required for all motorized vehicles. On-campus housing residents may only bring one motorized vehicle to campus.

    Excessive speed, stunt riding, or any other use of skateboards, skates, bicycles, or motorized vehicles that may cause property damage and/or endanger self or others is prohibited. Bicycles should be parked at any of the bicycle racks established throughout campus. Bicycles chained to trees, fences, handrails, etc., may be impounded. Users may not ride on stairways, patios, dock areas, benches, picnic tables, or irregular surfaces. Any person causing damage to University property through use or misuse of recreational equipment may face prosecution through the University Judicial process and/or the legal process to recover damages.

20. **Obstruction of Access.** Obstruction or disruption that interferes with the freedom of movement, either pedestrian or vehicular, on institutionally owned or controlled property is prohibited.
21. **Traffic and Parking Regulations.** Traffic rules and regulations as published by the University will be administered by the Office of Traffic and Parking. Students are required to obey these regulations as a condition of their enrollment. Any behavior that is unruly or demonstrates disrespect for their authority will be deemed a violation of the Code of Conduct.
22. **Fraud.** Knowingly passing a worthless check or money order, or fraudulent use of credit cards, including attempts to obtain any item of value under false pretenses or falsification of official university documents, is prohibited.
23. **Forgery.** Forgery, alteration, or misuse of University documents and records, including, but not limited to, electronic records, transactions, and/or communications, or identification, including student identification cards, is prohibited.
24. **Gambling.** Participation in any form of illegal gambling is prohibited.
25. **Violation of Laws.** The commission of acts that constitute a violation of local, state, and federal laws is prohibited. The University will review any conduct reported by members of the University community, law enforcement personnel, or citizens as being in violation of the law. Any student convicted of a criminal offense is subject to University judicial action.
26. **Violation of General Rules and Regulations.** Violation of any University policy, guideline, campus rule, or regulation of conduct that adversely affects the student's suitability as a member of the University community is considered a violation of the Code of Conduct.

Following the procedures of due process, if the WKU Student Code of Conduct is not followed, the alleged parties may go through the University's judicial process, which is intended to be a fair and educational experience.

JUDICIAL ACTIONS

The following list describes University sanctions that may be administered as a result of violating the WKU Student Code of Conduct. Sanctions may be imposed only after a conference at which the student has had the opportunity to review alleged violations, review any evidence, and respond.

Sanctions may be used independently or in combination depending on the particular circumstance of the violation. Chronic and/or multiple violations during the course of an individual student's college career may increase the level of sanctions applied.

1. **Warning and/or Reprimand.** Official notice to a student that conduct or actions are in violation. The continuation of such conduct or actions may result in further disciplinary action.
2. **Creative Sanction.** A sanction that may be used in lieu of, or in combination with, sanctions numbered three through six below. Creative discipline will be consistent with the offense committed. In some cases, at the discretion of the hearing officer, a student found in violation may attend special educational seminars, classes, or workshops offered in the subject area of the violation or be sanctioned in another way that is directly related to the violation. In these cases, the student must always submit written proof of completion of the sanction to the hearing officer. The University may also contact parents or legal guardians of students found in violation of policy concerning the possession of alcohol or controlled substances if the student is under 21.

3. **Disciplinary Agreement.** Behavior contract between the University and the student whereby the student agrees, in writing, to correct inappropriate behaviors.

4. **Restricted Use of Facilities.** Denial of on-campus use of an automobile for a specified period of time, removal from a living group, or denial of another privilege including the use of specific University facilities, consistent with the offense committed. Restricted use of facilities may be accompanied by other sanctions.

5. **Restitution.** Reimbursement by transfer of property or service to the University or a member of the University community in an amount not in excess of the damage or loss incurred. Reimbursement may be accompanied by other sanctions.

6. **Restricted University Participation.** Exclusion for a period of time from participating in extracurricular activities, including recognized student organizations and/or representing the University in any manner. Classroom attendance will be unaffected.

   The following sanction may be imposed upon groups or organizations:

   Deactivation—Loss of all privileges, including University recognition, for a specified period of time.

7. **Disciplinary Probation.** A period of observation and review of conduct in which the student demonstrates compliance with the provisions of University regulations. Any student found in violation of the Student Code of Conduct while on Disciplinary Probation in the same semester of academic probation may be subject to suspension or dismissal from the university immediately.

8. **Deferred Suspension.** In some cases, a sanction of suspension may be held in abeyance for a specified period. This means that, if the student is found responsible for any violation during that period, he or she will be subject to the deferred sanction without further review, in addition to the disciplinary action appropriate to the new violation.

9. **Separation.** Dismissal from the University for at least one semester. Students separated from the University are eligible to apply for reinstatement to the University. Readmission is not guaranteed.

10. **Interim Suspension.** Exclusion for a period of time, prior to a disciplinary hearing, from the residence halls or campus (including classes) and all other college activities or privileges of a University student.

    Interim suspension may be imposed only:

    - To ensure the safety and well-being of members of the University community or preservation of University property.
    - To ensure the student's own physical or emotional safety and well-being; or
    - If the student poses a definite threat of disruption of or interference with the normal operations of the University.

11. **Suspension.** Exclusion for a period of time, generally from one term to one year. A separation from the university is a time away for a number of academic semesters or until certain conditions are met.

    In certain circumstances, the Director of Judicial Affairs or the Vice President for Student Affairs may impose a University or residence hall suspension. All students who reach a level of sanction that includes any suspension may not be eligible to reside in the University Housing System.

12. Expulsion. Dismissal from the University for an indefinite period of time. Any student expelled may not, thereafter, be readmitted to the University except upon application to the Board of Regents through the President.

OFFICE OF JUDICIAL AFFAIRS CAMPUS RESPONSIBILITY

Following the procedures of due process, if the WKU Student Code of Conduct is violated, the alleged parties will go through the University's judicial process, which is intended to be a fair and educational experience.

Anytime a student is sanctioned by the University for inappropriate behavior, it is considered serious. Cases involving sanctions of warning, creative discipline, disciplinary agreement, restricted use of facilities, restitution, and disciplinary probation are usually not serious enough to warrant expulsion or suspension. Cases of this nature, which involve incidents occurring within the university residence halls, may be heard by the designee of the Executive Director of Housing and Residence Life and/or the Director of Judicial Affairs. With exception, all cases involving student arrests, drug violations resulting in arrest, sexual misconduct, physical assaults, unruly conduct, and academic dishonesty will be heard by the Office of Judicial Affairs or its designee. Those cases that involve serious incidents occurring off-campus and more egregious on-campus violations of the Student Code of Conduct will be heard by the University Disciplinary Committee under the direction of the Office of Judicial Affairs.

University Disciplinary Committee

A University committee for student disciplinary matters has been established by action of the Board of Regents of Western Kentucky University in accordance with the Kentucky Revised Statutes, which authorize the Board of Regents to invest the faculty/staff or a committee of the faculty/staff with the power to suspend or expel any student for severe violations of the WKU Student Code of Conduct or a gross disregard for the rights of others in the campus community. Therefore, this Committee will consider all cases involving sanctions of deferred suspension, suspension, and expulsion. In every case, the person suspended or expelled may appeal through the President if they meet the conditions for appeal.

The Committee is comprised of 13 members—six faculty, five staff, and two students—who are appointed by the President of the University. Faculty terms are three years and are staggered so that the term of one-third of the membership expires each year.

At least seven members of the Committee must be present before any official action is taken. Any decision will be made by a majority of those Committee members present. The Committee is to be notified of a meeting by the Office of Judicial Affairs or members of its staff immediately upon determination of the necessity for such a meeting.

Committee meetings are conducted in two parts. In the first part, only the information that bears on whether or not the student has engaged in specified violations or misconduct may be presented. If the Committee finds no violation or misconduct, the finding is recorded and the proceeding is concluded.

If the finding is that the student has, in fact, engaged in a violation or misconduct, the Committee shall, in the second part of the proceeding, hear and consider any information bearing upon circumstances of extenuation or mitigation. After this part is concluded, the Committee shall determine the appropriate sanction. The Committee will function in accordance with its own procedures.

EDUCATIONAL SANCTIONS

Alcohol 101

(Any student with a first-time violation of the alcohol code of conduct)

    Provides information regarding alcohol consumption of college students
    Educates students on alcohol statutes in the Commonwealth of Kentucky
    Educates students on policies/sanctions related to alcohol at WKU
    Offers suggestions and guidelines for practicing low-risk drinking habits

Prime For Life

(Any student with a major or second violation of the alcohol code of conduct or first violation of the drug code of conduct)

PRIME For Life is an alcohol and drug program for people of all ages. It is designed to gently but powerfully challenge common beliefs and attitudes that directly contribute to high-risk alcohol and drug use. The program goals are to reduce the risk for health problems and impairment problems by increasing abstinence, delaying initial use, and decreasing high-risk use.

A primary goal of **PRIME** For Life is prevention of any type of alcohol or drug problem. This includes prevention of health problems such as alcoholism, or impairment problems such as car crashes or fights. Emphasis is on knowing and understanding risks one cannot change and reducing risks one can change.

Many people who attend a **PRIME** For Life program already show signs of alcohol- or drug-related health or impairment problems. **PRIME** For Life is designed to effectively interrupt the progression of use with these audiences. **PRIME** For Life's intervention component focuses on self-assessment to help people understand and accept the need for change. Intensive prevention services, counseling, or treatment may be necessary to support these changes. For those who already need treatment, the program serves as pre-treatment and support for abstinence.

Using a persuasion-based approach, instructors use a variety of delivery methods, including interactive presentation and small group discussion. Participants use workbooks throughout the course to complete a number of individual and group activities. Material is presented using a DVD platform with animation, full-motion video clips, and audio clips to enhance the learning experience.

Several themes run throughout **PRIME** For Life. The first is an emphasis on the reality that while all of us can influence another person's drinking choices to some degree, none of us can directly control those choices. Therefore, the program is designed to maximize the influence of helping professionals, instructors, or family members.

Second, **PRIME** For Life is based on objective, documented research findings, not opinion, exaggerations, or scare tactics. Credibility (of program and instructor/counselor) is a key factor in initiating and maintaining behavior change. Instructors are trained to master the program to maximize program impact.

Third, **PRIME** For Life focuses on information that is needed to bring about behavior change. In fact, a casual observer might conclude that the program places too little emphasis on process and that there is too much information for the typical participant to remember. Participants are not expected to remember the details of the research cited. The content is only one of the tools used in the persuasion process. What participants will remember are the critical conclusions that come from hearing the information: Who can experience alcohol or drug problems? How do I estimate biological risk? How do I know what low risk is and how far my alcohol and drug choices have progressed? They remember the information they can use, even if some do not use it right away. The carefully selected, research-based information also provides the credibility needed to promote change.

PRIME For Life emphasizes both what is said and how it is said. Both content and process are keys to successful delivery of the program and to the ultimate goal, behavior change.

Prime for Life Class Information

Students assigned this sanction will be required to pay *$85.00* for educational materials provided in this nationally recognized and certified program. Successful completion of the program will provide students with useful information encouraging responsible and appropriate behavior when considering using alcohol or drugs. University policies regarding drug and alcohol use will also be addressed within the program.

Appropriate referrals include students found responsible for being drunk in the residence halls; a major violation of the alcohol policy; an alcohol-related offense with a previous judicial record for an alcohol violation, regardless of when that violation occurred; another violation of the WKU Student Code of Conduct for the same incident (i.e., noise violation, fighting, vandalism); providing alcohol to a minor; and/or selling alcohol illegally.

ACADEMIC DISHONESTY

Such as cheating, plagiarism, misrepresenting of oneself or an organization, knowingly furnishing false information to the University, or omitting relevant or necessary information to gain a benefit, to injure, or to defraud is prohibited.

Academic Integrity

The maintenance of academic integrity is of fundamental importance to the University. Thus it should be clearly understood that acts of plagiarism or any other form of cheating will not be tolerated and that anyone committing such acts risks punishment of a serious nature.

Academic Dishonesty

Students who commit any act of academic dishonesty may receive from the instructor a failing grade in that portion of the course work in which the act is detected or a failing grade in a course without possibility of withdrawal. The faculty member may also present the case to the Office of Judicial Affairs for disciplinary sanctions. A student who believes a faculty member has dealt unfairly with him/her in a course involving academic dishonesty may seek relief through the Student Complaint Procedure.

Plagiarism

To represent written work taken from another source as one's own is plagiarism. Plagiarism is a serious offense. The academic work of a student must be his/her own. One must give any author credit for source material borrowed from him/her. To lift content directly from a source without giving credit is a flagrant act. To present a borrowed passage without reference to the source after having changed a few words is also plagiarism.

Cheating

No student shall receive or give assistance not authorized by the instructor in taking an examination or in the preparation of an essay, laboratory report, problem assignment, or other project that is submitted for purposes of grade determination.

Other Types of Academic Dishonesty

Other types of academic offenses, such as the theft or sale of tests, electronic transmission of tests, test sharing, etc. will be reported to the Office of Judicial Affairs for disciplinary action.

ALCOHOL AND DRUG PREVENTION POLICY

Statement of Purpose

As a recipient of federal grants and contracts, the University has developed the following policy to ensure compliance with both the Drug-Free Workplace Act of 1988 and the Drug-Free Schools and Communities Act Amendments of 1989. Students are herein notified of the standards of conduct that shall be applicable while on Western Kentucky University property and/or participating in University-sponsored activities. Conduct that does not comply with this policy poses unacceptable risks and disregard for the health, safety, and welfare of the University community. Students may be subject to disciplinary sanctions up to and including expulsion and/or referral for prosecution for violation of this policy.

Alcohol and Drug Abuse Policy

Western Kentucky University prohibits the unlawful use (or as restricted by University policy), possession, manufacture, and distribution of illicit drugs and alcohol by its students and employees on its property or as part of any of its activities. Persons who violate this policy may be subject to campus disciplinary action and referral to law enforcement agencies. Students found to have committed a violation of this policy may be subject to University sanctions that may include probation, suspension, or dismissal. The level of sanction will be determined by assessing the seriousness of the breach of policy, the effect the conduct has on the institution, and the assessed probability that other violations will not be committed by the person(s) in the future. The minimum sanction for illegal sale or distribution of drugs includes separation from the University and referral for prosecution. Referral to treatment programs will be mandated when appropriate.

Distribution of Policy

At least annually, Western Kentucky University shall inform students of the dangers of drug and alcohol abuse on campus, the existence of this policy statement, its penalties for violations, and available drug and alcohol counseling, rehabilitation, and assistance through the following actions:

1. Appropriate publication, at least annually, of this policy in appropriate student publications and distribution to students in WKU's international programs and to study abroad participants;

2. Insertion of this policy in future editions of student class schedules and/or registration materials, student handbooks, and student catalogs;
3. Dissemination of this policy and related information at student orientation events and distribution of information concerning assistance programs and available rehabilitation programs; and
4. Continuation, and expansion, of the drug and alcohol awareness program and publication of pamphlets and other materials.

Health Risks Associated with Alcohol and Drug Abuse

1. Alcohol: **Effects**

   Information concerning alcohol and its effects appears on the WKU Student Wellness website.
2. Controlled Substances: **Effects**

   There are many serious and potentially irreversible or life-threatening effects from the use of controlled substances. A summary of these effects is available on the WKU Student Wellness website.

   Information regarding appropriate responses to students perceived to be under the influence of alcohol and/or illicit drugs while engaged in University activities or on University premises is available on the Judicial Affairs website.

Penalties and Sanctions

Internal

Under University regulations, students who violate the standards of conduct relating to alcohol and other drug use may be subject to disciplinary action under the student disciplinary process. Sanctions include, but are not limited to, warnings, restricted University participation, parental notification, suspension from the University, or probation, suspension, or termination of employment. Students who reside in Western Kentucky University housing are subject to additional disciplinary action that may vary from a warning to termination of their housing contract. Specifically defined sanctions for conduct violations appear in the Student Handbook.

External

In addition to University sanctions, individuals may face prosecution and imprisonment under state and federal laws that make such acts felony and misdemeanor crimes. Under University regulations, and state and federal drug laws, the gravity of the sanction depends on the classification of the controlled substance, the particular activity (possession or trafficking, which includes manufacture, sale, and possession with intent to sell) and amounts involved, and whether it is a first or multiple offense or conviction.

Charts detailing Federal Penalties and Sanctions for Illegal Possession of a Controlled Substance and Penalties of Kentucky Law for Driving under the Influence (KRS 189) appear on the Judicial Affairs website.

Additional information pertaining to federal penalties for certain drug-related offenses by the federal government appears on the U.S. Department of Justice, Drug Enforcement Administration website.

"Three Strikes" Alcohol Policy

- If you are under 21, it is against the Student Code of Conduct for you to drink.
- It is against the Student Code of Conduct for anyone to buy alcohol for someone under 21.
- It is against the Student Code of Conduct for anyone to be drunk in public or to drive while drunk.
- It is a violation of the Student Code of Conduct for your drunken behavior to disturb someone else's ability to sleep, study, or live peacefully.
- It is a violation of the Student Code of Conduct for you to hurt or endanger yourself or someone else through drinking.

HERE ARE THE *LIKELY* SANCTIONS

If you are found responsible for an alcohol violation that does not affect the health, safety, or welfare of yourself or others, you are **likely** to receive:

- Disciplinary Agreement and an educational experience for the first offense
- Probation and an educational experience for the second offense
- Separation or Suspension (referral to University Disciplinary Committee) for the third offense

If you are found responsible for an alcohol-related offense in which your own health or safety is affected, or in which you disturb, hurt, or endanger others through your drinking, you are **likely** to receive:

- Probation and an educational experience for the first offense (DUI arrests or getting so drunk that you become seriously ill or unconscious, hospitalization)
- Deferred Suspension for the first offense (alcohol-related fights or major violations related to alcohol use)
- If you are removed from an athletic event for alcohol-related problems, your privilege to attend events in the future **may** be suspended.

Zero Tolerance

Drug Policy

Drugs. Use, possession, production, manufacture, sale, possession with intent to sell, trafficking, or distribution of narcotics, dangerous drugs, or controlled substances, as defined in KRS Chapter 218A, including marijuana, and drug-related activities, including those involving drug paraphernalia, anabolic steroids, and non-prescription drugs except as expressly permitted by law, are prohibited. The manufacture or distribution or attempted manufacture or distribution of narcotics, dangerous drugs, or controlled substances on or off University property is prohibited.

SAFETY RESOURCES

Reporting Sexual Assault

Title IX

Title IX of the Education Amendments of 1972 is a federal law that prohibits sex discrimination in education.

It reads:

"No person in the United States shall, on the basis of sex, be excluded from participation in, be denied the benefits of, or be subjected to discrimination under any education program or activity receiving Federal financial assistance." Title IX of the Education Amendments of 1972, and its implementing regulation at 34 C.F.R. Part 106 (Title IX)
Sex discrimination includes sexual harassment and sexual assault.

WKU Code of Conduct related to Sexual Misconduct

Sexual misconduct is non-consensual sexual contact, including but not limited to sexual assault or abuse, rape, acquaintance rape, or sodomy.

The Investigation Process

It is also the position of the Office of Judicial Affairs that among the violations of misconduct considered to be of an especially serious nature are those that represent a threat to the safety and health of members of the University community. These include, but are not limited to, harassment, physical violence or threat of violence, non-consensual sexual contact, and rape.

Incidents of alleged sexual assault should be reported to a professional counselor or university official. WKU will investigate all reported sexual assaults or attempted assaults and, where appropriate, will hold individuals accountable for their actions according to the procedures outlined in the Student Code of Conduct. Following the procedures of due process, if the WKU Student Code of Conduct is violated, the alleged parties will go through the University's judicial process, which is intended to be a fair and educational experience. The accused and the complainant are entitled to the same opportunities to discuss their involvement in the alleged incident with the Office of Judicial Affairs and his/her designee. Those cases which determine a violation of the Student Code of Conduct will be heard by the University Disciplinary Committee. The range of sanctions up to and including suspension or expulsion from the University are possible depending upon the preponderance of the evidence and individual circumstances. Both the accuser and the accused shall be informed of the outcome of any on-campus judicial conference alleging a sexual assault or harassment.

The Office of Judicial Affairs and its designee(s) will address any complaint in a confidential, supportive, and timely manner. The Office of Judicial Affairs will oversee that fairness and due process are ensured while administering this process for both parties involved. All investigations will be conducted independently of one another.

Who to Contact

At WKU, students are encouraged to report to the following for confidential counseling with a professional counselor or university official. Here are some phone numbers to keep available:

- WKU Counseling and Testing Center: 270-745-3159
- WKU Housing and Residence Life: 270-745-4359
- WKU Office of Judicial Affairs: 270-745-5429
- WKU University Police: 270-745-2548
- WKU Health Services: 270-745-5641
- Hope Harbor: A Sexual Trauma Recovery Center: 270-782-5014 or 24-hour crisis line 270-846-1100 or 1-800-656-4673 (HOPE)
- WKU Department of Human Resources: 270-745-5360

Crisis Response

Sexual assault is an act of violence. The victim of an assault may be in a state of shock and disbelief, and may be feeling a variety or emotions such as fear, anger, helplessness, shame, and/or guilt. A victimized student may not know who to trust or where to turn for help. The student who has been sexually assaulted has many options in seeking assistance. A number of resources are available both on and off campus to assist assault victims. Although it is the student's option whether to seek legal, medical, and/or psychological services, students are encouraged to utilize these resources in order to make the most informed choices regarding prosecution, physical safety, and emotional recovery.

If you are the victim of a sexual assault, please know that you are in no way to blame for the criminal behavior. Here are some guidelines to help you in the aftermath of a sexual assault:

1. **GO TO A SAFE PLACE** as soon as possible.
2. **TRY TO PRESERVE ALL PHYSICAL EVIDENCE.** Do not wash, bathe, use the toilet, or change clothing if it can be avoided. If changing clothes is a must, put all clothing worn at the time of the assault in a paper bag, *not plastic*. A plastic bag can be used if paper is not available. However, do not seal the bag tightly, as that can cause a breakdown of the evidence.
3. **IF YOU BELIEVE YOU WERE GIVEN A DATE RAPE DRUG,** see a physician or nurse immediately. Wait to urinate until you arrive at the hospital. However, if you can't wait, collect your first urine in a clean container with a lid and take it to the emergency room or police station with you. Ask specifically for a drug screen that includes GHB, Rohypnol, and other common drugs used to facilitate sexual assaults. It is imperative that you be tested as soon as possible for the drug's presence in your body, as most of these substances can only be detected for a short period of time after ingestion.
4. **CONTACT SOMEONE** for support and information (family, friend, university staff, or campus police). You can also call 1-800-656-4673 or 270-846-1100 to talk with a rape counselor.
5. **SEEK MEDICAL ATTENTION** to address physical health needs, to ensure that you are disease- and injury-free, and to collect important evidence in the event of a later decision to take legal action. Hospital emergency rooms provide evidentiary exams, which include testing and treatment for sexually transmitted infections, pregnancy, and physical trauma. Emergency medical care can be received at the Medical Center of Bowling Green (250 Park Street or 270-745-1000) or Greenview Hospital (1801 Ashley Circle or 270-793-1000). For victims assaulted in the Commonwealth of Kentucky, these exams are free of charge. Should you need transportation, the University's Police Department (270-745-2548) can assist you. If you choose not to have an evidentiary exam conducted, please consider an appointment at a health department, Health Services (270-745-5641), or with your regular physician.
6. **CONSIDER COUNSELING** for support and to help you deal with a variety of feelings that often follow an assault. Free and confidential counseling services are available through WKU's Counseling and Testing Center (270-745-3159) or through Hope Harbor (270-846-1100) or Life Skills (270-237-4481).
7. If you choose to **REPORT THE ASSAULT,** you can contact law enforcement by calling 911 or WKU police at 270-745-2548. A call to the University Police does

not mean that you must bring criminal charges. The decision to file an official police report is yours to make. If the assault did not occur on campus, University law enforcement can assist you in determining how and where to file a police report. Timely notification helps the police in conducting their investigation and it provides a better chance of successful prosecution. You are encouraged to report the sexual assault and have it documented, even if you are not sure about filing formal criminal charges. Regardless of whether you report the incident to the police, you are still encouraged to seek medical attention to ensure your own personal safety.

Reporting an assault and receiving medical treatment does not require that the victim press charges. It does, however, allow the collection of data and information that can be used should the victim choose to press charges.

REFERENCES

http://www.wku.edu/judicialaffairs/mission.php
http://www.wku.edu/judicialaffairs/about.php
http://www.wku.edu/judicialaffairs/wkucreed.php
http://www.wku.edu/judicialaffairs/student-rights-responsibilities.php
http://www.wku.edu/judicialaffairs/student-code-of-conduct.php
http://www.wku.edu/judicialaffairs/sanctions.php
http://www.wku.edu/judicialaffairs/educationalsanctions.php
http://www.wku.edu/judicialaffairs/process-for-academic-dishonesty.php
http://www.wku.edu/judicialaffairs/u-d-c.php
http://www.wku.edu/judicialaffairs/alcohol-drug-preventionpolicy.php
http://www.wku.edu/judicialaffairs/plain-english-alcohol-policy.php
http://www.wku.edu/judicialaffairs/studentdrugcode.php
http://www.wku.edu/handbook/reportingsa.php
http://www.wku.edu/handbook/community_resources.php
http://www.wku.edu/handbook/crisisresponse.php

STUDENT ORGANIZATIONS

Student Activities: Life Outside of the Classroom!

You've come to college to obtain an education in your field of choosing; however, there is more to college than just going to class. While class is the most important item on your daily agenda, WKU offers a variety of ways to expand upon your classroom experience. Student organizations at WKU provide an incredible opportunity to meet new people, build leadership and event planning skills, share ideas, make connections across campus, and have fun!

WKU is home to over 300 student organizations providing opportunities for students to engage with a wide variety of interests and activities. Involvement with these organizations can give students a foundation for success, a passion for learning, and a commitment to responsible global citizenship, while fostering creativity and service. Organizations can provide not only membership but a safe home from where students can pursue their passions. Through cultural events, student organizations, and service learning opportunities, there is something out there for everyone.

Student Organizations at WKU

For a full listing of student organizations, please visit www.wku.edu/sao and click on "Registered Student Organizations" on the left-hand side of the page.

Listed below are just a few of the ways to get involved on the campus of Western Kentucky University.

Campus Ministries

WKU has over 20 active campus ministry organizations to meet the diverse spiritual needs of our students. Campus ministries offer weekly services on campus or at local churches. They also conduct retreats, mission trips, and local service projects for the participants.

Campus Activities Board

The WKU Campus Activities Board seeks to enrich the educational experience of students at WKU and support the overall mission of Western Kentucky University by offering a wide range of co-curricular experiences for students, faculty, and staff. CAB further seeks to provide leadership, involvement, and engagement opportunities for students in the planning, proposal, promotion, and presentation of a variety of activities. These activities are designated to serve the cultural, educational, and social interests of the WKU community. CAB traditionally sponsors, plans, promotes, and presents several major events yearly. Some of these include:

- Homecoming
- Concert Series
- Big Reds Roar
- CAB-OOM
- CAB After Dark Series
- Black History Lecture Series

Greek Life

The fraternity and sorority community has been a vital part of the student experience at WKU for the past 45 years. Over 1,500 students are members of our 17 fraternities and 14 sororities. Greek organizations produce outstanding leaders across all areas of campus life, and we hold high standards for academic achievement, leadership development, and community service. Joining a fraternity or sorority is a great springboard to other avenues of campus involvement such as the Student Government Association, Leadership and Volunteerism programs, campus-wide service projects, and intramurals.

Student Government Association

In 1956, Western Kentucky University students began actively participating in the administration of the university with the creation of the Student Advisory Council. Over the next 10 years, students struggled to achieve the influence they desired, but in 1966 the student body ratified the first version of its constitution and elected James P. "Jim" Haynes as the first president of the Associated Students. In 1992, the Associated Students changed its name to the Student Government Association. The Student Government Association of Western Kentucky University is an organization committed to the advocacy of every student that enters and subsequently exits WKU. SGA believes that each student has a vital opinion and voice, and the organization is fully committed to serving these students. Like the federal government, the SGA is comprised of three branches: executive, legislative, and judicial. These branches all have separate but fundamental duties; however, members of SGA—regardless of branch membership—collaborate often when developing new ideas to better serve the student population. SGA has developed numerous programs to help serve the needs of WKU. Campus Clean-Up, Campus Safety Walks, the Hall of Distinguished Seniors, Dine with Decision Makers, the Rally for Higher Education, Organizational Aid, Scholar Development, and Provide-A-Ride are examples of signature services provided by the SGA.

Leadership Development Opportunities

- **DLI (Dynamic Leadership Institute):** The Dynamic Leadership Institute began at WKU in the 1990s. The program is designed to teach students the basic interpersonal skills and knowledge needed to engage in various leadership roles on campus, within the community, and in their futures. Each of the four phases allows the students to view leadership from different perspectives and provides opportunities for them to examine and enhance their leadership skills.
- **LeaderShape:** This six-day, nationally recognized program focuses on developing an individual's goals and visions for a better future. The mission of LeaderShape states, "To transform the world by increasing the number of people who *lead with integrity*™ and a healthy disregard for the impossible." During these six days, students are immersed in intensive leadership training, which is centered on consideration for ethical values, developing meaningful relationships, and growing as an individual and as a leader. WKU holds a campus LeaderShape each spring following the week of graduation.
- **Leadership Conference:** In this one-day leadership conference, students from across campus come together to develop their leadership skills and network with fellow student leaders. This conference is designed to enhance current leadership opportunities available to students at WKU.
- **Weekend in the Woods:** This is a two-day retreat where first-year freshmen exchange leadership ideas, focus on special topics, and work on campus unity. This retreat is part of an invaluable process that helps ensure future leaders are working toward the same goal—a better WKU!

Can't find the right student organization for you? Then start your own!

At WKU, students have the distinct opportunity to start their own student organizations should they not be able to find one for them among all that are offered. The process to start a student organization is not overly complicated, either. The following must be submitted in order to start a new group on campus:

- Student Organization Form: This form identifies important contact information including the organizational spokesperson, as well as the permanent mailing address, email, and phone number. This form must be signed by the group's advisor.
- Constitution, Bylaws, and Charter: This document explains the organization's structure and procedures, along with the purpose and requirement for membership.

- Letter from the Advisor: Each organization must have a full-time faculty or staff member who is willing to serve in an advisory capacity. The advisor must write a letter stating that they are willing and able to serve as the advisor, along with their contact information.

Once all of the materials have been submitted to the Student Activities office, then the students should know within the next few weeks whether or not their organization has been approved. Once a student organization is approved and active, they can begin reserving rooms on campus and apply for Organizational Aid through the Student Government Association.

For more information on how to start your own organization, go to www.wku.edu/sao and click on the "Student Organization Guidebook" link on the left-hand side of the page.

SERVICE LEARNING

Service Learning: What Is It and Why Should It Be Important to Me?

The idea of service learning was developed to bring more depth and reflection to the community service activities in which students were participating. By enriching the experience of the students, it helps them learn to be more productive and responsible citizens and help build stronger communities. When students complete service learning projects, they also learn valuable teamwork, communication, and problem-solving skills. Since many of these projects can mimic real life situations, the lessons learned prove beneficial when students enter the real world after college.

Service learning thrives on the idea that to be a better society, we must be socially responsible individuals and truly care for each other's well-being. Students who volunteer to participate in service learning projects are providing a valuable service to a particular community. By getting out in the community and picking up trash, raising money for cancer research, walking the dogs at the animal shelter, or working with the elderly, volunteers are making a difference in the lives of others.

Students have been engaging in service learning on college campuses dating back to the 1800s. In the 1960s, there was a surge of individuals forging into the world of community service with intense passion, all due to the formation of the Peace Corps. College graduates would spend their first few years out of school traveling to make a difference in the world. While definitions of community service and service learning have developed over time, the same passion that was seen in college students in the 60s can be seen across campuses today.

Many universities have taken service learning to the next level by offering opportunities in the classroom. Here at WKU, students can earn a minor in Nonprofit Administration. With this minor, students complete at least 21 hours in coursework that relates to the field of nonprofit work. The philosophy of the department is "Where Passion Meets Opportunity." Many college graduates can find an entry-level position working for an organization that supports a cause they are passionate about. From animal welfare to cancer awareness, the options are unlimited in the nonprofit field.

There are a large variety of service learning opportunities outside of the classroom as well here at WKU. Whether it is activities that take place right here on campus, or in the Bowling Green and surrounding communities, there is an opportunity for everyone.

- **United Way Efforts:** The United Way's mission is "To improve lives by mobilizing the caring power of communities." Students help by competing in the United Way Penny War, which takes place in the fall. The goal is to be the group that collects the most pennies in their bucket. Pennies collected by a group count positively toward their total, while other coins and dollar bills are subtracted. In addition, "Jail & Bail" is where students nominate individuals to go to jail, and while there they must raise their bail!

- **VIP (Volunteering In Progress):** This initiative dedicates each month to a different cause. The monthly drives connect students to volunteer opportunities and service to the community, as well as on campus. Along with monthly drives, VIP sponsors monthly volunteer days where students can participate in a day of "action" by giving back to the community.

- **Up 'til Dawn:** This collegiate fundraising event benefits St. Jude Children's Research Hospital. Students raise money through a letter-writing campaign and other fundraising events. At the finale event, those who raised money stay up all night, with the notion that cancer never sleeps. Bands, games, food, and entertainment are provided to celebrate the year's success and to energize the students. Students also have the opportunity to serve on Up 'til Dawn's executive board.

- **National Volunteer Week & Make a Difference Week:** The purpose of these events is to stimulate and emphasize student engagement efforts in the community by building awareness and providing opportunities to serve. Each day highlights a variety of leadership activities on campus and within the community. The goal is to target a broader section of campus by offering different activities during both weeks. Make a Difference Week happens each fall and National Volunteer Week is held in the spring, co-sponsored by the WKU Alive Center.

- **Relay for Life:** As the American Cancer Society's signature event, Relay for Life is an overnight event that celebrates survivors, remembers those we have lost to cancer, and raises money for cancer research, patient services, education, and advocacy. WKU holds its campus Relay for Life each spring. Students, faculty and staff participate by forming a team or participating on the night of the event to support this great cause. Students can also serve on the event planning committee.

- **Alternative Breaks:** During the fall and spring breaks, students are given the opportunity to spend their time off of school giving back to various community service projects. Past breaks have included trips to Savannah, Georgia; Charleston, South Carolina; Memphis, Tennessee; Tuscaloosa, Alabama; and Mobile, Alabama. Students are selected based on their previous community service work and level of involvement and commitment.

ABOUT THE ALIVE CENTER FOR COMMUNITY PARTNERSHIPS

The ALIVE CCP is committed to bringing campus and community members together for the enrichment of both higher education and public life. We facilitate collaborative efforts that address local, regional, and global needs while enhancing the level of student learning and educational experience. We are dedicated to providing WKU students with opportunities that cultivate personal growth, ethical values, and public action for the common good. The ALIVE CCP supports public scholarship through service-learning and applied or community-based research as part of the WKU curriculum. We also provide numerous opportunities for volunteerism and ongoing community service.

Mission

The ALIVE CCP's mission is to support community development locally and abroad through campus and community partnerships. The ALIVE CCP connects students, faculty, staff, and community members to resources and opportunities for meaningful service and engaged scholarship.

Vision

Our vision is that campus and community members, from all sectors and backgrounds, will engage in successful applied-learning opportunities and work together to improve quality of life by acting as public problem-solvers and effective community-builders.

Creating Campus and Community Partnerships

The ALIVE Center seeks to facilitate campus and community partnerships that address issues in our local, regional, and global communities. We seek to accomplish our goal of facilitating partnerships by 1) having one-on-one meetings with individuals, groups, and organizations to get to know our constituents and learn what issues exist; 2) keeping an inventory of these individuals, groups, and organizations and the issues they work to address; 3) creating connections between individuals, groups, and organizations who seek to address interconnected issues to solve complex social problems; 4) providing an opportunity for individuals with similar interests to meet and share their stories; and 5) serving as a resource in ways that contribute to the success of partnership endeavors.

ALIVE CENTER PROGRAMS AND RESOURCES

Volunteerism

Perhaps you will have the opportunity to serve as a volunteer during your tenure at WKU. Whether is for a course requirement or just because you want to, there are literally hundreds of ways you can make a difference through service to others.

The ALIVE CCP maintains a listing of over 175 volunteer opportunities on our website, broken down by category, such as Clerical, Youth, Manual Labor, Animals, etc. We also maintain a listing of Event Volunteer Opportunities, which are one-time service opportunities in partnership with an organization hosting an event to raise money for their cause. All volunteer opportunities can be viewed at http://www.wku.edu/alive/volunteerism/index.php.

After viewing the volunteer opportunities online, you may contact the host organization directly. You may also call, visit, or email the ALIVE Center for additional information or assistance finding the right opportunity.

Sometimes it may take a few tries to find the right organization for you. Do not be discouraged if your first experience does not result in an ongoing connection. It is important to find an opportunity that is a good fit with your talents, energies, and skill set as a student.

Meeting Space

Who Can Use Meeting Space and Equipment?

Meeting space and equipment can be reserved by nonprofit organizations, WKU faculty/staff, and WKU student groups for University use free of charge.

The ALIVE Center offers two conference rooms free of charge. The conference rooms are available for meetings Sunday through Saturday, 8:00 a.m. to 10:00 p.m. Please contact us about reserving the room at 270-782-0082. The ALIVE Center office hours are Monday through Friday, 8:00 a.m.–4:30 p.m.

Public Scholarship

Educating to change the world by doing—that is what is required of institutions of higher education in order to meet the demands set forth by an ever-changing, complex society. The issues currently faced by societies locally and abroad require new responses and different types of relationships with the communities in which we serve as educators. We must engage with our surrounding communities in addressing social issues.

The AASCU's Task Force on Public Engagement offers the following definition of the publicly engaged institution: "The publicly engaged institution is fully committed to direct, two-way interactions with communities and other external constituencies through the development, exchange, and application of knowledge, information, and expertise for mutual benefit" (Jones, 2002, pp. 6–7).

At Western Kentucky University, the ALIVE Center for Community Partnerships provides opportunities for public scholarship by facilitating service-learning and community-based research with communities throughout the world. The Center staff offer programs and resources to improve the quality of the volunteer, service-learning, or research experience.

For specific information on these types of scholarships and how to apply, check the Alive Center website at www.wku.edu/alive.

Funding Categories

- Curricular or Co-Curricular Service-Learning Projects—Up to $1,000
- Community Development Projects—Up to $3,000
- Community-Based/Public Research Projects—Up to $5,000

Examples of approved Partnership Funds projects can be found online at http://www.wku.edu/alive/partnership_projects.php.
Institute for Citizenship & Social Responsibility

EXERCISE 1.1: JOURNAL ENTRY

Complete a journal entry answering the following questions (instructor will specify format, written or typed, and length).

- Why are you here? What are your **motivations** for being in college?

- What are three **goals** you have for this semester? For your academic career? Your life?

- Now that you're here, what are your biggest **challenges** in adjusting to a new learning environment (time management, personal life, finances, the college campus, etc.)?

- What is your **plan** for success? What actions will you take to ensure success?

- How can you use the information you have learned about the college and its resources to help you **achieve** your academic goals?

- How can you take what you learned in this chapter and apply it to another setting, such as beginning a new job?

EXERCISE 1.2: WHAT CAUSES SUCCESS OR FAILURE?

Consider the following situations:

A. After studying for two hours the night before the test, Bryan gets a D on the exam. When he finds out his grade, he is disgusted and says to himself, "I'll probably never do any better. I'll just quit trying in this class and spend time on my other classes."

B. Casey receives an A on her first math test. She is pleased until she learns the whole class did pretty well. She then feels that the test was too easy and that must be why she got an A.

C. Grace gets a C on her first history quiz. Because she did not do as well as she would like, she doubles the amount of time she studies for the next quiz. However, her next grade is only slightly higher. She is so frustrated that she wants to drop the class because she thinks that she will never be good in this class.

In your group, consider the following questions about each situation:

1. What did *each* student conclude was the main cause of his or her performance, and what effects will this probably have on the student?

   Bryan

   Casey

   Grace

2. Playing the role of the observer, what would *you* think was the main cause of their performance?

   Bryan

   Casey

   Grace

3. What advice would you give **each** student?

   Bryan

   Casey

   Grace

4. What are the top 3 reasons you feel that some students are more successful in college than others?

   (1)

   (2)

   (3)

NAME: _____ DATE: _____

EXERCISE 1.3: 3 × 5 NOTE CARDS

For each of the college terms discussed in ch. 1 (many of which are highlighted in bold), make 3×5 notecards. Write the term on side 1 and the definition on side 2 (see example below).

Course load

Side 1

The amount of credit hours you are taking

Side 2

Success strategies:

- Writing out the note cards (**note taking**)
- Periodic review of note cards (**time management** and **memory**)

EXERCISE 1.4: CALCULATING GPA

Complete the following GPA calculations.

FIRST SEMESTER

Course	Grade	Point Equivalent		Credit Hours		Total Quality Points
PSY 100	C	_____	×	3	=	_____
UCC 175C	A	_____	×	3	=	_____
DMA 096C	B	_____	×	3	=	_____
ENG 100	B	_____	×	3	=	_____

$$\text{GPA} = \frac{\text{Total Quality Points}}{\text{Total Credit Hours}} = \underline{\hspace{3cm}} = \underline{\hspace{3cm}}$$

SECOND SEMESTER

Course	Grade	Point Equivalent		Credit Hours		Total Quality Points
COMM 145	A	_____	×	3	=	_____
BIOL 113	C	_____	×	3	=	_____
MATH 116	E/F	_____	×	3	=	_____
ENG 300	B	_____	×	3	=	_____

$$\text{GPA} = \frac{\text{Total Quality Points}}{\text{Total Credit Hours}} = \underline{\hspace{3cm}} = \underline{\hspace{3cm}}$$

To calculate cumulative GPA, you divide the total quality points for all semesters attended by the total semester hours attempted. Calculate the cumulative GPA for these two semesters:

$$\text{Cumulative GPA} = \frac{\text{Total Quality Points Fall} + \text{Total Quality Points Spring}}{\text{Total Credit Hours Fall} + \text{Total Quality Hours Spring}} = \underline{\hspace{3cm}}$$

Cumulative GPA = _____

Calculate the second semester GPA again, except instead of the grade of E in Math, put in a grade of W (withdrawal).

SECOND SEMESTER (REVISED)

Course	Grade	Point Equivalent		Credit Hours		Total Quality Points
COMM 145	A	_____	×	3	=	_____
BIOL 113	C	_____	×	3	=	_____
MATH 116	W	_____	×	3	=	_____
ENG 300	B	_____	×	3	=	_____

$$\text{GPA} = \frac{\text{Total Quality Points}}{\text{Total Credit Hours}} = \underline{\hspace{3cm}} = \underline{\hspace{3cm}}$$

How did this change (from E/F to W) affect the GPA?

What are some key points to remember about Calculating GPA?

NAME: _____   DATE: _____

EXERCISE 1.5: CAMPUS AND COMMUNITY INVOLVEMENT

You will attend your choice of two campus or community activities this semester. These activities may be academic, social, or cultural. Refer to the Student Bulletin for ideas of activities available. Your instructor will also announce activities that might be of interest. After attending the activity, write a summary of the event and give your evaluation of it. The report should be approximately one typed page (double spaced) and it will be graded for completeness as well as correctness. Be sure to observe the rules of standard written English. Complete the following cover sheet and staple to your report.

Activity (please check):

☐ Theatre Department Play

☐ Campus Event (List: _____)

☐ Campus Workshop (Topic: _____)

☐ Community Event (List: _____)

☐ Other: (List: _____)

Signature from Sponsor of Event:

_____

Printed Name   Position Title

_____

Signature   Date

NAME: _____ DATE: _____

EXERCISE 1.6: GETTING TO KNOW YOUR COLLEGE/UNIVERSITY

Use your college catalog, university's web page, and/or other campus resources to answer the following questions relating to your specific college or university.

Campus Resources and Services

1. How do you access the following information?

College/university website address	
College/university email address	
Learning Management System (ex. TopNet or Blackboard)	
College Catalog	
Library Databases	
Student Bulletin/Newsletter	
Student Code of Conduct	
Register for Emergency Text Messages or Alerts	

2. List the buildings on your campus and name one service located in each building.

Building	Service

3. Complete the chart about the resources at Your college or University:

Office Title	Location (building and room number)	Function (assists with)
Admissions Office		
Advising Center		
Assessment Center		
Bookstore		
Bursar's (Cashier's) Office		
Campus Security		
Career Center		
Counseling Center		
Disabled Student Services		
Financial Aid Office		
Records Office/Registrar		
Tutoring Program		
Learning Center		

4. List two (2) types of financial aid students may receive.

    (1)

    (2)

    List two (2) other methods of payment students can use to finance their education.

    (1)

    (2)

5. List two (2) student activities and/or student organizations on your campus.

    (1)

    (2)

General Information

6. What types of degrees are offered at your college?

7. How would you get information about school closings/delays? (list at least 2 ways)

8. Where can a student park on campus? (be specific)

    How much does it cost to get a parking permit?

    Where do you go to get your parking permit?

Policies and Procedures

9. How much does it cost to attend JCTC as a full-time student?

   How many credit hours are considered full time?

   How much is tuition per credit hour?

10. What is the procedure to withdraw from a class?

    Where do you turn in your withdrawal form? (Office and location)

11. What is the policy regarding release of student information? Be specific.

Academic Calendar

12. What is the last date this semester you can withdraw and receive 100% tuition refund?

    What is the last date this semester you can withdraw **without** your instructor's signature?

    What is the last date this semester you can withdraw **with** your instructor's signature?

13. When is **midterm** this semester (based on information in **academic calendar**)?

14. What is the **final exam schedule** for this class (based on information in the academic calendar—day, date, and time)?

15. What dates are **classes cancelled** (academic holidays, school closings, etc.) for this semester?

College Administration

16. Who are the key leaders on your campus?

Administrator/Title	Name
College President	
Provost and Vice President for Academic Affairs	
Vice President for Student Affairs	
Registrar	

In addition to these leaders, who are the key leaders on your campus?

Administrator/Title	Name

17. Using the Internet, perform a search to obtain information regarding statistics and educational attainment (ex. % of Americans who have a college degree). Summarize your findings below. Cite your source.

EXERCISE 1.7: RECOGNIZING CHALLENGES AND SOLUTIONS

List 5 challenges you think you will have this semester that could impact your academic success. It may be a certain class you are taking, finances, personal issues, etc. Then, come up with at least 2 possible solutions to help overcome each challenge. Remember, part of being a successful student is recognizing your challenges and also coming up with a plan to overcome them.

CHALLENGES	SOLUTION #1	SOLUTION #2
Example: Math class	*Contact tutoring office to sign-up to get a tutor*	*Network with students in my math class and form a study group*

Chapter 2

Introduction to Technology and Information Resources – How Do I Find It?

INTRODUCTION

Research in the 21st century is very different from research in the past. Now, students have access to **information** like never before. Technology has made this possible and students are the beneficiaries of these advances. **Information** is everywhere. The Internet, television, radio, newspapers, magazines, billboards, and T-shirts are just some of the places where you can access information. In terms of information literacy and libraries, professors expect their students to know the difference between popular information and scholarly information. Students are expected to utilize scholarly information sources to support their ideas within papers and projects.

INFORMATION LITERACY

One of the most important skills you can develop is learning how to access information. This information often comes in a variety of resource formats ranging from Internet to campus publications to library resources, and forms a body of knowledge known as **information literacy**. This section focuses on research, use of Internet, and use of information resources.

"I've never set foot in a library before . . . and I hate asking people for help."

"I hear you really don't need to use the library until your junior or senior year. Thank goodness! I'll probably just look things up on the computer anyway."

We would like to suggest two avenues for researching—the physical use of the college/university library, as well as the online version. Both are and will be essential to building your knowledge base as a college student. And like any other skill, practice develops that skill. Sometimes it is easier and faster to use the library, other times a quick scan on the computer will help start your search—it all depends on the type and depth of research you are conducting. Tapping into the wealth of info found in both your campus library and the Internet will increase your chances of finding the key info you need.

HOW TO CONDUCT RESEARCH

Conducting research is another critical thinking skill you will need to develop. This section highlights two important resources that will aid you in learning to conduct research: your library and computer resources.

USING YOUR LIBRARY

Academic libraries are said to be central to the mission of the college or university or, at least, of central importance to the academic success of students. They are important for resources, research, and learning about virtually any subject taught in the school. While the academic library building or learning resource center, as it is sometimes called, is usually a building located in the physical center of the campus, it is more than just a building. The library is a combination of information resources, people, and points of access.

© Tyler Olson/Shutterstock, Inc.

The information resources are in both print and non-print formats. The print resources are probably quite familiar to students and include books, magazines, newspapers, and a whole range of pamphlets and special files. The common characteristic of this type of resource is that they are printed on paper. Unfortunately, paper resources deteriorate when they become old and are easily damaged. The non-print information resources include microfilm, microfiche and electronic materials. While it is harder to browse through non-print resources, they last a long time and are often easier to access, especially the eResources.

Most libraries, both public and academic, are also computing centers. Part of the reason for libraries to have lots of computers is that they are open long hours and many research materials are now in electronic form. Electronic catalogs, subscription databases for articles, search engines, idea organizers, and word processors may all be found on library computers. A student may explore a topic, create an outline, research for information, write a paper and print it just by using the variety of print and non-print tools that are conveniently located in the library.

Access to library materials is not only through the front door of the library building but also through the library Internet portal. In fact, many of the popular research tools are now available only in electronic formats. A benefit of eResources is that these materials are accessible remotely from off campus or from home. All you need is the Internet address for the subscription database or library site, and the user identification and password. This information can be requested at the library service desk and is available to all students.

The library service desk or circulation desk is usually located very close to both the entrance and the exit. You can get a library card so you can check out library materials, request the database access codes, pick up printouts, check out reserve material for your classes, or ask a question. It is a place to get information, ask for assistance or directions, and to learn about the library and research.

Academic libraries are at the center of the college or university and are at the center of the learning activity. In order to fully succeed as a student and as a life-long learner, one of the first disciplines that must be learned is literacy. All learners should be able to read with comprehension, interpret images, calculate mathematically and search for information. Using appropriate search strategies and resources to find, evaluate and use information involves knowledge of the library, print and non-print resources and thinking. This discipline and general academic competency is called "managing information" or "information literacy." It is an essential skill for academic success.

Do not overlook the fact that librarians are educators who provide instruction outside the classroom. You can learn from them just as you do from faculty inside the classroom. Furthermore, the library is a place where you can acquire skills for locating, retrieving, and evaluating information that you may apply to any course you are taking or will ever take.

TIPS FROM A FELLOW STUDENT . . .

Academic Research

You should familiarize yourself with the library early in your college experience. Since the Internet explosion, people have forgotten about the library. You cannot always find everything you need on the Internet. In addition, you cannot believe everything you read on the Internet. You must consider the sources you use to cite information, and make certain the source is reputable. Colleges/Universities now allow you use the Internet to access information through automated databases. Usually information obtained in this manner is easier to cite, and comes from reputable sources.

SOME BASICS ON RESEARCH

The Internet is not the same thing as the Web. Think of the former as a highway of information—the physical network, and the Web as an easy pass tollbooth, which you go through when you are traveling on that highway. The Web is a multimedia interface linking resources worldwide. It adds a visually (and often sound) pleasing "face" to the info available on the computer. We are "served" by either Netscape Navigator or Internet Explorer (two common Web browsers), which channel and organize that raw data on the Internet into a more appealing and, in many cases, a more usable form. Lest we think that the Web is the only way to go—the Internet can take us:

- to other library computers where we can look up information
- to info files on other connected computers
- to info organized by software for usually one computer system but able to connect to other computers
- to the Web

When we search for information on the computer we typically enter the address of the site (if we know and remember it)—which is called the URL, or Uniform Resource Locator at the top of the page. Or we can utilize available indexes or "search engines"— web page file cabinets that have already been organized for us beforehand. We do not have to search randomly into all corners of the net. We can open only a few file drawers to find info. Try the following helping tools on a regular basis. They should speed up your searches.

Indexes, sometimes referred to as "directories," are organized in broad categories and can be best used when we are looking for general information about a topic. For this reason it is a good place to start when we are beginning a search for information. A category like "recreation" can be selected from a group of categories found on the first page of an Index (like Yahoo) and then entering "art" followed by "cinema," will further narrow that search to permit us to view documents on that final subject. There is usually an assortment of categories in the middle of an Index's page . . . like "sports," "entertainment," "education," and "news."

Search engines can best be used when we are searching for more specific information after we have done an initial search and know something about our topic and some search terms to use. We enter our search terms as "keywords" (using quotation marks) that relate to our topic, rather than categories. We can add Boolean terms, such as "and," "not," or "or" to get more hits if you need them or fewer if you are swamped with too many to scan. You can then view the documents that pertain to your search. Examples of popular search engines are: WebCrawler, HotBot, and Alta Vista. We find engines by entering the name of the engine in the subject line or by referring to the library homepage.

Online Databases accessed from your library homepage are collections of files about a certain topic or discipline. They can link you to full documents or abstracts of articles appropriate to your topic. **CD-ROM databases** may be housed at separate computer stations in your library or available online through any computer. Your library may have to "rent" these databases for you. Finally, the online catalog, available through your library homepage, is your base of operations to access any materials that your library holds or has access to through **interlibrary loan**.

Organize Your Sources

When you find a source, write down its location or bookmark it. It is likely that you will have to come back to it sooner or later. Think about the 5 Ws of research: Who is the project about? Who can you get information from? Who is likely to review your information? Who is likely to have the information you are seeking? What is the kind of information you need (statistics, news sources, interviews, etc.)? What information do you need? What information will be most useful? What are the sources of data for your information? What do you do if you cannot find the information you need? When do you need your information? When was the information you get last updated (how old is it)? When do you do the search (peak/off hours)? Where have you looked for information? Where did the information you are researching take place? Why are you looking for this information? Why was the information originally collected and posted?

Start early! Sites occasionally (and sometimes often) go down. The earlier you start, the sooner you will know where to find your information. You may have more time to expand your knowledge and information base than if you start doing research the night before something is due.

Know when to stop. The Internet is way big. There is absolutely no way you are going to find every tidbit of information relating to your source that exists on the Internet. Keep in mind the "when," too. If you are researching a topic with constantly breaking news (medicine, politics, the Internet), you should figure out where the breaking news is and periodically check it as your paper or project progresses.

Don't get sidetracked. The Internet can be amazingly engaging, addicting, and fascinating. It helps to keep a written sheet of paper with an idea of the types of information you are looking for.

Paraphrase

Some papers use direct quotes—word-for-word ideas from an author. Obviously you must give credit to the author—you put his words in quotation marks and reference the actual source and page. Sometimes you want to summarize either one author's idea or several at the same time. Anytime you use someone else's idea/concept/words you need to give credit—in your paper itself AND at the end in the list of sources you used. It is good practice early in your college career to learn how to "paraphrase" material that you want to use in your paper. Here's how:

- read the info
- look away from it and
- in your *own* words, say what idea the author gave you

You can decide later whether to use that idea or whether it agrees with another author's ideas, etc. In paraphrasing, you cannot use the author's words exactly or some of his words intermittently. Failure to give appropriate credit to someone else's ideas or words is called **plagiarism** and is considered academic "stealing." It always carries a fine—discredit of a paper, report (written or oral) and/or failure of a course.

Evaluating the "Worth" of Your Sources of Information

Collect more information than you think you will need. Balance your sources with conflicting viewpoints from various authors. Check to see if your premise can only be supported by one author while many authors offer contradictory information.

For the critically thinking student, the warning light should go on. You want to find corroboration among your supporting info. It lends strength to your position. Check, especially on Internet sources, for who is authoring the info you find. Whether it is a "com," "org," or even "gov" site it will have a certain viewpoint. Is what you found opinion or fact, an interpretation or an unbiased record of events? Is it evident that the author is an "expert" in her field? Is there evidence of research? Are there other documents (in the bibliography) that support her position? Is the Web page you found organized, maintained recently, and are its links active?

AFTER (A)

Continue to *review*, *revise,* and *self-modify* as needed.

- **Do I evaluate the resources I am using?**
- **Am I using the library, the Writing Center, and other services?**
- **What changes can I make to what I am doing now that will help me become better at using the university library and online resources that will also help me become a better researcher?**

SUMMARY

Of the many goals of college/university, learning how to conduct research, utilizing the library and online resources, and developing in the area of scholarly research is at the top of the list. Developing these skills will not only help you become a critical thinker and problem-solver, but will also aid you in graduate school and in the workforce.

SUGGESTED READINGS

Handbooks on conducting research (MLA, APA, etc.)
College/university student code of conduct

HOW DO I FIND IT? WESTERN KENTUCKY UNIVERSITY

How Do I Find It?

Western Kentucky University

WKU STUDENT HANDBOOK*

Academic Offenses

The maintenance of academic integrity is of fundamental importance to the University. Thus it should be clearly understood that acts of plagiarism or any other form of cheating will not be tolerated and that anyone committing such acts risks punishment of a serious nature.

Academic Dishonesty

Students who commit any act of academic dishonesty may receive from the instructor a failing grade in that portion of the course work in which the act is detected or a failing grade in a course without possibility of withdrawal. The faculty member may also present the case to the Office of the Vice President for Student Affairs for disciplinary sanctions. A student who believes a faculty member has dealt unfairly with him/her in a course involving academic dishonesty may seek relief through the Student Complaint Procedure.

Plagiarism

To represent written work taken from another source as one's own is plagiarism. Plagiarism is a serious offense. The academic work of a student must be his/her own. One must give any author credit for source material borrowed from him/her. To lift content directly from a source without giving credit is a flagrant act. To present a borrowed passage without reference to the source after changing a few words is also plagiarism.

Cheating

No student shall receive or give assistance not authorized by the instructor in taking an examination or in the preparation of an essay, laboratory report, problem assignment, or other project that is submitted for purposes of grade determination.

Other Types of Academic Dishonesty

Other types of academic offenses, such as theft or sale of tests, should be reported to the Office of the Vice President for Student Affairs for disciplinary sanction.

WKU TECHNOLOGY RESOURCES

Accounts and Logins

As a faculty, staff, student or alumni of WKU, you Could have several IT accounts and IDs assigned to you that enable you to login to various computer systems, applications and online services, at WKU. These accounts will typically have a username (login ID) and a password or PIN. It is your responsibility to manage and protect your IT accounts and login Information. You need to become knowledgeable on how to use your accounts to login to the many online services at WKU and to change and reset your passwords and PIN. Here are some bullet points you really need to know and understand:

- **WKUID and PIN**—The WKUID (800#) Is your main identification number at WKU. You need to memorize it and your PIN.
- **NetID account**—The NetID is the "Universal" login account for accessing most WKU systems and services. Examples of major systems and services you access with your NetID are:
    - Blackboard (Ecourses)
    - TopNet
    - WKU Portal
    - Email
    - Computer Labs
    - Wireless Network
    - MyStuff
- **LDAP Account (formerly called Email Account).** LDAP accounts (which are typically constructed in the form of Firstname.Lastname999@wku.edu) are being phased out. Most users will use their NetID to login to email now and most other applications and systems, Please pay attention to login screens of the various applications, for instructions on whether to use your NetID or LDAP account to login to a given systems. Eventually, all web forms and other services will use the NetID.

For Help, please call the Help Desk @ 270-745-7000.

Account FAQS

What is my WKUID?
What is my WKU PIN?
How do I login to TopNet?
What is my NetID account and how do I use it?
What is My Email Account/Address?
What is LDAP?
What is the difference in my LDAP account and my Email account?
Why do I have so many accounts at WKU?

What Is My WKUID?

Your WKUID (800#) is your main identification number at WKU and is printed and encoded on your WKUID card. All employees are issued a WKUID upon hire and students are issued a WKUID upon application to the University. You need to memorize your WKUID and your PIN.

You must know your WKUID and PIN to change and reset passwords on other WKU Accounts such as your NetID account. Visit What's My WKUID? for more information.

What Is My WKU PIN?

Your WKUID and PIN are used to access TopNet. The first time you use TopNet, your PIN will be the last 6 numbers of your Social Security Number. If you do not have a social security number, it will be set to the fast 6 digits of your WKUID. The first time you login to TopNet, you will be required to change your PIN. Please memorize your PIN and change it often. Visit I forgot my TopNet PIN for more information.

How Do I Login to TopNet?

If you are a *New WKU student* registering for the first Time or you are a newly readmitted student, you **MUST** login to TopNet using your WKUID and PIN. Visit What is my WKUID Account? for more information.

If you are a *current WKU student or employee*, you may login to TopNet using your NetID and Password **OR** you may use your WKUID and PIN. Visit What is my NetID Account? for more information.

What Is My NetID Account and How Do I Use It?

All active faculty, staff and students are issued a NetID. NetID accounts for employees are created automatically when they are hired. NetID accounts are created for new students within 24–48 hours of their initial course registration. The NetID and password are used to login to most major WKU computer systems and services including Blackboard, TopNet. WKU Portal, Email, Computer Labs, and the WKU Wireless Network to name a few. It is your responsibility to manage and protect your NetID and password. Your NetID password will expire periodically and you will be required to pick a new password. Visit www.wku.edu/netid for more information.

What Is My Email Account/Address?

Email addresses are in the format of firstname.lastname(999)@wku.edu. Student accounts typically have the random three digits (999), while employee accounts do not. **Please lookup your email address at "What's My Email Address?".**

Active employees and students will login to email using their NetID and password. Visit www.wku.edu/netid for more info.

Alumni, Retirees, Affiliates will access their email using their LDAP account. Visit www.wku.edu/ldap for more info.

What Is LDAP?

LDAP stands for Lightweight Directory Access Protocol. **LDAP is being phased out at WKU.** LDAP accounts are in the format of firstname.lastname and many accounts have a random three digit number on then end to make them unique. Some applications still require you to login with your LDAP account. This will change over time as all applications login screens are converted to NetID login. Visit www.wku.edu/ldap for more info.

What Is the Difference in My LDAP Account and My Email Account?

This can be confusing, Email accounts and LDAP accounts are both in the format of firstname.lastname. Historically, email was accessed by logging in with your LDAP account (your firstname.lastname) which was also the same as your **Email** account name. We are replacing the LDAP login with the NetID ID login. **Active employees and students login to email using their NetID and password NOT LDAP.** Alumni and Retirees still use their LDAP account but we will eventually phase that out also.

Why Do I Have So Many Accounts at WKU?

Historically, in most IT environments, each individual application and/or system used or required a separate userid account and password. At WKU we are moving toward a single sign-on environment using your NetID.

Your **WKUID** account and PIN will allow you access to TopNet and will be used to authenticate other logins.

Your **NetID** account and Password will allow you single sign-on via the Portal to various applications such as TopNet, email, Blackboard, and Mystuff.

Your LDAP Account (formerly called Email Account) is being phased out. Most users will use their NetID to login to email now and most other applications and systems. Please pay attention to login screens of the various applications for instructions on whether to use your NetID or LDAP account to login to a given system. Eventually, all web forms and other services will use the NetID.

NAME: _____ DATE: _____

EXERCISE 2.1: LEARNING TO USE THE LIBRARY

Note: Please read the assignment instructions CAREFULLY and follow the instructions.

Research

Choose an occupation that interests you as a future career. Research the topic using the following information sources as your guide:

a. One book that you accessed using TOPCAT, WKU's online catalog

b. One journal article that you have accessed online through WKU Libraries' web-accessible databases

c. One FREE resource that you have accessed online (through Google, Yahoo!, etc.)

d. *The Occupational Outlook Handbook,* available online at http://www.bls.gov/oco

The Assignment

Prepare a one- to two-page typed paper (12 point font) that summarizes the differences between the information sources you identified and discusses how your perceptions about the career have changed after researching the topic. Which, sources were easiest to use and most beneficial? Did they give salary ranges for the career you chose? Did they include educational requirements? What other information was listed in relation to your topic? Do not forget to tell how the information has helped shape your opinion of the career and the choices you will make for the future. Also, list each information source you used to complete this assignment on a **Works Cited Page**.

EXERCISE 2.2: WEBSITE EVALUATION CHECKLIST

Why Evaluate Websites?

No one has judged the quality or accuracy of most information you find on the World Wide Web before you come across it, so you must evaluate the information you find. Some websites are created by experts: for example, the WKU Libraries website is authored by librarians who have expertise in the field of information science. However, the vast majority of WWW sites are designed and authored by non-experts.

Directions:

1. Search the web and choose a site to evaluate.

2. Read each question and answer carefully.

3. Return this checklist to your instructor.

4. Attach a printout of the first page of the website you are evaluating to this checklist.

What is the URL or web address of the website you are evaluating?

What is the title of the website?

Authority and Accuracy

Anyone who knows a little HTML coding and has access to a server can create and load a website. It is important to find out the author's identity and qualifications or expertise, in order to determine the credibility and reliability of the information.

Who is the author of the website?

☐ I couldn't tell

☐ The author is:

What part of the URL (web address) gave you clues about authorship? Check all that apply:

☐ .com—a company   ☐ .org—a nonprofit organization

☐ .edu—an academic institution   ☐ .uk—a country-sponsored site

☐ .gov—a U.S. government agency   ☐ ~/al's—a personal web page

☐ .mil—a U.S. military site   ☐ Other? Please describe:

☐ .net—a network of computers

What are the qualifications of the author or group that created the site?

☐ I couldn't find this information

☐ The author's qualifications are:

Purpose and Content

Determine the purpose of the website by looking closely at the content of the information. Some sites provide links to information in the form of an "about our organization" page or a mission statement that details the purpose for creating the website. The purpose of other sites may not be obvious at first. Take time to thoroughly explore a website to determine if the information is subjective (biased or opinionated), objective (factual), or mixed.

What is the purpose of the web page or site? Check all that apply:

☐ a personal web page

☐ a company or organization website

☐ a forum for educational/public service information

☐ a forum for scholarly/research information

☐ for entertainment

☐ an advertisement or electronic commerce

☐ a forum for ideas, opinions, or points of view

☐ Other? Please explain:

In your own words, briefly describe the purpose of the website:

What does the website provide? Check ONE:

☐ Balanced, objective, or factual information

☐ Biased, subjective, or opinionated statements

Are the arguments well supported?　　☐ Yes　　☐ No

☐ Both objective and subjective information

☐ I couldn't tell

☐ Other? Please explain:

Does the website provide any contact information or means of communicating with the author or webmaster?

☐ Yes

☐ No

Currency

The currency or regularity of updating information is vital for some types of websites, and not so important for others. For example, websites that provide historical information, such as the presidential papers of George Washington, do not have to be updated as often as sites that provide news stories or stock market information.

When was the website last revised, modified, or updated?

☐ I couldn't tell

☐ It was updated:

Is currency important to the type of information available on this website?

☐ Yes—Please explain:

☐ No—Please explain:

Is the site well maintained?

☐ I couldn't tell

☐ Yes

☐ No

Are links broken (Error 404 messages)?

☐ I couldn't tell

☐ Yes

☐ No

Design, Organization, and Ease of Use

Design, organization, and case of use are important considerations. Websites can provide useful sources of information; however, if websites are slow to load and difficult to navigate, their contribution and usefulness in providing information will be lost.

In your opinion, how does the website appear overall? Check all that apply:

☐ Well designed and organized   ☐ Poorly designed and organized

☐ Easy to read and navigate   ☐ Difficult to read and navigate

☐ Help screens are available   ☐ Help screens are unavailable

☐ A search feature/site map is available   ☐ A search feature/site map is unavailable

Characteristics of Popular Magazines and Scholarly Journals

	Popular Journal Article	*Scholarly Journal Article*
Purpose:	Report current events Entertain Summarize research of general interest	Report results of research
Audience:	General population	Scholars, researchers, and students in a particular field of study
Authors:	Journalists Often unnamed	Researchers Always named
Characteristics:	Short Pictures, advertisements No citations (sources) Everyday language Not peer-reviewed*	Long (5 pages +) Describes research methodologies Citations Technical or specialized language Peer-reviewed*

*Peer-reviewed articles are those that have been reviewed and accepted for publication in a journal by a selected panel of recognized experts in the field of study covered by that journal.

EXERCISE 2.3: LIBRARY SKILLS SCAVENGER HUNT

Completion of this scavenger hunt will require a visit to Helm-Cravens Library. The online catalog databases may be accessed via the Internet. However, to successfully complete the Reference and Periodicals sections, you will need to visit these areas of Helm-Cravens Library.

Cravens library

| 9 |
| 8 |
| 7 |
| 6 |

Helm library

2	2–5	5
1	1–4	4
G		3
		2
		1

http://www.wku.edu/Library/security/hcfloor.htm

Helm library

Ground floor: Government documents/law library

1st floor: Reference center/Java city

2nd floor: Periodicals/ student technology center

Most materials are non-circulating

Cravens library

1st floor: Dean's office

2nd floor: VPAL (Visual and performing arts library)

3rd floor: Departmental offices

4th floor: Circulation

5th floor: Stacks

6th floor: Stacks

7th floor: Stacks

8th floor: Stacks

9th floor: Stacks

Online Catalog

1. How many books by William Faulkner can be found via the online catalog?

2. What is the Library of Congress call number for the book *Gone with the Wind*?

3. Who is the author of *Coming of Age in Mississippi*?

4. What is the call number and location of the *9/11 Commission Report*?

Databases (EBSCOhost and JSTOR)

1. List the titles of three articles from EBSCOhost that appear after a search on "cholesterol."

2. Provide the author(s), article title, journal title, volume number, issue number, and publication date for an EBSCOhost article pertaining to sunscreen and skin cancer.

3. Using the JSTOR database, give the author(s), article title, journal title, volume number, issue number, and publication date for an article pertaining to the Dust Bowl.

Reference

(Answers to the following questions must be found in print materials housed within the Reference Room of Helm Library. Sources, including titles and publication dates, must be provided with answers.)

1. What is the mailing address of Apple, Inc.?

2. When and where was Winston Churchill born?

3. Who won the Oscar (Academy Award) for Best Actress in 1964? What character did she play?

NAME: _____ DATE: _____

EXERCISE 2.4: PRACTICE YOUR RESEARCH SKILLS IN A TEAM SETTING (GROUP ACTIVITY)

Below are ten statements to verify for truth or falsity. Use each other and/or library reference materials in your critical thinking process. Problem solve how you will verify the statement, and how confident you are in the accuracy of the source(s) you use and how confident you are in its truth or falsity. The group should come to a consensus for each statement and can record either individual student responses or group responses to the following questions:

- Is the statement true or false?

- How confident are you about your answer? (Use a 1 to 5 scale, with 1 being no confidence to 5 being extremely confident.)

- What source(s) of information was used to locate your answer?

1. Doctor-assisted suicide is the same as euthanasia.

2. World courts settle trade disputes between countries.

3. There are over four-hundred species of sharks.

4. Intrastate commerce is the same as interstate commerce. (Both controlled by the federal government)

5. The greenhouse effect has been scientifically proven.

6. A convicted felon can never possess a firearm.

7. Date rape and statutory rape are the same.

8. 70% of college students cheat at some time during their college years.

9. HIV and AIDS mean the same thing.

10. The number-one growth industry is the prison industry.

Evaluate the reliability and validity of your sources.

Critically assess your team for the above exercise; were your team members adamant about the answer they chose? Did others agree immediately? Did they back up their answer with evidence and/or sound logical reasoning? Or did they agree to just agree?

Chapter 3

Critical Thinking – What's the Problem?

INTRODUCTION

Your college experience will help you to develop critical and creative thinking skills. Critical thinking involves analyzing data, generating alternatives, and solving problems. Creative thinking helps you to find new ideas to solve problems in your personal and professional life.

Critical thinking involves questioning established ideas, creating new ideas, and using information to solve problems. In critical thinking, reasoning is used in the pursuit of truth. Part of obtaining a college education is learning to think critically. Understanding the concepts of critical thinking will help you to be successful in college courses in which critical thinking is used.

Beyond college, critical thinking is helpful in being a good citizen and a productive member of society. Throughout history, critical thinkers have helped to advance civilization. Thoughts that were once widely accepted were questioned, and newer and more useful ideas were introduced. For example, it was once assumed that blood-sucking leeches were helpful in curing diseases. Some critical thinkers questioned this practice, and the science of medicine was advanced. It was not so long ago that women were not allowed to vote.

Critical thinkers questioned this practice so that women could participate in a democratic society.

A lack of critical thinking can lead to great tragedy. In his memoirs, Adolf Eichmann, who played a central role in the Nazis' killing of six million Jews during World War II, wrote:

> *From my childhood, obedience was something I could not get out of my system. When I entered the armed services at the age of 27, I found being obedient not a bit more difficult than it had been during my life at that point. It was unthinkable that I would not follow orders. Now that I look back, I realize that a life predicated on being obedient and taking orders is a very comfortable life indeed. Living in such a way reduces to a minimum one's own need to think.*

Critical and creative thinking are closely related. If you can think critically, you have the freedom to be creative and generate new ideas. The great American jurist and philosopher Oliver Wendell Holmes noted:

> *There are one-story intellects, two-story intellects, and three-story intellects with skylights. All fact-collectors who have no aim beyond their facts are one-story men. Two-story men compare, reason, generalize, using the labor of the fact-collectors as their own. Three-story men idealize, imagine, predict—their best illumination comes from above through skylights.*

Use the information in this chapter to become a three-story intellect with skylights. And by the way, even though Oliver Wendell Holmes talks about men, women can be three-story intellects too.

BEFORE (B)

Before you begin the critical and creative thinking process, you should know the following (which relate to *preparation, self-awareness,* and *planning*):

- **Fallacies in reasoning**
- **The levels of thinking expected of you in college**

FALLACIES IN REASONING

To think critically, you need to be able to recognize fallacies in reasoning. Fallacies are patterns of incorrect reasoning. Recognizing these fallacies can help you to avoid them in your reading, thinking and writing. You can also become aware of when others are using these fallacies to persuade you. They may use these fallacies for their own purpose, such as power or financial gain.

Appeal to authority

It is best to make decisions by reviewing the information and arguments and reaching our own conclusions. Sometimes we are encouraged to rely on experts for a recommendation because they have specialized information. Obviously, we need to have trust in the experts to accept their conclusions. However, when we cite some person as an authority in a certain area when they are not, we make an appeal to a questionable authority. For example, when a company uses famous sports figures to endorse a product, a particular brand of athletic shoes or breakfast cereal, they are appealing to a questionable authority. Just because the athletes are famous, does not mean they are experts on the product they are endorsing. They are endorsing the product to earn money. Many commercials you see on TV use appeals to a questionable authority.

Jumping to conclusions

When we jump to conclusions, we make hasty generalizations. For example, if a college student borrows money from a bank and does not pay it back, the manager of the bank might conclude that all college students are poor risks and refuse to give loans to other college students.

Making generalizations

We make generalizations when we say that all members of a group are the same, as in

> *All lawyers are greedy.*
> *All blondes are airheads.*

Of course, your occupation does not determine whether or not you are greedy, and the color of your hair does not determine your intelligence. Such thinking leads to harmful stereotypes and fallacies in reasoning. Instead of generalizing, think of people as unique individuals.

Attacking the person rather than discussing the issues

To distract attention from the issues, we often attack the person. For example, during the Clinton administration, much time was spent attacking the President rather than discussing the issues. Rather than focusing attention on health care and education, attention was focused on the President's real estate deals and extramarital affairs. Political candidates today are routinely asked about personal issues such as extramarital affairs and drug use. Of course personal integrity in politicians is important, but attacking the person can serve as a smokescreen to direct attention away from important political issues. Critical thinkers avoid reacting emotionally to personalities and use logical thinking to analyze the issues.

Appeal to common belief

Just because something is a common belief does not mean that it is true. At one time people believed that the world was flat and that when you got to the edge of the earth, you would fall off. If you were to survey the people who lived in that period in history, the majority would have agreed that the earth was flat. A survey just tells us what people believe. The survey does not tell us what is true and accurate.

Common practice

Appealing to common practice is the "everyone else is doing it" argument. Just because everyone else does it doesn't mean that it is right. Here are some common examples of this fallacy:

> *It is okay to cheat in school. Everyone else does it.*
> *It is okay to speed on the freeway. Everyone else does it.*
> *It is okay to cheat on your taxes. Everyone else does it.*
> *It is okay to text or talk on the phone when driving. Everyone else does it.*

Appeal to tradition

Appeal to tradition is a variation of the "everyone else is doing it" argument. The appeal to tradition is "we've always done it that way." Just because that is the way it has always been done doesn't mean it is the best way to do it. With this attitude, it is very difficult to make changes and improve our ways of doing things. While tradition is very important, it is open to question. For example, construction and automotive technology have traditionally been career choices for men but not for women. When women tried to enter or work in these careers, there was resistance from those who did not want to change traditions. This resistance limited options for women.

Two wrongs

In this fallacy, it is assumed that it is acceptable to do something because other people are doing something just as bad. For example, if someone cuts you off on the freeway, you may assume that it is acceptable to zoom ahead and cut in front of his or her car. The "two wrongs" fallacy has an element of retribution, or getting back at the other person. The old saying, "Two wrongs do not make a right," applies in this situation.

The slippery slope or domino theory

The slippery slope or domino theory is best explained with an example. A student might think: If I fail the test, I will fail this class. If I fail this class, I will drop out of college. My parents will disown me and I will lose the respect of my friends. I will not be able to get a good job. I will start drinking and end up homeless. In this fallacy, the negative consequences of our actions are only remotely possible, but are assumed to be certain. These dire consequences presented influence people's decisions and change behavior. In this situation, it is important to evaluate these consequences. One does not necessarily lead to the other. If you fail the test, you could study and pass the next test. As a child you were probably cautioned about many slippery slopes in life:

- **Brush your teeth or your teeth will fall out.**
- **Do your homework or you will never get into college and get a good job.**

Wishful thinking

In wishful thinking an extremely positive outcome, however remote, is proposed as a distraction from logical thinking. For example, a new sports stadium may be proposed. Extremely positive outcomes may be presented, such as downtown redevelopment, the attraction of professional sports teams, increased revenue, and the creation of jobs. Opponents, on the other hand, might foresee increased taxes, lack of parking, and neglect of other important social priorities such as education and shelter for the homeless. Neither position is correct if we assume that the outcomes are certain and automatic. Outcomes need to be evaluated realistically.

Appeal to fear or scare tactics

Sometimes people appeal to fear as a way of blocking rational thinking. I once saw a political commercial that showed wolves chasing a person through the forest. It was clearly designed to evoke fear. The message was to vote against a proposition to limit lawyers' fees. The idea was that if lawyers' fees were limited, the poor client would be a victim of limited legal services. This commercial used scare tactics to interfere with rational thinking about the issue.

Appeal to pity

In an appeal to pity, emotion is used to replace logic. It is what is known as a "sob story." Appeals to pity may be legitimate when used to foster charity and empathy. However, the sob story uses emotion in place of reason to persuade and is often exaggerated. College faculty often hear sob stories from students having academic difficulties:

- *Please don't disqualify me from college. I failed all my classes because I was emotionally upset when my grandmother died.*
- *Please don't fail me in this class. If you fail me, my parents will kick me out of the house and I will not be able to get health insurance.*
- *If you fail me in this class, I won't be eligible to play football and my future as a professional will be ruined.*

Appeal to loyalty

Human beings are social creatures who enjoy being attached to a group. We feel loyalty to our friends, family, school, communities, teams, and favorite musicians. Appeals to loyalty ask you to act according to the group's best interests without considering whether the actions are right or wrong. Critical thinkers, however, do not support an idea just to show support for a group with which they identify.

Peer pressure is related to the loyalty fallacy. With peer pressure, members of a group may feel obliged to act in a certain way because they think members of the group act that way. Another variation of the loyalty fallacy is called the bandwagon argument. It involves supporting a certain idea just to be part of the group. This tendency is powerful when the group is perceived to be powerful or "cool." In elections, people often vote for the candidate that is perceived to be the most popular. If everyone else is voting for the candidate, they assume the candidate must be the best. This is not necessarily true.

Appeal to prejudice

A prejudice is judging a group of people or things positively or negatively, even if the facts do not agree with the judgment. A prejudice is based on a stereotype in which all members of a group are judged to be the same. Speakers sometimes appeal to prejudice to gain support for their causes. Listen for the appeal to prejudice in hate speeches or literature directed against different ethnicities, genders, or sexual orientations.

Appeal to vanity

The appeal to vanity is also known as "apple polishing." The goal of this strategy is to get agreement by paying compliments. Students who pay compliments to teachers and then ask for special treatment are engaging in apple polishing.

Post hoc reasoning, or false causes

Post hoc reasoning has to do with cause and effect. It explains many superstitions. If I play a good game of golf whenever I wear a certain hat, I might conclude that the hat causes me to play a good golf game. The hat, however, is a false cause of playing a good game of golf. I may feel more comfortable wearing my lucky hat, but it is a secondary reason for playing well. I play well because I practice my golf skills and develop my self-confidence. In scientific research, care is taken to test for false causes. Just because an event regularly follows another event does not mean that the first event caused the second event. For example, when the barometer falls, it rains. The falling barometer does not cause the rain; a drop in atmospheric pressure causes the rain. If falling barometers caused the rain, we could all be rainmakers by adjusting our barometers.

Straw man or woman

Watch for this fallacy during election time. Using this strategy, a politician creates a misleading image of someone else's statements, ideas, or beliefs to make them easy to attack. For example, politicians might accuse their opponents of raising taxes. That may only be part of the story, however. Maybe their opponents also voted for many tax-saving measures. When politicians or anyone else uses the straw man fallacy, they are falsifying or oversimplifying. Use your critical thinking to identify the straw man or woman (political opponent) in the next election. Of course you don't have to be a politician to use this strategy. People use this strategy when they spread gossip or rumors about someone they want to discredit.

Burden of proof

Burden of proof refers to the evidence for the truth of a statement. Generally the person making the statement is the one who should provide the evidence of its truth. However, the speaker may attempt to shift the burden of proof to another person to distract attention. Here is an example of shifting the burden of proof from the popular TV show "The X-Files":

Scully: *Your sister was abducted by aliens? Mulder, that's ridiculous!*

Mulder: *Well, until you can prove it didn't happen, you'll just have to accept it as true.*

Mulder is making a claim but he shifts the burden of proof to Scully. If she can't prove it didn't happen, it must be true. It is actually Mulder who needs to provide the evidence for or against the possibility of alien abduction.

False dilemma

This fallacy is sometimes called the "either-or fallacy" or the "black-and-white fallacy" because you think that you have only two choices. For example, think about this statement:

> *My country, love it or leave it.*

In this statement you are presented with two opposite choices. Are these the only options? Maybe if I disagree with my country's policies, I could work to change them or exercise my right to vote for a different political leader. Maybe I could leave my country and still love it. Most social issues today are so complex that we need to examine many options to find the best answers. When students say that they need an A or will drop the class, they are presenting a false dilemma. It is possible to earn other grades and still make progress toward graduation. Critical thinkers are not limited by either-or choices but look to find creative solutions.

Viruses of the mind

No, it's not a real virus; it just acts like one. Viruses of the mind refer to beliefs for which hard evidence is lacking. These beliefs survive like viruses in that they need a host to ensure their survival. Some person or group believes the idea and promotes it. The ideas jump from person to person. An example is the Heavensgate cult:

> *It all seems perfectly ludicrous: 39 people don their new sneakers, pack their flight bags and poison themselves in the solemn belief that a passing UFO will whisk them off to Wonderland.*

Cults and doomsday forecasters spread unorthodox and sometimes harmful beliefs with great fervor. These thoughts are perpetuated through mind-control techniques. With mind control, members of a group are taught to suppress natural emotions and accept the ideas of the group in exchange for a sense of belonging. These groups do not allow members to think critically or question the belief system. Mind control is the opposite of critical thinking. It is important to use critical thinking when you encounter beliefs for which there is no hard evidence.

LEVELS OF THINKING

Table 3.1 Taxonomies of the Cognitive Domain

Bloom's Taxonomy 1956	Anderson and Krathwohl's Taxonomy 2000
1. Knowledge: Remembering or retrieving previously learned material. Examples of verbs that relate to this function are: know define record identify recall name relate memorize recognize list repeat acquire	**1. Remembering: Retrieving, recalling, or recognizing** knowledge from memory. Remembering is when memory is used to produce definitions, facts, or lists, or recite or retrieve material.
2. Comprehension: The ability to grasp or construct meaning from material. Examples of verbs that relate to this function are: restate identify illustrate locate discuss interpret report describe draw recognize review represent explain infer differentiate express conclude	**2. Understanding:** Constructing meaning from different types of functions be they written or graphic messages activities like **interpreting, exemplifying, classifying, summarizing, inferring, comparing, and explaining.**
3. Application: The ability to use learned material, or to implement material in new and concrete situations. Examples of verbs that relate to this function are: apply organize practice relate employ calculate develop restructure show translate interpret exhibit use demonstrate dramatize operate illustrate	**3. Applying:** Carrying out or using a procedure through **executing, or implementing.** Applying related and refers to situations where learned material is used through products like models, presentations, interviews or simulations.

(Continued)

Table 3.1 Taxonomies of the Cognitive Domain (*Continued*)

Bloom's Taxonomy 1956	Anderson and Krathwohl's Taxonomy 2000
4. Analysis: The ability to break down or distinguish the parts of material into its components so that its organizational structure may be better understood. Examples of verbs that relate to this function are:	**4. Analyzing:** Breaking material or concepts into parts, determining how the parts relate or interrelate to one another or to an overall structure or purpose. Mental actions included in this function are **differentiating, organizing, and attributing**, as well as **being able to distinguish between** the components or parts. When one is analyzing he/she can illustrate this mental function by creating spreadsheets, surveys, charts, or diagrams, or graphic representations.

analyze	differentiate	experiment
compare	contrast	scrutinize
probe	investigate	discover
inquire	detect	inspect
examine	survey	dissect
contrast	classify	discriminate
categorize	deduce	separate

Bloom's Taxonomy 1956	Anderson and Krathwohl's Taxonomy 2000
5. Synthesis: The ability to put parts together to form a coherent or unique new whole. Examples of verbs that relate to this function are:	**5. Evaluating:** Making judgments based on criteria and standards through **checking and critiquing**. Critiques, recommendations, and reports are some of the products that can be created to demonstrate the processes of evaluation. In the newer taxonomy evaluation comes before creating as it is often a necessary part of the precursory behavior before creating something. **Remember this one has now changed places with the last one on the other side.**

compose	plan	propose
produce	invent	develop
design	formulate	arrange
assemble	collect	construct
create	set up	organize
prepare	generalize	originate
predict	document	derive
modify	combine	write
tell	relate	propose

Bloom's Taxonomy 1956	Anderson and Krathwohl's Taxonomy 2000
6. Evaluation: The ability to judge, check, and even critique the value of material for a given purpose. Examples of verbs that relate to this function are:	**6. Creating:** Putting elements together to form a coherent or functional whole; **reorganizing** elements into a new pattern or structure through **generating, planning, or producing**. Creating requires users to put parts together in a new way or synthesize parts into something new and different a new form or product. This process is the most difficult mental function in the new taxonomy. **This one used to be #5 in Bloom's known as synthesis.**

judge	argue	validate
assess	decide	consider
compare	choose	appraise
evaluate	rate	value
conclude	select	criticize
measure	estimate	infer
deduce		

A major distinction between the high school and college class environment is that college faculty expect students to assume responsibility for their own learning of information. Instructors do not check to see if students have purchased textbooks, if they are taking notes, keeping up with the reading assignments, or studying for tests. Attending classes is the responsibility of the student, and many instructors do not penalize students for absences. At first, students may not perceive that the classes are difficult, but this perception often changes after the first exam. College classes often require a level of learning that students may not have incorporated into their previous learning strategies. Most high school courses focus on lower levels of understanding. Often students only needed to recognize the correct answer or restate information. Postsecondary coursework assumes students already know how to do that. They require you to think differently and at higher levels.

Many students find that the self-taught study strategies that enabled them to be successful in high school do not transfer to the college environment. Your high school or job-related experiences developed skills that you can now build upon and expand. Also, your previous study skills can be used as a base to learn more strategies. When you learn more about effective learning and study skills, then you can design your learning time to produce results. *You will not have to work harder, but you will be working smarter.*

Bloom's Taxonomy

Luckily, you already know how to think and are aware that different tasks require different degrees of thinking. The thinking you do when you remember a phone number differs from the thinking you do to solve a math story problem. If you can identify the level of thinking you already do, the level you may need to achieve, then you can apply this knowledge to areas involved in studying coursework. Each level builds on the previous level. That is, students cannot speak and comprehend a foreign language until they have memorized the basic vocabulary. Effective students are aware of learning strategies that incorporate the level of thinking required for success in each course. This chapter uses examples from a Geography textbook to demonstrate the thinking levels and practical application to studying and learning material.

Knowledge and recognition of information are the first level and form the basis of understanding. It requires you to remember what you heard or read, but not necessarily to understand it. It is as simple as remembering the name of the person you just met or what you need at the grocery store. In coursework, this level is necessary to build information for any subject. Many general education courses you select will require you to learn the basic vocabulary and principles of the course. Memorization can achieve this, but this is not meaningful learning, which requires understanding of the material. In the section from the Geography 152 textbook (Figure 3.2), the text discusses climatic classification systems. A student operating at the recognition/knowledge level may memorize the name of "Köppen" and the contribution that he made to science. Possibly, you will form a study group for the course. When you compare your notes for the course, each of you lists Köppen as an important person. You practice asking each other key names and other definitions from that chapter. The GEO 152 test and the essay question never ask what Köppen did. The test asks you to apply his classification system to describe a particular type of climate. To answer this question, the study group needed to do more processing of information. Simply memorizing the conditions and episodes was not sufficient. In Anderson and Krathwohl's taxonomy (2000), this domain is called **Remembering**.

The comprehension level emphasizes studying for an understanding of the material you are trying to learn. In this level of Bloom's taxonomy, you become more focused on what the material is trying to explain to you. During your geography study group time, you may explain to each other the characteristics of each type of climate mentioned in the GEO 152 lecture. Then you can answer the essay question that asks you to describe the different climatic types. At this level, you can explain information to someone else. You can share the plot of a movie or a novel, report the homework assignment to a roommate who missed class, or explain the course syllabus. In Anderson and Krathwohl's taxonomy (2000), this domain is called **Understanding**.

The third level in Bloom's taxonomy is **application**. When you apply what you understand, you begin to link the information you gained to examples in your own life. After seeing a movie or reading a novel, you connect with similar personal experiences. Your ability to see a parallel between the example in the text and the experience in your own life is the thinking skill of application. At this level, math courses require students to solve word problems or solve problems different from those previously seen. You are asked to compare and contrast information on an essay test question. In GEO 152 an essay test question might ask you to "describe the major differences between the classification systems." Many courses will ask you to provide examples from your own life of the information you study, determine causes and effects, or draw analogies. The more ways you apply the information, the longer you will retain the concepts. In Anderson and Krathwohl's taxonomy (2000), this domain is called **Applying**.

Analysis requires you to break apart and examine the components of a concept in depth. Depth is the key element that true analysis demands. If when discussing a movie or novel with a friend, you discuss the main theme and what made the leading character so evil, then you are using analytical thinking skills. If your friend disagrees with your analysis and questions your theory, the friendly debate that may follow requires additional analytic thinking. In GEO 152, the instructor may ask you to "calculate the climatic classification based on temperature and precipitation for a particular region." To analyze the problem, you need to gather facts, translate information, look at relationships, and apply rules and principles concerning weather patterns. In Anderson and Krathwohl's taxonomy (2000), this domain is called **Analyzing**.

Synthesis is the creative level of thinking. You combine different ideas to create a new whole. When you synthesize, you combine your current understanding of concepts with new information that you create. Many instructors assign group projects where students must design, create, or propose a solution to a problem. In GEO 152 the instructor may require that you work in a group to generate solutions to farming problems that have developed because of global warming. Examples that require that you operate at a synthesizing level include using music or art to express yourself, developing a topic for a research paper, or answering essay questions that ask you to "tie together" all the information you have learned to solve a problem. In Anderson and Krathwohl's taxonomy (2000), this domain has changed places with the next level of Bloom's, is considered the highest level and is called **Creating** (Table 3.1).

Evaluation forms the highest level of thinking in Bloom's taxonomy. At this level, you must use your personal judgment regarding an issue's relevance, depth, value, or other qualities. To do this, you would review all the relevant "facts" and review sources for their contribution to the topic under discussion. You often use evaluation to make judgments and decisions in your personal life. Choosing to attend Utah State University, whether to live on or off campus, or how many hours you can work and still do well in school require evaluation. Coursework may ask you to evaluate decisions in court cases or whether a social policy is adequate in providing aid and assistance to poor people. Geography classes may require you to judge what types of vegetation could adapt to climatic changes. Although this text describes the levels of Bloom's taxonomy separately, few learning situations depend solely on one level or another. Generally, as the information increases in complexity, the effort needed to learn also increases. Your classes will increase in complexity as will the levels of thinking required, as you specialize in a content area. This information will help you as a learner continually decide what you know, what you still need to learn, and the ways in which you must learn. However, in Anderson and Krathowal's taxonomy (2000), this domain has changed places with the previous level of Bloom's, is considered the 2nd highest level of thinking, and is called **Evaluating** (Table 3.1).

Background

In the late 1950s into the early 1970s here in the US there were attempts to dissect and classify the varied domains of human learning—*cognitive* (knowing, head), *affective* (feeling, heart) and *psychomotor* (doing, hand/body). The resulting efforts yielded a series of taxonomies in each area. A taxonomy is really just a word for a form of classification.

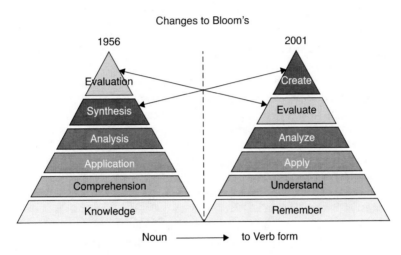

Figure 3.1 Visual Comparison of the Two Taxonomies.

The Cognitive Domain

In Table 3.1 are the two primary existing taxonomies of cognition. The one on the left, entitled **Bloom's**, is based on the original work of Benjamin Bloom and others as they attempted in 1956 to define the functions of thought, coming to know, or cognition. This taxonomy is over 50 years old.

The taxonomy on the right is the more recent adaptation and is the redefined work of one of Bloom's former students, Lorin Anderson, working with one of Bloom's partners in the original work on cognition, David Krathwohl. That one is labeled **Anderson and Krathwohl.** The new taxonomy was a larger group effort lead by Anderson and Krathwohl as they worked on this task from 1995–2000. The group was assembled by the primary authors and included people with expertise in the areas of cognitive psychology, curriculum and instruction, and educational testing, measurement, and assessment.

As you will see the primary differences are not just in the listings or rewordings from nouns to verbs, or in the renaming of some of the components, or even in the repositioning of the last two categories. The major differences in the updated version is in the more useful and comprehensive additions of how the taxonomy intersects and acts upon different types and levels of knowledge—factual, conceptual, procedural, and metacognitive.

The Köppen System ———————

Vladimir **Köppen** began devising a climatic classification system with his doctoral dissertation and continued to refine it until his death. An ethnic German from Russia, Köppen received formal training as a botanist. His system of climatic classification is based largely on the responses of biological activity to certain critical temperatures and moisture. Köppen reasoned that the world distribution of vegetation closely resembles the world distribution of climates. His attempt was to quantify climatic boundaries evidenced by the global distribution of vegetative groups.

Figure 6.1 illustrates the spatial distribution of global climates according to the **Köppen climatic classification** system. Köppen's labelling system begins at the equator with climates designated with the letter "A" which are macrothermal and humid. Straddling the wet and warm equatorial climates are the dry climates dominated by the subtropical high pressure represented by the symbol "B." Poleward of the B-type climates are the "C" climates characterized by humid, mesothermal atmospheric conditions with mild winters. At higher latitudes, Köppen's "D" climates are mid/latitude humid, mesothermal climates having cold winters. Finally, the "E" climates are those with microthermal characteristics dominated by low temperatures due to polar regions. Sites with climates dominated by altitude are represented by the letter "H." For precise definitions for the Köppen classification system, see End Note 6.

A Geography of Climates ———————

Although a case could be made for 30 to 35 different climatic types, this textbook describes only the climatic types covering significant portions of the earth's surface making them important to an introductory study of climates. Each of the following climatic types are products of earth/atmospheric processes at work in the area. As each climatic region is discussed, some explanation is offered as to the atmospheric mechanism controlling the manner in which the climate behaves. An understanding of various climatic types is basic to a comprehension of the distribution of people, plants, soils, and many other natural phenomena across the surface of the earth.

(Koeppen)

*

Köppen climatic classification: empirical climatic groups based on temperature and precipitation regimes.

A = tropical
B = desert/steppe
C = Mediterranean (mild-mes)
D = meso-cold
E = arctic/polar/ tundra
H = Highland (altitude)

Figure 6.1

Figure 3.2 Geography 152 Textbook Sample Annotated Page Example.

Climate and Climatic Classification   135

Figure 6.2 Humid tropical climate (Af).

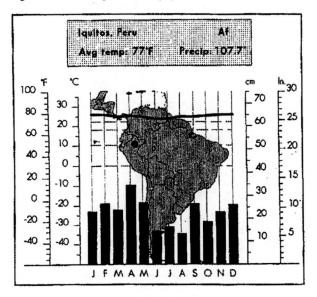

The Humid Tropical Climates

Generally located as a continuous belt near the equator, tropical (A) climates display high daily temperatures and significant annual precipitation. Dominated by proximity to the ITCZ, tropical climates are characteristically humid and warm. With average annual precipitation amounts greater than the annual potential for evapotranspiration, mean monthly temperatures exceed 18 degrees Celsius (64.4 degrees Fahrenheit). High temperatures are a function of the vertical rays of the sun while the high precipitation totals are caused by intertropical convergence.

The **humid tropical climate (Af)** is found in locations where daily, weekly, monthly, and annual conditions are continuously hot and humid. Figure 6.2 is a climograph illustrating the monthly temperature and precipitation of humid tropical climate. Due to the dominance of the ITCZ, precipitation is evenly distributed throughout the year which normally sup-

humid tropical climate: warm and moist year-round

Figure 3.2 (*Continued*)

136   Principles of Physical Geography

Figure 6.3 Humid wet-dry tropical climate (Aw).

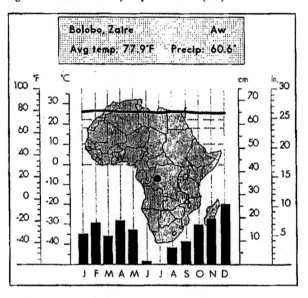

ports large expanses of rainforest accompanied by luxuriant undergrowth. Even though precipitation is received year round, the time of maximum precipitation occurs shortly after the time of the summer solstice. So little change occurs in daily weather patterns that the terms weather and climate are nearly synonymous. Indeed, the daily temperature range typically exceeds those of the annual temperature ranges causing reference to the nighttime as the "winter" of the tropics. Humid tropical climates occur in much of Central America, the equatorial belt of West Central Africa, and Indonesia.

humid wet-dry climate: warm year-round with dry winter season

Poleward of the humid tropical climate is the **humid wet-dry tropical climate** (Aw) which displays two distinct seasons of precipitation (Figure 6.3). During the wet season, precipitation rivals that of the humid tropical climate. However, the wet-dry tropical climate has a distinct dry winter during which precipitation is reduced to 30 percent or less of the annual total. The dry season lasts from three to six months and occurs during the time when the sun is not directly overhead, improperly

Figure 3.2 (*Continued*)

Climate and Climatic Classification   137

Figure 6.4   Tropical monsoon climate (Am).

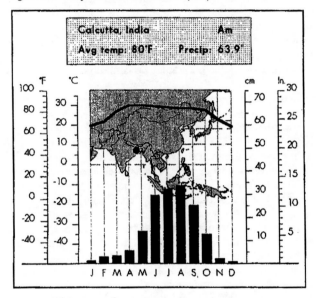

referred to as the tropical "winter." The shifting ITCZ is the climatic control of seasonal precipitation. When the ITCZ is present during the high-sun season, it brings with it abundant precipitation; when the ITCZ is absent during the low-sun season, dryness prevails. During the dry winter season, many of the trees lose their leaves and grasses experience stress. Tropical wet and dry climates are found in South America (central Brazil, Colombia and Venezuela), North and South Central Africa, India and Southeast Asia, Northern Australia, and parts of the Caribbean.

The **tropical monsoon climate** (Am) is characterized by a very short low-sun dry season during which the precipitation is reduced to less than 1/10 of the wet, high-sun season (Figure 6.4). The climate of India is perhaps the best example of a true monsoon. Though not experiencing reversals in regional winds, locations in Northern Brazil, the Guianas, Burma, and much of the Philippines are characterized as having tropical monsoon climates. In order for these locations to experience true mon-

tropical monsoon climate: warm year-round with extremely wet summer season

Figure 3.2 (*Continued*)

soonal weather, seasonal reversals of wind must accompany these wet-dry seasons which, in the locations cited above, seldom occurs. Often associated with the mechanisms responsible for the precipitation regime of the true monsoon climate is the presence of high ground (such as a mountain range) located near a coastal plain initiating orographic precipitation.

The Dry Climates

Covering more than a fourth of the total land surface area of the earth, the dry climates are symbolized by the letter "B." Although they can be found at much higher latitudes, the dry climates are concentrated between 20 and 30 degrees north and south latitude (Figure 6.1). A geographic site has a dry climate regime when the annual total precipitation is less than the potential for evaporation from natural surfaces and transpiration (water loss) from plants. The potential for evaporation and transpiration is often combined into one term, **evapotranspiration**. In dry climatic regions, potential evapotranspiration amounts exceed the total accumulations of precipitation. Not only do dry climates experience little precipitation, but they also exhibit great variation in annual precipitation totals and distribution. Because of the general absence of clouds, dry climates receive intense insolation which effectively heats the atmosphere and reduces relative humidity.

evapotranspiration: combined water loss by evaporation and transpiration from plants.

The principle controlling mechanisms establishing dry climates on the earth's surface include: (1) high atmospheric pressure caused by the subsidence of air in the subtropical high pressure cells, (2) the rainshadow on the leeward side of the prevailing winds over a major mountain range, and (3) interior continental positions some distance from marine water sources. The dry climates are of two general varieties: the steppe and the desert. The steppe (BS) has a semiarid moisture regime where total annual precipitation is less than potential evapotranspiration but greater than one-half that value making it capable of supporting stumpy woodlands with small communities of grass. Most steppe climates function as transitional zones between humid and arid climates. The desert (BW) has an arid moisture regime with an average annual precipitation less than one-half the annual potential for evapotranspiration.

Figure 3.2

DURING (D)

Commit to the following *actions*:

- **Become a critical thinker**
- **Think creatively**
- **Understand your emotional intelligence**
- **Solve problems**
- **Construct and evaluate arguments**
- **Conduct research**
- **Use your library**

HOW TO BECOME A CRITICAL THINKER

The Critical Thinking Process

When thinking about a complex problem, use these steps in the critical thinking process:

1. **State the problem in a clear and simple way.** Sometimes the message is unclear or obscured by appeals to emotion. Stating the problem clearly brings it into focus so that you can identify the issue and begin to work on it.
2. **Identify the alternative views.** In looking at different views, you open your mind to a wider range of options. For every issue, there are many points of view. The larger circle represents these many points of view. The individual point of view is represented by a dot on the larger circle. Experience, values, beliefs, culture, and knowledge influence an individual's point of view.
3. **Watch for fallacies** in reasoning when looking at alternative views.
4. **Find at least three different answers.** In searching for these different answers, you force yourself to look at all the possibilities before you decide on the best answer.
5. **Construct your own reasonable view.** After looking at the alternatives and considering different answers to the problem, construct your own reasonable view. Practice this process using the critical thinking exercises in this chapter.

> ### Elements of Thought
>
> - Point of View
> - Purpose
> - Question at issue
> - information
> - Interpretation and inference
> - Concepts
> - Assumptions
> - Implications and Consequences
>
> http://www.criticalthinking.org/ctmodel/logicmodel1.htm

© Kheng Guan Toh/Shutterstock, Inc.

Use the Following Tips to Improve Your Critical Thinking Skills

1. **Be aware of your mindset.** A mindset is a pattern of thought that you use out of habit. You develop patterns of thinking based on your personal experiences, culture, and environment. When the situation changes, your old mindset may need to change as well.

2. **Be willing to say, "I don't know."** With this attitude you are open to exploring new ideas. In today's rapidly changing world, it is not possible to know everything. Rather than trying to know everything, it is more important to be able to find the information you need.

3. **Practice tolerance for other people's ideas.** We all have a different view of the world based on our own experiences and can benefit from an open exchange of information.

4. **Try to look for several answers and understand many points of view.** Remember the false dilemma fallacy of reasoning? The world is not either-or or black-and-white. Looking at all the possibilities is the first step in finding a creative solution.

5. **Understand before criticizing.** Life is not about justifying your point of view. It is important to understand and then offer your suggestions.

6. **Realize that your emotions can get in the way of clear thinking.** We all have beliefs that are important to us. It is difficult to listen to a different point of view when someone questions your personal beliefs. Open your mind to see all the alternatives. Then construct your reasonable view.

7. **Notice the source of the information you are analyzing.** Political announcements are required to include information about the person or organization paying for the ad. Knowing who paid for an advertisement can help you understand and evaluate the point of view that is being promoted.

8. **Ask the question, "What makes the author think so?"** In this way you can discover what premises the author is using to justify his or her position.

9. **Ask the question, "So what?"** Ask this question to determine what is important and how the author reached the conclusion.

Critical Thinking over the Internet

The Internet is revolutionizing the way we access and retrieve information today. Through the use of search engines, websites, electronic periodicals, and online reference materials, it is possible to find just about any information you need. The Internet is also full of scams, rumors, gossip, hoaxes, exaggerations, and illegal activity. Anyone can put anything on the Internet. You will need to apply critical thinking to the information that you find on the Internet. Author Reid Goldsborough offers these suggestions for thinking critically about material on the Internet:

- **Don't be fooled by appearances.** It is easy to create a flashy and professional-looking website. Some products and services are legitimate, but some are scams.
- **Find out about the person or organization providing the information.** There should be links to a home page that lists the author's background and credentials. You need to be skeptical if the author is not identified. If you cannot identify the person who authored the website, find out what organization sponsored the site. Most of the Internet resources cited in this text are provided by educational or government sources. It is the goal of these organizations to provide the public with information.
- **Look for the reason the information was posted.** What is the agenda? Keep this in mind when evaluating the information. Many websites exist to sell a product or influence public opinion.

HOW TO RECOGNIZE A SCAM

Use your critical thinking skills to recognize a scam or hoax. How can you recognize a scam? Here are some signs to watch for:

- **Be aware of big promises.** If something sounds too good to be true, it probably is a hoax. If you are promised $5,000 a month for working part time out of your home, be careful. If you are offered a new TV in a box for $50, the box may contain stolen goods or even rocks!
- **The word "free" is often used to catch your attention to make a sale.** Few things in life are free.
- **A similar tactic is to offer money or a prize.** The scam goes like this: "Congratulations! You have just won a . . ." Be especially careful if you have to pay money to claim your prize.
- **Beware of high-pressure tactics.** A common scam is to ask you to pay money now or the price will go up. Take your time to think carefully about your expenditures. If the deal is legitimate, it will be there tomorrow.
- **To avoid identity theft, be careful about disclosing personal information such as social security numbers and credit card numbers.** Disclose this information only to people and organizations you know and trust.
- **If you suspect a scam, research the offer on the Internet.** Use a search engine such as yahoo.com or google.com and type in the word "scam." You can find descriptions of many different types of scams. You can also find information on the latest scams or file a complaint at the Federal Trade Commission website at www.ftc.gov.

- **Look for the date that the information was created or revised.** A good website posts the date of creation or revision because links become outdated quickly.
- **Try to verify the information elsewhere, especially if the information is at odds with common sense or what you believe to be true.** Verify the information through other websites or your local library.

CREATIVE THINKING

What Is Creativity?

The creative individual asks why and uses divergent thinking. **Divergent thinking** is the ability to discover many alternatives. J. P. Guilford, a researcher on creativity, said that "the person who is capable of producing a large number of ideas per unit of time, other things being equal, has a greater chance of having significant ideas." Divergent thinking is useful in careers requiring creativity, such as the arts, science, and business. Creativity helps in the enjoyment of outside activities such as hobbies that help us to lead satisfying lives. Creativity and divergent thinking are important in generating alternatives necessary for effective problem solving and coming up with creative solutions to the challenges we all face in life.

The Three S's of Creativity: Sensitivity, Synergy, and Serendipity

The creative process involves sensitivity, synergy, and serendipity. Creative persons use their **sensitivity** to discover the world and spot problems, deficiencies, and incongruities. A person who is sensitive asks, "Why does this happen?" Sensitive persons are also

inventive and ask the question, "How can I do this?" They are problem finders as well as problem solvers.

Synergy occurs when two or more elements are associated in a new way and the result is greater than the sum of the parts. For example, imagine a machine that combines the telephone, the computer, and the television. The combining of these familiar devices into one machine will soon change the way we live. Another example of synergy is the old saying, "Two heads are better than one." When two or more people work together and share ideas, the result is often greater than what one person could produce alone. This is the essence of creativity.

The word **serendipity** is attributed to Horace Walpole, who wrote a story about the Persian princes of Serendip. The princes made unexpected discoveries while they were looking for something else. Serendipity is finding something by a lucky accident. You can only take advantage of a lucky accident if you look around and find new meaning and opportunity in the event. An example of serendipity comes from a story about the famous musician Duke Ellington. He was playing at an outdoor concert when a noisy plane flew over the stage. He changed the tempo of the music to go with the sounds of the airplane and directed the plane along with the orchestra. Another example of serendipity is Alexander Fleming's discovery of penicillin. He was growing bacteria in his lab when a spore of *penicillium notatum* blew in the window, landed on the bacteria, and killed it. Instead of throwing away a ruined experiment, he discovered the antibiotic penicillin, one of the most important medical discoveries ever made.

Creative Thinking Techniques

Brainstorming

One of the most important components of creativity is the ability to use divergent thinking to generate many ideas or alternatives. Brainstorming is one of the most frequently used techniques to develop divergent thinking. The key to brainstorming is to delay critical judgment to allow for the spontaneous flow of ideas. Critical judgment about the merit of ideas can hinder the creative process if it is applied too early. Here are the rules of brainstorming:

- *Generate a large quantity of ideas without regard to quality.* This increases the likelihood that some of the ideas will be good or useful.
- *Set a time limit to encourage quick thinking.* The time limit is generally short, from three to five minutes.
- *Set a goal or quota for the number of ideas you want to generate.* The goal serves as a motivator.
- *The wilder and more unusual the ideas, the better.* It is easier to tame down crazy ideas than to think up new ideas.
- *Use synergy by brainstorming with a group of people.* Build on other people's ideas. Sometimes two ideas combined can make one better idea.
- *Select the best ideas from the list.*

Relaxed attention

Can you imagine being relaxed and paying attention at the same time? Robert McKim describes this as the paradox of the Ho-hum and the Aha! To be creative it is first necessary to relax. The brain works better when it is relaxed. By relaxing, the individual releases full energy and attention to the task at hand. Athletes and entertainers must master the art of relaxation before they can excel in athletics or entertainment. If the muscles are too tense, blood flow is restricted and energy is wasted. However, totally relaxed individuals cannot think at all. They might even be asleep!

Some tension, but not too much, is needed to think and be creative; hence the term "relaxed attention." In the creative process, the person first thinks about a task, problem, or creation and then relaxes to let the ideas incubate. During this incubation period, the person often gets a flash of insight or feeling of "Aha!"

As a student you can apply the principle of relaxed attention to improve your creativity. If you are thinking about a problem and get stuck, relax and come back to it later. Take a break, do something else, or even sleep on it. You are likely to come up with creative inspiration while you are relaxing. Then get back to solving the problem and pay attention to it.

Use idea files

Keep files of ideas that you find interesting. People in advertising call these "swipe files." No one creates in a vacuum. Some of the best creative ideas involve recombining or building on the ideas of others or looking at them from a different perspective. This is different from copying other people's ideas; it is using them as the fertilizer for creative thinking.

As a college student, you might keep files of the following:

- *Interesting ideas and their sources for use in writing term papers*
- *Information about careers*
- *Information for your resume*
- *Information that you can use to apply for scholarships*
- *Ideas related to your hobbies*
- *Ideas for having fun*
- *Ideas for saving money*

Practice using visualization and imagination

Visualizing and imagining are important in the creative process. Young children are naturally good at these two skills. What happens as we grow older? As we grow older, we learn to follow the rules and color between the lines. We need rules to have an orderly society, yet we need visualization and imagination to move forward and create new ideas. Don't forget to use and practice visualization and imagination.

Visualization and imagination can be fun and interesting activities to help you relax. We have often been told not to daydream, but daydreams can be a tool for relaxation as well as creativity. It is important to come back to reality once we are finished daydreaming. The last step in the creative process is doing something with the best of our creative ideas.

Read

One of the best ways to trigger your creativity is to read a wide variety of materials, including newspapers, magazines, novels, and nonfiction books. The ideas that you discover will provide background information, helping you gain perspective on the world, and give you ideas for making your own contributions. When you read, you expose your mind to the greatest people who have ever lived. Make reading a habit.

Keep a journal

Keep a journal of your creative ideas, thoughts, and problems. Writing often will help you think clearly. When you write about your problems, it is almost like having your own private therapist. In college your journal can be a source of creative ideas for writing term papers and completing assignments.

Think critically

Approach learning with a sense of awe, excitement, and skepticism. Here is another paradox! Creative and critical thinkers have much in common. Both ask questions, look at the world from different perspectives, and generate new alternatives.

EMOTIONAL INTELLIGENCE (EI)

Another strategy for becoming a critical thinker is your ability to manage your emotions and determining your emotional intelligence. Emotional intelligence . . . "is a type of social intelligence that involves the ability to monitor one's own and others' emotions, to discriminate among them, and to use the information to guide one's thinking and actions" (Mayer & Salovey, 1993: 433). According to Salovey & Mayer (1990), emotional intelligence subsumes Gardner's inter- and intrapersonal intelligences, and involves abilities that may be categorized into five domains:

1. **Self-awareness:**
   Observing yourself and recognizing a feeling as it happens.
2. **Managing emotions:**
   Handling feelings so that they are appropriate; realizing what is behind a feeling; finding ways to handle fears and anxieties, anger, and sadness.
3. **Motivating oneself:**
   Channeling emotions in the service of a goal; emotional self control; delaying gratification and stifling impulses.
4. **Empathy:**
   Sensitivity to others' feelings and concerns and taking their perspective; appreciating the differences in how people feel about things.
5. **Handling relationships:**
   Managing emotions in others; social competence and social skills.

PROBLEM SOLVING

Problem solving involves critical thinking. Are problem solving and critical thinking the same? Not really. Problem solving is about having the ability and skills to apply knowledge to pragmatic problems encountered in all areas of your life. If you were trying to solve a financial problem or decide whether or not to change roommates, you probably would not need a model of thinking as extensive as the one previously described. The following steps offer an organized approach to solving less complex problems.

1. **Identify the problem. Be specific and write it down.**
2. **Analyze the problem.**
3. **Identify alternative ways to solve the problem.**

4. **Examine alternatives.**
5. **Implement a solution.**
6. **Evaluate.**

Identify the Problem

What exactly is the problem you wish to solve? Is it that your roommate is driving you crazy, or is it that you want to move into an apartment with your friend next semester? Be specific.

Analyze the Problem

Remember, analysis means looking at all the parts. It is the process by which we select and interpret information. Be careful not to be too selective or simplistic in your thinking. Look at all the facts and details. For example, suppose you want to move into an apartment with your friends. Do you need permission from anyone to do so? Can you afford to do this? Can you get a release from your dorm lease? Your answer to all the questions might be yes, with the exception of being able to afford it. You want tomove, so now the problem is a financial one. You need to come up with the financial resources to follow through on your decision.

Identify Alternative Ways to Solve the Problem

Use convergent and divergent thinking. You are engaging in **convergent thinking** when you are narrowing choices to come up with the correct solution (e.g., picking the best idea out of three). You are engaging in **divergent thinking** when you are thinking in terms of multiple solutions. Mihaly Csikszentmihalyi (1996) says, "Divergent thinking leads to no agreed-upon solution. It involves fluency, or the ability to generate a great quantity of ideas; flexibility, or the ability to switch from one perspective to another; and originality in picking unusual associations of ideas" (1996, p. 60). He concludes that a person whose thinking has these qualities is likely to come up with more innovative ideas.

Brainstorming is a great way to generate alternative ways to solve problems. This creative problem-solving technique requires that you use both divergent and convergent thinking. Here are some steps to use if you decide to brainstorm.

- **Describe the problem.**
- **Decide on the amount of time you want to spend brainstorming (e.g., 10 minutes).**
- **Relax (remember some of the best insights come in a relaxed state).**
- **Write down everything that comes to your mind (divergent thinking).**
- **Select your best ideas (convergent thinking).**
- **Try one out! (If it does not work, try one of the other ideas you selected.)**

Students have successfully used the process of brainstorming to decide on a major, choose activities for spring break, develop topics for papers, and come up with ideas for part-time jobs. Being creative means coming up with atypical solutions to complex problems.

Examine Alternatives

Make judgments about the alternatives based on previous knowledge and the additional information you now have.

Implement a Solution

Choose one solution to your problem and eliminate the others for now. (If this one fails, you may want to try another solution later.)

Evaluate

If the plan is not as effective as you had hoped, modify your plan or start the process over again. Also look at the criteria you used to judge your alternative solutions.

DEVELOPING A PROBLEM-SOLVING ACTION PLAN

Based on the info from the chapter—NOW what research do you want to or need to conduct for a class this term?

> ### THE SPECIAL PROBLEM-SOLVING ACTION PLAN
>
> S   Set the Stage and Self-Assess
>
> P   Prepare your Plan
>
> E   Explore strategies
>
> C   Choose strategies and Commit
>
> I   Investigate resources
>
> A   Act and Announce!
>
> L   What have you Learned?

What are you willing to do to get it? Do you want/need a PLAN to do it?
Here is our guideline to help you make your research easier (focus on your research).

S   Set the Stage and Self-Assess

What grade do you want in this assignment? Are you researching for personal reasons or for general improvement of your research skills? What type of info do you think you should get? Set YOUR goals. Do your goals match what you are required to get for your assignment? Are you up to speed?

P   Prepare your Plan

Organize by listing your tasks (i.e., method of recording info you find, due dates, backward time plan) and estimate how long it will take you to do each (find all sources, etc.). Do you need to go to the library to get it? Search the Web? Both?

E   Explore strategies

Dividing this step up for a big research assignment:

Strategies for choosing a topic (unless one is assigned to you) Collecting general info on your topic (baby research) Strategies for beginning the writing process itself

What is the best way to record the info that I find? The best way for me? Note cards? Doodles on loose-leaf? What do I need to record?

C   Choose strategies and Commit

Make a decision on which strategies you will use. If I'm stuck on choosing—do I need more info to make a good decision? List strategies.

What is my level of commitment for each strategy?

I   Investigate outcomes and other resources

Can I predict how long this assignment will take me? If I run into snags can I get help? From whom? When? Are my current strategies getting me what I want? Are there any negative outcomes or roadblocks?

A   *Act and Announce!*

What are you doing? Are you still on track?

What are your actions on choosing a topic?

What exactly is your "writing process"—are you doing this at a certain time/day each week?

Are you booking in computer time to research? To write?

Are you finding, then recording key information?

Making note cards? Outlines, concept maps?

Who have you told (announced) about this assignment? Have your actions included:

Talking to your professor—to let her know how you are doing, or for more help?

Talking to the librarian (online or in person)?

Checking in with fellow classmates?

L   *What have I Learned?*

So far—have you set a realistic goal (grade, due date, paper length, number of sources) for yourself?

Have you correctly assessed your abilities in terms of **skills** to get what you want in this assignment?

- How do you feel about your ability to evaluate Internet sources for reliability?
- Do you now know how to summarize info, paraphrase info, and cite sources correctly?

Have you checked your original and current priority list regarding academic activities? Has this assignment changed in its level of importance to you?
What have you learned about your choice of strategies?

- Did you build in a reward to help motivate you through a "big" project? (This, too, is a strategy.)
- Did you organize a timetable to get this done? What else did you actually DO?
- Were you able to ask for help? Go to the library and find sources?
- Did you or do you still need to revise your work? Who is going to proofread it?

So, now—is what you are doing getting you what you want? Are there any changes that you want to make?

- Different goals?
- Quick catch-up on skills?

- New timetable to get/stay organized?
- New strategies?
- More information/use of resources available to you?
- "Just DO It"

ARGUMENTS

Critical thinking involves the construction and evaluation of arguments. An argument is a form of thinking in which reasons (statements and facts) are given in support of a conclusion. The reasons of the argument are known as the **premises**. A good argument is one in which the premises are logical and support the conclusion. The validity of the argument is based on the relationship between the premises and the conclusion. If the premises are not credible or do not support the conclusion, or the conclusion does not follow from the premises, the argument is considered to be invalid or fallacious. Unsound arguments (based on fallacies) are often persuasive because they can appeal to our emotions and confirm what we want to believe to be true. Just look at commercials on television. Alcohol advertisements show that you can be rebellious, independent, and have lots of friends, fun, and excitement by drinking large quantities of alcohol—all without any negative consequences. Intelligence is reflected in the capacity to acquire and apply knowledge. Even sophisticated, intelligent people are influenced by fallacious advertising.

AFTER (A)

Continue to *review*, *revise,* and *self-modify* as needed.

- **How am I thinking** (critically, creatively, emotionally)**?**
- **Do I examine every possibility and determine at least 5 ways to solve a problem?**
- **What changes can I make to what I am doing now that will help me become a critical and creative thinker that will also help me be a better employee and person?**

SUMMARY

One of the goals of college is to produce critical thinkers. This chapter has covered the essence of critical thinking: fallacies in reasoning; levels of thinking (Bloom's Taxonomy); how to become a critical thinker; creative thinking; emotional intelligence (EI); problem-solving and decision making and arguments. Applying these critical thinking strategies will help you achieve academic, professional, and personal success.

SUGGESTED READINGS

Barell, John. *Developing More Curious Minds.* Alexandria, VA: Assoc. for Supervision and Curriculum Development, 2003.

Mitroff, Ian I. *Smart Thinking for Crazy Times: The Art of Solving the Right Problems.* San Francisco: Berrett Koehler, 1998.

Elder, Linda, and Paul, Richard. *25 Days to Better Thinking & Better Living: A Guide for Improving Every Aspect of Your Life.* Upper Saddle River, NJ: Pearson Education, Inc., 2006.

EXERCISE 3.1: CASE STUDY—CHRIS CROSSED?

Chris is an 18-year-old freshman who plans to major in pre-med. He is taking a 16-hour course load as well as working 30 hours a week. Chris received a partial scholarship which is tied directly to his grade point average. He lives in a small apartment three miles from campus and just bought his first new car. There are only three (3) weeks left in the semester. Chris is struggling through an important exam in "Introduction to Human Anatomy." His boss asked him to work late last night and close the store. Even though he studies until 4:00 a.m., Chris is not well prepared for the exam. Halfway through the hour, Chris glances up to notice Tracy is copying answers from a cheat sheet on her exam. Shortly after the exam, Chris sees Tracy in the Student Union. He knows that the professor grades on a curve and his grade is crucial to his future career. Chris is furious.

Resolve the scenario by answering the questions below.

- *What is the problem(s)?*

- *What is the root of the problem(s)?*

- *What are some potential <u>assumptions</u> and/or <u>fallacies in reasoning</u> that should be uncovered?*

- *What are some <u>mistakes in logic</u> that Chris made?*

- *What should he do? Think of at least 3 answers and describe below:*

  1.

  2.

  3.

EXERCISE 3.2: CREATIVE THINKING

The following exercises are opportunities for you to practice creative thinking and problem-solving. Stretch yourself! Think of as many ideas as you can for each section.

Be Creative

Think of as many uses for a toothpick as you can.
(For now, just come up with eight.)

1. _____
2. _____
3. _____
4. _____
5. _____
6. _____
7. _____
8. _____

By completing this exercise, we have gotten some valuable ideas for what you can do with a toothpick. For example, one of our favorites is to use them to roast tiny marshmallows over a tiny fire or use them to make wind chimes. Now that you have a few more ideas, go back to the previous exercise and come up with a few more uses before going any further.

1. _____
2. _____
3. _____
4. _____
5. _____
6. _____
7. _____
8. _____

Now that you have completed the exercise the second time, look back and compare the two sets of answers. Are they different? How? What we have found is that the answers given the first time around are usually the more common and conventional uses such as picking up food and the ever popular cleaning of teeth. But the second time, after we have given some of our favorite examples, the answers get more, shall we say, wild. What happened to make things different? Well, when we shared our ideas, we brought down the walls of conventional thinking. You were no longer confined to just that small realm of ideas and were free to "roam" around a bit and consider uses that you may have eliminated previously because you felt that they were irrelevant. Here are a few more exercises you can use to help bring those walls down.

Job Interview

You have a job interview at 10:00 a.m. the next morning, but your car just broke down that afternoon and won't be fixed for two weeks. The place is 20 miles away, and you need to be dressed well. Also keep in mind that the traffic will be horrible between 8:00 and 10:00 in the morning. List as many possible ways you can get to the job interview.

_____

_____

_____

_____

_____

_____

_____

_____

_____

_____

_____

_____

_____

_____

_____

_____

_____

_____

_____

_____

_____

_____

Term Paper

You've been working on a term paper for weeks and as you arrive at school that morning, you realize that you left it at home sitting on top of the computer. This paper means everything. If you get an A, you get an A in the class; if you fail, you don't graduate. The bell for class starts to ring and you realize that you're stuck since you won't be allowed to leave for any reason. What do you do? (Don't forget to use those creative juices that are flowing now.)

_____

_____

_____

Here are some things to keep in mind as you are working on things in the future:

- **Be original.** Look for new ways to do the same thing. Examine the problem from different points of view and go beyond the conventional. You may find a new solution that works just that much better than the one you just had. It's going to be a bit difficult at first, but it'll get easier and easier the more you practice.

- **Remember not to be judgmental when you're brainstorming.** Jot down your ideas. Many great ideas can be lost at this stage by making quick judgments. Make the judgment calls later on.

- **Be flexible to change.** Change is another one of those double-edged swords, so be careful as to how you wield it. Make sure you know when it is time for change and when you need to stay with convention. Keep in mind that something is only effective as long as it is effective.

- **Keep an eye out for opportunities to use your creativity.** There are opportunities everywhere. This one might be difficult at first, but the more you get in the habit and practice, the easier it is going to get.

Keep in mind these four steps and keep reminding yourself that you can do this, because you can. You do it every day and probably don't even recognize it.

EXERCISE 3.3: CASE STUDY—THE LAB PARTNER

Pat Collins reluctantly handed in his lab assignment to the teaching assistant. The lab today had been a complete disaster, and Pat worried that his grade would begin to be affected by the poor work that he and his lab partner were performing. But Pat had to do all of the work himself while his partner just showed up to class assuming that everything would be done for him. "I can't go on like this," Pat thought, "I'll never get a good grade if I am forced to do everything myself."

Pat was in the middle of his first semester at Mercury University. He came to MU from Maryland with a very good academic record, and decided to major in pharmacy after his experience working part-time in a drug store while in high school. He knew college would be challenging but did not know exactly how challenging it would be. Regardless, Pat was coming to school to study—not to party—so he was ready to accept the challenge.

During the first couple of weeks of the semester, Pat was without a lab partner for his chemistry class. A very conscientious student, he was worried that not having a lab partner would require additional work and would affect his grade. He had already called his mother to tell her that he had done poorly on a biology test, so he felt that he could not afford more work than would have been the case if he had a lab partner. But, Pat was very particular, so not having a partner allowed him to do the lab work exactly like he wanted it done. Two weeks into the course, Pat was finally assigned a partner and figured that things would begin to fall into place. But, instead of falling into place, things began to fall apart.

Pat's new lab partner was never prepared for class. He never read over the experiments or material before class and did not attend recitations. He did not study nor take any of the quizzes. He just came to the lab each week without any idea of how to perform the experiments. Unlike Pat, he was not in the least concerned about getting good grades. Pat wondered, "How can I possibly survive this semester in lab with this slacker?"

This week's experiment did not work the way it was supposed to and Pat blamed his lab partner's lack of preparation. Pat tried to save the experiment (without his partner's help), but it still did not come out right. That was not all; chemical problems and equations also had to be completed before the end of lab. Pat knew how to do the problems, but the failed experiment made doing the equations correctly much more difficult. As he worked through the problems he could feel the clock ticking away the time; he was running out of time.

Pat felt frustrated and angry. He was already in a bad mood when he arrived in lab, feeling tired and a little homesick. He missed his friends and family in Maryland. Making friends at Mercury was not as easy as he would like because he saw himself as somewhat more quiet and conservative than most others at the university. He did not really want to alienate his lab partner, and did his best not to be rude even though he was angry. He kept from confronting him because he was afraid that would make it too awkward to work with him in the future.

Pat turned in the assignment expecting a bad grade. The teaching assistant noticed the frustration and asked what was going on. Pat hesitated as he struggled for a way to respond.

The Lab Partner

What is this case about?   Get into the case by putting yourself in Pat Collins' place as he tries to figure out what to do about his lab partner who won't do any of the work.

Get the facts.   List the facts that you know about Pat and his situation:

1. _____
2. _____
3. _____
4. _____
5. _____

State the problem, issue, or question that needs to be resolved.

_____

_____

List several ways that the problem might be resolved.

1. _____
2. _____
3. _____

Write down the best way to solve the problem and why you would solve it that way.

_____

_____

_____

_____

EXERCISE 3.4: GROUP ACTIVITY—PRACTICE YOUR RESEARCH SKILLS IN A TEAM SETTING

Below are ten statements to verify for truth or falsity. Use each other and/or library reference materials in your critical thinking process. Problem solve how you will verify the statement, and how confident you are in the accuracy of the source(s) you use and how confident you are in its truth or falsity. The group should come to a consensus for each statement and can record either individual student responses or group responses to the following questions:

- Is the statement true or false?
- How confident are you about your answer? (Use a 1 to 5 scale, with 1 being no confidence to 5 being extremely confident.)
- What source(s) of information was used to locate your answer?

1. Doctor-assisted suicide is the same as euthanasia.

2. World courts settle trade disputes between countries.

3. There are over four-hundred species of sharks.

4. Intrastate commerce is the same as interstate commerce. (Both controlled by the federal government)

5. The greenhouse effect has been scientifically proven.

6. A convicted felon can never possess a firearm.

7. Date rape and statutory rape are the same.

8. 70% of college students cheat at some time during their college years.

9. HIV and AIDS mean the same thing.

10. The number-one growth industry is the prison industry.

Evaluate the reliability and validity of your sources.

Critically assess your team for the above exercise; were your team members adamant about the answer they chose? Did others agree immediately? Did they back up their answer with evidence and/or sound logical reasoning? Or did they agree to just agree?

EXERCISE 3.5: JOURNAL ENTRY

Write/type a one-page journal entry discussing the following:

Identify a **problem** you are currently having (academic or personal). Using information found in this chapter, **create an action plan** to solve this problem. Discuss possible **solutions** you discovered and how you determined the best way to effectively solve this problem.

Chapter 4

Learning Styles – How Do I Learn Best?

INTRODUCTION

This chapter focuses on learning styles, personality and multiple intelligences and how these affect your learning. As you read the chapter and complete the exercises, keep in mind that there are no right or wrong answers. The goal is to help you complete self-analysis to discover how you learn best. In the process, you will also find out more about your strengths and weaknesses. The more you know about yourself and the ways you learn, the more effectively you can put that information to use in your college courses and in your career.

BEFORE (B)

How do you complete the *preparation, self-awareness,* and *planning* needed for your learning styles?

- **Know what a learning style is**
- **Know why it is important to examine your learning style**
- **Know the types of learning styles**
- **Complete a self-analysis of your learning styles**

WHAT IS A LEARNING STYLE?

Before continuing, it is necessary to make clear just what is meant by learning style. Scholars have different opinions regarding what should or shouldn't be included in the definition. For our purposes, **learning style** is the characteristic and preferred way one takes in and interacts with information, and the way one responds to the learning environment. Think of your particular learning style as the way you prefer to learn new or difficult information, and the way you find it easiest and most comfortable to learn.

To illustrate, suppose that you are given a learning task. What is the first thing you would prefer to do to get the new information—read about it in a book; listen to someone talk about it; or do something with the information to prove that you know it? None of the ways is the right or best way, they are simply examples of different ways to learn. You may prefer one, or a combination of those listed. There is no best way to learn, just different ways. The goal for you is to find your preferred learning style.

Depending on which expert you ask, there are many different ways to consider learning styles and many ways to analyze them. This chapter will only touch on a few.

Your learning style may be more difficult to determine now than it would have been in elementary school. The reason is that as you get older and become a more mature learner, your learning style becomes more integrated. You have probably learned that you have to use many different ways to get information depending on the learning situation. When you answer the questions on the various learning style inventories given later in this chapter, keep in mind that you want to answer them thinking about your preferences. Answer them based on what you are most comfortable doing, and what's easiest for you. The more accurate the picture of your learning style, the more you can use it to help you.

WHY SHOULD YOU KNOW ABOUT YOUR LEARNING STYLE?

One of the goals of a college education is to make you an independent learner. There will be many things you will have to learn after you complete your degree, and helping you learn HOW to learn is an important aspect of your education. Knowing how you learn will help you begin to monitor your learning. The more aware you are of the way you learn, the better you can be at determining where you need help and where you don't.

As you study information by reading a textbook for example, if you are not understanding what you are reading, you need to make adjustments in the method you are using. You may try one of several options—reading the material aloud, silently reading it over again, asking someone from your class to explain it, or whatever might work. If you know what your learning style is, you will have a better idea about the one or two strategies more likely to work for you. This makes you more efficient (you don't have to try everything to find a strategy that works) and it makes you more effective because you can change strategies and understand the difficult material more clearly.

Some research indicates that grades are better, and the learner is more motivated when taught using the preferred learning style. The research also indicates a tendency in learners to retain the information better. Although you can't usually make choices about how your instructors will present information to you, you can choose how you will study on your own. This independent studying is the way you will be getting more of your information in college.

STRENGTHS AND WEAKNESSES

Knowing your learning style can also help you understand why certain types of information are easier or more difficult for you to learn. Being aware of weaknesses can help you be prepared for them. For example, if you know that you have trouble with numbers, then you know that your math class (necessary for meeting general education requirements) is going to be difficult for you. You can be better prepared by scheduling the class at a time when you are most alert, finding a tutor early on in the class, or scheduling it during a semester when you can devote the necessary time and effort to it. Your awareness of weak areas will help you be prepared for problems and prevent some, instead of being caught by surprise.

By knowing your strengths, you can overcome the problems and weaknesses. If you know the ways you are most comfortable learning, you can use those to help you learn difficult material. If you know, for example, that you need to read information to really understand it, then you know that you have to read the text chapter before you go to the lecture class. Hearing about something is not your preferred way to get information. You have to prepare yourself to be a better listener by reading first (using a strength).

As indicated earlier, as you mature, your learning style becomes more integrated. This does not mean that you don't have preferences. It only means that you have learned how to get information and use your weaker areas better. You will not always get information in your preferred style, so you must learn to use those styles which are less comfortable for you. Some students learn this easier and more quickly than others. By helping you see your style, you can also find the areas which need attention. The ultimate goal for a student is to use any learning style comfortably depending on what's best for the situation. That may not be practical, but you need to be fairly competent getting and using information in several ways. This will help you with instructors who use only one method of getting information across, and will give you more options when faced with difficult material to learn. Most of us learn better when we use more than one mode or style to get it.

There are styles that can impact your learning. These include **personality, sensory preferences, and multiple intelligences**.

PERSONALITY*

Each person is unique. Each person thinks differently, acts differently, has various wants and needs, finds different things to be sources of pleasure and frustration, and conceptualizes and understands things differently. The psychotherapist Carl Jung said that beneath the surface of all of these differences are preferences about ways of interacting with people, perceiving information in the surrounding environment, making decisions, and acting on decisions that give rise to various personality types. These different personality types influence the way you learn. Jung's theory about personality types is the basis for a personality assessment developed by Isabel Myers and Katharine Briggs, named the Myers-Briggs Type Indicator (MBTI) (Myers, 1995).

The MBTI identifies 16 personality types based on individual preferences. Four dimensions differentiate personality types: introversion-extroversion, intuition-sensation, thinking-feeling and judging-perceiving. Complete the personality assessment in Exercise 4.2 at the end of the chapter to discover your type. Then read through the following descriptions of the four dimensions to learn more about the influence of personality and learning.

Introversion-Extroversion

When solving a problem, do you prefer to talk with others or think it through alone? Do you tend to be more aware of what is going on around you or more aware of what you are thinking and feeling? The dimensions of introversion and extroversion are related to how people energize themselves in different situations, including learning.

Introversion (I). Introverts are reflective learners, scanning inwardly for stimulation. They become energized as they reflect and think about ideas. In an academic setting, introverts prefer working alone because they can comprehend better if they take the time to organize and think about the information before them. Introverts have a tendency not to speak up in class, as all their energy is spent on thinking and reflecting about ideas. Introverts plan out thoughts and words before writing, stop frequently to think as they write, prefer quite places to study, and dislike interruptions. They spend so much time thinking and reflecting that they may start daydreaming about how things might be, and opportunities sometimes pass them by.

Extroversion (E). Extroverts are active letters who focus their attention outwardly for stimulation. They learn new information best when they can apply it to the external world. Extroverts are energized by people and thus prefer interacting with others while learning. They tend to participate in class, enjoying group projects, discussions, and study groups (similar to the interactive learner). Extroverts tend to jump into things enthusiastically, including writing assignments, and learn best in active learning situations that are filed with movement and variety. Because of this, they may get frustrated with long tasks that require a lot of reading and reflection.

Intuition-Sensation

Do you consider yourself to be more of a practical person or an innovative person? Is it easier for you to learn facts or concepts? This dimension tells you about how you perceive information in your environment.

Intuition (N). Intuition refers to use of the "sixth sense," an unconscious way of knowing the world. Intuitive people learn best when instruction is open-ended with a focus on theory before application. Intuitive learning can be characterized as a creative, right-brain approach to learning. Intuitive learners often work in bursts of energy that yield quick flashes of insight. They want and need to see how everything works together; they look at the big picture and tend to engage in divergent thinking as opposed to convergent thinking. Creative approaches to writing are preferred; their writing also tends to be full of generalities (and facts might not be too accurate!). On multiple-choice tests, intuitive learners follow their hunches but can make errors involving facts (too many details can bore them). If you happen to be an intuitive learner, it is good idea to read each question twice to make sure you read it correctly.

Intuitive learners may be negligent about details at times, but they are generally good at drawing inferences when reading. They prefer to read something that gives them ideas to day-dream about.

Sensation (S). Sensation refers to the process of acquiring information through your five senses (sight, sound, smell, touch, and taste). Sensing people learn best when there is an orderly sequencing of material that moves slowly from concrete to abstract. Sensing people prefer to process concrete, factual information and can become impatient with theories or examples that are not oriented to the present. In an academic setting, they tend to work steadily and focus on details and facts. If not aware of this tendency when reading and taking notes, they can end up neglecting important concepts and miss the broader picture. When completing a writing assignment, sensing people prefer explicit, detailed directions. They prefer to read something that teaches new facts or tells how to do something. Sensing people are good at memorizing facts, and on multiple-choice tests they search for clues that relate to practical knowledge and personal experience. Because they rarely trust their hunches, they generally lose points by changing answers.

Thinking-Feeling

When you make a decision, do you tend to be more impersonal and objective or personal and subjective? We all use our cognitions (thoughts) and emotions (feelings) when making decisions, but we generally use one more than the other.

Thinking (T). Thinking people tend to discover and gather facts first and then make decisions based on logic. They enjoy problem solving, analyzing situations, weighing the pros and cons, and developing models for deeper understanding. In writing assignments they are task-oriented, organizing thoughts and focusing on content. When reading, they tend to engage in critical thinking and can stay engaged in reading even if the information does not personally engage them.

Feeling (F). Feeling people tend to make decisions based on feelings, values, and empathy. Feeling types are motivated by personal encouragement, and in making decisions, they consider the effect of the impact of the decision on others. In writing they tend to rely on personal experience and focus on the message and how it will affect the reader. In reading, they prefer material that is personally engaging, otherwise, there is a chance they will become bored and quit reading.

Perceiving-Judging

Once decisions have been made, based on thoughts and feelings, how do you act on them? Do you seek closure and act quickly, or do you prefer to keep your options open and maybe even procrastinate?

Perceiving (P). Perceivers tend to be adaptable and spontaneous, preferring open, spontaneous learning situations. They like gathering additional information before acting on a decision and because of their flexible, tentative nature, they are good at seeing multiple perspectives. Perceiving types tend to start many tasks at once and tend not to be good with deadlines. They prefer the process more than the completion of the task, can easily get distracted, and often need help in organizing. On multiple-choice tests, each answer can be a stimulus for more thought (gathering more information), so it is often difficult for the perceiver to choose the correct answer. When writing, perceivers tend to choose expansive topics that sometimes do not have a clear focus.

Judging (J). The judging type wants to get things settled and wrapped up. Judging types are goal-oriented and generally set manageable goals. Their first drafts tend to be short and underdeveloped. When reading, judging types may be too quick to interpret a book. They tend to gauge their learning by how many pages they have read or how much time they have spent on it. They generally enjoy planning and organizing and prefer to work on one task at a time. Judging types prefer well-defined goals and get frustrated with a lot of ambiguity.

Personality clearly affects learning patterns. In Exercise 4.2, the score for each personality dimension suggests the extent to which that dimension affects your learning style. In the process of discovering your learning style, try to see if it matches your professor's teaching style. If your professor lectures in a roundabout way, using metaphors and analogies and trying to get you to see the big picture through theories and concepts, an intuitive teaching style is being used. If you are a sensing student who wants facts presented in an orderly, sequential manner beginning with concrete information, you may have to adapt your learning style to avoid feeling frustrated and discouraged. If your teacher presents a lot of facts and detailed information in a sequential, organized lecture format, a sensing teaching style is being used. If you are an intuitive learner who needs examples and theories first, you will need to adapt your learning style so as not to become bored and start daydreaming in class. Students who are sensing and judging (SJ) have a strong need for order and thus need a lot of structure in learning. Students who are intuitive and perceiving (NP) need more creative and autonomous learning styles would match, but as well all know, this is not a perfect world. The Swiss developmental psychologist Piaget wrote much about the power of adaptation. *Adaptation* is making adjustments to fit a new situation. We do it all the time as we assimilate new information into preexisting learning patterns. The more flexible your learning style, the greater your capacity to learn.

Sensory Preferences

Sensory preferences concern the way or ways in which you like to acquire information—by seeing (**visual**), hearing (**aural**), reading/writing, or through physical experiences (**kinesthetic**). Some learning activities, for example, mapping or charting, combine visual, reading/writing, and kinesthetic styles. Table 4.1 provides suggestions for using your sensory preferences in classroom, study, and exam situations. If you have no clear preferences for a single type, consider using a **multisensory** approach, one that combines two or more senses (for example, talking yourself through the steps in constructing a model, drawing a diagram for later visual review, or talking yourself through the connections in constructing a map).

You also should remember that depending on the subject matter or situation, you might change from one preference to another. In actuality most successful students learn to use a multi-sensory approach and adapt as needed to different learning situations.

The VARK Questionnaire below and Exercise 4.2 provide you with assessments of your sensory preferences and how these preferences can be used in various learning situations.

Table 4.1 Applying VARK Sensory Preferences to Classroom Study and Exam Situations

	In Class	When Studying	During Exams

Visual	Underline
	Use different colors
	Use symbols, charts,
	  arrangements on a page
		Use the "In Class" strategies
		Reconstruct images in
		  different way
		Redraw pages from memory
		  with symbols and initials
			Recall the "pictures of pages"
			Draw or sketch
			Use diagrams where
			  appropriate
			Practice turning visuals back
			  into words

Aural	Attend lectures and tutorials
	Discuss topics with students
	Explain new ideas to other
	  people
	Use a tape recorder
	Describe overheads, pictures,
	  and visuals to somebody
	  not there
	Leave space in notes for
	  later recall
		Expand your notes
		Put summarized notes on
		  tape and listen
		Read summarized notes
		  out loud
		Explain notes to another
		  person
		Compare notes with other
		  students for
		  completeness and clarity
			Listen to your inner voices
			  and write down what you
			  say to yourself
			Speak your answers
			Practice writing answers to
			  old exam questions

Reading/
Writing
	Use lists, headings
	Use dictionaries and
	  definitions
	Use handouts and textbooks
	Read
	Use lecture notes
		Write out the words again
		  and again
		Reread notes silently
		Rewrite ideas into other
		  words
		Organize diagrams into
		  statements
			Practice with multiple-choice
			  questions
			Write out lists
			Write paragraphs, beginnings,
			  endings

Kinesthetic	Use all your senses
	Go to lab, take field trips
	Use trial-and-error methods
	Use hands-on approach
	Listen to real-life examples
		Put examples in note
		  summaries
		Use pictures and photos
		  to illustrate
		Talk about notes with
		another person
		Compare notes with other
		  students for
		  completeness and clarity
			Write practice answers
			Role-play the exam situation
			  in your room

Source: From Neil Fleming and Colleen Mills who teach at Lincoln University, New Zealand.

THE VARK QUESTIONNAIRE (VERSION 7.2)

How Do I Learn Best?

Choose the answer which best explains your preference and circle the letter(s) next to it. **Please circle more than one** if a single answer does not match your perception.
Leave blank any question that does not apply.

1. You are helping someone who wants to go to your airport, the center of town or railway station. You would:
   a. go with her.
   b. tell her the directions.
   c. write down the directions.
   d. draw, or show her a map, or give her a map.

2. You are not sure whether a word should be spelled 'dependent' or 'dependant'. You would:
   a. see the words in your mind and choose by the way they look.
   b. think about how each word sounds and choose one.
   c. find it online or in a dictionary.
   d. write both words down and choose one.

3. You are planning a vacation for a group. You want some feedback from them about the plan. You would:
   a. describe some of the highlights they will experience.
   b. use a map to show them the places.
   c. give them a copy of the printed itinerary.
   d. phone, text or email them.

4. You are going to cook something as a special treat. You would:
   a. cook something you know without the need for instructions.
   b. ask friends for suggestions.
   c. look on the Internet or in some cookbooks for ideas from the pictures.
   d. use a good recipe.

5. A group of tourists want to learn about the parks or wildlife reserves in your area. You would:
   a. talk about, or arrange a talk for them about parks or wildlife reserves.
   b. show them maps and internet pictures.
   c. take them to a park or wildlife reserve and walk with them.
   d. give them a book or pamphlets about the parks or wildlife reserves.

6. You are about to purchase a digital camera or mobile phone. Other than price, what would most influence your decision?
   a. Trying or testing it.
   b. Reading the details or checking its features online.
   c. It is a modern design and looks good.
   d. The salesperson telling me about its features.

7. Remember a time when you learned how to do something new. Avoid choosing a physical skill, eg. riding a bike. You learned best by:
   a. watching a demonstration.
   b. listening to somebody explaining it and asking questions.
   c. diagrams, maps, and charts - visual clues.
   d. written instructions – e.g. a manual or book.

8. You have a problem with your heart. You would prefer that the doctor:
   a. gave you a something to read to explain what was wrong.
   b. used a plastic model to show what was wrong.
   c. described what was wrong.
   d. showed you a diagram of what was wrong.

9. You want to learn a new program, skill or game on a computer. You would:
   a. read the written instructions that came with the program.
   b. talk with people who know about the program.
   c. use the controls or keyboard.
   d. follow the diagrams in the book that came with it.

10. I like websites that have:
    a. things I can click on, shift or try.
    b. interesting design and visual features.
    c. interesting written descriptions, lists and explanations.
    d. audio channels where I can hear music, radio programs or interviews.

11. Other than price, what would most influence your decision to buy a new non-fiction book?
    a. The way it looks is appealing.
    b. Quickly reading parts of it.
    c. A friend talks about it and recommends it.
    d. It has real-life stories, experiences and examples.

12. You are using a book, CD or website to learn how to take photos with your new digital camera. You would like to have:
    a. a chance to ask questions and talk about the camera and its features.
    b. clear written instructions with lists and bullet points about what to do.
    c. diagrams showing the camera and what each part does.
    d. many examples of good and poor photos and how to improve them.

13. Do you prefer a teacher or a presenter who uses:
    a. demonstrations, models or practical sessions.
    b. question and answer, talk, group discussion, or guest speakers.
    c. handouts, books, or readings.
    d. diagrams, charts or graphs.

14. You have finished a competition or test and would like some feedback. You would like to have feedback:
    a. using examples from what you have done.
    b. using a written description of your results.
    c. from somebody who talks it through with you.
    d. using graphs showing what you had achieved.

15. You are going to choose food at a restaurant or cafe. You would:
    a. choose something that you have had there before.
    b. listen to the waiter or ask friends to recommend choices.
    c. choose from the descriptions in the menu.
    d. look at what others are eating or look at pictures of each dish.

16. You have to make an important speech at a conference or special occasion. You would:
    a. make diagrams or get graphs to help explain things.
    b. write a few key words and practice saying your speech over and over.
    c. write out your speech and learn from reading it over several times.
    d. gather many examples and stories to make the talk real and practical.

The VARK Questionnaire Scoring Chart

Use the following scoring chart to find the VARK category that each of your answers corresponds to. Circle the letters that correspond to your answers

e.g. If you answered b and c for question 3, circle V and R in the question 3 row.

Question	a category	b category	c category	d category
3	K	(V)	(R)	A

Scoring Chart

Question	*a* category	*b* category	*c* category	*d* category
1	K	(A)	(R)	V
2	V	A	(R)	(K)
3	(K)	(V)	R	A
4	K	A	(V)	R
5	A	V	(K)	R
6	(K)	R	(V)	(A)
7	(K)	(A)	V	R
8	(R)	(K)	(A)	(V)
9	R	A	(K)	V
10	(K)	(V)	R	(A)
11	V	(R)	A	(K)
12	A	(R)	(V)	K
13	K	A	(R)	V
14	(K)	(R)	A	V
15	(K)	A	R	V
16	V	(A)	(R)	K

Calculating your scores

Count the number of each of the VARK letters you have circled to get your score for each VARK category.

Total number of **V**s circled = **6**

Total number of **A**s circled = **6**

Total number of **R**s circled = **8**

Total number of **K**s circled = **11**

MULTIPLE INTELLIGENCES

Upon examination of your learning style, you are then able to match your preferred method of learning with your preferred type of intelligence.

    Dr. Howard Gardner, a psychologist and professor at Harvard University, is one of many researchers who have studied how people learn and what makes them successful in school and in life. His theory that there are multiple ways a person can be intelligent might help you understand your own abilities. While most people have all of the intelligences, a couple of them are usually more developed than the others. Tapping into your strongest intelligences to learn new material will help you understand and master it more readily. Think of them as special talents. If you are talented in a certain area, doesn't that usually mean that it is easier to learn and perform in that area? That's what the multiple intelligence theory is all about. So far Dr. Gardner has identified eight different kinds of intelligence.

You will have a chance to complete an assessment to identify your top intelligences at the end of the chapter.

- **Verbal/Linguistic**—relates to written and spoken words. People who are good at reading, writing, speaking, debating, or learning foreign languages have a high level of this type of intelligence. The ACT, SAT, IQ tests, and/or other standardized tests taken in school have parts that measure verbal ability. High scores on these tests are considered accurate predictors of college success because verbal ability is one of the two kinds of intelligence emphasized in school. Those who have it fit our traditional notions of "smart."
- **Logical/Mathematical**—has to do with reasoning, critical thinking, problem solving, recognizing patterns, and working with abstract symbols such as numbers or geometric shapes. This is the other type of intelligence that is measured by virtually all standardized tests and is usually the ticket to college success and a good job. Schools place the utmost importance on teaching and developing this in students. Science, math, and computer science majors usually have high levels of logical/mathematical intelligence.
- **Visual/Spatial**—relies on eyesight and also the ability to visualize things/places. It is valued by those in our culture who appreciate the visual arts such as painting, drawing, and sculpture. It is useful in situations where you need to be able to use space or get around somewhere such as in navigation, map-making, architecture, computer-aided drafting, graphic arts, and so forth. It is also an ability that is used in games or puzzles where seeing things from different angles is an advantage. People with strong visual/spatial intelligence can look at something and see how it could be improved or see beyond what *is* to what *could be*. This intelligence is often considered synonymous with a good imagination.
- **Bodily/Kinesthetic**—the ability to express oneself through movement or to do things using the body, or to make things. This intelligence is seen in athletes, dancers, actors/actresses, artists, skilled craftspeople, and inventors. People with this intelligence are often very physically active. The ability to use the capabilities of one's body, sometimes even without conscious thought, is another characteristic of this intelligence.
- **Musical/Rhythmic**—being able to "tune in" to sounds and rhythms and use them to create mood changes in the brain. For example, creating soothing melodies, stirring marches, or stimulating raps requires strong use of this intelligence. Expressing yourself with sounds from nature, musical instruments, or the human voice or being able to differentiate tone qualities are more examples of this intelligence. Often people with this intelligence enjoy listening to music as they work on other things or seem to have an "ear" for it. Unfortunately, this intelligence is often not emphasized in school curriculums and is an "extra" that usually gets cut from tight budgets, even though research has shown that learning to play an instrument stimulates connectors in the brain that enhance other learning. Music and rhythm make up a universal language that can transcend culture and touch people's lives. This can be a powerful intelligence to develop.
- **Interpersonal**—the capacity to communicate effectively with others through verbal and nonverbal expression. Persons who have a high degree of this intelligence

can work effectively in groups. They notice and understand things about other people such as their moods, facial expressions, posture, gestures, inner motivations, and personality types. They can also listen to others and make them feel valuable and appreciated. Although teachers like students to get along, children with a naturally high level of interpersonal intelligence may have gotten in trouble for being "too social" in school. Though it is invaluable in many occupations, people who have this talent are often drawn into the helping professions.

- **Intrapersonal**—probably the least understood and/or valued in our educational system, this intelligence deals with knowing and understanding oneself. It involves being able to analyze our own thinking and problem solving processes, being aware of our inner thoughts, feelings, and internal state. It is also a sensitivity to and understanding of spiritual realities, and experiencing wholeness and unity as a person. Being able to anticipate the future and contemplate our unreached potential requires this type of intelligence. Because people with high levels of this intelligence enjoy solitude, meditation, and quiet, their abilities may not be recognized. They probably don't mind, though. Their self-concept and self-confidence does not come from what others think of them. They set their own goals and agendas and know exactly why they do and say the things they do.

- **Naturalistic**—the ability to live in harmony with the natural world and appreciate nature. People who have a "green thumb," or a "way with animals," or who could survive in the wilderness without modern conveniences have naturalistic intelligence. It also includes people who are perceptive about differences in the natural world such as being able to recognize the many kinds of flowers, trees, birds, etc. and can use this ability productively. Farmers, biological scientists, and hunters might utilize naturalistic intelligence. In addition, Dr. Gardner believes that people in our materialistic, consumer culture display naturalistic intelligence when they can distinguish even subtle differences among car styles, athletic shoes, and the like.

MULTIPLE INTELLIGENCES—WHAT DOES IT MEAN FOR YOU?

When you read these descriptions, can you pick out your strongest type of intelligence from Gardner's list? What do you think would happen if our school systems actually taught in ways that emphasized all of the intelligences? Even though the traditional ways of being smart have always been a pathway to success, it is interesting to note that the types of intelligence least emphasized by schools in the United States, when developed fully, provide some of the greatest income potential and social status. Professional athletes, entertainers, musicians, actors, actresses, and artists have a lot more visibility in our society than doctors, judges, scientists, or mathematicians. Think of a few examples of people who achieved fame, fortune, and sometimes even greatness for maximizing their various intelligences.

Let's start with the richest person in the world. Bill Gates's visual/spatial intelligence led him to create a whole new approach to using computers where icons (pictures) replaced typed (verbal) commands. Tiger Woods's bodily/kinesthetic intelligence has made him a legend in the golf world while still in his 20s. Oprah Winfrey and Barbara Walters have used their interpersonal intelligences to pursue lucrative and successful careers in a business that wasn't traditionally open to women (especially women of color) when they began. Mahatma Gandhi in India and later Martin Luther King, Jr. in the United States both used their intrapersonal and interpersonal intelligences to change the course of history.

While you may seem a long way from these examples, recognizing your natural gifts and using the intelligences you have can lead you to a more productive, fulfilling life. If you haven't done so before now, start to appreciate your own ways of being intelligent. Then, use your strengths to help you comprehend new material. For example, if you have great musical/rhythmic intelligence, put your lessons to music. If you excel at interpersonal intelligence, talk to others and learn from the dialogs you initiate. If you have strong intrapersonal intelligence, think through your goals and recognize that doing well in each of your classes will help you achieve them.

Don't ever put yourself down for not being as talented as someone else is. Learn to make the most of what you can do, and always try to do your best. Motivation, desire, and hard work are always the surest pathways to success.

DURING (D)

Commit to the following *actions*:

- **Use the information about your learning style to help you in the classroom and with studying/review (as identified in the previous section)**
- **Learn what other factors influence learning**
- **Discover that knowledge is power**

WHAT OTHER FACTORS INFLUENCE LEARNING?

In addition to your preferred learning styles, there are other factors which affect your learning. There are factors which affect your ability to study effectively and efficiently. Some of these will affect you more than others. Some may not be an issue for you at all, but you will find some you should consider when planning where, when, how and what to study.

Consider the answers to these questions regarding your preferences. Are writing assignments easier for you than oral ones? Would you rather write a paper or give a talk on a subject? (Tough choice!) Do you feel that you do a better job when you write or when you speak on a subject? Is it easier to get your thoughts down on paper or to talk about them? The answers to those questions will help you determine your preference for oral or written expressiveness. You will have to do some of both, but you can make course choices based on this knowledge.

Another option you may have in some of your classes is whether to participate in study groups. If you are the type of person who is comfortable in a group, then they will help you. Others, who learn better alone, may find a study group a liability. There are times when working with a group can help you understand material because the group can exchange ideas. Material may become clearer as you discuss it among the group members. Know your preferences and study accordingly.

Motivation

Motivation plays a role in your learning. Are you learning for the pleasure of learning—to become more aware of the world around you, and to broaden your knowledge? Or are you learning with that one goal in mind—a degree? If the achievement of that goal is the only reason you are learning, you are approaching your education differently than the person who is learning to increase knowledge.

Being aware of your locus of control can help you understand your motivation. Locus of control is your perception of what accounts for the successes or failures in your life. It can be either external or internal. If external, then you attribute success or failure to outside forces (family, peers, fate, enemies). If internal, you attribute success or failure to the consequences of your own actions. You probably have a tendency toward one or the other, but do not see everything one way or the other. If this is a problem for you, you may need to work on changing your outlook.

Other factors which may influence your ability to learn or study are given in the following list.

Noise level—from complete quiet to lots of noise

Light—from low to bright

Temperature—from warm to cool

Time—early morning to late evening (the time you feel most alert)

Position—sitting to lying down

Developing Active Learning Strategies

Your instructors also expect you to become an active learner, illustrated by the following situation. A first-year student who had always thought of himself as a B student was getting low Cs and Ds in his business course. The instructor gave weekly quizzes; each was a practical problem to solve. Every week the student memorized his lecture notes and carefully reread the assigned chapter in his textbook. When he spoke with his instructor about his low grades, the instructor told him that his study methods were not effective and that he needed to become more active and involved with the subject matter. Memorizing and rereading are passive approaches. The instructor suggested that he try instead to think about content, ask questions, anticipate practice uses, solve potential problems, and draw connections between ideas.

	Passive Learners	Active Learners
Class lectures	Write down what the instructor says	Decide what is important to write down
Textbook assignments	Read	Read, think, ask questions, try to connect ideas
Studying	Reread	Consider learning style, make outlines and study sheets, predict exam questions, look for trends and patterns
Writing class assignments	Only follow the professor's instructions	Try to discover the significance of the assignment, look for the principles and concepts it illustrates
Writing term papers	Do only what is expected to get a good grade	Try to expand their knowledge and experience with a topic and connect it to the course objective or content

Figure 4.1 Characteristics of Passive and Active Learners.

Active versus Passive Learning

How did you learn to ride a bike, play racquetball, or change a tire? In each case you learned by doing, by active participation. College learning requires similar active involvement and participation. Active learning is expected in most college courses and can often make the difference between barely average grades and top grades. Figure 4.1 lists common college learning situations and contrasts the responses of active and passive learners. The examples in Figure 4.1 show that passive learners do not carry the learning process far enough. They do not go beyond what instructors tell them to do. They fail to think about, organize, and react to course content.

Active Learning Strategies

When you study, you should be thinking about and reacting to the material in front of you. This is how you make it happen:

1. **Ask questions about what you are reading.** You will find that this helps to focus your attention and improve your concentration.
2. **Consider the purpose behind assignments.** Why might a sociology assignment require you to spend an hour at the monkey house of the local zoo, for example?
3. **Try to see how each assignment fits with the rest of the course.** For instance, why does a section called "Amortization" belong in a business mathematics textbook chapter entitled "Business and Consumer Loans"?
4. **Relate what you are learning to what you already know from the course and from your background knowledge and personal experience.** Connect a law in physics with how your car brakes work, for example.
5. **Think of examples or situations in which you can apply the information.**

Active learning also involves active reading. In Chapter 7 you will learn specific strategies for becoming an active reader.

Instructional Styles

While it would be wonderful if every teacher were trained to teach to all of the learning styles and to present material that appealed to each of the intelligences, this is the real world, and that isn't going to happen. Just as learners have different styles, your instructors will also have different instructional styles. These styles will be influenced by their personalities, their own learning styles, the intelligences they possess, their education, and/or previous teaching experiences. They may vary their approach, or they may use the same methods semester after semester. The three styles used most often are **Independent, Student Centered/Interactive, and Cooperative Learning**. Let's take a look at each one:

Independent—An instructor with an independent style delivers course material primarily by lecturing. S/he may use prepared audio-visual aids or PowerPoint presentations to add a visual component to the auditory delivery. Class sessions are usually formal with little or no input from the students. This style is typically used in large classes such as those at a state university where several hundred students may be seated in a large lecture hall. The instructor is independent of the students, may not take attendance, get to know them personally, or be concerned if they miss class. Therefore, those students must be independent learners. They must motivate themselves to go to class, take notes, read the textbook, do the assignments, prepare for exams and quizzes, and

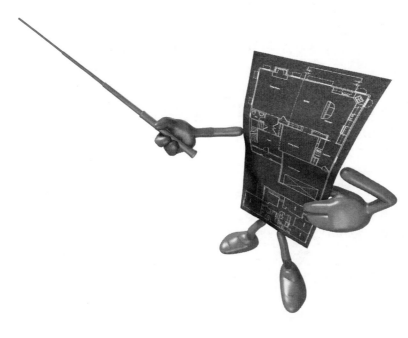

do their own research to get answers to their questions.

Student Centered/Interactive—Instructors using this style are less formal and want students to be involved during class. They may use a lecture/discussion format or prefer questions and answers. They may use the board or an overhead projector to illustrate points but are willing to stop the lecture to field questions and comments. If students don't voluntarily participate, the instructor may call on them. S/he usually tries to get to know each student's name to facilitate this process. Small classes may be asked to move their desks into a circle or semi-circle so students can see each other and discuss issues face-to-face. Class participation and attendance may be part of the final course grade because much of the learning is done in class.

Cooperative Learning—Instructors who break their classes into small groups or learning teams are using a style that places more emphasis on discovery learning and student involvement. Instead of the instructor being the authority figure, imparting wisdom to the class, students are encouraged to take charge of their learning and help each other achieve. With guidance from the instructor, students work together with their teammates to find the information they need. Each person may have a different role (leader, recorder, spokesperson) and is responsible for carrying out his/her portion of the assignment. Team members teach each other, making sure each one has mastered the content. Students are responsible to their teammates to attend class and complete their portion of the assignments. Sometimes they take their exams as a team, or they may all receive the same grade on an assignment.

People in teams who stay together for the entire semester tend to form strong bonds with one another and develop close friendships that last beyond the duration of the course. That is one of the main benefits of this style. Instructors who use cooperative learning point out that it is more like the real world where people have to work together to get a specific job accomplished.

While it's nice to have an instructor whose instructional style matches your learning style, if you don't, you can still achieve satisfaction and success in the course. Use the knowledge you have gained in this chapter to understand what works best for you. Make learning as easy as you can, and use your preferred style and strongest intelligence to master new content. Adapt your class and textbook notes to your style. If the assignments given by the instructor don't get through to you, give yourself additional assignments that will force you to learn thoroughly. Remember that you should always do more than the minimum. This is your education. Take charge of it. As you work from your strength areas, try also to develop and improve your weaker areas. Review previous lessons using a different modality than your preferred one. Explore areas of personal interest/hobbies in one of your less-developed intelligences. College and life are all about learning and growing as a person.

KNOWLEDGE IS POWER

If knowledge is power in the 21st Century, who would choose to enter it weak? You wouldn't really want to go off to battle without a weapon, would you? Well, you'll be entering the next century unarmed if you're not well educated. To prosper in the Information Age, you must know how to acquire, process, and use knowledge. The best jobs will require knowledge. Do you really want to condemn yourself to a series of low paying, menial jobs that do not offer security and lead nowhere?

You must keep up with advancing knowledge in order to be a player in the Information Age, but it is very easy to drown in it. (Getting a degree from a competitive university today has been likened to getting a drink of water from a fire hose.) This information overload implies at least two things:

1. **You must be capable of learning rapidly.** Otherwise, you'll be left behind. For example, just a few years ago our management majors were graduating without knowing how to do spreadsheets on their computers. While they were getting their degrees, the technology changed and required a new skill of them. The best ones made it a point to learn spreadsheets on their own or from a friend. Some sat in on classes they had already taken so they could learn the new software, which was by this time a course requirement.
2. **You must be selective in what you learn.** No matter how rapidly you acquire new information, there is too much to keep up with all of it. You must develop learning strategies that permit you to stay abreast of key trends without drowning in a sea of information.

The Rand Institute recently conducted a study of what college graduates need to know to be ready to compete in the global economy. They asked academicians from leading universities and managers from multinational corporations. Both professors and corporate leaders agreed the number one requirement was what they called general knowledge. They meant by this that the graduates had learned how to learn, how to think critically, and how to solve complex problems, and that they had acquired the habit of ongoing learning.

AFTER (A)

Each term (and throughout your life) you will be presented with new learning situations. You will need to continue to *review, revise,* and *self-modify* as needed. Ask yourself these reflection questions:

☐ What study strategies am I using based on my learning styles?

☐ How can I get the most out of my instructor's lecture if he/she does not teach the way I learn best?

☐ What am I doing to move from being a passive to an active learner?

☐ Am I using the instructor's office hours and other campus resources when I need help?

SUMMARY

Learning style has been defined as the way you perceive or take in information, the way you process that information, and the way you react to the learning environment. You have inventories at the end of the chapter to determine your personality, sensory preferences, and multiple intelligences. Knowing about your learning style is important to you because it can make you aware of your strengths and weaknesses. You can use this information to be a better learner by using your strengths to help you with difficult material. Your weak areas are where you need to develop or improve your skills to become more integrated. Being more integrated means being able to adapt to the best learning strategy for the learning situation.

Self-analysis is also important when choosing a major or career. By analyzing your personality, preferences for learning, etc. you can critically evaluate whether or not you will be satisfied in your chosen career field. Seek out guidance from advisors and your college's career center to help you with this process. You do not want to pursue a career only to find out that it really does not match well with your personality and values. Real self-assessment can help you in all areas of your life – not just learning.

SUGGESTED READINGS

Goreman, D. *Emotional Intelligence: Why It Can Matter More Than IQ*. New York: Bantam Books, 1995.

Nomura, Catherine, Waller, Julia, and Shannon Waller. *Unique Ability: Creating the Life You Want*. Chicago: The Strategic Coach Inc., 2003.

EXERCISE 4.1: LEARNING STYLES RESEARCH

Using your college library and Internet research, locate a book or journal article about learning styles.

Complete two paragraphs about the information you found.

The first paragraph should describe the book or journal, including the author and title; what the book or article is about; and what specific topics or features interest you. Remember to evaluate your article using skills learned in Chapter 2 to determine if this is "credible" (good) information. (*Option: Use MLA or APA format to Cite your source*).

For your second paragraph, summarize the information you learned from the book or article.

EXERCISE 4.2: LEARNING STYLES PROJECT

Step 1: Complete Self-Analysis

Personality

Use your college's library, career center, or Internet search to research and complete an online personality assessment. (Note: Your instructor may assign a specific assessment for you to complete.) Be sure to print out your results as many on-line assessments do not save.

Sensory Preferences (Learning Styles)

Use your college's library, career center, or Internet search to research and complete an online learning styles assessment. (Note: Your instructor may assign a specific assessment for you to complete.) Be sure to print out your results as many on-line assessments do not save.

Multiple Intelligence

Use your college's library, career center, or Internet search to research and complete a multiple intelligence assessment. (Note: Your instructor may assign a specific assessment for you to complete.) Be sure to print out your results as many on-line assessments do not save.

Step 2: Reflection Paper (typed—double spaced—10, 11, or 12 point font only)

For the 3 assessments completed in Step 1, submit a typed reflection paper that includes the following:

- Introductory paragraph (brief description of yourself with information about your personality, background, major, hobbies/interests, etc.)

- Summary paragraph for each assessment explaining your results (3 paragraphs total). What did the assessment say about you?

- Paragraph discussing whether or not you agreed with the results. Explain why or why not. How do you think your learning style was formed? What past experiences (favorite teacher, classroom activities, parenting styles, etc.) influenced or created your current preferred learning style?

- Paragraph discussing strategies that you will begin to use to help strengthen your learning based on your assessment results.

- Paragraph discussing how these results relate to other areas of your life (besides being a student) such as possible choices of career and how you relate to others.

- Concluding Paragraph – What were the most surprising/interesting things you learned about yourself by completing this project? How will you use what you learned to help in your future academic work? What impact did this project have on your possible career choice and why?

Step 3: Illustration

Create a visual illustration of yourself that represents you: your learning style, your personality and your multiple intelligences. Note: Your illustration should have a good balance of words and pictures. Examples include, but are not limited to, the following…(keep from current text)

Step 4: Presentation:

Present the result of your self-assessments to your classmates. When presenting your project, remember to follow basic rules of effective communication:

- Body language: Face your audience at all times/do not chew gum.

- Eye contact: Make eye contact with your classmates

- Voice: Speak slowly, clearly, and loud enough to be heard across the room.

- Length: Follow instructor's directions as to the appropriate length

- Professional Dress: Dress for success (business dress - i.e. dress slacks, button down shirt, tie)

NAME: _____ DATE: _____

EXERCISE 4.3: DETERMINING INSTRUCTIONAL STYLES

Complete the chart for each class you are taking this semester and write a reflection paragraph.

Course/ Instructor	Instructor's Teaching Style (Independent, Interactive, Cooperative or Combination)	Instructor's VARK Style (To which of the four VARK styles does this instructor teach - visual, auditory, read/ write, kinesthetic?)	Instructor's Style vs. Your Style (Does this instructor's style match your learning style, personality, multiple Intelligences?)	Your Progress (How are you doing in this class so far? What is your current grade?)	Your Strengths and Weaknesses in the Class (What are your academic strengths and weaknesses in this class?)	Completing the Semester (Do you antici- pate that it will get harder or easier as the semester progresses?)

Reflection Paragraph:

How will you use this information to plan for your success? If your Instructor's Style does not match your preferred style, what will you do to get the most out of the class? How can you maintain or improve your current grade? How can you use your academic strengths to your advantage and how can you improve on your weaknesses?

EXERCISE 4.4: WHAT SHOULD YOU DO?

Pretend you have a friend in each of the following situations. You are discussing with your friend what s/he should do to achieve the greatest degree of success in each course. Write out at least two recommendations. (Dropping the course is not an option.)

1. The class is Introduction to the Visual Arts. The instructor shows many slides of famous works of art to the class. They are also supposed to look up information on the Internet about the works of art. Tests are based on textbook reading assignments and identifying works of art and the artist from slides. Your friend is not a good visual learner. S/he is more of a tactile/kinesthetic learner.

   _____

   _____

   _____

   _____

   _____

   _____

2. The class is history. The instructor lectures every day. The course grade is determined by two main scores: the mid-term and the final exam, both of which are based on notes from the class lectures. Your friend is primarily a visual learner.

   _____

   _____

   _____

   _____

   _____

3. The course is computer science. Everything is hands-on and independent learning. The instructor expects the students to look at the book and do the exercises. S/he doesn't fully explain things to the whole group but instead walks around to make sure the students are working. Your friend has never really been a tactile/kinesthetic learner. His/her preferred learning modality is auditory. Besides that, s/he has very little computer experience and is embarrassed to constantly be the one asking the instructor questions. Everyone else seems to enjoy the no lecture/hands-on format of the class.

   _____

   _____

   _____

   _____

   _____

   _____

Chapter 5

Effective Time Management – Where Does the Time Go?

Using our time wisely is as important as using our money wisely. Like money, time is something you can only spend once. When it is gone, you can't get it back. Fortunately, we receive a new supply of time every day, but unlike money, it can't be stored or accumulated. It must be spent each day. What you get in return for your time is up to you. Unfortunately, failure to plan is one of the top reasons students do not succeed in college.

In this chapter, we will take a look at ways to control the use of time. You will be asked to examine how you currently spend time. We will explore how our goals should form the foundation for the way we "budget," or plan to use time. Once you have established your goals, there are three scheduling tools that will help you get organized. They are the weekly schedule, the semester schedule, and the daily to-do list. Common time management problems such as procrastination and distractions will be discussed, and suggestions will be given on how to avoid these problems. We hope that you will learn to make the best use of your time while you are in college. It's an investment for life.

BEFORE (B)

What types of *preparation, self-awareness,* and *planning* are needed to become an effective time manager?

- **Making time for college**
- **Setting your goals**

MAKING TIME FOR COLLEGE

One of the biggest adjustments many students have to make when they start college is how to structure their time. Most college classes don't meet every day. You may be taking a late starting class that begins two weeks after the semester is underway or a combination of day, twilight, and evening classes, and, unlike high school, you might not have a "regular" schedule. Some courses require assignments that must be completed in a lab or that require a significant amount of reading or research beyond what is covered in the textbook. Don't expect your instructors to give you class time to do homework. It is your responsibility to spend time out of class doing assignments and studying for tests.

Remember the rule of thumb, "for every hour of class time, you should expect to spend at least two hours outside of class doing independent work." For those difficult courses in chemistry and calculus, you may need as much as four hours of study time per class hour. That's why you are considered a full-time student when you are taking 12 or more credit hours of coursework. Twelve hours of class time per week plus 24 hours of studying equals a 36-hour time commitment. If you are enrolled in 15 credit hours of coursework, you have made a 45-hour per week commitment. This can become a problem if you were not prepared to devote that much time to college. Most of you have other factors, sometimes called "having a life," that impact the amount of time you devote to your education.

Working Students

In addition to attending classes, many college students work 20 hours per week or more. Generally, if you are a full time student, you should only work part time. If you must

work full time, it would be better to attend college as a part-time student. People who try to take on too much often end up getting worse grades, failing, or dropping courses. Although it may seem that it will take you much longer to complete your degree if you take the minimum course load each semester, it will be faster and less expensive to take only the amount of coursework you can realistically accomplish. Dropping, failing, and having to repeat classes ends up costing you more time and money in the long run.

If you are receiving financial aid, getting poor grades and failing to successfully complete classes each semester will put you on probation or result in termination of your benefits. With the new federal regulations, you may even be required to repay some of your financial aid if you do not meet the Standards of Progress each semester. Remember, it is better to get A's and B's in a few classes than to get C's or lower in several classes.

Other Demands on Your Time

Those of you who are not traditional age college students probably have many life roles in addition to that of student. You may be married and/or have children to support. You may be responsible for running a household and do most of the chores such as grocery shopping, cooking, cleaning, laundry, yard work, home maintenance and repairs, chauffeuring others back and forth to activities/events, etc. Even those of you who are in the 18- to 21-year-old age group probably have significant demands on your time in addition to classes, homework, and a job. Learning how to prioritize your time to do the things that are most important is one of the most valuable skills you can develop.

SETTING YOUR GOALS

Your Personal Life Mission

Before you devote time to any activity, you should think about how it fits into your life, and whether it helps you accomplish any of your goals. If you don't know what your goals are, now is the time to give thoughtful consideration to what you want to do with your life. In his book, *The Seven Habits of Highly Effective People* (we highly recommend that all students read this book), Dr. Stephen Covey discusses finding your purpose in life and writing out a personal mission statement. Knowing what you want from your life will help you evaluate how to invest your time. Once you have decided what is important, it's time to set some goals.

How to Get Started

When asked to state their goals, many people can only generate one or two vague wishes or dreams. To be a successful college student, you need to move beyond the dream stage and set goals that will be the basis for action. A goal should be your destination or end point. It should be specific and measurable enough to let you know when you've achieved it. For example, we've had countless students tell us that their goal in life is to be happy. That's nice, but what are you going to do to get happiness? How will you know when you've achieved ultimate happiness? When you get there, can you stop pursuing happiness? Maybe happiness isn't the goal. Maybe happiness is a consequence or byproduct—something you get from achieving your real goals.

Let's consider some basic criteria for a well-written goal statement:

1. It needs to be **specific**. You need to know exactly what it is you plan to accomplish. *Example: I will earn a Bachelor of Science in Nursing.*
2. It needs to be **realistic**. Your goal has to be something you can actually accomplish; otherwise you will just frustrate and discourage yourself. Also, you must believe that you can achieve your goal in order for it to be realistic.
3. It needs to be for **yourself and within your control.** You can only set goals for one person—you. You cannot control other people's thoughts or actions. Even if it is your parents' fondest wish that you graduate from college, it will only happen if you decide to make it happen. They can encourage you, but earning your degree must be *your* goal.

4. It needs to be **measurable**. You will want to know when you're there so you can stop pursuing that one and move on to your next goal. It also needs to identify the costs involved. Everything you will want to accomplish has a cost. Sometimes it is money. Most often the cost is time and effort. Sometimes it is giving up something to get something else.

Taking our example of getting a college degree, the goal statement might read: I will earn a Bachelor of Science Degree in Nursing from Western Kentucky University in 4 years by taking 15–18 credit hours per semester. To accomplish this goal, I plan to have $_____ (fill in the blank) for tuition, fees, books, housing, and transportation and 30–36 hours per week of study time to maintain a 3.0 GPA.

This goal statement is right on target, reflecting all of our criteria. We already said that it is specific and within your control. It is measurable; you will receive a degree when you are done. It identifies the major costs, although some of you may have other costs.

Goal setting.   Managing time and setting goals go hand-in-hand. Using your time wisely helps you to achieve what you want, when you want. Knowing what your goals are for college and your future career help guide decisions regarding the use of your time.

There are several types of goals:

- **Short-term:** Goals you want to achieve tomorrow, next week, or within the year. (Attend class each week, find a study partner for each class, or locate the free math tutor services.)
- **Mid-term:** Goals you want to achieve within 2–5 years. (Complete all the College/University Studies requirements.)
- **Long-term:** Goals you want to achieve within 5–20 years. (Obtain a degree in biology.)

Planning.   Your goals indicate where you want to go. Creating an action plan tells you how to get there. The saying, "if you don't know where you are going, you may end up somewhere else," is a good reminder of what happens without planning. The plan may consist of your "to-do lists," as well as your daily and semester planning schedules. Using these planning tools, write down specifically what you will do, and when and where you will do it. It is through a plan that "time management" becomes tangible and visible. It is no longer a "wish" or a "hope." Plans put you in charge of your time. The time management exercise at the end of this chapter gives you an opportunity to assess your time needs for this semester and create plans that enable you to reach your goals.

Values.   To accomplish major tasks in one's personal, academic, social, and professional life requires consideration of one's values. When goals are in line with our values, they have **values-congruence**. Achieving a values-congruent perspective will help you maximize your academic performance and your overall potential. Another outcome is likely to be greater general happiness.

Steps necessary to achieve values-congruence are the following:

1. *Identify the most significant values in your life (e.g., financial security, working with others, utilizing creative ability, supervising others, influencing others, working with computers).*
2. *Identify how your academic preparation and choice of a major ties to your values.*
3. *Identify all the steps, activities, and academic opportunities involved in accomplishing lifelong educational and career objectives.*

DURING (D)

Commit to the following *actions:*

- **Managing your time**
- **Deciding when to study**
- **Eliminate the thieves of time** (procrastination, distractions, over scheduling, poor time management/organization skills)

MANAGING YOUR TIME

Do you ever feel like a hamster on a wheel, always running, but never really getting anywhere? You're constantly busy, but never accomplish everything you need to do? When people talk about managing time, what they really mean is managing your activities to make the best use of your time. Think about this for a moment: how you spend your time is a direct reflection of your priorities. Is that true for you? Or are you giving priority to things that you don't truly value? Do you allow low-priority activities to use up time that could be spent doing better things? If so, you need to make a lifestyle change. Begin to make conscious choices about how you invest your time. By setting goals and systematically working toward achieving them, you will find that your life will have more purpose and meaning. You will accomplish more. We all have the same number of hours each day. The difference between people who are productive and those who seem to drift along not getting much done is the way they view and use those hours.

The Use of Scheduling Tools

Most people need some visual aids to help them plan how to use their time. It's too hard to remember everything, especially now that you've added schoolwork to your already busy life. Writing things down is much more effective. There are so many wonderful organizational notebooks and planners on the market, finding something practical to use should not be that difficult. It doesn't have to be expensive, either. The three major tools that work for most people are a weekly schedule, a semester schedule, and a daily "To-Do" list.

A **Weekly Schedule** is the cornerstone of your time/activity management plan. It is an outline that allows you to see how your time is budgeted. Start by filling in your fixed time commitments. These are things like your classes, work hours, time spent commuting, eating, grooming, and anything else you do regularly every week. If you go to temple, mosque, or church every week, put that on your schedule. If you have band practice every Monday evening, a club meeting on Thursdays, or family dinner on Sunday afternoons, include these activities. Be sure to write in study sessions for your classes. Set aside specific hours each week to do your homework and study—don't just hope you have time left over after all of your other activities are done. When you have finished filling in your fixed time commitments, you will easily see where you have discretionary time. Figure 5.1 is an example of a weekly schedule.

The **Semester Schedule** allows you to see everything at once. We like the month-at-a-glance type calendars, though some people prefer the big poster size calendars that show several months (or even the whole year) on one page. Choose whichever seems right for you, and start to fill in known deadlines and future activities: a family wedding coming up next month, your psychology paper due three weeks before the end of the semester, your midterm exams, the church bazaar you volunteered to help with, the

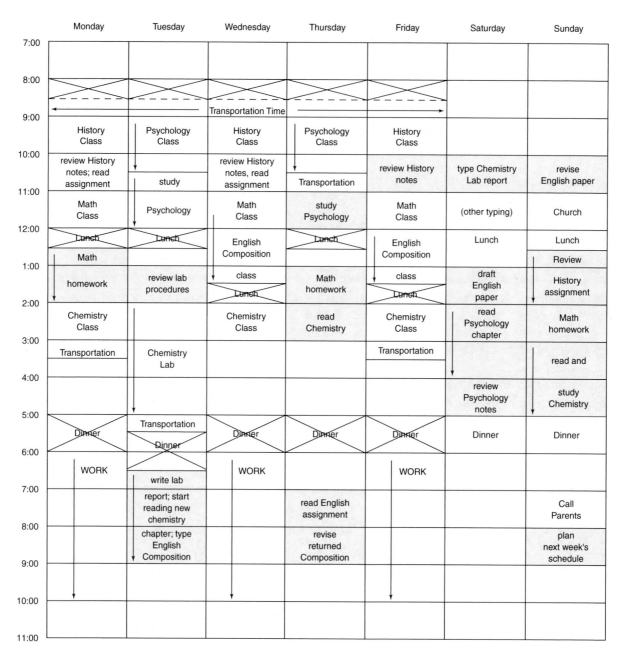

	Monday	Tuesday	Wednesday	Thursday	Friday	Saturday	Sunday
7:00							
8:00							
			Transportation Time				
9:00	History Class	Psychology Class	History Class	Psychology Class	History Class		
10:00	review History notes; read assignment	study	review History notes, read assignment	Transportation	review History notes	type Chemistry Lab report	revise English paper
11:00	Math Class	Psychology	Math Class	study Psychology	Math Class	(other typing)	Church
12:00	Lunch	Lunch	English Composition	Lunch	English Composition	Lunch	Lunch
1:00	Math homework	review lab procedures	class	Math homework	class	draft English paper	Review History assignment
2:00	Chemistry Class		Chemistry Class	read Chemistry	Chemistry Class	read Psychology chapter	Math homework
3:00	Transportation	Chemistry Lab			Transportation		read and
4:00						review Psychology notes	study Chemistry
5:00	Dinner	Transportation Dinner	Dinner	Dinner	Dinner	Dinner	Dinner
6:00	WORK	write lab report; start reading new chemistry chapter; type English Composition	WORK	read English assignment	WORK		Call Parents
7:00							
8:00				revise returned Composition			plan next week's schedule
9:00							
10:00							
11:00							

Figure 5.1 Example of a Weekly Time Schedule.

neighborhood watch meeting and potluck, your six-month dental check-up, and anything else you've made a commitment to do. Putting all of these down on a calendar helps you see in advance what you have to do so you aren't "surprised" by a deadline you forgot. If you are a parent with children who are involved in a variety of activities, you have probably already discovered the value of a centrally located calendar that becomes the family's master schedule.

As you put together your weekly and semester schedules, follow these two rules when planning your college study time:

1. **Never schedule yourself to work more than four hours in any one day on the same assignment. Three hours would be better and more reasonable.**
2. **Always give yourself an extra day.**

Most of us want to avoid living in a constant crisis-management mode. You never know what might happen. If you wait until the last day to do a major assignment, an unforeseen emergency could occur that would prevent you from completing your assignment on time. Even minor irritations such as getting sick, having car trouble, getting stuck in traffic for hours, weather complications, etc. can use up those last moments you were counting on to get your work done. If you allow extra time, you won't have to worry. In addition, getting an assignment done early allows you to proofread it to make sure it is your best work.

Let's look at Carol's semester schedule. She has chosen the month-at-a-glance type calendar. From her student handbook, she has identified holidays and other important college dates and transferred them to her calendar. Next, she looked at all of her course syllabi and entered major deadline dates for assignments and tests. Then, she considered her family obligations and social commitments. Finally, she noted when she would be likely to have to work overtime at her job. She realized she'd have to plan her study time carefully during the weeks before the holidays.

This semester Carol is taking Biology, English Composition, Math, and a History telecourse. She meets with her math tutor every week, has a weekly biology lab, and an essay due every other Friday in her English class. She has specific deadline dates for taking exams and turning in the research paper in History.

Carol's cousin, Jennifer, is getting married in November. Carol is going to be in the wedding. She will need to go for a dress fitting and attend a bridal shower, the rehearsal dinner, and the wedding. Her boyfriend has invited her to a holiday party in December, and she has some family gatherings during the semester.

One of the most effective ways to stay on track and actually get things done is to use a **daily to-do list**. While the Time Monitor/Time Plan is a general picture of the week, your daily to-do list itemizes specific tasks you want to complete within 24 hours. Keep the list with you at all times, crossing off activities when you finish them and adding new ones when you think of them.

Write out your daily to-do list the night before. That way, when your day begins, so will you. List everything you want to accomplish on a sheet of paper or a daily planning calendar, or in a special notebook. You can also use 3 × 5 cards. Cards work well because you can slip them into your pocket.

Rate each task by priority. One way to do this comes from an excellent book, *Take Control of Your Time and Life,* by Alan Lakein: Simply label each task A, B, or C.

A's on your list are those things that are most important. These are assignments that are coming due or jobs that need to be done immediately. Also included are activities that lead directly to your long-, mid-, or short-term goals.

The B tasks on your list are important, but less so than the A's. B's might someday become A's. For the present, these tasks are important, but are not as urgent as A's. They can be postponed, if necessary.

C's do not require immediate attention. C priorities include activities such as "shop for a new blender" and "research genealogy on the Internet." C's are often small, easy jobs with no set timeline.

Once you've labeled the tasks on your list, schedule time for all of the A's. The B's and C's can be done randomly during the day when you are in between tasks and are not yet ready to start the next A.

Use your to-do list to keep yourself on task, working on your A's. Don't panic or berate yourself when you realize that in the last six hours, you have completed 11 C's and not a single A. Calmly return to the A's.

As you complete tasks, cross them off your list. Crossing off tasks can be fun—a visible reward for your diligence—and can also foster a sense of accomplishment.

SEPTEMBER

Sunday	Monday	Tuesday	Wednesday	Thursday	Friday	Saturday
1	2 *Holiday*	3	4 view history video	5	6	7
8	9 math tutoring	10 view history video	11 math test	12 biology lab	13 English essay due	14 block party
15 7:00 Mom's birthday party	16 math tutoring	17 biology test	18 English test	19 biology lab	20 history test 1	21 view history video
22	23 math tutoring	24 view history video	25 math test	26 biology lab	27 English essay due	28 11:00 dentist appt.
29 8:00 walk-a-thon	30 math tutoring					

OCTOBER

Sunday	Monday	Tuesday	Wednesday	Thursday	Friday	Saturday
		1 view history video	2 math test	3 biology lab	4 English essay due	5
6	7 math tutoring	8 biology test	9 view history video	10 biology lab	11	12 2:00 dress fitting
13 view history video	14 math tutoring	15 math test	16 history test 2	17 biology lab	18 English essay due	19
20	21 math tutoring	22 view history video	23 English test	24 biology lab	25	26 11:00 dog to vet
27 12:30 bridal shower	28 math tutoring	29 biology test	30 view history video math test	31 biology lab		

NOVEMBER

Sunday	Monday	Tuesday	Wednesday	Thursday	Friday	Saturday
					1 English essay due	2
3 pancake breakfast	4 math tutoring	5 view history video	6 English test	7 biology lab *Register for Spring classes*	8 Rehearsal & dinner	9 Jennifer & Mike's Wedding
10	11 ***Holiday***	12 rough draft of research paper due	13 view history video math test	14 biology lab	15 English essay due	16 history test 3
17	18 math tutoring	19 biology test	20 *last day to drop classes*	21 ***Holiday***	22 ***Break*** work overtime	23 → work overtime
24 view history video	25 math tutoring	26 math test	27 view history video	28 biology lab	29 English essay due	30 work overtime

DECEMBER

Sunday	Monday	Tuesday	Wednesday	Thursday	Friday	Saturday
1	2 math tutoring	3 research paper due	4 math test	5 biology lab	6 view history video	7 Christmas party w/Joe
8	9 math tutoring	10 history test 4 biology test	11	12 biology lab	13 English essay due	14
15	16 ←	17 *FINAL*	18 *EXAM*	19 *WEEK*	20 → work overtime	21 work overtime
22 work overtime	23 work overtime	24 work overtime	25 ***Christmas***	26 work overtime	27 work overtime	28
29 dinner at Aunt Sally's	30	31 ***New Year's Eve***				

At the end of the day, evaluate your performance. Look for A priorities you didn't complete. Look for tasks that repeatedly turn up as B's or C's on your list and never seem to get done. Consider changing these to A's or dropping them altogether. Similarly, you might consider changing an A that didn't get done to a B or C priority.

In any case, make starting your own to-do list an A priority.

Example A

Example B

Things to do Today Today's Date: Sept. 9	Priority
Math Tutoring	A
Organize notes & study for math test	A
Go shopping for mom's birthday gift	B
Go to store – need snacks for block party	C
Set up a study group for next week's biology test	B
Write intro. and outline for English essay	A
Get supplies for biology lab	B
Call jennifer about wedding shower	C
Laundry	C

Figure 5.2 Two Examples of To-Do Lists.

HOW DO I DECIDE WHEN TO STUDY?

1. The **OPTIMUM TIME** for the most efficiency is usually **RIGHT AFTER THE CLASS**. To study the subject right **BEFORE THE CLASS** meets can be very advantageous for discussion classes, or even just a quick review of notes before a lecture can make those classes more beneficial. To pick a time slot right after class can increase your efficiency and decrease the time needed to study. For example, a 30-minute study immediately after class could be worth one hour of study later. You tend to be more interested in the subject at that time, need less warm-up time to get involved in the studying, and there tends to be less confusion about assignments if they are started quickly.

2. Try planning a time to **REVIEW** your notes immediately **BEFORE YOU GO TO SLEEP.** Plan on learning new material when you are fresh, but review right before you retire. Studies have shown that you retain this reviewed material better if you sleep on it. In fact, the shorter the delay between study and bed, the more likely you are to retain the material!

3. **Plan on studying your MOST DIFFICULT CLASSES IN THE EARLY AFTER-NOON,** for the most part. Long-term memory seems to be more effective then, as well as hand-eye coordination and physical strength. If you need to memorize or juggle words or figures, your short-term memory is more effective in the morning, so plan those types of activities for earlier hours. Beware of general low-energy time zones—for most people these center around 2–5 pm (when neural functions decline and blood sugar levels are lower) or 2–7 am (when most

accidents that can be attributed to human error occur). These might not be the optimum times to write that difficult research paper.

4. **FOLLOW YOUR BIOLOGICAL CLOCK.** Find your prime times and work with your body rather than fighting against its natural tendencies. To find whether you are a night person (an owl) or a morning person (a lark), take the inventory and then plan to study for tests at your peak periods. Morning people tend to jump out of bed early in the morning with a drive to have a productive morning. They tend to lead controlled, structured, well-regulated lives. They begin to slow down about mid-afternoon and believe and follow the old adage of "Early to bed, early to rise . . ."

   On the other hand, night people (or owls) crawl rather than jump out of bed, barely survive mornings, begin to wake up about noon and become their normally extroverted selves, peak in mid-afternoon, and wind down quite a bit later. No one tendency is the correct one, but you must work with your preference or it will defeat you. Don't plan on getting up early and cramming for the big final if you are a night owl. You probably won't make it up! And if you are a morning lark, you'd better not go ahead and attend the big party with lofty plans to study all night long. Your body won't make things easy for you to follow through with your plans. Consider these factors when you schedule classes.

   One final thought about your body's biological clock is that most people tend to find benefit in keeping in step with the sun. There seems to be some added benefits to working during daylight hours and resting during night hours.

5. Make sure you **SPACE YOUR STUDYING PROPERLY**. Remember to plan and use breaks that vary greatly from what your study activity was. Alternate different types of study activities. For example, plan to study an activity subject (such as math or composition) between subjects that require a lot of reading. And make sure you space out the studying required for each subject. It will usually be more effective to study biology in three one-half hour sessions rather than one and one-half hour session. Don't forget to include a time to review past notes also. Otherwise, you will be practically starting over when it is time for testing.

6. **DOUBLE TIME ESTIMATES AS YOU PLAN.** Things always seem to take longer than originally thought. In fact, you need to guard against "Parkinson's Law"—work always stretches to fill whatever time is available. Instead of planning on studying one hour, plan how much you will get accomplished in one hour. Set goals and limits and you will be able to achieve more.

7. Plan to **STUDY EACH SUBJECT AT THE SAME TIME, ON THE SAME DAYS, AND IN THE SAME PLACE** (one place with everything you need close at hand). Again, the idea is to work with your body instead of against it, and you can condition your body to not resist studying so much if you establish very firm habits. If you have psychology on Mondays, Wednesdays, and Fridays, the best time to study would be on those days at whatever time you designate would fit your biological clock, your time schedule, and be closest to psychology class time.

8. In general, plan to study the **WORST FIRST, EASIEST (OR MORE INTERESTING) LAST**. Prioritize, and then plan on getting the tough stuff over while your energy and initiative are at their peaks.

THIEVES OF TIME

Sometimes even your best efforts at scheduling don't produce the results you want. Have you ever had one of those days where nothing on your To-Do list got done? What happened? It's as though a thief broke into your life and stole those minutes and hours that you planned to use for homework and study.

Procrastination

This is probably the number one time thief. Although it manifests itself in many ways, procrastination comes in two common varieties: **inertia** and **avoidance**. **Inertia** is a word you might remember from science class. It is the physics property that says unless acted upon by a greater force, things in motion stay in motion, and things at rest (motionless) stay at rest. If you've ever had to push a stalled car, you know that it takes more effort to get it going when it's stopped. Once it starts to roll, it takes less effort to keep it going.

How does this relate to you and your use of time? If your body is at rest (such as on the couch watching TV), it will stay at rest unless you force it into action. Sometimes stopping to watch your favorite half-hour show turns into several hours in front of the TV. Once you stop working, it takes more effort to get back to work. That's why many students prefer to schedule breaks between classes so they can study in the library or LRC, rather than wait until they get home. If you tend to put things off because it is easier to be lazy, you need to look at your goals and remember your priorities. Tell yourself, "I need to be doing _____ right now."

Avoidance is the other reason people tend to put off getting things done. They really don't want to do it at all. Have you ever avoided doing something because:

- The task is too hard or too overwhelming?
- If you can't do it perfectly, you don't want to do it at all?
- You don't see any real value in doing it?
- You would rather be doing something else?
- You dislike the task or find it unpleasant?
- You don't want to/are afraid to deal with the problem/situation?
- A distorted self-concept, conscious or unconscious, makes you feel inadequate?
- You are afraid of someone else's judgment of your work?

Procrastination is not an unusual event. Everyone procrastinates from time to time (e.g., scheduling a doctor's appointment may be consistently put off), but procrastination can become a vicious cycle. This vicious cycle can become a mental and behavioral prison. Individuals caught in such a cycle reveal its strength when they say things such as, "There's no point in getting started—I can't get anything done," "I feel overwhelmed and stressed out and don't know where to start." Such self-defeating thoughts and behaviors tend to intensify the problem and frequently contribute to lower self-esteem. For example, a student puts off doing math homework because he does not like math. Because less time is being devoted to math, the student starts to do poorly in math. This drop in performance leads to longer delays and increased avoidance of the topic, which results in another drop in grade average. The student now repeatedly states self-defeating messages about math whenever confronted with the topic. Sometimes these statements are made to others, but most of the time they are simply repeated silently, as if a taped message were playing over and over inside this person's head. According to David Burns (1980), a **mind set** has been established.

Mind sets interfere with motivation and can be fueled by many different things, according to Burns. A syndrome is created, in which a group of signs are found together. The procrastination mind set is characterized by a feeling of hopelessness, a sense of being helpless, magnification of events leading to feeling overwhelmed, a tendency to jump to conclusions, negative self-labeling ("I am a loser"), undervaluing rewards due to perceiving outcomes as not worth the effort, self-coercion in the form of shoulds and oughts (e.g., "I should do X; otherwise I am a rotten person"), low tolerance of frustration, and a general sense of guilt and self-blame.

According to Burns, procrastination can be effectively dealt with. He suggests taking actions such as these:

1. **Use a schedule.** Prioritize tasks and do so using a weekly/monthly/annual planner.

2. **Keep a record of dysfunctional thoughts.** Record the self-defeating language you are feeding yourself and use cognitive restructuring techniques to break this pattern. This involves changing the negative scripts in your head and creating and using self-affirming scripts ("I am a capable person, so I can find ways to learn math!")

3. **Endorse one's self.** If you find yourself operating from a perspective of "what I do doesn't count," you should argue with yourself. Turn the old perspective around. ("I have always thought others were more deserving, but there is no reason to not place myself in the deserving group of people. The people I have been placing on a pedestal also have strengths and weaknesses. I am just as deserving as they are!")

4. **Avoid the oughts and shoulds that are governing your behavior.** Albert Ellis has referred to the destructive impact on one's quality of life because of absolutes ("I must always be the A student. Less than an A means I am a failure.") by saying we are performing "*must*erbation."

5. **Use disarming techniques.** If something or someone is contributing to a negative mind set, disarm it or the person by taking its or the person's power away. In cases involving others, you can call upon assertiveness skills to change the situation.

6. **Think about little steps.** Seeing too far into the future sometimes leads to procrastination. If you have to write a 25-page term paper for an early American history class, you might see the finished product in your mind and become overwhelmed, wondering "How can I ever write that 25-page paper?" When this takes place, stop and think about the task a step at a time. Break up what you see as the end product into manageable smaller stages.

7. **Visualize success.** Envision yourself completing the task. See yourself as succeeding when you start to experience self-doubt.

8. **Test your can'ts.** When you say you cannot do something, stop and do a specific assessment of what is involved in completing something. Often when we carefully assess what is required, we start to understand exactly what steps are needed to succeed, and the feeling of "I can't" loses its power.

Distractions

Even the most dedicated student can be thrown off course by distractions. These also come in two varieties: *external* and *internal*. **External distractions** come from our surroundings or other people and things. Noise, music, TV, computer games, or anything that catches your attention can distract you. Sometimes the distractions are a room temperature that is too hot or too cold, uncomfortable furniture, or poor lighting. Physical problems or limitations can take your mind off the task at hand. Interruptions (whether in person or on the telephone) by family members, friends, salespeople, etc. are some of the most common and irritating external distractions.

Internal distractions come from within. They interfere with your ability to concentrate. They could be emotional or relationship problems that upset you and cause you stress; physical needs such as hunger, thirst, fatigue, or illness; negative attitudes about your assignment, instructor, or the course; daydreaming; thinking about other things; worrying; or whatever keeps you from focusing your attention on your studies.

Over Scheduling

This is a common time thief for many students. Because there are so many conflicting demands for our time and energy, we often get overwhelmed with things that appear on our to-do list as either "urgent" or "responsibilities." Trying to do too much at once to meet real or imagined obligations can cause burnout and stress. The inability to say "no" to things/activities may cause us to spend time meeting other people's expectations and not meeting our own. When we get overwhelmed or overly fatigued, our bodies often succumb to a cold or the flu, and we end up "wasting" time being sick.

Set daily goals, objectives, and priorities. If you do not have priorities you could be spending too much time on minor things. Many times, though, we try to do too much, only to find that we do them half-heartedly, instead of being thorough and complete. There are some things, however, that we can leave undone or only partially completed. There are others that you could delegate to someone else. For example, run your household as you would a business. Get your family members to act as a team and help each other out. When one person has a super busy week, someone else could "cover" for him/her with the agreement that the favor will be reciprocated. It could not only reduce your workload, but may even lead to a more harmonious life at home.

Poor Time Management/Organizational Skills

This time thief is subtle. You may not even realize all of the time it consumes. However, if you've ever spent an hour searching for something you "lost" because it wasn't put away properly, you may start to get the idea. Being disorganized with your schoolwork could be hazardous to your grade. For example, your returned quizzes and homework papers can be great study aids for your final exams, but if you aren't able to find them, you can't use them. Your notes and all related papers for each class should be kept together in a notebook. Have a filing system to organize returned, graded papers and keep them until *after you receive your final grade* for the course. If there is a grade dispute, the burden of proof will be up to you.

For many students, the inability to set priorities, confusion about or lack of goals/direction, and poor planning cost a lot of time and money. Sometimes students wait to do academic planning with a counselor or advisor until after they have already spent two or more semesters in college. They are frustrated and angry when they discover that they have taken courses that do not count toward their chosen degree. For students receiving financial aid, the consequences may be especially daunting because the Pell grant will only pay for 150% of the credit hours required for a specific degree. Courses that you fail or from which you withdraw after the refund date count toward the total.

There are many old maxims such as "an ounce of prevention is worth a pound of cure," or "a stitch in time saves nine" that attempt to teach us some truths about time management. Putting things off and not taking time to plan or prepare properly have proven to be much more time consuming in the long run.

Overcoming Thieves of Time

1. **Find the first step for whatever it is you have to do.** Start there without contemplating the whole project yet. Just get the momentum going.
2. **Set a short time limit.** Commit to working on your task for 10 or 15 minutes. Sometimes you'll get involved and work longer.
3. **Break tasks into smaller chunks.** Set a pace and reward yourself for what you have accomplished. When you become bored with what you are studying, change the task.
4. **Remember the To-Do list.** As you cross off those items you complete, you will feel a sense of accomplishment. It will allow you to see and chart your progress and will provide self-satisfaction that might become one of your best motivators.
5. **Plan a ten-minute break between each study hour.** Reward yourself when you have satisfactorily completed an assignment.
6. **Make appointments with yourself and keep them.** Do it NOW. Set deadlines for yourself.
7. **Try to understand why you are avoiding a task.** Learn to compensate for whatever the reason. If you do not understand, ask the instructor to explain. Perhaps your fellow classmates might be able to help out. Ask them what they know or understand about a given assignment. Seek out tutoring if you need it.
8. **Get a study circle going for a particular class or find a study partner.** When you make a commitment with others to spend time on a particular class or assignment, it will be easier to stick with a schedule.
9. **If you are too tired, be sure to get enough rest at night.** Studying all night is not as productive as you might think. Research has found that students who got a full night's sleep after studying remembered information twice as well as students who pulled an "all-nighter."
10. **Be aware of your internal and external distracters.**
11. **Learn to say "NO" to interruptions.**
12. **Choose a study location that is as free from external distractions as possible.** Have all of your supplies and study materials ready, too, so you won't waste time or get distracted looking for them.
13. **Use positive self-talk to encourage yourself.** Instead of thinking, "I'll never get all of this work done," think, "I know I can at least read the chapter; I'll get that done first."
14. **If you lack confidence and self-esteem, make an appointment to talk with a counselor.**
15. **Experiment with your own techniques.** Only you know what works best for you. Build on your successes. Profit from your failures. Learn to study smarter.

AFTER (A)

Time management is something that will need to be continually *reviewed, revised,* and *self-modified* as needed.

- **Am I writing down my commitments and tasks in my planner?**
- **Do I prioritize my "to-do list"?**

- **How am I eliminating the thieves of time** (procrastination, distractions, over scheduling, poor time management/organization skills)?
- **What type of planning system will I continue to use as a result of what I've learned about time management** (i.e. style, features)?
- **Have I practiced saying "no"?**
- **What changes can I make to what I am doing now that will help me become an effective time manager that will also help me be a better employee and person?**

SUMMARY

Most students have multiple roles (student, employee, family member, etc.) and have many demands on their time. Unfortunately, study time is often sacrificed to do other things. **Careful use of your time is critical to success in college.** Learning to set specific, realistic, and measurable goals is the first step toward developing a workable time management plan. Identify your goals, and give priority to the activities that assist you in achieving them. This chapter introduced three scheduling tools, **the weekly schedule, the semester schedule, and the daily To-Do list,** that can help you keep track of how you wish to spend your time in order to achieve your goals.

SUGGESTED READINGS

Allen, David. *Getting Things Done: The Art of Stress-Free Productivity.* New York: Penguin Books, 2001.

Emmett, Rita. *The Procrastinator's Handbook: Mastering the Art of Doing It Now.* New York: Walker & Co., 2000.

NAME: _____ DATE: _____

EXERCISE 5.1: DEVELOPING A PERSONAL MISSION STATEMENT

This exercise is to develop your own personal mission statement (setting your own personal standard or guide for living your best life regardless of life's challenges). Begin by asking yourself the following questions:

What are your values? (refer to p. 116, #1 for examples)

What kind of person do you want to be?

What talents do you have (or would like to have)?

How can you contribute to your family, your job, and the world?

Based on your responses to the above questions, write your own personal mission statement. Be specific and detailed when explaining your mission.

Sample Mission Statement: *To fulfill my Christian duty by displaying love, fighting for justice, and being a community servant to and for my fellowman; by using my writing talent to create poetry, plays, novels, and movies to communicate and share this love; and to devote my time to help those in need.*

_____
_____
_____
_____
_____
_____
_____
_____
_____
_____
_____
_____
_____
_____
_____

EXERCISE 5.2: GOAL SETTING AND TIME MANAGEMENT

The chapter emphasized the importance of goal setting and how goal setting is related to time management. This exercise will give you an opportunity to identify your specific goals (short term, mid-term, and long term). Many people think goal setting begins with the identification of short term goals. However, you actually need to begin with your long term goals in order to develop a plan for achieving these goals.

Part One: Long-Term Goals

Long-term goals represent major targets in your life. These goals can take **five to twenty years** to achieve. In some cases, they will take a lifetime. They can include goals in education, careers, personal relationship, travel and financial security, whatever is important to you. Include answers to the following questions in your long-term goals:

What do you want to accomplish in your life? Do you want your life to make a statement? What is it?

Brainstorm

Begin with an eight-minute brainstorm. For eight minutes, write down everything you think you want in your life. Write as fast as you can, and write down everything that comes into your mind. Leave no thought out. Don't worry about accuracy. The purpose of a brainstorm is to generate as many ideas as possible.

Evaluate

Look over your list. Analyze what you wrote. If you left something out, add it. Look for common themes and relationships between goals. Select three long-term goals that are very important to you—goals that will take many years to achieve. Write those goals below:

1. **Long-term goal:**

2. **Long-term goal:**

3. **Long-term goal:**

Now, reflect on the process you just used. What criteria did you use to select your top three goals? (These are core values such as love, wealth, or happiness.) Write those values here:

Part Two: Mid-Term Goals

Mid-term goals are objectives you can accomplish in **two to five years**. They include goals such as completing a course of education or achieving a specific career level. These goals usually support your long-term goals.

Brainstorm

Read the three long-term goals you selected in Part One. Choose one of them. Now brainstorm a list of goals you might achieve in the next two to five years that would lead to the accomplishment of that one long-term goal. These are mid-term goals. Remember, neatness doesn't count. Go for quantity!

Evaluate

Now, analyze your brainstorm of mid-term goals. Select three that you estimate to be most important in meeting that long-term goal you picked. Write your selections here:

1. **Mid-term goal:**

2. **Mid-term goal:**

3. **Mid-term goal:**

Now, pause for reflection before going on to the next part of this exercise. Why did you see these three goals are more important than the other mid-term goals you generated?

Part Three: Short-Term Goals

Short-term goals are goals you can accomplish in **one year or less**. These goals are specific achievements such as completing a particular course or group of courses. A short-term financial goal would include an exact dollar amount. Whatever your short-term goals are, they will require action now or in the near future.

Brainstorm

Review your list of mid-term goals and select one. Generate a list of short-term goals—those you can reach in a year or less that will lead you to the accomplishment of that one mid-term goal. Write down everything that comes to mind. Do not evaluate or judge these ideas yet. For now, the more ideas you write down, the better.

Evaluate

Analyze your list of short-term goals. Cross out any bizarre ideas. Next, evaluate your remaining short-term goals to determine which ones you can accomplish and are willing to accomplish. Select three and write them below.

1. **Short-term goal:**

2. **Short-term goal:**

3. **Short-term goal:**

Finally, write a list of small, achievable steps you can take to accomplish each short-term goal. Make these steps specific enough to include a time line. Then return to your steps in a few weeks and note your progress.

Steps for short-term goal #1:

Steps for short-term goal #2:

Steps for short-term goal #3:

The more you practice, the more effective you can be in choosing goals that have meaning for you. You can repeat this process using the other long-term goals you generated, or you can create new ones.

EXERCISE 5.3: TIME MANAGEMENT AND THE INTERNET

Activity #1—Basic Internet Search

Perform a web search on one of the following:

- *Procrastination*

- *Time Management*

- *Long-Term Academic Planning*

- *Goal Setting*

Copy source information from three (3) different websites regarding one of these topics.

Write a short summary (one paragraph) on what new information you learned and how you will apply it in your learning strategies.

Activity #2—Advanced Internet Search (Boolean)

Use the Boolean operators *AND, OR,* and *NOT* to search for articles on *time management strategies for college students.* (Possible subtopics could be anything from Chapter 4 such as procrastination, to-do lists, goals, motivation, etc.).

Choose two of the following four search engines: Altavista, Google, Hotbot, Excite.

Find and print out one article from each of the search engines you choose (2 articles total). Printouts should be no more than 5 pages each. One or two pages is fine if the information is relevant and interesting.

Write a two or three paragraph summary of each article.

Search Strategy Tips:

Step 1: State what you want to find.

Step 2: Identify keywords.

Step 3: Select synonyms for your keywords.

Step 4: Combine keywords, synonyms, and Boolean operators.

Step 5: Perform your searches and print out two (2) articles of your choice.

Step 6: Write a two or three paragraph summary of each article.

Special Note: Be creative with your word choices and combinations. Read and satisfy your curiosity about the topic. Let this be a fun activity.

EXERCISE 5.4: MONITORING AND PLANNING YOUR TIME

1. Complete a daily log for a full week indicating how your time and energy were spent. Follow these directions:

   a. List all fixed obligations—classes, meetings, work hours, meals, travel time to and from commitments, family obligations, etc.—as you complete them.

   b. Consider and indicate time spent on class review if you prepared for class.

   c. Don't forget to indicate any time spent on health essentials such as recreation, sleep, and exercise.

   d. Be sure 24 hours per day are accounted for in your log.

Monitoring Your Time

Fill in each time block **AFTER you have completed the activity**. Use the following categories of activities.

Class	Travel	Exercise
Work	Eating	Personal (getting dressed, bathing,
Housework	Sleep	brushing teeth, etc.)
Meeting	Recreation	Other (explain)

Date Hours	Monday	Tuesday	Wednesday	Thursday	Friday	Saturday	Sunday
7:00 A.M.							
7:30							
8:00							
8:30							
9:00							
9:30							
10:00							
10:30							
11:00							
11:30							
12:00 Noon							
12:30 P.M.							
1:00							
1:30							
2:00							
2:30							
3:00							
3:30							
4:00							
4:30							

Date							
Hours	**Monday**	**Tuesday**	**Wednesday**	**Thursday**	**Friday**	**Saturday**	**Sunday**
5:00 P.M.							
5:30							
6:00							
6:30							
7:00							
7:30							
8:00							
8:30							
9:00							
9:30							
10:00							
10:30							
11:00							
11:30							
12:00 MIDN.							
12:30 A.M.							
1:00							
1:30							
2:00							
2:30							
3:00							
3:30							
4:00							
4:30							
5:00							
5:30							
6:00							
6:30							

(Continued)

Analyzing Your Time Monitor

According to your personal summary log, how did you spend your time?
Identify the eight areas where you spent the greatest amounts of time. Explain why.

1. _____

2. _____

3. _____

4. _____

5. _____

6. _____

7. _____

8. _____

In what areas should you increase the amount of time you spend if you are going to accomplish your goals?

_____

_____

_____

List and discuss any other factors you should consider before actually planning and taking control of your time (i.e., child care, work, travel, overcommitting).

_____

_____

Planning Your Time

This is a very important exercise because if you really follow the time management tips and are highly motivated, there is no way you can fail. The purpose of a time schedule is to give you a framework for bringing order and discipline into your life, not to make you into a robot. It will give you time to do the things you need to do. It can break the pattern of procrastinating and cut down on worrying time. **Assume that you are basically planning how the rest of your weeks will look during the semester** with the exception of a few changes for unplanned events.

1. Complete a To-Do List for one week.

2. Complete a daily log for a full week indicating how you **PLAN** to spend your time.
    a. List all fixed obligations—classes, work, domestic chores, travel to and from commitments, sleep, and meals—you know you must complete.
    b. Don't forget to allow time for yourself (personal time), recreation, religion, and exercise.
    c. Based on class times, indicate when you plan to study and review school work. Don't forget to consider the amount of time you need for every hour in class and when you should review for information to move from short-term to long-term memory.
    d. Go back to Analyzing Your Time and use the information from your analysis.
    e. Be sure to plan for 24 hours a day.

3. Now summarize the time you plan to spend each day on the various activities according to the planning summary log sheet.

CONSTRUCTING A TO-DO LIST

Start the planning process by thinking of all of the tasks that need to be completed this week. Now, construct a to do list of at least 10 items that need to be done this week. Use **A, B,** and **C** to indicate each task's importance (**A = top priority**).

Importance	Check if completed on time	List tasks here
_____	_____	1. _____
_____	_____	2. _____
_____	_____	3. _____
_____	_____	4. _____
_____	_____	5. _____
_____	_____	6. _____
_____	_____	7. _____
_____	_____	8. _____
_____	_____	9. _____
_____	_____	10. _____

Were any of the items you listed not completed by the specified date? Explain why for each item. Briefly discuss any feelings of accomplishment or frustration you experienced in completing or not completing the tasks listed. Suggest at least one change you would make in the future when you use a to-do list.

Planning Your Time

This week, your assignment is to create a plan for an entire week. After creating your plan, you will monitor this plan to see if you completed the things you have listed. If an action is different than what you wrote, highlight and make a note of what you did using different colored ink. Use the following categories of activities.

Class	Travel	Exercise
Work	Eating	Personal (getting dressed, bathing,
Housework	Sleep	brushing teeth, etc.)
Meeting	Recreation	Other (explain)

Date							
Hours	**Monday**	**Tuesday**	**Wednesday**	**Thursday**	**Friday**	**Saturday**	**Sunday**
7:00 A.M.							
7:30							
8:00							
8:30							
9:00							
9:30							
10:00							
10:30							
11:00							
11:30							
12:00 Noon							
12:30 P.M.							
1:00							
1:30							
2:00							
2:30							
3:00							
3:30							
4:00							
4:30							

(Continued)

Date							
Hours	Monday	Tuesday	Wednesday	Thursday	Friday	Saturday	Sunday
5:00 P.M.							
5:30							
6:00							
6:30							
7:00							
7:30							
8:00							
8:30							
9:00							
9:30							
10:00							
10:30							
11:00							
11:30							
12:00 MIDN.							
12:30 A.M.							
1:00							
1:30							
2:00							
2:30							
3:00							
3:30							
4:00							
4:30							
5:00							
5:30							
6:00							
6:30							

ANALYZING YOUR TIME PLAN

List activities that you planned but did not complete.

What priority were these activities? How would completing these activities have helped you achieve your goals?

What mistakes did you make (overplanning; inability to say "no"/ delegate; did not schedule adequate study time; did not plan for the unexpected; etc.)?

List activities that you procrastinated on completing.

Why do you think you procrastinated on these activities?

Explain why you get more things accomplished once you have a plan.

What are the advantages of using a planner?

How can you use *your* student planner more effectively?

EXERCISE 5.5: TIME MONITOR WORKSHEET

Analyze your time usage by answering these questions based on your time monitor.

		YES	NO
1.	I often study at a time when I am not at peak efficiency due to fatigue.	_____	_____
2.	I have failed to complete at least one assignment on time this semester.	_____	_____
3.	This week I spent time watching TV, visiting, or napping that really should have been spent otherwise.	_____	_____
4.	Often, lack of prioritizing tasks causes me some difficulty in completing tasks on time.	_____	_____
5.	Social or athletic events cause me to neglect academic work fairly often.	_____	_____
6.	At least once this semester, I have not remembered that an assignment was due until the night before.	_____	_____
7.	I often get behind in one course due to having to work on another.	_____	_____
8.	I usually wait until the night before the due date to start assignments.	_____	_____
9.	My studying is often a hit-or-miss strategy which is dependent on my mood.	_____	_____
10.	I normally wait until test time to read texts and/or review lecture notes.	_____	_____
11.	I often have the sinking realization that there is simply not enough time left to accomplish the assignment or study sufficiently for the test.	_____	_____
12.	Often I rationalize that very few people will make the A/get the project done on time/really read the text, etc.	_____	_____
13.	I catch myself looking forward to study interruptions rather than trying to avoid them.	_____	_____
14.	I have failed to eliminate some time wasters this past week that I could have controlled.	_____	_____
15.	I often feel out of control in respect to time.	_____	_____
16.	I have procrastinated at least twice this week.	_____	_____
17.	I find myself doing easier or more interesting tasks first, even if they are not as important.	_____	_____
18.	I feel I have wasted quite a lot of time—again—this week.	_____	_____
19.	I studied EACH course I am currently taking this week.	_____	_____
20.	I spent some time this week reviewing previous weeks' notes even though I did not have a test.	_____	_____
21.	The time of day that I am the most alert is _____, so I tried to study my hardest subjects then.	_____	_____

	YES	NO
22. I studied approximately 1–2 hours out of class for every hour in class.	_____	_____
23. My most sluggish period during the day is _____, so I used these times to relax or participate in sports or hobbies.	_____	_____
24. I often make out daily lists of tasks to be completed, and I prioritize these lists.	_____	_____
25. I use small blocks of time (10–30 min.) between classes to review notes, start assignments, or plan.	_____	_____

To calculate your score, score 1 point for each yes from items 1–18, and 1 point for each no from items 19–25. The higher your score, the more you need a Master Time Schedule! Consider these categories for your score:

15–19 YOU'RE IN DESPERATE NEED OF A PLAN! How do you ever get anything accomplished? (Or do you?)

10–14 YOU NEED A PLAN! Life could be simpler if you took the time to plan it out.

5–9 A PLAN WOULD HELP! The going could be smoother, and more could be accomplished.

0–4 A PLAN COULDN'T HURT! You're doing pretty well, but give yourself the gift of organization, and you may give yourself the gift of more time.

Please write a paragraph that reflects on your results.

(What specific actions you will take, how you can use your planner to help.)

_____

_____

_____

_____

_____

_____

_____

_____

_____

_____

_____

_____

_____

_____

EXERCISE 5.6: MORNING LARK VS. NIGHT OWL

This questionnaire can help you determine if you are a morning person (a lark) or a night person (an owl). "Larks" usually lead well-structured, controlled lives. They jump out of bed and usually have productive mornings, tending to wind down about mid-afternoon. "Owls," on the other hand, tend to crawl out of bed, barely live through mornings, but have more productive afternoons. They also tend to be more extroverted than larks. Which are you? Find out by circling the answer most appropriate for you and adding up your points.

		Points Possible	Points Earned
1.	I feel best if I get up around:		_____
	5–6:30 am	5	
	6:30–7:30 am	4	
	7:30–9:30 am	3	
	9:30–11 am	2	
	11–noon	1	
2.	If I had to describe how easy it is for me to get up in the morning, I would say:		_____
	It is not easy at all!	1	
	It is not very easy.	2	
	It is fairly easy.	3	
	It is very easy.	4	
3.	The way I feel for the first half-hour after I wake up is:		_____
	very tired	1	
	fairly tired	2	
	fairly refreshed	3	
	very refreshed	4	
4.	If I could choose the best time to take a difficult test, it would be:		_____
	8–10 am	4	
	10 am–1 pm	3	
	1–5 pm	2	
	7–9 pm	1	
5.	If my job would require that I work from 4–6 am one day, I would choose to:		_____
	not go to bed until after I worked	1	
	take a nap before and sleep after	2	
	sleep before work and nap after	3	
	get all the sleep I need before work	4	

		Points Possible	Points Earned

6. If someone asked me to jog with them at 7 am one morning, I would perform: _____

	Points Possible
well	4
reasonably well	3
not very well	2
not well at all	1

7. If I have to wake up at a specific time each morning, I depend on my alarm clock: _____

	Points Possible
not at all	4
slightly	3
quite a lot	2
desperately	1

8. I am usually tired and wanting to go to bed by: _____

	Points Possible
8–9 pm	5
9–10:30 pm	4
10:30 pm–12:30 am	3
12:30–2 am	2
2–3 am	1

TOTAL NUMBER OF POINTS EARNED _____

A score of 20 is halfway between owl and lark. The higher your score, the more of a morning lark you are. The lower your score, the more of a night owl you are.

EXERCISE 5.7: PROJECT PLANNING SHEET

The goal of project planning is to assist you with completing big projects and assignments. The first step is to list the start and due dates. Completion of the project should be 3 days from the due date. The next step is to make a list of ALL tasks and things needed to do, buy, research, type, etc., in order to complete the project. The final steps are to rank these tasks in priority order and assign dates of completion.

Project Start Date (when did you receive the project/assignment?) _____

Things to Do List	Rank	Deadline Date
(make a list of things to do to complete project)	(rank in order of first to last)	(when will you complete each item on the list?)

-
-
-
-
-
-
-
-
-
-
-
-
-
-
-

Now that you have the list, In the next column, rank them in order and of importance

Now that you have ranked in order of importance, establish a deadline date of when you would complete

Completion Date (3 days before due date): _____

Due Date (When is the project/assignment due to instructor?) _____

EXERCISE 5.8: JOURNAL ENTRY: UNDERSTANDING PROCRASTINATION

Complete the following reflection journal on your own paper:

List 3 situations in which you typically find yourself procrastinating, or, putting off what you need to do. Reflect on how you feel about putting off what needs to be done in these situations (e.g., guilty, angry, depressed)? What thoughts come to mind when you think about these situations (e.g., "I tell myself I'll get started, but I never do")?

Discuss what steps you should consider using to overcome procrastination (e.g., "I need to divide the work up into amounts I can handle"). Also reflect on what obstacle is preventing you from doing what needs to be done (e.g., "I feel like a failure in math, so I delay doing homework"). Commit to a specific action that you will take to overcome the obstacle that prevents you from doing what you need to do.

Chapter 6

Improving Memory – Why Can't I Remember?

INTRODUCTION

As college students, you are required to pay attention to classroom lectures and to concentrate while reading your many textbooks. Several weeks later, or perhaps even as late as mid-term, you are asked to "remember" the information you've learned from all those lectures and reading assignments. In simplistic terms, learning is the acquisition of knowledge/information, and memory is the vehicle that allows you to store and retrieve that knowledge. Learning depends upon input, and each word you read or hear and each sight you experience will change your memory in some way. This chapter should help you understand how you receive information, process it, and store it in your memory. In addition we'll look at some strategies for enhancing your memory for classroom use.

BEFORE (B)

To improve your memory, you must complete *preparation, self-awareness,* and *planning* strategies as follows:

- **Self-analysis of your current memory**
- **Understand why you forget**
- **Know ways to enhance your memory**

Pretest

Directions: Check Yes or No to the following questions.

		Yes	No
1.	Do you remember appointments without having to check?		
2.	Do you remember names/faces easily?		
3.	Do you know your social security number?		
4.	Do you remember birthdays, anniversaries, and other important dates easily?		
5.	Do you remember special events that happened several years ago clearly and distinctly?		
6.	Do you intend to remember lecture and reading material for your classes?		
7.	Do you pay attention while studying?		
8.	Do you recite material aloud to boost your memory?		
9.	Do you force yourself to pay attention in class even when you find the class boring?		
10.	Do you study in short, concentrated sessions for 45–50 minutes and then take a break?		
11.	Do you use memory prompts (acronyms, rhymes, etc.) to help you remember data for tests?		
12.	Do you organize your study material into meaningful categories?		
13.	Do you review notes and reading material on a regular basis—at least once a week?		
14.	Do you use note cards to review class material when time allows?		
15.	Do you use your preferred learning style to boost study strategies?		

Questions 1–5 ask about your memory ability for personal situations, while questions 6–15 relate to memory habits and strategies that you use in school. Did you have 7 or more "Yes" responses to questions 6–15? If so, you're on the right track! If not, you need to focus on the strategies covered in this chapter to help you improve your memory.

A study conducted at Southwest Missouri State University by Dr. Charles Tegeler revealed information on the value of review to help you remember. Students were given information and they studied it until they had 100 percent mastery. The group was

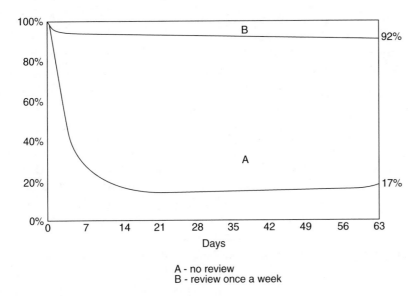

A - no review
B - review once a week

Figure 6.1

divided into two groups. One group did not review the material and at the end of 63 days when they were retested, they averaged 17 percent comprehension. The other group -reviewed once a week. At the end of the 63-day period, they averaged 92 percent comprehension! (See Figure 6.1.)

WHY DO YOU FORGET?

Forgetting can be defined as a failure or loss of memory. Your mind remembers only what you need and discards the rest. Do you remember grades you made in your classes in the eighth grade? Do you even remember what classes you had? You probably don't remember. Information that is not used is forgotten.

Research has proven over and over that the greatest amount of forgetting occurs during the first day. Remembering what you have heard is even more difficult to remember than what you have read. When you read, you have control over the material. You can slow down, regress, or speed-up your reading.

People often say they forgot something when they actually never knew it. If you just met someone and didn't really catch their name, you didn't forget it—you probably never knew it.

There are a variety of theories about forgetting. Think about these as you read them and see if you can understand how the theory relates to your own "forgetful" experiences.

1. **It's There Somewhere!**—Some psychologists believe once we have thoroughly learned something, it remains in our memory our entire life. This theory suggests that the concept is there, but we are just having trouble finding it in order to be able to retrieve it.

2. **Interference Theory**—Old facts and ideas cause us to forget new facts and ideas. The reverse is also true. New ideas and facts can cause confusion with old ones. We are continually adding ideas to our memory bank. If you learn three similar facts at three separate times, the middle one will have the most difficult time surviving. This is also true of lists you need to remember. The first and last items are easier to remember than the middle ones.

3. **Use It or Lose It**—If you don't use a fact you have learned, it gets more difficult to remember it. This is why review is so important!

4. **Motivation and Attitude Theory**—Here are our two favorite words again! Sometimes we choose to forget. Things we associate with unpleasant memories or mistakes we have made we would like to forget. A poor attitude in class can definitely affect memory ability. You have the power to influence both remembering and forgetting.

An understanding of how memory works and effective ways to use your memory will increase your ability to memorize information. All incoming information enters the **sensory memory**, which holds an exact copy of everything you see or hear for several seconds. On the way to class, you may notice a squirrel in a tree, but you can't recall that experience several moments later. Generally, your sensory memory will hold information just long enough for your **short-term memory** to register it. Short-term memory is the temporary storehouse for information. If your brain does not identify the information as meaningful or important, it quickly disappears. Your short-term memory lets you concentrate on the task at hand, but prevents you from collecting too much information in temporary storage. You are introduced to several people, but can't use their names in talking with them. You did not retain their names beyond sensory memory. Information that your mind identifies as meaningful or important makes its way into **long-term memory**. In order to enter information into your long-term memory, it must be actively processed through your short-term memory. "Active processing" in short-term memory is the key to the successful transfer of information into long-term memory.

Long-term memory can store an unlimited amount of information for long periods of time. Information is stored in long-term memory on the basis of meaning and importance. Information you don't really understand or consider significant will most likely not find its way into long-term memory. This means that your ability to remember what you study depends on your willingness to make sure you thoroughly understand the material and can relate it to existing information in long-term memory.

Functions of Memory	Stages of Memory		
	Reception Getting Information	Retention Storing Information	Recollection Recalling Information
Sensory Memory	Register perceptions	Quickly lost without selective attention	Automatic from second to second
Short-Term Memory	Focuses on facts and details	Quickly lost unless recited or reviewed	Possible for short time only until information is lost
Long-Term Memory	Forms general ideas images and meanings	Integrates information transferred from short term memory for storage	Possible for long periods of time or for a lifetime

Figure 6.2 Your Memory Box.

How Can You Enhance Your Memory?

Our most powerful attack against forgetting is cognitive processing. This simply means deep thinking. It is deep thinking that makes a long-lasting memory trace. According to Walter Pauk, there are three steps in cognitive processing or deep thinking:

1. Understand the fact thoroughly; be able to explain it in your own words.
2. Analyze the fact by viewing it from all sides.
3. Relate the fact to information you already have.

Using memory effectively is being able to recall information at the right time. Our memory system needs to be flexible.

The following ideas should help improve your memory:

1. *Organization*—The first step in organizing is to get a broad overview. Learn general concepts before you learn specifics. If you have a "feel" for the general idea, the details will have a place to fit.

   Research has shown that our short-term memory has a limited capacity. Seven unrelated items are about maximum for most people to remember. In various college classes, you will need to remember more than seven unrelated items. The way to handle this is through meaningful organization.

   Chunking or Clustering—This is a method whereby you categorize similar items you need to know. For example:

   As you walked to the grocery store, you realized you didn't have your list with you. You did remember there were twelve items. The items you had on your list were: onions, lettuce, ice cream, bananas, green beans, eggs, cheese, peas, apples, grapefruit, milk, and oranges.

   Look at these items for 15 seconds. Close the book and see how many you can recall. You are doing well if you remember 6 or 7.

   By clustering or chunking these items, we can make them manageable. We can have 3 major items instead of twelve.

   When we think of the major headings, the individual details fall in place. The thought of dairy products automatically reduces our thoughts to dairy products. This procedure will work well in your textbooks. Learn to associate details with the major headings.

Vegetables	Dairy	Fruits
onions	ice cream	bananas
lettuce	milk	apples
green beans	eggs	grapefruit
peas	cheese	oranges

2. *Visualize Relationships and Associations*—Knowing individual facts does not help you understand a topic. Relating details provides a basis for the main idea. Also, it is important to relate new ideas to what you already know. Visualizing uses a different part of your brain than when you just read. This will also aid in retention. Often students will remember a picture, table, or graph that explains a theory- easier than they will remember the words that described it. The better our background, the easier this will be.

3. *Make It Meaningful*—We remember things better when we can apply them to ourselves. If we can match the information we need to remember to a goal we have set, it will be easier to recall.

4. *Intend to Remember*—Your mental attitude plays an important role in your memory. Intending to learn can create a positive attitude that will include other important characteristics, such as active learning, paying attention, and writing to understand.

5. *Motivated Interest*—Research has shown that interest is important to learning, but remembering is almost impossible without interest. If you are not interested in a class you are taking, find some way to create an interest. We tend to forget information that contradicts our opinions. If you feel bored, consider the possibility that you are creating your boredom. Take responsibility for your attitudes.

6. *Recitation*—This technique is probably the most powerful one that will allow transfer from short-term to long-term memory. When you want to remember something, repeat it aloud. Recitation works best when you put concepts you want to remember into your own words.

   Arthur Gates did a series of recitation experiments in 1917. His experiments suggest that when you are reading a general text (psychology, sociology, history), 80 percent of your time should be spent in reciting and 20 percent in reading. It is also more effective to start recitation early in the reading process. Do not wait until you have read everything before you start to recite.

7. *Spaced Study*—Marathon study sessions are not effective. It is much better to have intermittent spaced review sessions. A practical application of this would be using the small blocks of time you are now wasting during the day. It is also important to take breaks while you are studying. After 45–50 minutes, reward yourself with a short break. When you come back, you will be more alert and more efficient. If significant learning is taking place and you are really engrossed, go for it! You don't have to stop, but memory is more productive when you space your studying instead of trying to accomplish everything in one long session.

8. *Brainstorming*—If you are having a problem recalling an answer on a test, try brainstorming. Think of everything you can that is related to what you are trying to remember. For example, if you are trying to remember your fifth grade teacher's name, think of other elementary teachers you had. By association the name you are trying to remember should pop up during this brainstorming.

9. *Reflecting*—It is important to give information time to go from short-term memory to long-term memory. This is considered consolidation time. Researchers vary on their opinions, but a safe rule is to leave information in your short-term memory 4–15 seconds. This gives information time to consolidate and transfer to your long-term memory. This is important to remember when you are reading quickly and not stopping to think about what you have read. The information will be discarded quickly if you do not allow time for transfer. Stop and think about what you have just read, recite it, paraphrase it, and relate it to what you already know.

10. *Use All Your Senses*—The more senses you involve in studying, the better your memory process will work. Read and visualize, recite key concepts, devise questions, and write answers.

11. *Combine Memory Techniques*—You can combine organizing, reciting, and reflecting in one task. Different techniques can reinforce each other.

12. *Repetition*—Simply repeating things will aid memory. Advertisements hook us in this way. We learn a jingle by hearing it repeated again and again. For example:

    "You Deserve a Break Today" . . . *McDonalds*

    "It's the Real Thing" . . . *Coke*

    "Ring around the Collar" . . . *Wisk Detergent*

    "You've Got the Right One, Baby" . . . *Diet Pepsi*

13. *Mnemonics*—Mnemonics are easily remembered words, rhymes, phrases, sentences, or games that help you remember difficult lists, principles, or facts.
    - *Acronyms* are words created by the first letters of a series of words. For example: FBI, CIA, IRS, USU. By using acronyms, you can create your own cues for recalling a series of facts or words. Be sure to create an acronym that is simple enough to not be forgotten or confused.
    - *Acrostics* are creative sentences that help you remember a series of letters that stand for something. You can create acrostics to remember a specific item, such as the planets in our solar system in sequence (Mercury, Venus, Earth, Mars, Jupiter, Saturn, Uranus, Neptune, and Pluto.) Taking the first letter of each word, you would have m, v, e, m, j, s, u, n, and p. Make up a nonsensical phrase to help you remember the exact order, such as, "My very elegant mother- just served us nine pies." A good sense of humor will help you remember your sentence.
    - *Rhymes and Songs.* Rhymes are used to help remember facts. For example: "In fourteen hundred and ninety-two, Columbus sailed the ocean blue." "Fifty Nifty United States" is an example of a song that helps us to remember many isolated facts, such as the names of all the states.
    - *Loci and Peg Systems.* Loci is a strategy where you associate a concept with a place. This includes where you were when you heard the concept, how it looked in your notes, which graphics were on the page containing the information, etc. You can create a visual association between the material to be learned and a familiar place or routine. For instance, suppose you want to learn a list of chemical elements. You choose a familiar route, such as the route from the TSC to the Business Building. As you pass each building along the way, you assign it a chemical element. Later in your class, you visualize your route. As you "see" each place, you recall the element it represents. The method of loci helps you to remember things in a particular order. This is especially helpful when trying to remember steps in a process. Peg systems work by visualizing pegs or hooks in a closet. You hang information on each peg, and then recall what's on each one.

    Mnemonic devices have some limitations. First, the technique is often difficult to learn and remember. You may forget the technique. Second, mnemonic techniques don't work well for remembering technical terms in math and science. And third, mnemonic techniques won't necessarily help you get beyond the knowledge level of thinking. You won't necessarily understand or comprehend the material you are trying to recall.

14. *Use Your Preferred Learning Style:* In a previous chapter, you read about learning styles and completed exercises to help you identify how you learn best. Use this knowledge to help you process information in your "strength" mode. For example, if you know you learn best by hearing the information (auditory

learner), using recitation techniques should be a major part of your review efforts. If you know you learn best by reading or seeing the information visually (visual learner), use charts, graphs, and diagrams to organize your lecture notes and textbook material.

Use of Mind Maps

From *Advantages of Mind Maps and Uses of Mind Maps* by Peter Russell. Copyright © by Peter Russell. Reprinted by permission.

Notes. Whenever information is being taken in, mind maps help organize it into a form that is easily assimilated by the brain and easily remembered. They can be used for noting anything—books, lectures, meetings, interviews, phone conversations.
Recall. Whenever information is being retrieved from memory, mind maps allow ideas to be quickly noted as they occur, in an organized manner. There's no need to form sentences and write them out in full. They serve as quick and efficient means of review and so keep recall at a high level.

Figure 6.3 Sample of a Mind Map by Dan Kesterson.

Creativity. Whenever you want to encourage creativity, mind maps liberate the mind from linear thinking, allowing new ideas to flow more rapidly. Think of every item in a mind map as the center of another mind map.

Problem solving. Whenever you are confronted by a problem—professional or personal—mind maps help you see all the issues and how they relate to each other. They also help others quickly get an overview of how you see different aspects of the situation, and their relative importance.

Planning. Whenever you are planning something, mind maps help you get all the relevant information down in one place and organize it easily. They can be used for planning any piece of writing from a letter to a screenplay to a book (I use a master map for the whole book, and a detailed sub-map for each chapter), or for planning a meeting, a day, or a vacation.

Presentations. Whenever I speak I prepare a mind map for myself of the topic and its flow. This not only helps me organize the ideas coherently; the visual nature of the map means that I can read the whole thing in my head as I talk, without ever having to look at a sheet of paper.

DURING (D)

When it comes to memory, there is one specific *action* to take:

- **Concentration**

CONCENTRATION

Students often cite lack of concentration as a major barrier to learning information. Some common laments are "I can only concentrate for a few minutes." "Studying is boring." Some common concentration problems include: fatigue, distractions, and poor time management.

Distractions are those things in the environment that compete for attention. These distractions may be external or internal. An inappropriate learning environment will definitely decrease your ability to concentrate. Learning new material requires your complete and focused attention. Being distracted by personal problems and frequent daydreaming divides your attention and causes a decrease in your ability to concentrate.

Concentration Strategies

Concentration is giving material your complete and focused attention. This focus is necessary to store information. Without concentration and focus, information is not put into long-term memory for later recall. Often, knowing that we are not concentrating begins a cycle of frustration. "Tomorrow is the test. I don't want to sit here and read this. I can't think at all. I'm going to fail." The fear of failure adds an additional barrier to concentration. Knowing the common causes of poor concentration may help you to focus during your study time. Ineffective time management has a great deal to do with concentration. By setting goals and establishing priorities, you will be better able to schedule time for studying. Procrastination causes stress, which in turn affects your ability to concentrate. Knowing how to pace yourself and prioritize your commitments will directly increase your ability to concentrate.

Barriers to Concentration

The major barriers to concentration come under four main categories: distractions, attitude, poor time management, and fatigue. Knowing what is causing your inability to focus may aid you in choosing strategies to solve the problem.

Distractions are those things in the environment that compete for our attention. Minor distractions can be small environmental problems that are simple to control: the phone ringing, the noise of the TV, roommates chattering, the room too hot or too cold, a great view, being hungry, tired, or thirsty. Major distractions absorb your thoughts and are more difficult to manage. Anticipating an upcoming vacation is just as distracting as worrying about relationships or financial problems. Major or minor distractions can make it difficult to remember what you just read in U.S. History.

Strategies to eliminate distractions:

- **Be physically prepared to study. Are you sleepy? Hungry?**
- **Find a place to study that is free of distractions.**
- **Deal with personal problems before or after studying.**
- **Write down your problem and set it aside for later.**
- **Study with a partner to increase motivation.**
- **Practice increasing your "focused" concentration time. Set a timer and start with short times that will bring you success.**
- **Practice effective time management strategies, such as creating a study schedule and daily "to-do" lists.**

Students often confuse "concentration" problems with "interest and attitude" problems. The reality is that not every course will be on a favorite subject. Having a negative attitude about a course creates a concentration barrier. To the extent that you can convince yourself that there is something of interest in each of your classes, you will find that you can concentrate at a higher level. You may have to create a reward system for yourself to overcome an attitude. Rewards can vary from candy bars to time with friends, but many students find they work effectively.

Strategies to overcome attitude problems:

- **Accept your responsibility for learning the information.**
- **Accept your instructor's limitations. He/she does not have to "entertain" you.**
- **Relate the course to your goals. "After this class, I can take a class in my major."**
- **Break long assignments into smaller parts.**
- **Set specific study goals for a time block. (For example: finish reading three sections of chapter seven in the history text, or complete two math problems.)**
- **Study the least interesting subject first.**
- **Promise yourself a small reward for your concentrated study time.**
- **Talk about the problem with a friend or professional counselor.**

Proper rest, exercise, and nutrition are essential to maintaining a healthy body. Inattention to any of these three areas may result in fatigue and the decreased ability to concentrate. Eat well-balanced meals, include exercise as part of your daily routine, and allow enough time for rest and recreation.

Strategies to prevent fatigue:

- **Schedule study times when you are not tired.**
- **Eat well so you won't be hungry.**
- **Sign up for a physical education course.**

- **Exercise with a partner to increase motivation.**
- **Take advantage of the college/university exercise facilities.**

Causes of poor concentration can also include lack of academic, listening, or note-taking skills. In this text, we list many suggestions to help you in these areas. If you identify your problem area, you can then decide to make changes. Start with a small change. Perhaps you will decide to study longer on a difficult subject. Start with a manageable time to give you success, then increase the time gradually. Be sure to reward yourself for each gain.

What are External and Internal Distractors?

A learner must be able to cope with internal and external distractors before starting to concentrate and learn.

Internal Distractors

Any form of negative self-talk is an internal distractor. In order to concentrate, your mind must be quiet and controlled. Sometimes a small voice inside that should be full of confidence blurts out, "You are probably going to say something stupid," and, sure enough, this proves to be true. But luckily, there is also another voice hiding in there. You feel confident and knowledgeable about what you are about to say, and it comes out right! These inside voices determine to a great extent the "tone" of your world—whether it is good, bad, or indifferent. We can change how we feel by what we say to ourselves.

Negative self-talk can be produced by insecurity, fear, anxiety, frustration, defeatist attitudes, indecision, an ger, daydreams, and personal problems. This self-talk is obviously influenced by your feelings. If your self-talk seems to lean more on the negative side, you are not alone! Richard Fenker says 80–90 percent of students with learning problems have self-talk that is predominantly negative. Fenker believes you can control these negative voices using your right brain and substituting more positive self-talk. If you are afraid of speaking in public, imagine yourself giving a report in front of a class. If you have test anxiety, imagine or picture yourself being relaxed and calm in that testing situation. Spend a few days listening to yourself. When a negative opinion surfaces, try to replace it with a neutral or a positive thought!

What Internal Distractors Affect You?

Take a look at the following list of internal distractors. Do any of these distractors seem to be a problem for you? If so, note the possible answer for this distractor.

Please note that some of these distractors can be eliminated if you anticipate your needs!

Hunger	Eat before you study.
Fatigue	Plan study time when you are most alert and get at least 7 to 8 hours of sleep. Don't forget some exercise!
Illness	Postpone until you feel better.
Worrying about grades or work	Try to focus on the task and better grades will be the result. Focus on work while you are at work.

(Continued)

Hunger	Eat before you study.
Stress	Attempt to focus on what you are trying to accomplish.
Physical discomfort	Study in a comfortable place.
Not understanding assignment	Always clarify assignments before you start.
Personal problems	Make a note of the problem and tell yourself you will cope after you study.
Lack of interest	Try studying with someone else, find something that you can relate to, or look at related material.
Negative attitude	Remember negative thoughts take away from getting a job done! Convince yourself there is something positive in the class.

External Distractors

External distractors originate outside of you. They are those things that draw your attention away from a learning task.

Take a look at the following list of external distractors. Do some of them seem familiar? Many of these problems can also be eliminated if you anticipate your needs.

Lack of proper materials	Before you start your study session, have paper, pencil, etc. in place.
Music, television, noise, lighting too bright or too dim, temperature too high or too low, people talking, telephone	Choose your study location carefully. These should be eliminated by just choosing a proper spot.
Party or activity that you want to attend, family or friends wanting you to do something	If possible, plan your study session ahead of activity and use it as a reward.

Why Is a "Place of Study" So Important?

By looking at internal and external distractors, you can see how many can be controlled by the place you choose to study. It is important to have a definite and permanent place to study. Psychologists believe a conditioning effect is created between your desk and you. Do not do any other activities at your study desk. You should associate your study place with studying alone. Don't write letters, daydream, plan activities, or visit with friends in your study place. You need a study place where you feel comfortable and where you are likely to have few distractions.

What are Some Strategies to Strengthen Concentration?

1. **Learn to beat boredom**—If boredom is causing a problem with concentration, study in small groups occasionally, buy review manuals and workbooks, and look at the material from a different angle. Perhaps a tutor could provide new insights.
2. **Become more active in studying**—Highlight, underline, make questions out of the material, paraphrase, construct mnemonics, and/or form imagery associations. Think about your learning style and put it to work.
3. **Ignore external distractions**—A vibrating tuning fork held close to a spider's web sets up vibrations in the web. After the spider makes a few investigations and doesn't find dinner, it learns to ignore the vibrations. If a spider can control external distractors, a student should be able to eventually ignore external distractions.

AFTER (A)

Memory works with other college study skills (i.e., critical thinking, time management) and needs to be *reviewed, revised,* and *self-modified* as needed.

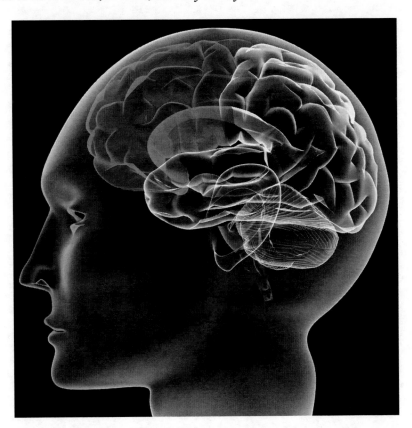

- Have I developed an intent to remember?
- Do I have enough time built into my schedule for daily, weekly, and major reviews?
- How am I eliminating internal and external distractions?
- Do I have a designated study area?
- What changes can I make to what I am doing now that will help me to remember?

SUMMARY

Retrieving information from long-term memory is a complicated process, but we can use memory strategies to help you "remember" the necessary information. Keeping the four principles of learning in mind—intent to remember, meaningfulness, organization of information, and spaced learning—will help us process information for better retention and retrieval. You were also introduced to barriers to concentration and how to handle internal and external distractors. It is clear that you, the student, are in charge of your memory, and that practicing these memory strategies can make a difference in your academic success.

SUGGESTED READINGS

Buzan, Tony. *Use Your Perfect Memory.* New York: Penguin Books, 1991.

Eprile, Tony. *The Persistence of Memory.* New York: Norton & Co., 2004.

Lorayne, Harry. *How to Develop a Super-power Memory.* New York: Frederick Fell, 1997.

Lorayne, Harry, and Jerry Lucas. *The Memory Book.* New York: Ballantine Publishing Group, 1974.

EXERCISE 6.1: YOUR MEMORY

Answer yes or no to the following questions:

		YES	NO
1.	Do you intend to remember your course work?	_____	_____
2.	Do you try to get interested in your classes?	_____	_____
3.	Do you honestly focus your full attention while studying?	_____	_____
4.	Do you review lecture and textbook notes once a week or more?	_____	_____
5.	Do you use organization in your study sessions?	_____	_____
6.	Do you study in short spaced (45–50 minutes) sessions with breaks?	_____	_____
7.	Do you keep an open mind when being introduced to new material?	_____	_____
8.	Do you recite material you are trying to remember?	_____	_____
9.	Do you make an effort to understand the material, not just read it?	_____	_____
10.	Do you use several methods to reinforce memory, i.e., reciting, discussing with friends, and effective note taking?	_____	_____

If you answer yes to 7 or more of these, you are on the right track! If you have 3 or more no answers, you need to evaluate your study habits.

Journal
Use your critical thinking skills and information you learned about yourself through self-assessment to develop a plan to take charge of your memory. Write a brief paragraph explaining what you intend to start doing to develop your memory.

_____

_____

_____

_____

_____

_____

_____

EXERCISE 6.2: CREATING A MIND MAP

Create a mind map of the textbook chapter on Geography used in Chapter 3 which appears on pages 100–104.

EXERCISE 6.3: CONCENTRATION WORKSHEET

During your next study session, keep a record of internal and external distractors. On the chart below, write what the distractor was. After your study session, determine whether the distractor was internal or external. Write a brief solution.

Distraction	External/Internal	Solution
1.		
2.		
3.		
4.		
5.		
6.		
7.		
8.		
9.		
10.		

(continued)

When considering the solutions—how many do you feel you can control? Write a brief paragraph explaining how you can possibly prevent these distractions.

_____

_____

_____

_____

_____

_____

_____

_____

_____

_____

_____

_____

_____

_____

_____

_____

_____

_____

_____

_____

NAME: _____ DATE: _____

EXERCISE 6.4: STUDY AREA ANALYSIS

List the three places you use most frequently for studying:

A. _____

B. _____

C. _____

Now check the column that applies to each of these places:
T = True F = False

	Place A		Place B		Place C	
1. Other people often interrupt me.	T	F	T	F	T	F
2. The environment reminds me of things not related to studying.	T	F	T	F	T	F
3. I can often hear radio or TV.	T	F	T	F	T	F
4. I can often hear the phone ringing.	T	F	T	F	T	F
5. I take too many breaks.	T	F	T	F	T	F
6. I seem to be especially bothered by distractions.	T	F	T	F	T	F
7. My breaks tend to be long.	T	F	T	F	T	F
8. I tend to start conversations.	T	F	T	F	T	F
9. Temperature conditions are ideal.	T	F	T	F	T	F
10. Chair, table, and lighting arrangements are not conducive to studying.	T	F	T	F	T	F

Journal: By analyzing my study areas, I learned that . . .

_____

_____

_____

_____

_____

_____

_____

_____

_____

Chapter 7

Reading – Do I Have To?

INTRODUCTION

You may have arrived on campus feeling confident in your academic reading skills. Having a reading section in this book may appear unnecessary to you. Reading in your high school courses may have varied, from being able to pass the class without looking at the text, to required reading of several texts, novels, or supplemental readings. You may have heard rumors that college reading is "different," however, the only problem you currently anticipate is the expense of the text.

Often, by mid-semester, students realize why college reading may require more skills than they previously had to demonstrate. This chapter explains active study/reading approaches to textbooks that will involve you in using your textbooks to gain information. College classes usually require a text, often expensive, and reading assignments that must be completed in order to pass the class. You may find the text difficult to comprehend. The reading assignments contain more facts and ideas per page and are written at a higher reading level than high school texts. In fifteen weeks, you may have to be responsible for the amount of information you covered in an entire year in high school. The chart in Figure 7.1 lists common reading problems and suggested study strategies to help you with this area.

Causes of Reading Problems	Active Reading Strategies
1. Lack of motivation.	• Evaluate your reading purpose, your background knowledge, your interest in the material, and the difficulty of the reading. • Do the most difficult reading first. • Arrange your schedule so that you read at your most productive study time. • Find a way to personalize the information. • Join a study group, divide the reading responsibility so that each person creates a summary and study guide for the group.
2. Lack of background knowledge and understanding of the subject.	• Skim the chapter headings, pictures, charts, graphs, and diagrams. • Read the summary or conclusion first. • Get a tutor to explain difficult concepts. • Form a study group to discuss topics.
3. Inability to concentrate.	• Formulate a purpose for reading. • Practice a study strategy. • Annotate the text. • Look for signal words to follow the organization of the text. • Break the reading time into manageable blocks.
4. Frustration with inability to recall the information.	• Make connections between old and new information. • Review the main concepts daily. • Create study guides that reflect the type of test for that class.
5. Course and textbook contain difficult vocabulary and terminology.	• Make a course vocabulary notebook or 3x5 card system, listing new words and definitions. • Review the vocabulary daily. • Learn common prefixes, suffixes, and root words to help you build your vocabulary. • Use color to highlight similarities and differences in word parts.

Figure 7.1 Reading Comprehension Problems and Strategies.

Active study reading is not "speed-reading." Research has shown that speed-reading is only effective when you are reading information that you already know and understand. What students do need are active reading/study strategies and a flexible reading rate. In some instances, you will be able to speed up your reading, but often new information requires more than one reading and an interactive approach. Active reading strategies involve you in the reading process, so that you are able to effectively read and comprehend the material in the textbook. With the use of time management skills, concentration techniques, and study strategies, you can feel in charge of all the reading required in college.

WHAT AFFECTS READING COMPREHENSION?

You should check your readiness to comprehend textbook material by identifying your **Purpose, Background, Interest, and Difficulty (PBID)**. Assessing yourself in each area, then developing strategies to improve each area, will help you read effectively. You will be able to recall and use the information from the textbook.

Purpose

Students often sit down to read with only the thought that they have to "study" this chapter and hopefully retain "something." Take a minute to identify the purpose of the reading, that is, what is your reason for reading the textbook? Textbooks are read for different reasons:

- To build background knowledge so you can understand the lecture.
- To add supplemental information to your class notes.
- To learn details, such as the classification of types of rock or the time sequence of events that led up to the Civil War.
- To be prepared for a class discussion: the causes of the Civil War and the effect it had on the future politics of the South.
- To understand principles, processes, and concepts, such as Mendel's Law of Genetics, Newton's Three Laws of Motion, or the properties of real numbers.

How do you know the purpose of the text for each class?

1. Read the syllabus, and pay careful attention to the relationship between the reading assignments and the class topics.
2. Talk to the instructor.
3. Talk to other students who have had the class or are in class with you. Find out how they used, or are using, the text for the class.
4. If Supplemental Instruction sessions are available for the class, attend, and the SI leader will model how to use the textbook.

Background

Your reading comprehension is strongly affected by your background knowledge or what you already know about the subject. This is why:

- If you have high knowledge of the subject, it may be easier for you to read the material. You will be able to meet your purpose quicker than if the information is totally new to you.

- If your knowledge of the subject is low, you will have to build up your knowledge base. Some lectures are intended to build background before attempting textbook reading. However, you will often be expected to do this on your own. Time management becomes a factor, as you may have to reread your text three times to build up enough knowledge to comprehend the information.

How do you check your background for reading?

1. Before reading the chapter, skim the chapter headings, pictures, charts, graphs, and diagrams.
2. Read the summary and think about what you know about the subject.
3. Read the syllabus, and mark the topics that you know something about.
4. Review your notes, and look for connections between the lecture and the reading.
5. Discuss new information with other students in a study group or at a Supplemental Instruction (SI) session. This will enhance your knowledge base and help you comprehend the information.

Interest

Students often complain that they don't like to read the text because it is not interesting. In many cases this is a true statement, but it doesn't remove the fact that in many classes, if you do not read the text, you will not pass the class. If you avoid the text because of lack of interest, then you need to take some action to make the reading bearable for that semester.

How do you create interest in what you need to read?

1. Break your reading session into small time units: twenty minutes of concentrated reading, then a small break, then twenty minutes more of focused reading.
2. Create questions before you read. Pretend they are real test questions, and you must know the answers to pass the class.
3. Use a specific reading strategy, such as SQ4R, to keep focused.
4. Do something with the information as you read the text. Write lists or notes in the margins. Create a picture of the information in your mind. Write an outline or draw pictures of the process.
5. Share the reading with study partners. Divide up the chapter into sections, and make each student responsible for reading and teaching the concepts from their section to the other members of the group. Be aware that the section you learn best will be the one that you teach.
6. Talk to the instructor and ask questions about the subject matter. Ask him/her for advice about how to read and comprehend the text. The instructor may say something to spark your interest.
7. Reward yourself for reading and studying material that is not interesting to you.

Difficulty

The difficulty of the reading material can encourage or discourage a student from reading and studying the text. Sometimes the format of the text is more difficult than the actual course material. You have little control over the choice of the text, but you do have options if the reading is difficult.

How do you cope with difficult reading material?

1. Think again about your purpose for reading, your prior knowledge of the subject, and your interest in the course and material. Are any of these factors making the reading difficult? Reread the suggestions in this section and the reading solutions chart in Figure 7.1.

2. Get a tutor for the class or attend Supplemental Instruction sessions. At these sessions, difficult information is explained and discussed. This may make the reading less complex and more interesting.

3. Read another text that is on the same subject, but is written in a different style or at a different reading level. You can check out textbooks at the library.

BEFORE (B)

College textbook reading strategies involve the following *preparation, self-awareness, and planning* strategies:

- **Evaluate concentration level and environment**
- **Assess organizational structure of text and course**
- **Preview the text**
- **Ask preview questions**
- **Make predictions about the reading passage**
- **Set reading goals**
- **Activate prior knowledge**

EVALUATE CONCENTRATION LEVEL AND ENVIRONMENT

Reading a college textbook is not the same as reading a magazine, comic book, or novel; text messages from your friends; or tweets on Twitter/messages on Facebook. In order to get the most from your reading, you should assess your concentration level and your environment. As mentioned in the previous chapter, you must give the material your complete and focused attention.

How Do You Improve Concentration while Reading?

Dr. Walter Pauk, noted study skills expert, believes the best way to gain and maintain concentration while you read is by having a lively conversation with the author. (No one will have to know!) Agree or disagree with the author. Interject your thoughts and ideas. This will also lead to more comprehension.

One reason your mind may wander during reading is because material is unfamiliar or too difficult. You cannot concentrate on what you can't comprehend. Formulate a purpose for reading! It also never hurts to look up words when you do not know the meanings!

You should also assess your environment. As mentioned in the previous chapter, it is important to have an area devoted to studying—in this case, reading. Your reading area should be a place where you are comfortable and likely to have few distractions.

ASSESS ORGANIZATIONAL STRUCTURE OF TEXT AND COURSE

Before* jumping into your assigned reading, look at how it fits into the overall organizational structure of the book and course. You can do this efficiently by taking a quick look at the book's table of contents to see where the chapter you're about to read is placed in the overall sequence of chapters, especially its relation to chapters that immediately precede and follow it. Using, this strategy will give you a sense of how the particular part you're focusing on connects with the bigger picture. Research shows that if learners gain access to advanced knowledge of how information they're about to learn is organized—if they see how its parts relate to the whole—*before* they attempt to start learning the specific parts, they're better able to comprehend and retain the material (Ausubel, Novak, & Hanesian, 1978; Mayer, 2003). Thus, the first step toward improving reading comprehension and retention of a book chapter is to see how it relates to the whole book before you begin to examine the chapter part by part.

PREVIEW THE TEXT

Just as the preview for a movie gives you an idea of what the movie is about, previewing the text you will be reading gives you an idea of what the chapter is about. When you preview, take a look at the following:

- *Chapter outline*
- *Objectives*
- *Headings*
- *Subheadings*
- *Graphics*
- *Chapter summary*
- *Questions at the end of the chapter*

Preview the chapter you're about to read, by reading its boldface headings and any chapter outline, objectives, summary, or end-of-chapter questions that may be included. Before jumping right into the content, get in the habit of previewing what's in a chapter to gain an overall sense of its organization. If you dive into the specific details first, you lose sight of how the smaller details relate to the larger picture. The brain's natural tendency is to perceive and comprehend whole patterns rather than isolated bits of information. Start by seeing how the parts of the chapter are integrated into the whole. This will enable you to better connect the separate pieces of information you encounter while you read, similar to seeing the whole picture of a completed jigsaw puzzle before you start assembling is pieces.

* From *Thriving in College and Beyond: Research-Based Strategies for Academic Success and Personal Development* by Jospeh B. Cuseo, Aaron Thompson, Michele Campagna, and Viki S. Fecas. Copyright © 2013 by Kendall Hunt Publishing Company. Reprinted by permission.

ASK PREVIEW QUESTIONS

In order to help you focus your reading, it is important to ask preview questions. Preview questions can be formed by turning the headings and subheadings into questions. Use the journalism questions: Who? What? When? Where? Why? How? For instance, using the sample Geography 152 textbook chapter (pp. 100–104), you could turn the bold-faced headers into the following questions:

- *What is the Koppen System?*
- *What is geography of climates?*
- *Where are the humid tropical climates?*
- *Where are the dry climates?*

MAKE PREDICTIONS ABOUT THE READING PASSAGE

Based on what you already know about the subject you are reading (your prior knowledge), what do you think the text is going to be about? Make your predictions about the reading passage.

SET READING GOALS

As you know, goals are connected to time management. Just as you have educational and career goals, you should have reading goals. Say you are a Nursing major and you are taking Anatomy & Physiology. On the first day of class, the instructor assigns you to read the 1st chapter which has 50 pages. In addition to attending college, you may also work, have children, and have other commitments on your time. How will you divide this reading task into manageable chunks so that 1) you complete the assigned reading and 2) you understand what you read? When dividing the chapter, make sure you stop at the end of a section. You can use post-it notes or paper clips to help you divide the chapter.

The following chart will help you set reading goals:

# of pages I will read:	When I will read these pages (day/time)

You should also log this information in your planner.

ACTIVATE PRIOR KNOWLEDGE

Much of the information that you learned in the Memory chapter will help you when you are reading. You can only learn new information when you connect it to something you already know. Ask yourself, what do I already know about this subject/topic?

Also, it is easier for the brain to learn new information when you help it organize the information where it should be stored.

DURING (D)

Reading college textbooks requires the following *actions* while you are reading:

- **Read selectively to find important info**
- **Take written notes on what you're reading**
- **Pause periodically to summarize and paraphrase what you're reading in your own words**
- **Answer metacognition questions**
- **Use elaboration strategies**
- **Highlight and annotate the text**
- **Follow the organization/thought patterns of the text**
- **Read and interpret graphics**
- **Determine the meaning of new vocabulary**

READ SELECTIVELY TO FIND IMPORTANT INFORMATION

Rather* than jumping into reading and randomly highlighting, effective reading begins with a plan or goal for identifying what should be noted and remembered. Here are three strategies to use while reading to help you determine what information should be noted and retained.

- **Use boldface or dark print headings and subheadings as cues for identifying important information.** These headings organize the chapter's major points; thus, you can use them as "traffic signs" to direct you to the most important information in the chapter. Better yet turn the headings to questions and then read to find answers to these questions. This question-and-answer strategy will ensure that you read actively and with a purpose. (You can set up this strategy when you preview the chapter by placing a question mark after each heading contained in the chapter.) Creating and answering questions while you read also keeps you motivated; the questions help simulate your curiosity and finding answer to them serves to reward or reinforce your reading (Walter, Knudsbig, & Smith, 2003). Lastly, answering questions about what you're reading is an effective way to prepare for tests because you're practicing exactly what you'll be expected to do on exams—answering questions. You can quickly write the heading questions on separate index cards and use them as flash cards to review for exams. Use the question on the flash card as a way to flash back and trigger your recall of information from the text that answers the question.
- **Pay special attention to words that are *italicized*, <u>underlined</u>, or appear in boldface print**. These are usually signs for building-block terms that must be understood and built on before you can proceed to understand higher-level concepts covered later in the reading. Don't simply highlight these words because their special appearance suggests they are important. Read these terms carefully and be sure you understand their meaning before you continue reading.
- **Pay special attention to the first and last sentences in each paragraph.** These sentences contain an important introduction and conclusion to the ideas covered in the paragraph. It's a good idea to reread the first and last sentences of each paragraph before you move on to the next paragraph, particularly when reading sequential or cumulative material (e.g., science or math) that requires full comprehension of what was previously covered to understand what will be covered next.

Reread your chapter notes and highlights after you've listened to your instructor lecture on the material contained in the chapter. You can use your lecture notes as a guide to help you focus on what information in the chapter your instructor feels is most important. If you adopt this strategy, your reading before lectures will help you understand the lecture and take better class notes, and your reading after lectures will help you locate and learn information in the textbook that your instructor is emphasizing in class—which is likely to be the information your instructor thinks is most important and is most likely to show up on your exams. Thus, it's a good idea to have your class notes nearby when you're completing your reading assignments to help you identify what you should pay special attention to while reading.

Remember

Your goal when reading is not merely to cover the assigned pages, but to uncover the most important information and ideas contained on those pages.

TAKE WRITTEN NOTES ON WHAT YOU'RE READING

Just as you should take notes in class you should take notes in response to the author's words in the text. Writing requires more active thinking than highlighting because you're creating your own words rather than passively highlighting words written by somebody else, Don't get into the habit of using your textbook as a coloring book in which the artistic process of highlighting what you're reading with spectacular kaleidoscopic colors distracts you from the more important process of learning actively and thinking deeply.

If you can express what someone else has written in words that make sense to you, this means that you're relating it to what you already know—a sign of deep learning (Demmert & Towner, 2003). A good time to pause and summarize what you've read in your own words is when you encounter a boldface heading, because this indicates you've just completed reading about a major concept and are about to begin a new one.

> **Remember**
>
> *Effective reading isn't a passive process of covering pages: it's an active process in which you uncover meaning in the pages you read.*

* From *Thriving in College and Beyond: Research-Based Strategies for Academic Success and Personal Development* by Jospeh B. Cuseo, Aaron Thompson, Michele Campagna, and Viki S. Fecas. Copyright © 2013 by Kendall Hunt Publishing Company. Reprinted by permission.

PAUSE PERIODICALLY TO SUMMARIZE AND PARAPHRASE WHAT YOU'RE READING IN YOUR OWN WORDS

If you can express what someone else has written in words that make sense to you, this means that you understand what you're reading and can relate it to what you already know—which is a telltale sign of deep learning (Demmert & Towner, 2003). A good time to pause and paraphrase is when you encounter a boldface heading that indicates you're about to be introduced to a new concept. This may be the ideal place to stop and summarize what you read in the section you just completed.

ANSWER METACOGNITION QUESTIONS

Metacognition is "thinking about your thinking" by asking yourself the following questions as your read:

5 Questions Designed to Stimulate Metacognitive Thinking While Reading

When you come to the end of a sentence, or punctuation in a complex sentence, stop and ask yourself:

1. **Do I understand what I just read?**
2. **What do I already know about what I just read?**
3. **Can I say it in my own words?**
4. **Can I think of another example?**
5. **Is it important enough to put in my notes (or to map, to chart, or to use another organizational tool)?**

Strategies to Help Metacognition and Comprehension

1. **Divide reading into manageable chunks.** When previewing decide places that would provide good breaks. Try to read in 15–20 minute blocks. Take a break, get up, stretch, let your mind relax a minute and then begin again. Overall comprehension is better using this strategy.
2. **Stop and ask yourself questions as you read.** Can you say it in your own words, do you understand it, what do you know about it, should you include this in your map—What can you do if you don't understand or cannot say it in your own words?
3. **Organize the information.** Look how the ideas are structured, identify main ideas and supporting details, compare and contrast information, and create maps.
4. **Elaborations.** Help to store the information so that you can recall it and work with it.

USE ELABORATION STRATEGIES

Elaborations are thinking strategies designed to help you tie new information to information you already know. These thinking processes make new information "meaningful" and therefore useful. What are the elaboration strategies you should use as you read?

- *Answer preview questions—While you are reading, your brain will automatically start to answer the preview questions. Stay focused so that you can answer the questions.*
- *Ask deeper level questions about the reading—These are the metacognition questions (see previous section) that ensure your understanding of the text.*
- *Talk about the material with yourself—Always have a conversation going on in your head about what you are reading. This is a very powerful way for your brain to connect new information to information already stored in the brain. It is also a powerful memory strategy.*
- *Compare and contrast—Think about how what you are learning is similar to and different from what you already know. This is one of the key strategies for understanding what you are reading, being able to recall it later, and for being able to use the information.*
- *Visualize—Create mental pictures of everything you are learning.*
- *Transform—Take the time to create a visual map of the information you are learning. Anytime you change the shape of the information you are learning (i.e., creating a visual map and using pictures in the visual map; creating a diagram; creating lyrics (song, rap) or poems), the brain really works to store the information.*
- *Explain the material in your own words—The single most powerful elaboration strategy for improving memory of what you are learning is to "say it in your own words, out loud." Many studies on memory have found that changing headings and subheadings into questions, reading to answer those questions, and saying the answer to those questions in your own words as you find them improved memory of that information. Without using this information, the average student remembers about 20% after two weeks. Students who use this strategy remember around 80%.*

HIGHLIGHT AND ANNOTATE (MARK) THE TEXT

To learn how to highlight textbooks effectively, start with the following guidelines.

1. **Read first; then highlight.** As you are reading to develop skill in highlighting, it is better to read a paragraph or section first and then go back and highlight what is important to remember and review. Later, when you've had more practice highlighting, you may be able to highlight while you read.

2. **Read the boldface headings.** Headings are labels, or overall topics, for what is contained in that section. Use the headings to form questions that you expect to be answered in the section.

3. **After you have read the section, go back and highlight the parts that answer your questions.** These will be parts of sentences that express the main ideas, or most important thoughts, in the section. In reading and highlighting the following section, you could form questions like those suggested and then highlight as shown.

Questions to Ask

What are primary groups?

What are secondary groups?

PRIMARY AND SECONDARY GROUPS

It is not at all surprising that some students used their families as a reference group. After all, families are the best examples of the groups Charles Cooley (1909) called *primary* chiefly because they "are fundamental in forming the social nature and ideals of the individual." In a primary group the individuals interact informally, relate to each other as whole persons, and enjoy their relationship for its own sake. This is one of the two main types of social groups. In the other type, a secondary group, the individuals interact formally, relate to each other as players of particular roles, and expect to profit from each other.

—Thio, *Sociology,* p. 100

---

4. **As you identify and highlight main ideas, look for important facts that explain or support the main idea, and highlight them too.**

5. **When highlighting main ideas and details, do not highlight complete sentences.** Highlight only enough so that you can see what is important and so that your highlighting makes sense when you reread. Note how only key words and phrases are highlighted in the following passage.

CAUSES OF HOMELESSNESS

The causes of homelessness can be categorized into two types: larger social forces and personal characteristics. One social force is the shortage of inexpensive housing for poor families and poor unattached persons. This shortage began in the 1970s and accelerated in the 1980s. Another social force is the decreasing demand for unskilled labor in the 1980s, which resulted in extremely high unemployment among young men in general and blacks in particular. A third social force is the erosion of public welfare benefits over the last two decades. These three social forces do not directly cause homelessness. They merely enlarge the ranks of the extremely poor, thereby increasing the chances of these people becoming homeless.

—Thio, *Sociology,* p. 232

ASPECTS OF EFFECTIVE HIGHLIGHTING

For your highlighting to be effective and useful to you as you study and review, it must follow four specific guidelines.

1. *The right amount of information must be highlighted.*
2. *The highlighting must be regular and consistent.*

3. *It must be accurate.*
4. *It must clearly reflect the content of the passage.*

Suggestions for implementing these guidelines and examples of each are given in the following paragraphs.

Highlight the Right Amount

Students frequently make the mistake of highlighting either too much or too little. If you highlight too much, the passages you have marked will take you too long to reread when you are studying later. If you highlight too little, you won't be able to get any meaning from your highlighting as you review it.

TOO MUCH HIGHLIGHTING

Iran, which had served as an area of competition between the British and the Russians since the nineteenth century, became a bone of contention between the United States and the Soviet Union after World War II. As the result of an agreement between the British and the Russians in 1941, Shah Mohammad Reza Pahlavi (1919–1980) gained the Iranian throne. After the war he asked foreign troops to withdraw from his country, but following the slow return of the Soviet army to its borders, aggressive activities of the Iranian Communist party (Tudeh), and an assassination attempt on the Shah's life, Iran firmly tied itself to the West.

—Wallbank et al., *Civilization Past and Present,* pp. 1012–1013

TOO LITTLE HIGHLIGHTING

Iran, which had served as an area of competition between the British and the Russians since the nineteenth century, became a bone of contention between the United States and the Soviet Union after World War II. As the result of an agreement between the British and the Russians in 1941, Shah Mohammad Reza Pahlavi (1919–1980) gained the Iranian throne. After the war he asked foreign troops to withdraw from his country, but following the slow return of the Soviet army to its borders, aggressive activities of the Iranian Communist party (Tudeh), and an assassination attempt on the Shah's life, Iran firmly tied itself to the West.

EFFECTIVE HIGHLIGHTING

Iran, which had served as an area of competition between the British and the Russians since the nineteenth century, became a bone of contention between the United States and the Soviet Union after World War II. As the result of an agreement between the British and the Russians in 1941, Shah Mohammad Reza Pahlavi (1919–1980) gained the Iranian throne. After the war he asked foreign troops to withdraw from his country, but following the slow return of the Soviet army to its borders, aggressive activities of the Iranian Communist party (Tudeh), and an assassination attempt on the Shah's life, Iran firmly tied itself to the West.

Almost all of the first passage is highlighted. To highlight nearly all of the passage is as ineffective as not highlighting at all, because it does not distinguish important from unimportant information. In the second passage, only the main point of the paragraph is highlighted, but very sketchily—not enough detail is included. The highlighting in the third passage is effective; it identifies the main idea of the paragraph and includes enough details to make the main idea clear and understandable.

As a rule of thumb, try to highlight no more than one-quarter to one-third of each page. This figure will vary, of course, depending on the type of material you are reading.

DEVELOP A REGULAR AND CONSISTENT SYSTEM OF HIGHLIGHTING

As you develop your textbook highlighting skills, you should focus on this second guideline: Develop a system for deciding what type of information you will highlight and how you will mark it. First, decide what type of information you want to mark. Before marking anything, decide whether you will mark only main ideas or mark main ideas and details. You should also decide whether you will highlight or mark definitions of new terminology and, if so, how you will distinguish them from other information marked in the paragraph. Second, it is important to use consistently whatever system and type of highlighting you decide on so that you will know what your highlighting means when you review it. If you sometimes mark details and main ideas and other times highlight only main ideas, at review time you will find that you are unsure of what passages are marked in what way, and you will be forced to reread a great deal of material.

You may decide to develop a system for separating main ideas from details, major points from supporting information. When you review highlighting done this way, you will immediately know what is the most important point of the paragraph or section, and you will not get bogged down in the details—unless you need to. One such system uses one color of marker for main points and a different color for details. Another approach is to use asterisks and brackets to call attention to the main points.

HIGHLIGHT ACCURATELY

A third guideline for marking textbooks is to be sure that the information you highlight accurately conveys the content of the paragraph or passage. In a rush, students often overlook the second half of the main idea expressed in a paragraph, miss a crucial qualifying statement, or mistake an example or (worse yet) a contrasting idea for the main idea. Read the following paragraph and evaluate the accuracy of the highlighting.

It has long been established that the American legal court system is an open and fair system. Those suspected to be guilty of a criminal offense are given a jury trial in which a group of impartially selected citizens are asked to determine, based upon evidence presented, the guilt or innocence of the person on trial. In actuality, however, this system of jury trial is fair to everyone except the jurors involved. Citizens are expected and, in many instances, required to sit on a jury. They have little or no choice as to the time, place, or any other circumstances surrounding their participation. Additionally, they are expected to leave their job and accept jury duty pay for each day spent in court in place of their regular on-the-job salary. The jury must remain on duty until the case is decided.

In the preceding paragraph, the highlighting indicates that the main idea of the paragraph is that the legal system that operates in American courts is open and fair. The paragraph starts out by saying that the legal system has long been established as fair, but then it goes on to say (in the third sentence) that the system is actually unfair to one particular group—the jury. In this case, the student who did the highlighting missed the real main statement of the paragraph by mistaking the introductory contrasting statement for the main idea.

MAKE YOUR HIGHLIGHTING UNDERSTANDABLE FOR REVIEW

As you highlight, keep the fourth guideline in mind: Be certain that your highlighting clearly reflects the content of the passage so that you will be able to reread and review it easily. Try to highlight enough information in each passage so that the passage reads smoothly when you review it.

Read these two examples of highlighting of the same passage. Which highlighting is easier to reread?

VERSION 1

Capital may be thought of as manufactured resources. Capital includes the tools and equipment that strengthen, extend, or replace human hands in the production of goods and services. Hammers, sewing machines, turbines, bookkeeping machines, and component parts of finished goods—all are capital goods. Even the specialized skills of trained workers can be thought of as a kind of human capital. Capital resources permit "roundabout" production: producing goods indirectly by a kind of tool rather than directly by physical labor.

To construct a capital resource requires that we postpone production of consumer goods and services today so that we can produce a tool that will enable us to produce more goods and services in the future. To postpone production of wanted goods and services is sometimes a painful decision, particularly when people are poor and in desperate need of goods and services today.

—McCarty, *Dollars and Sense*, pp. 213–214

VERSION 2

Capital may be thought of as manufactured resources. Capital includes the tools and equipment that strengthen, extend, or replace human hands in the production of goods and services. Hammers, sewing machines, turbines, bookkeeping machines, and component parts of finished goods—all are capital goods. Even the specialized skills of trained workers can be thought of as a kind of human capital. Capital resources permit "roundabout" production: producing goods indirectly with a kind of tool rather than directly by physical labor.

To construct a capital resource requires that we postpone production of other goods and services today so that we can produce a tool that will enable us to produce more goods and services in the future. To postpone production of wanted goods and services is sometimes a painful decision, particularly when people are poor and in desperate need of goods and services today.

A good way to check to see if your highlighting is understandable for review is to reread only your highlighting. If parts are unclear right after you read it, you can be sure it will be more confusing when you reread it a week or a month later. Be sure to fix ineffectual highlighting in one paragraph before you continue to the next paragraph.

TEST YOUR HIGHLIGHTING

As you are learning highlighting techniques, it is important to check to be certain that your highlighting is effective and will be useful for review purposes. To test the effectiveness of your highlighting, take any passage that you have highlighted and reread only the highlighting. Then ask yourself the following questions.

1. *Have I highlighted the right amount or do I have too much or too little information highlighted?*
2. *Have I used a regular and consistent system for highlighting?*
3. *Does my highlighting accurately reflect the meaning of the passage?*
4. *As I reread my highlighting, is it easy to follow the train of thought or does the passage seem like a list of unconnected words?*

ANNOTATE (MARK) A TEXTBOOK

Highlighting alone is not sufficient, in many cases, to separate main ideas from details and both of these from new terminology. You may have seen that highlighting does not easily show the relative importance of ideas or indicate the relationship between facts and ideas. Therefore, it is often necessary to annotate (mark), as well as highlight, selections that you are reading. Suggestions for annotating (marking) are shown in Figure 7.2.

When you highlight, you are operating at the knowledge and comprehension levels of thinking. Annotating (marking) is an opportunity to record your thinking at other levels.

Type of Annotating (Marking)		Example
Circling unknown words	*def*	. . . redressing the apparent (asymmetry) of their relationship . . .
Marking definitions	*def*	To say that the balance of power favors one party over another is to introduce a disequilibrium.
Marking examples	*ex*	. . . concessions may include negative sanctions, trade agreements . . .
Numbering lists of ideas, causes, reasons, or events		. . . components of power include self-image[1], population[2], natural resources[3], and geography[4]
Placing asterisks next to important passages	*	Power comes from three primary sources . . .
Putting question marks next to confusing passages	? →	. . . war prevention occurs through institutionalization of mediation . . .
Making notes to yourself	*check def in soc text*	. . . power is the ability of an actor on the international stage to . . .
Marking possible test items	*T*	There are several key features in the relationship . . .
Drawing arrows to show relationships		. . natural resources . . . control of industrial manufacturing capacity
Writing comments, noting disagreements and similarities	*Can terrorism be prevented through similar balance?*	. . . war prevention through balance of power is . . .
Marking summary statements	*sum*	. . . the greater the degree of conflict, the more intricate will be . . .

Figure 7.2 Textbook Annotating (Marking).

ANNOTATING (MARKING) AND LEVELS OF THINKING

Here are some examples of the kinds of marginal notes you might make.

Level of Thinking	Marginal Notes
Application	Jot notes about how to use the information.
Analysis	Draw arrows to link related material.
Synthesis	Record ideas about how topics fit together; make notes connecting material to lectures; condense ideas into your own words.
Evaluation	Comment on the worth, value, relevance, and timeliness of ideas.

WRITE SUMMARY NOTES

Writing summary words or phrases in the margin is one of the most valuable types of textbook annotating (marking). It involves pulling ideas together and summarizing them in your own words. This process forces you to think and evaluate as you read and makes remembering easier. Writing summary phrases is also a good test of your understanding. If you cannot state the main idea of a section in your own words, you probably do not understand it clearly. This realization can serve as an early warning signal that you may not be able to handle a test question on that section.

The following sample passage has been included to illustrate effective marking of summary phrases. First, read through the passage. Then look at the marginal summary clues.

CROSS-CULTURAL CONCLUSIONS

At this juncture, after analyzing organized crime in various societies, we may reach several conclusions about the subject.

hierarchical

First, organized crime is basically the same across societies in being a hierarchical organization that engages in crime activities. Organized crime differs from one society to another only in intraorganizational unity and criminal activities. Members' loyalty to the crime organization seems stronger in Japan and Hong Kong than in the United States and Italy today. The Hong Kong Triads engage in drug trafficking much more extensively than their counterparts in other countries. The Triads, along with their peers in Japan, Italy, and Russia, seem to have penetrated legitimate business and politics more deeply than the crime organizations in the United States.

not uniquely American

Second, there is no validity to the suggestion of Bell's well-known theory that organized crime is a uniquely American way for ambitious poor people in the United States to realize the American dream. There is nothing unique about American organized crime as a ladder of success for the ambitious poor. Organized crime serves the same function in other countries.

stronger outside U.S.

Third, organized crime is more pervasive, influential, or powerful in Italy, Japan, and Hong Kong than in the United States. The reason may be partly cultural in that organized crime in foreign countries is more socially acceptable and integrated into the legitimate world of business and politics. The reason may also be partly economic: the less mature the capitalism of a country is, the less controllable and hence more prevalent its organized crime is. This point shows most clearly in the contrast between the United States and Russia.

difficult to get rid of

Fourth, it is extremely difficult, if not impossible, to get rid of organized crime, as shown by the failure of anti-syndicate measures in various countries. This is particularly true in Japan and Hong Kong because of the underworld's deeper penetration into the conventional upperworld. By comparison, however, the American authorities are more successful in prosecuting mobsters, especially in recent years. Does this mean that we can ever hope to eradicate organized crime in the United States? Let us take closer look at this issue.

—Thio, *Deviant Behavior*, pp. 311–312

Summary notes are most effectively used in passages that contain long and complicated ideas. In these cases, it is simpler to write a summary phrase in the margin than to highlight a long or complicated statement of the main idea and supporting details.

To write a summary clue, try to think of a word or phrase that accurately states, in brief form, a particular idea presented in the passage. Summary words should trigger your memory of the content of the passage.

FOLLOW THE ORGANIZATION/THOUGHT PATTERNS OF THE TEXT

Making Sense of a Paragraph

The typical paragraph contains a topic sentence stating the author's major point, the body of the paragraph, consisting of one or more sentences providing supporting detail, and the conclusion, which restates the main idea or serves as a transition to the next paragraph.

Let's look at a paragraph from a college catalog discussing the Illinois Articulation Initiative:

Transferring to another institution is a complex process. In order to understand the process of course transferability, students should use two sources of data.	*Topic sentence* states the main idea.
First, students should consult the www.itransfer.org website for specific information about the General Education Core requirements and certain academic majors. Second, students should meet with a counselor or advisor to seek out information on how courses will be used when transferring to another institution. Once a student narrows down the choices of transfer institutions, s/he should consider how well his/her selected courses fit the requirements of the four-year college. While the approved IAI General Education Core Curriculum allows for completion of the transfer institution's lower level general education requirements, there are specific course selections in general education, the major, and electives, which can enhance the transfer process.	*Body* of sentences to support the main idea. *Conclusion* supports the point that course transfer is a complex process.

Not all paragraphs will contain a clearly stated topic sentence. Some may use a series of supporting sentences that lead to a conclusion. Try to identify topic sentences or main ideas as you read, and pay special attention to any conclusions drawn by the author.

When reading critically, try to identify whether the supporting detail provides facts or just the author's opinion. Try to restate the author's main idea in your own words.

READ AND INTERPRET GRAPHICS

Look at the visual aids provided in the textbook, such as charts, graphs, pictures, timelines, cartoons. Don't fall into the trap of thinking that visual aids can or should be skipped because they're merely secondary supplements to the written words in the body of the text Visual aids are powerful learning and memory tools for a couple of reasons:

1. they enable you to "see" the information in addition to reading (hearing) it.
2. they organize and connect separate pieces of information into an integrated whole.

Compare these visuals to the information in the text. What do you notice? Often, these visuals summarize the information in the text and help visual learners see them in a different way. Furthermore, this occasional change of sensory input brings variety to the reading process, which can recapture your attention and recharge your motivation

DETERMINE THE MEANING OF NEW VOCABULARY

When you see new words that you don't know the meaning of, it is important to use a dictionary and a thesaurus (print and/or online) to aid in your understanding of this new vocabulary. Many students put these words on 3x5 flashcards. However, to ensure you have a deeper understanding of the word meaning, you can use charts or vocabulary word maps, which typically ask for you to predict what the word means, define the word, use it meaningfully in a sentence, find the synonyms and/or antonyms, and even draw a picture.

AFTER (A)

Continue to *review, revise,* and *self-modify* your college textbook reading strategies as needed.

- **Determine what is important to learn**
- **Create study tools**
- **Compare reading notes with lecture notes**
- **Recite**
- **Review what you've read**
- **Locate other information sources**
- **Form discussion/study groups**

DETERMINE WHAT IS IMPORTANT TO LEARN

Now that you've read the textbook, what concepts or information are important to learn, to create a study tool, to review and remember for an exam, etc.? This will include information that answers your before and during reading questions.

CREATE STUDY TOOLS

Study tools eliminate the need to re-read the text. Study tools come in a variety of forms, such as:

- *Mind maps*
- *Diagrams*
- *Charts*
- *Outlines*
- *Cornell notes*

Use your preferred learning style to decide which study tool to create.

COMPARE READING NOTES WITH LECTURE NOTES

You should compare the notes you take in class with the notes you take from the readings. Ask yourself:

- *How closely does the instructor follow the textbook?*
- *Do I need to do additional research on the topic?*
- *Do I need to edit my notes (lecture and/or reading)?*
- *What information was presented in both the text and the lecture?*
- *What are the key concepts?*
- *What information could be a possible exam question?*
- *What information will I present to my study group?*
- *What information needs to be clarified?*

RECITE

One of the best ways to transfer information to long-term memory is to recite, say it out loud and in your own words. What will you recite? Your reading and lecture notes, answers to the preview and metacognition questions, study tools.

REVIEW WHAT YOU'VE READ

End a reading session with a short review of the information you've noted or highlighted. Most forgetting that takes place after you receive and process information occurs immediately after you stop focusing on the information/and turn your attention to another task (Baddeley, 1999; Underwood, 1983). Taking a few minutes at the end of your reading time to review the most important information works to lock that information into your memory before you turn your attention to something else and forget it.

Another powerful way to increase your memory is to complete periodic reviews of the text. Periodic reviews allow time to think about and organize the information you need to know. There are three (3) periodic review periods:

- *Daily reviews—review information from previous class (lecture notes, reading notes, visuals, etc.) and review your syllabus, textbook, and Blackboard for upcoming assignments.*
- *Weekly reviews—your weekly reviews are to help you get organized, develop your study tools, and practice reciting information.*
- *Exam reviews—your exam reviews are an extension of your daily and weekly reviews, and should be used to make sure you understand the deeper concepts and relationships*

that were presented in the readings and lectures; and for taking the time to develop practice exam questions and answer those questions so you feel confident for the test.

LOCATE OTHER INFORMATION SOURCES

For difficult-to-understand concepts, seek out other information sources. If you find you can't understand a concept explained in your text, even after rereading and repeatedly reflecting on it, try the following strategies:

- **Look at how another textbook explains it.** Not all textbooks are created equally: some do a better job of explaining certain concepts than others. Check to see whether your library has other texts in the same subject as your course, or check your campus bookstore for textbooks in the same subject area as the course you're taking. A different text may be able to explain a hard-to-understand concept much better than the textbook you purchased for the course.
- **Seek help from your instructor.** If you read carefully and made every effort to understand a particular concept but still can't grasp it, most instructors should be willing to assist you. If your instructor is unavailable or unwilling, seek help from the professionals and peer tutors in the Learning Center or Academic Support Center on campus.

FORM DISCUSSION/STUDY GROUPS

A good way to ensure that you understand the readings, have learned key information, and are prepared for exams and projects, is to form a discussion/study group. Keep the following tips in mind when you participate in discussion/study groups:

- *Conduct the discussion/study group like a meeting! Have an agenda; assign roles and action item; discuss team rules (what you will do if there is a slacker, etc.); know the topics you will discuss; and ask everyone to bring their planners to set up future meetings.*
- *Complete a dress rehearsal! If at all possible, have your meetings in the classroom so that you are prepared on the day of the exam. The environment will be a lot less intimidating.*
- *Reduce stress! Discussion/study groups are designed to reduce stress, not become another stressor. Make it engaging and a fun way to learn! Utilize different learning styles!*

SUMMARY

If "Do I Have To [Read]?" is your question, then this chapter answered with a resounding and emphatic "YES!" If your next question is to ask why you have to read, this chapter answered by explaining how reading is important to you as a student and as a professional in your field. If you're questioning how to get the most from your reading, the text answered by including strategies for reading college textbooks. The ultimate answer is this (to use an old cliché): reading truly is fundamental to your success.

SUGGESTED READINGS

Your college textbooks ☺
McWhorter, Kathleen. *College Reading and Study Skills.* 11th ed. New York: Pearson, 2010.

EXERCISE 7.1: THINKING ABOUT YOUR READING

Assigned reading: pages _____ (assigned by instructor)

Before You Read

Before reading, take a few minutes to analyze your active learning potential and answer the following questions:

Physical Environment

Where are you and what time is it?

What are your external distractions at this time?

Internal Distractions

What is popping into your mind and interfering with your concentration?

Spark Interest

Glance at the selection and predict what it will cover. What about it might be of interest to you?

What is the purpose of this selection?

Write down what you already know about the topics in this section after previewing.

(Continued)

Set Time Goals

How long do you think it will take you to read the selection? _____minutes
Record your starting time _____:_____

While You Read

Read for understanding. Then record your ending time and calculate how long it took you to read the assigned selection.

_____:_____ Ending time   Total reading time _____:_____

After You Read
Summary

Summarize what you read.

Evaluation

What adjustments did you make as you were reading?

Are there places where there are "blanks" in your understanding?

Concentration

Evaluate your concentration. How well did you do?

What could you have done differently?

What did you do well?

EXERCISE 7.2: LEARNING COLLABORATIVELY

DIRECTIONS: Your instructor will choose a reading and divide the class into two groups for an out-of-class assignment. One group should highlight the reading but make no other markings. The second group should both highlight and mark the reading. During the next class session, students may quiz each other to determine which group is better prepared for (1) an essay exam, (2) a multiple-choice exam, and (3) class discussion.

EXERCISE 7.3: WORD MAP - 8 STEPS TO LEARNING NEW VOCABULARY

http://www.rit.edu/~w-asc/documents/VocabularyStrategies.pdf

College textbooks often include unfamiliar terminology and vocabulary. When you locate a word that you cannot determine the meaning from context, use the word map on the link above which contains 8 steps to learning new words:

Chapter 8

Listening and Note Taking – Should I Write That Down?

Do I need to write this down?

—scene from every course ever taken throughout academic history

INTRODUCTION

Perhaps you have not been concerned about your note taking skills in the past. You may have managed to get by without even taking notes. However, now that you are in college, your instructors will hold you responsible for knowing the course content and the concepts presented in class. Your tests may cover several chapters at a time. In some courses, the only tests are a midterm and a comprehensive final exam that includes material from the entire semester. It is difficult to remember everything that is said in class. That is why you need to have good notes.

Academically successful college students are not necessarily the most intelligent students in the class, but are students who use good study skills. Many students who made good grades without too much effort in high school don't do as well in college. Becoming a better notetaker is a big step toward increasing your success in the classroom. Developing good note taking skills requires **being prepared for class, actively listening** to the lecture material, **selecting a note taking style**, and learning to use your notes as a part of your total study system.

This chapter will help you check your note taking strengths and weaknesses and will introduce several note taking systems for you to try. You'll also learn how to identify your instructor's lecture style and to develop the note taking style that works best for you.

BEFORE (B)

In order to become a better note taker, you must complete *preparation, self-awareness,* and *planning* strategies as follows:

- **Analyze your current note taking skills**
- **Prepare yourself to take notes**
- **Plan to become an active listener**

Pre-test: Assessing Your Note Taking Skills

Check Yes or No for each item to describe your note taking habits	Yes	No
1. I check my course syllabus before each class to make sure I'm ready for each assignment.		
2. I read the text chapter(s) before class to make sure the lecture material will be familiar.		
3. I use a three-ring binder and loose-leaf paper for note taking.		
4. I review and edit my notes on a daily basis.		
5. I understand my notes when I look them over several days or weeks later.		
6. I take notes in my own words rather than trying to write down everything the instructor says.		
7. I use abbreviations and symbols so that I can note all of the important information.		
8. I make sure to include examples and all key information the instructor puts on the board.		
9. I leave enough space to fill in or add to my notes later.		
10. I pay attention in class even if the instructor wanders from the point or makes remarks with which I don't agree.		
11. I use my notes to think of possible test questions.		
12. I ask questions if I don't understand the material presented in class.		
13. I identify introductory and concluding statements and recognize transition words and phrases when the instructor is lecturing.		

Look over your responses to the pre-test. Can you honestly say that you practice most of these note taking habits? If not, use the information provided in this chapter to better your skills.

PREPARATION FOR NOTE TAKING

Preparation for note taking starts before you actually begin the class. When you purchase supplies at the beginning of the semester, don't buy a spiral notebook! Why not? Spiral notebooks are limiting; they don't offer the flexibility for using your notes in study sessions that a three-ring binder and loose-leaf paper will provide. In addition, write on only one side of the paper. Our sample notes provided later in this chapter will show you how to use your loose-leaf notes for test review.

Once you get to class and the lecture starts, you have to decide quickly what information needs to be recorded. In addition to having read the material ahead of time, you need to be able to follow the instructor's lecture. S/he will use *verbal and nonverbal* signals or clues to help you pick out the information you should record.

Non-Verbal Signals include:

- *Visually Presented Information:* If the instructor puts information on the board, uses an overhead projector, or distributes handouts, s/he is giving you a signal that the information presented is important. Remember that some instructors just jot down key words or phrases. Be sure to get down enough information to prompt your memory later.
- *Instructor Mannerisms:* Frequently when instructors are about to introduce a new topic, they will pause for a minute or glance down at their notes to gather their thoughts. This is a clear signal that you should space down and get ready for a new topic.

Verbal signals include the following:

- *Definitions:* Terms or definitions frequently show up as test questions, whether in multiple choice, matching, or true-false formats.
- *Repetitions:* You can usually assume information is important if it's repeated. Make a notation in the margin, like a circled R, to show that the information was repeated.
- *Examples:* Examples help you to understand the material when you review it later.
- *Enumerations:* Your instructor may use signals like "Five characteristics of … ," or "The three steps in the process are …". Make sure you clearly identify the topic and get down each item listed.
- *Transitional Words:* Be alert for words like "consequently," "furthermore," or for phrases like "another reason for …". These words and phrases are clear signals to record the information provided.
- *Direct Announcement:* Some instructors may simply tell you up front that something is important, with a lead-in like "Pay attention to … ," "This is important," or literally, "note this in your book, or put it in your notes."

Some instructors are not great lecturers and tend to stray from the point, but paying attention to the clues they provide can help you to record the information you need.

In addition to using a loose-leaf binder and learning to "read" your instructor's signals, advance preparation includes developing some personalized note taking short cuts. Most instructors speak at a rate of about 125–150 words per minute when giving a typical lecture. You can't possibly record every word, but you do want to write down as much information as possible. Using a system of abbreviations and symbols will help you to increase your note taking speed. Some common abbreviations and symbols are listed in the following chart.

Word or Term	Abbreviation or Symbol	Word or Term	Abbreviation or Symbol
About	~	Introduction	Intro.
Amount	Amt.	Months	Mo(s).
And	&	Number or Pound	#
Chapter	ch.	Organization	Org.
Company	Co.	Page(s)	Pg., p., pp.
Continued	Cont'd.	Psychology	Psyc.
Decrease	Decr.	Principal	Princ.
Definition	Def.	Significant	Sig.
Economic	Econ.	Social or sociology	Soc.
Example	Ex. or X or e.g.	Summary/ summarize	Sum.
General	Gen.	Versus	Vs.
Government	Gov.	Volume	Vol.
Hour/hourly	Hr./hrly.	Year	Yr.
Illustrate	Illus. or e.g.	Equal/Not Equal	= and =/=
Important	Imp.	Less than/more than	< and >
Increase	Inc.	Positive/negative	+ and –
Information	Info.	With/without	w/ and w/o

Other personalized short cuts include using a ? in any place where you think you missed something important, using a B to indicate work from the board, and an X for examples. Using abbreviations can become especially important in later semesters when you develop a specialized terminology for your major.

ACTIVE LISTENING

How do we listen actively? What does this term mean? For now, we'll use the term to mean paying attention to what the speaker *means* as well as to what s/he *says*.

Remember

When you enter a class; you have a choice about where you're going to sit. Choose wisely by selecting a location that will maximize your attentiveness to the instructor and the effectiveness of your note taking.

In the classroom, you are given directions and assignments, and you listen to presentations and lectures. How well you understand the material will help determine the Fgrade you will receive in the class. When working, you listen to instructions that will help you do your job. In your personal life, you listen to the concerns and problems of your friends and family members. Listening, therefore, is an essential life skill, and developing that skill can make you a better student.

We can improve our listening skills for classroom use by practicing the following strategies:

- *Read the Text:* Make sure you know the topic for upcoming lectures and that you've completed the reading assignment. Your instructor gives you a course syllabus for just this reason! Being familiar with the topic can help you follow the instructor's lecture.

- *Concentrate:* We all know it's easy to "drift off," so you need to concentrate on paying attention. Many instructors test primarily from lecture notes rather than from the book, so you need to keep focused. Make sure you record all main points and supporting ideas. You need to be actively involved in listening to the lecture, and writing will help you to keep your concentration.

- *Respond to the Message, not the Messenger:* Don't let your instructor's appearance, mannerisms, or lecture style detract you from your task—writing down the relevant information.

- *Be Accepting of Different Ideas and Viewpoints:* Many college classes will introduce you to new ideas or to value systems that differ from yours. While questions are always appropriate, the classroom is not intended for personal arguments. Don't be defensive or aggressive in class if the instructor is presenting material that differs from your beliefs. You're responsible for learning the information presented in class—not for arguing with the instructor or monopolizing class time. If you have an honest difference of opinion on an issue, make an appointment to discuss it with your instructor during his/her office hours.

- *Pay Attention to Instructional Clues:* As discussed earlier, your instructor will use "signals" or clues to guide you through the lecture. Keeping up with these transitions will help you to write down the important facts.

Physically Present

Being physically present means attending class regularly. If you are not attending regularly, you need to honestly evaluate your situation. Circumstances often necessitate a change in plans. If attending class is not a priority, maybe you need to sit down with an advisor and discuss your academic goals.

Physical presence also means sitting in class where you can hear and see the speaker, focusing on the speaker, and maintaining eye contact. Finding a place to sit where you can see and hear enhances your ability to concentrate. As a general rule, the closer to the front you sit, the more focused and attentive to the lecturer you will remain. In fact, research on college students and academic success has proven that students who sit closer to the instructor achieve higher grades. Those students appear to be more focused on the instructor. From the instructor's perspective he/she may feel that a rapport has been established with those students.

Mentally Alert

Being mentally alert means avoiding distractions, thoughts, and behaviors that inhibit or block your ability to listen effectively. Bringing your body to class and allowing your mind to be someplace else sabotages your goals for effective listening. If you are preoccupied, worried, daydreaming, or thinking about something else while trying to listen, you will most likely miss a lot of the information being given. Financial concerns, academic difficulties, family problems, roommates, weekend plans, etc., etc., are all examples of things that compete for a student's attention. For some students, class time is the only quiet time they have. It is during this quiet time that personal problems and concerns begin to enter into consciousness and compete for attention. What can you do when you are sitting in class and your mind begins to wander, or you begin to think about things unrelated to the class?

- Jot down these thoughts on a piece of paper. Tell yourself that you will get back to them later.
- Give yourself permission to attend to these problems at a later time.
- Set aside time during the day to work on problems.

Aside from personal distractions, many students have difficulty listening to lectures because they lack the basic course knowledge. They are unfamiliar with the material being presented and become overwhelmed. This is often the result of failing to do assigned readings or poor class attendance. By attending class regularly, doing supplemental readings to build background, and coming prepared, you are able to keep on top of assignments and avoid being overwhelmed.

You can learn to listen more effectively.

Research indicates that the following statements are true (Carmen and Adams, 1972).

1. **We listen in spurts.** Your attention wanders so that you listen intently for 30 seconds or so, tune out for a short time, and then return. You are usually not aware this is happening.
2. **We hear what we expect to hear.** Your prejudices, past experiences, expectations, and beliefs determine what you hear. You tune out what you do not want to hear.
3. **We do not listen well when we are doing other things.**
4. **We listen better when we are actively involved in the process.** When we listen to satisfy a purpose, we hear more and better.

You may first need to identify the instructor's purpose in lecturing. Is it to show you how the course material relates to your own life, to help you solve a particular problem, to discuss and raise questions, to demonstrate certain trends, to encourage you to think critically and analytically? The instructor often states the purpose of the lecture on the syllabus as well as at the beginning of the lecture.

When you go job hunting, you need to hear what the employer is going to require of an employee. Employment expectations and knowledge generated while listening and communicating in an interview is very valuable. Hours to be worked need to be understood, responsibilities must be clarified and clearly defined, and work hours, environment, benefits and advancement opportunities all need to be discussed.

DURING (D)

The following ***action*** is required in note taking:
Take notes actively using your preferred note-taking style

TAKING NOTES FROM LECTURE

In the previous section, we discussed the important skill of listening. You spend about half of your college time doing this vital task, and yet it has been called the most used and least taught of communication skills. It has even been noted that, in respect to amount of words, we listen a book a day, speak a book a week, read a book a month, and write a book a year. Yet have you ever heard of a class called Listening 101? Somehow it is assumed that we need classes to improve our speaking, reading, and writing skills, but we all know how to listen and do not need improvement in this area.

We hope you realize by now that the skill of listening can be improved, but only by practice and hard work! You can't really listen half way—it's either on or off. Unless you mentally rehearse material you are trying to listen to, you can't retain the information in short-term memory for more than twenty seconds! Yet listening comprehension affects your college grades more than reading comprehension does! Evidentally, something must be done to give us a back-up system, since we cannot count on our memories.

Some of you may not be convinced of this fact. You may feel that if you really set your mind to it, you WILL remember that lecture. An interesting study was done several years ago to see how well we really can remember when we are interested and pay attention. The members of the Cambridge Psychological Society (obviously, intelligent people!) had an enjoyable discussion one day that was secretly taped by the experimenters, and two weeks later they were asked to write down all the specific points of the discussion they could remember. These learned members—who spend their lives learning and remembering—could only remember 8 percent of the major points, and what is even more startling was that 42 percent of those points were wrong! Do you really think you could do much better? **The simple truth is this: if you want to remember, you must <u>write it down</u> so that you can review it. In short, you've <u>got to take notes!</u>**

What Are Some Common Mistakes in Note Taking?

It has been said that most of us do one of two things when it comes to taking notes: we suddenly become a stenographer who feels that we must get everything down word-for-word, or we do the other thing—absolutely nothing! Both of these practices are incorrect and will lead to problems in learning. Another common problem involves worrying too much about grammar or spelling, and thus not getting enough information down on paper. A possible solution to this problem is to spell phonetically (or the way the word sounds) and correct it later that day. If you have no idea how to spell the word, leave a blank and write the first consonant. Then rely on the rest of the phrase or sentence to clue you in later that day as you look the word up and find out how to spell it. We have also seen problems with students who take notes, but do not take **enough** notes. They wait for the professor to write on the board before they write any information down, or they keep waiting to write the BIG idea only. Try to get as much information down as possible while still keeping up with the lecturer. You can always delete, but it is much more difficult to add on later.

Two final note taking mistakes are the failure to review notes and relying on tape-recorders. It defeats the purpose of note taking if you do not review the notes. Although it is beneficial just to write the information down, don't leave out the review step! As to whether to tape record lectures, our advice is that it is usually not a good idea. For one thing, if you rely on a machine you will probably not listen as actively. Secondly, if you find it difficult to listen to a live lecturer, how are you going to make yourself listen to an inanimate object? That is even more boring than the most boring of lectures! Finally, when will you find the time to listen to (and hopefully take notes from) the tape? You may soon find that you have a whole set of tapes to listen to and that is just one more thing to get you behind! If the lecturer speaks very quickly, you write very slowly, or the lecturer is difficult to understand due to an accent or other condition, it might be beneficial to tape record, as long as you follow these guidelines:

1. *Take notes as if you did not have the tape recorder so you will promote active listening on your part.*
2. *Revise your notes with the tape THAT SAME DAY.*
3. *Only use 1 tape per subject so that you will be forced to stay caught up with your notes.*

What's the Best Way to Take Lecture Notes?

The first item that is needed in order to take good notes is a well-organized notebook. It is best to have a separate notebook for each subject, preferably one with pockets or a three-ring binder so that you can add handouts to the proper place in your notes. At the very minimum, you need a separate section in the notebook for each subject. It has been stated that you can tell how a woman keeps house by the way that she keeps her purse organized. We're not sure how accurate that is, but it is fairly safe to say that a well-organized notebook helps to promote well-organized thinking, and should also promote the possibility for a higher GPA! If your notebook is similar to the organization of a flea market, perhaps there is a reason for that confusion in your brain!

Now that you are armed with the proper notebook, consider the following suggestions as you begin to take notes and fill up that notebook:

1. **ASSUME A POSITION OF ALERTNESS.** This statement involves two suggestions: watch WHERE you sit, and watch HOW you sit. If you want to give yourself every advantage, SIT FRONT AND CENTER. Students who sit closer to the lecturer get higher grades—it's just that simple. No one seems to know for sure why this is true. Could it be because there are less distractions, or could it be that better students naturally navigate closer to the front? For whatever reason, it will be to your advantage to DO IT! Besides watching where you sit, make sure you also watch your posture. For the most part, an alert body helps to promote an alert mind, and outward manifestations of interest may even create genuine internal interest, so watch how you sit. Slump in your seat, and your mind may slump with you! As you sit alertly, INTEND TO REMEMBER what you will be hearing. Pretend you are going to have a pop quiz after the lecture. It **will** make a difference in how carefully you listen!

2. **BE PREPARED!** Have all your SUPPLIES together. You will need your trusty notebook, of course, and a pen with which to take notes. But you also need to prepare by making sure you have kept up with your TEXTBOOK READING, and also by REVIEWING YOUR PAST LECTURE NOTES before class. These two suggestions will make a large difference on how easily you can follow the lecturer. Keep your class SYLLABUS handy and refer to it often. It is a contract between the professor and yourself, and you are both obligated by what it says. Make sure *you* know what it says! Part of class preparation starts before the beginning of the semester by trying to SCHEDULE your classes in an organized fashion. Consider your own biological clock as you decide when the best time

would be to take each class. If it is at 12:00 pm, you may have difficulty concentrating due to hunger. So, as much as you can, prepare adequately before you start the class by considering all possibilities. Finally, prepare by ASSUMING YOUR RESPONSIBILITY. You will decide how much you get out of the lecture largely by this one act. If you are a responsible, self-motivated student, you will FIND reasons to listen and take notes. If you do not assume this responsibility, you will be a more passive listener who expects the instructor to GIVE you reasons to listen by motivating you and capturing your interest. Don't count on this happening. It's nice when it does, but the responsibility has to be yours—as is the education you gain or lose.

3. **ATTEND CLASS AND BE PUNCTUAL.** You can skip class physically (as many do), or you can realize from the very start how much you are paying for each class period, and that it's your loss if you skip. Unfortunately, the habit of skipping is an easy one to get into and a hard one to stop. Don't start it. Be there, and be there on time! You need to also be aware of the fact that you can skip mentally even if you do not skip physically. If you do not listen actively or if you do not take notes, you might as well have skipped the class.

4. **KEEP YOUR EYES ON THE INSTRUCTOR.** It does take PRACTICE to listen, watch, and write, but your skill will improve with practice. It is important to WATCH THE PROFESSOR FOR THOSE VISUAL CLUES mentioned earlier, and to NOTE THOSE as you take notes. Mark things with which you tend to disagree. For some reason we tend to remember best the things we agree with and ignore the rest. Try to listen with your mind, not your feelings. Is the lecture boring? You have some control over that, believe it or not, by your attitude and by your facial expressions. You can ENCOURAGE THE LECTURER by nodding your head, smiling, and looking alive and interested, and the lecture may improve. If you want it to get even more boring, try looking bored or even putting your head down on your desk. You can spice up the lecture by making your face look interested! Try it! VISUALIZE AND CATEGORIZE as you listen. See it as well as hear it and write it, and you will be planting it more firmly in your mind. Since the mind can only retain about seven "chunks" of information at a time, try to think in main ideas. These main topics will be easier to organize in your notes AND in your mind. Lastly, NEVER HESITATE TO ASK a professor to explain a point if you've read your assignment and been listening to the lectures. You're probably not the only one who has that question!

5. **TAKE NOTES AGGRESSIVELY!** Do not wait for something important to be said. It will be too late to get it down if you put your pen down and wait. You never know the importance of the statement until it is past, so keep your pen in hand, and use it! Perhaps the most crucial component of this suggestion is your attitude. The proper attitude has been called the most important requirement for good note taking. Realize that the lecture is supposed to save you time and effort, and that the teacher is a partner in your future success for your chosen career. This will make it a little easier to share the responsibility of the communication and cooperate in active listening. Take advantage of your professor's knowledge and time. It will add to yours—and we're speaking both of knowledge and time! Don't just write down what you think will be on the test. You are trying to learn all you can learn, remember?

6. **WRITE IN TELEGRAPHIC STYLE.** Even though it is important to get down all the information you can in the time you have, it is beneficial to leave out words that are not crucial to the meaning of the message—like you would if you were paying for each word in a telegram. Invent your own symbols and

abbreviations to make your notes more meaningful. For example, put a star by material that the lecturer mentioned might be test material, or put a box around material that was written on the board. Abbreviate words such as without (w/o), because (b/c), or a name that is used repeatedly can just be the first initial with a blank after you have used it several times. Make sure you USE YOUR OWN WORDS. If you try to copy the professor's words down word-for-word, you may bypass your brain! Rephrase the main idea into your own words, and you will increase your learning power. All of the above take practice, but you will improve with each good set of notes that you take.

7. **NEATNESS COUNTS!** Don't waste valuable study time trying to decipher notes that can only be read by a mind-reader. BLOCK PRINTING is often more easily read than cursive, and can also be much faster to write, so consider printing your notes in manuscript. Be sure to LEAVE PLENTY OF WHITE SPACE. Use blanks for words or ideas missed and fill them in after class by asking your professor or a friend for clarification, or by looking it up in your text. Review your notes as soon as possible after class so you can do some fix-ups. Add to or correct whatever is needed. "White space" aids in this revision process. KEEP YOUR NOTES DATED AND NUMBERED to avoid confusion at a later time and to be able to tell where test coverage will start. Remember, if the problem of spelling slows you down, use the first letter plus a blank space, or use phonetic spelling. Also, USE INK as you take your notes. It is less likely to smudge or fade, and you will not have as much difficulty reviewing your notes several weeks later—or even years later, as the case may be!

8. **DON'T DOODLE!** If you do doodle—or write letters, or sleep, or knit, or whatever—you are making a judgment call that what you are doing is more important than the lecture, and you may be right! But remember, you must also be willing to accept the consequences of your actions, and usually that's a high price to pay. If you get bored, try reviewing your notes, questioning them, or predicting what's going to be said next. All of these strategies are important comprehension tools, and may help to revive your interest. Even if that doesn't happen, you are not wasting your time as you are with the doodling syndrome!

9. **GO FOR MAIN IDEAS, NOT DETAILS.** Note taking is a process of selection, condensation, and compression, and this very process is a wonderful learning experience. If you do it correctly, the act of note taking is a valuable study tool. Try to think in terms of headings and sub-headings, and USE SOME TYPE OF AN OUTLINE SYSTEM to show the overall organization of the lecture. Headings or labels are extremely important! If you are not sure what the topic is, leave a blank, get down the information, and come back to create a heading later. You need to see some visual organization in order to think in an organized fashion. The outline form itself is not important—that there is some organization for main points and sub-points is vital!

10. **ALWAYS COPY EXAMPLES AND BOARD WORK.** These will tend to be the items that make the most sense to you and will be more easily remembered. They may help to clarify the rest of the material.

11. **LISTEN CAREFULLY TO THE VERY END** of the lecture! Professors typically get behind in a lecture, and they may be cramming in two last pages of notes while you are busy gathering up all your junk! Or they may be reviewing some important test questions right at the last minute, so you must listen until the "bitter end." Some of the most important information may be squeezed into the last few seconds. Take a few minutes to get the full benefits, or you may live to regret it!

NOTE TAKING STYLES

You've spent a number of years taking classroom notes already and may have a format or style that really works for you. Many students use a formal numbered outline format, grouping main ideas or topics, secondary topics, and supporting details. This is one of the oldest notetaking systems in use, and it can be very effective if the instructor is well organized and presents the information in an easy-to-follow, step-by-step manner.

Our sample notes will present information regarding the stages of memory in two variations of the formal outline system. We'll also take this same information and present it in a visual format that may work very well in certain classes or for certain topics in a given class. Remember that you don't need to use exactly the same note taking style for every class or even all the time in the same class.

Informal Outline

The informal outline (also known as the indented topic system) shows major topics and lists secondary points and supporting details by indenting them under the major topics, without using a numbering system. This format leaves a 2½ inch margin on the *right* side of the paper. After class, you can jot down key words or terms in this space for use as memory prompts when you review your notes. The following notes are written in the *informal outline* style.

Date _____ Course *PSY. 100* Stages of Memory A. Sensory Memory • First point of information intake—sight, sound, touch • Lasts for a few seconds as exact copy B. Short-Term Memory • Temp. storage of small amts. of info.—5-7 "bit" avg. • "Chunking" helps us to remember more—e.g. S.S. #'s are 3 bits, 2 bits, and 4 bits • Provides a "working" memory—e.g.—Looking up phone #'s • Sensitive to interruption—phone # lost if someone interrupts us before we dial • After 18 secs the info. is lost w/o coding or rehearsal—e.g. Meaningless syllables experiment (in text). C. Long-Term Memory • Permanent storage • Rehearsal process (repetition, etc.) required • Limitless storage capacity • Info. stored on basis of meaning & imp.	Digit-span exp. Chuncking—grouping bits together Sensitive to -interruption Info. lost after 18 secs. Permanent Requires rehearsal Limitless

Figure 8.1 Informal Outline System.

Cornell System

Developed by Dr. Walter Pauk of Cornell University, the Cornell System is a widely used note taking system. The example below shows a blank notebook page divided into the three sections of the Cornell system, and the next page shows our stages of memory notes recorded using this system. As the sectioned paper shows, this format leaves a blank column on the *left* side of the page. This space is used to develop questions about the material presented for later review. You can also include key words, graphic signals, and vocabulary words. The horizontal column across the bottom of the page is used to jot down a quick summary of key points.

Date _____

Course <u>PSY. 100</u>

	Stages of Memory
Sensory Memory	Sensory Memory
	1. First point of information intake—sight, sound, touch
	2. Lasts for a few seconds only as exact copy
	Short-Term Memory
How does the process of chunking help us to remember?	1. Temp. storage of small amts. of info.—5–7 bit avg.—digit span experiment
	2. "Chunking" like bits of info. together makes it easier to remember—e.g. S.S. # has 3/2/4 bits grouped
	3. Info. from sensory memory is selected for attention—phone # you've looked up, etc.
	4. Serves as working memory
What happens to info. entering STM?	5. Sensitive to interruption—someone interrupts before you make the phone call, and the # is gone
	6. After 18 secs. w/o rehearsal, info. is lost and doesn't get to LTM.
	7. Coded, rehearsed info. goes into LTM
Long-Term Memory	Long-Term Memory
	1. Permanent storage
How does info. get moved from STM to LTM?	2. Limitless storage capacity
	3. Rehearsal process (repetition, etc.) required
	4. Info. stored on basis of meaning & imp.

Info. must go through 3 stages—sensory, S/T, and L/T. Rehearsal process required for retention. Info. stored on basis of meaning & imp.

Figure 8.2 Notes Using Cornell Note Taking System.

```
┌─────────────────────────────────────────────────────┐
│              Cornell Page Set-up                      │
│                 ← 8½" →                               │
│ ┌─────────────────────────────────────────────────── │
│ ← 2½" →  ┊            ← 6" →                          │
│          ┊                                            │
│          ┊                                            │
│ Questions┊                                            │
│          ┊                                            │
│ Key Words┊                                            │
│          ┊                                            │
│ Graphic  ┊                                            │
│ Signals  ┊                                            │
│          ┊                                            │
│ Vocabulary┊                                           │
│ Words    ┊                                            │
│          ┊    ↑                                       │
│          ┊                                            │
│ Area C   ┊   9"          Area A                       │
│          ┊                                            │
│          ┊    ↓          Notes                        │
│          ┊                                            │
│          ┊                                            │
│ ─ ─ ─ ─ ─┊─ ─ ─ ─ ─ ─ ─ ─ ─ ─ ─ ─ ─ ─ ─ ─ ─          │
│   ↑      ┊                                            │
│   2"     ┊              Area B                         │
│   ↓      ┊              Summary                        │
└─────────────────────────────────────────────────────┘
```

The Cornell Note Taking System

1. On the page on which you're taking notes, draw a horizontal line about 2 inches from the bottom edge of the paper.
2. If there's no vertical line on the left side of the page, draw one line about 2½ inches from the left edge of the paper (as shown in the scaled down illustration here).
3. When your instructor is lecturing, use the large space to the right of the vertical line (area A) to record your notes.
4. After a lecture, use the space at the bottom of the page (area B) to summarize the main points you recorded on that page.
5. Use the column of space on the left side of the page (area C) to write questions that are answered in the notes on the right and/or to mark key words, graphic signals, and vocabulary words.
6. Quiz yourself by looking at the questions listed in the left margin while covering the answers to them that are found in your class notes on the right.

Note: You can use this note taking and note-review method on your own, or you could team up with two or more students and do it collaboratively.

Charting, Mind Mapping, and Clustering

These note taking systems allow you to "picture" the information visually. Mind mapping and clustering usually begin with the main topic circled in the middle of the page, with arrows or smaller circles radiating out from the middle to show supporting topics or details. Charting is a more linear format, using horizontal or vertical arrows or lines to show a sequence of events. The figure below shows our memory notes in a horizontal chart, with the process moving from left to right and top to bottom across the page.

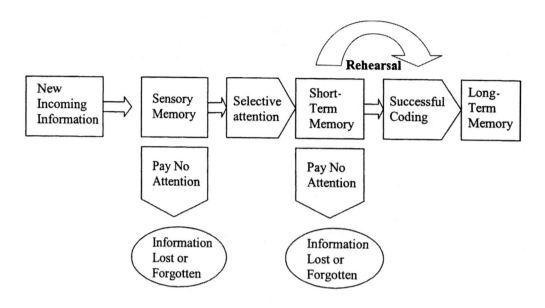

AFTER (A)

Continue to *review, revise*, and *self-modify* your note taking style and strategies as needed.

- **Am I getting the key points/main ideas on my notes?**
- **How am I using my notes?**
- **Am I evaluating my notes?**
- **Have I built in time to review and edit my notes from the lecture?**
- **What changes can I make to what I am doing now that will help me to become a better reader and retain the information that I have read?**

USING YOUR NOTES

Developing a good note taking system doesn't help you do well in your classes if you don't learn to use your notes as a part of your total study system. Follow the steps below to maximize the usefulness of your class notes.

- **Editing**: Your first review of your notes should take place as soon as possible after class. Use this time to rewrite illegible words, finish incomplete thoughts or ideas, clarify any abbreviations you used that you may not remember, and fill in any information you might have missed getting down. This first review is a repetition step that serves as a rehearsal, and it will help you move the information into long-term memory.
- **Weekly Review**: At the end of each week, you should complete a second review of your notes. Concentrate on relationships, time sequences, and organizational patterns at this point. Think about how your notes and your text material overlap. This second review is critical to processing the information for long-term memory storage.
- **Test Preparation**: If your instructor has notified you of the test format, try to predict both objective and essay type questions. For math class, try straight calculating as well as word problems. Remember to look over your notes for information that was put on the board or that the instructor announced was important.

Pg. 1	Pg. 2	Pg. 3
Which memory stage holds information for only a few seconds?	Why can you remember your social security number when shorter strings or numbers or information may be forgotten?	What did the meaningless syllable experiment prove?
Describe the effect of interruptions on short-term memory.	What process is necessary to transfer information from S/T to L/T memory?	How is information in LTM stored?
How does the digit-span test affect memory?		

Test Review with Cornell Note-taking System

It is at this point that the questions developed from the Cornell note taking system can be especially useful if you've followed our advice to use loose-leaf paper for your note taking. Remove your one-sided notes from your binder and overlap them so you can only see the question or key word column as shown in the example that follows.

Use a blank sheet of paper to cover your notes from the top sheet. Quiz yourself by answering the questions listed. If you're not sure, you can quickly flip the page to find the correct answer. Once you're sure you know the material, put those notes back in your binder. Continue working on the material you still haven't mastered.

- **After the test:** Your final review should come after your test has been returned. Were you prepared? Were your notes adequate? If not, what kind of information was missing from your notes? What percentage of test questions seemed to come from lectures? What percentage came from the text? Think about what you need to do to improve your test scores next time.

EVALUATING YOUR NOTES

Even if you are on the right track, you'll get run over if you just sit there.

—*Anonymous*

Finally, even with all these steps, you need to assess your level of note taking ability. The most obvious indicator of this is whether you are performing well on the portion of your exams that come from class lectures. If you are doing *really well*, your note taking technique is probably sufficient—at least for this class! If your grades are poor, you need to decide where you are going wrong and correct it *now*. Here are ideas for evaluating your notes.

Get Feedback from Others

Compare your notes with those of peers and/or teaching assistants. See whether you have the same coverage of important information. How clear is your content? How effective and memorable are your abbreviations and symbols? Is your organization sufficient? Do your self-originated examples really fit the material? You may also benefit from showing your notes to your course professor. Just be sure to do so well before an exam so that feedback will be useful.

Take a Course

Most college/universities have courses on study skills and note taking, in addition to other student support services. The time invested (which may even qualify for credit toward graduation) can pay off dramatically in future performance and time savings. Again, note taking is a *skill* that can always be improved. Get a jump on the competition by honing this skill!

SUMMARY

This chapter stressed that taking good notes requires being prepared for class, actively listening to the lecture, selecting a note taking style, and using your notes as a part of your total study system. You learned to key in to the verbal and nonverbal signals your instructors use to guide you through the lecture, and you were encouraged to use abbreviations, symbols, and other shortcuts to help you record as much information as possible.

Remember that your notes are only as good as the information you record and the way in which you use them. Students who test well have usually practiced the editing and review techniques covered in this chapter.

SUGGESTED READING

Pauk, Walter. "Taking Good Notes." *How to Study in College*. 7th ed. New York: Houghton Mifflin Co., 2001.

NAME: _____ DATE: _____

EXERCISE 8.1: CHECKING OUT YOUR INSTRUCTOR'S LECTURE STYLE

DIRECTIONS: Use the statements below to evaluate the lecture style used by one of your instructors for this semester.

Course Name _____

	Yes	No
1. My instructor begins each class with a quick review of the last session.		
2. My instructor is well organized and clearly introduces each new topic.		
3. My instructor lectures at a comfortable pace; s/he doesn't speak too slowly or too fast.		
4. My instructor speaks clearly and at a voice level I can understand.		
5. My instructor is focused and doesn't wander off the topic.		
6. My instructor includes illustrations and examples that help me to understand the material s/he is presenting.		
7. My instructor uses a vocabulary (words) that I can understand and defines new terms when needed.		
8. My instructor is open to questions and encourages classroom discussion.		
9. My instructor frequently provides visual input by his/her use of the board, an overhead projector, or handouts.		
10. My instructor uses the last few minutes of the period to summarize main ideas and/ or to clarify new assignments.		

How do your instructors measure up? If your responses cluster on the "No" side, the note taking strategies presented in this chapter are especially important. They should help you to make the most of your classroom time.

What specific note taking strategies from this chapter will I attempt to start using in this class?

EXERCISE 8.2: NOTE TAKING PRACTICE

Complete one of the four exercises below:

1. Interview a successful upper-class student (GPA of 2.75 or higher). Find out what kind of note taking style she has chosen for one of her tough classes. Have her describe:
   a. its format; how she created the notes; what she "attends" to during class in order to encode the important information.
   b. whether her note taking gets her the grades on tests that she wants. That should lead you to ask her other pertinent questions regarding her choice of note taking …
   c. what she did with them after class and until test time.

2. Choose one course that demands that you take notes—useful notes. Go to the professor of that course and with his help, choose one of our suggested formats to practice and ask that professor for any suggestions on improving note taking for THAT class.

   Name of course: _____

   Note taking format I have chosen to practice: _____

   What specific recommendations does this professsor give you?

   _____

   _____

   _____

   _____

   _____

   How do you know what is important to encode in his class?

   _____

   _____

   _____

   _____

   _____

3. Use the sample Geography Chapter from Ch. 3 (pp. 80–84) to practice each of the note taking styles: outline, Cornell system, and mind map.

4. Use the videotaped lectures provided by your instructor to practice note taking using the different formats: outline, Cornell system, and mind map.

EXERCISE 8.3: CREATE AN ACTION PLAN FOR EDITING

Choose one of your courses and using one of the note taking styles, make notes and then plan to edit them before the next class period. You may want to choose a class you are not doing well in or you may be concerned about the amount of info or difficulty of the next test in that class. Make this a purposeful exercise for yourself!

You may use the following prompts to get you started. Reviewing your own notes may prompt other questions and "wants" that you may address …

• What info do I want to record? What info do I need to record for the next quiz or test?

• What am I going to do to get that info?

• How will I encode it? What style (format) will I choose?

• How will I store this info in 24-hour service; what is my "editing" process?

• How will I practice rehearsal of this info and plan retrieval cues for the test?

The SPECIAL Problem-Solving Action Plan

S   Set the Stage and Self-Assess

P   Prepare your Plan

E   Explore and Examine strategies

C   Choose strategies and Commit

I   Investigate resources

A   Act and Announce!

L   What have you Learned?

Note: *Special Problem-Solving Action Plan is described in detail in Chapter 3.*

EXERCISE 8.4: JOURNAL—NOTE TAKING

Note taking is a critical skill you continue to develop throughout your academic career. It is essential to survival in college. Compare your present style of note taking with the approach suggested in this chapter. Where are you having the most success in taking satisfactory notes which are a good resource when you are studying for exams. Why? Discuss at least two of the note taking suggestions you will implement immediately to improve your note taking skills.

_____

_____

_____

_____

_____

_____

_____

_____

_____

1. Why is it a good practice to make a habit of reviewing all of your notes within a 24-hour period?

_____

_____

_____

2. What is the purpose of a recall column?

_____

_____

_____

3. List several verbal and visual cues the instructor may use to indicate certain -information is important and belongs in your notes.

_____

_____

_____

_____

4. How do you want to improve your note taking skills?

_____

_____

_____

_____

5. What factors would you consider important to take notes on when researching careers?

_____

_____

_____

_____

6. Describe the importance of the skill of writing and listening when succeeding in a career.

_____

_____

_____

_____

NAME: _____ DATE: _____

EXERCISE 8.5: TOO FAST, TOO FRUSTRATING: A NOTE-TAKING NIGHTMARE

Susan Scribe is a first-year student who is majoring in journalism, and she's enrolled in an introductory course that is required for her major (Introduction to Mass Media). Her instructor for this course lectures at a rapid rate and uses vocabulary words that go right over her head. Since she cannot get all her instructor's words down on paper and cannot understand half the words she does manage to write down, she becomes frustrated and stops taking notes. She wants to do well in this course because it's the first course in her major, but she's afraid she will fail it because her class notes are so pitiful.

Reflection and Discussion Questions

1. Can you relate to this case personally, or do you know any students who are in the same boat as Susan?

2. What would you recommend that Susan do at this point?

3. Why did you make the preceding recommendation?

Chapter 9

Taking Tests – What's On It?

INTRODUCTION

Oh, no! Not another test. Whose idea are tests anyway? Who needs them? I sure don't! Have you ever found yourself thinking these very thoughts? Most people do not like tests, but they are a necessary part of the learning process, and they do have a purpose. One reason instructors give tests is to motivate students to learn. If you knew that you were not going to be tested on the textbook or lecture materials, chances are you would not spend as much time reading, studying, or taking notes in class. In other words, you probably would not try as hard to learn, even though you are in college for that very purpose. Another reason for giving tests is that they help the instructor assess how much and how well you have learned the course content and its applications. Homework alone is not always a proper gauge of a student's knowledge. Instructors do not have any real way to know that you are the one who did the assignment or that you know and understand the material.

Taking tests gives both you and your instructor some feedback on what you have learned. It helps you to know what you need to review. It helps the instructor to know what material was confusing to the class, what topics may need to be repeated, or whether or not his/her style of delivery needs to be changed. Test results also help to determine the grade you will receive for the class. Test scores combined with your homework, projects, participation, and attendance indicate how well you achieved the course objectives. This total effort determines whether or not you are ready for the next course. In a very real sense, a test is—first and foremost—a learning device.

Properly preparing for tests and learning the skills and strategies presented in this chapter will make you test-wise, contribute to improved test scores, and help you become a more confident student. When you have learned how to develop good study habits, take good notes, and practice the strategies from this chapter, you will no longer have any reason to fear or hate taking tests.

BEFORE (B)

The *preparation, self-awareness,* and *planning* strategies needed to be a good test taker are as follows:

- **Self-analysis of your current test taking skills**
- **Knowing what to do before the test**

Pretest

How test-wise are you? Check yourself on the following:

	Yes	No
1. I never miss class, especially when I know we will be reviewing a test.		
2. I get as much information about the test as I can. I ask questions about the test format and what it will cover.		
3. I study and review for tests throughout the semester so I don't have to cram.		
4. I have well written, understandable class notes to use when I study.		
5. I make up practice tests for myself.		
6. I get enough sleep the night before every test.		
7. I always survey tests before I take them.		
8. I plan and use my testing time wisely. I allow more time for the questions that are worth the most points. I skip questions I am unsure of and return to them later.		
9. When I don't know the answer to a test question, I know how to increase my odds of guessing correctly.		
10. I know how to get a better score on essay tests.		
11. I double check my test before turning it in to make sure I have followed the directions, finished all of the questions, and to see if my answers make sense.		
12. I always review tests when they are returned and correct my mistakes so I won't make them again.		

The above are things good test-takers do automatically. How many of them do you practice regularly? If you checked NO five or more times, your test scores may not be an accurate reflection of your ability, and you may really benefit from implementing the skills you will learn in this chapter.

> Since testing is such an important college survival skill, you need to know just how it is done and what the rules are for succeeding.

BEFORE THE TEST

Know the Planning Rules for Effective Studying.

Start studying for exams from the first day of class. When talking with the instructor after you have received the course syllabus, be sure to ask the following questions:

- *What are the major goals of the course?*
- *What kinds of exams do you normally give? Do you have any copies of some of your old exams I may use to help me prepare for your exams?*
- *How many units or chapters are usually covered on an exam if it is not already in the syllabus?*
- *Does the instructor expect you to remember general or specific detail, deduction and/or opinions?*
- *Will the tests normally cover class texts, lecture, and other assigned materials such as films, periodicals, etc.?*
- *Will make-up exams be allowed if I fail or miss a test?*
- *How much will each exam count toward passing the course?*

If you do not develop a system, it will be difficult for you to be a successful test taker. Use the following rules to develop your system.

- **Learn the vocabulary of the course.** Many students fail because they do not understand the vocabulary on exams.
- **Establish a study group or find a study partner from the class.** Never go through a class without connecting with at least one other person in that class. You will have a built-in system for getting class notes you missed or for cross-checking information. In a study group, each person is responsible for units of information which they must share/teach to others in the group. This is good because when you have to teach information to someone else, you are more likely to learn it.
- **Always scan your chapter before you read.** Then read the introduction and summary. These two parts of the chapter should help you to zero in on what you need to know. Do not read your textbooks as if you are reading a suspense or romance novel. Read with the knowledge or understanding of what is on the next page. Make connections.
- **Always read with a question and/or objective in mind.** Never read aimlessly. Take the information in like your exam is tomorrow. Know the objectives your instructor wants you to cover. For each unit covered, ask the instructor to share the *must know* items.
- **Always do a quick review before going to class.**
- **Take good notes from lecture and/or assigned readings.**
- **Immediately after each lecture/reading assignment, organize your information the way it should be remembered.** Rewrite your notes if necessary. Preferably a rewrite should be done within 24 hours of the class/review.

Nicole is enrolled in PSY100 and Professor Cooper has just announced a test for next Friday. He has given them thirty items to study and has indicated that the test will be a combination of objective and essay questions. Nicole works 12–16 hours a day on weekends. The only time she has for studying is during the week. So today she needs to make sure she has all of the notes and information from which the test will be drawn. Based on the test information, she has 4 days to prepare. She must also begin to determine which items may be asked objectively or in essay form.

Mon.	Tues.	Wed.	Thurs.	Fri.
10 items	10 items	10 items	Test/Rev	Test Day

Day One	Master the 1st 10 items/test yourself
Day Two	Review the 1st 10 items
	Master the 2nd 10 items/test yourself
Day Three	Review the 1st 20 items
	Master the 3rd 10 items/test yourself
Day Four	Retest yourself on all items/review
Day Five	Arrive early enough to relax/then take test

Note: You should use a realistic time table that takes into consideration your daily responsibilities and the difficulty of the material to be learned.

- **Once material is organized, master it before you go back to class and take in new information. Mapping** is a method that can help you organize material. Why don't you try making one for all of your courses?
- **It is a good practice to take weekly tests on new information.** This will help in moving information from short-term to long-term memory.
- **This is the time to develop mnemonics if necessary.**
- **Use flash cards.** You may use these cards to review or test. You can take them places where you are not allowed to take books or tablets. A flash card is a 3" × 5" card with the question on one side and the answer on the opposite side.

Strategies That Promise Good Grades

The only way to ensure success is by thoroughly preparing for a test. Here are several important suggestions to help you.

Attend Class

This is crucial. Even though you may read the textbook, the instructor often explains the material. S/he may give examples that are not in the book, expand on the information already provided, present a different point of view, or provide your class with additional handouts and other materials. You need to be there! Anything covered in class may be included on the exam.

Class attendance also proves to the instructor that you are putting forth the effort to learn the material and that you want to earn a good grade. Often the class prior to the exam is used for review. The instructor usually will give you information to properly prepare for the test. This is the time for you to ask those questions that your classmates will be glad you asked.

Study Throughout the Semester

If you start studying from the first day and consistently review it, the material will stay in your mind. Cramming the night before a test opens the door for failure. The material is only in your short-term memory; therefore, you may not retain the information as readily or retrieve it as easily. Data may become confused, and you will become tense and tired from staying up all night.

- **Study the most difficult concepts first.** You have a better chance of learning difficult material when you first begin to study, before you get tired.
- **Review before you go to sleep.** Recent studies about brain function and memory show that your mind continues to work on problems during dream stages of sleep. Memory and problem solving ability improved with 6 or more hours of sleep. Each extra hour—up to 9 hours—of sleep provided significantly better results.
- **Find a study partner or group.** You will learn better when you study together. It will force you to put your thoughts into words. In the exchange of notes, ideas, questions, and other materials, you will learn from each other. Helping others will help you on test day.
- **Don't just memorize; try to understand the relationship between ideas, facts, and/or problems.** You need to understand the material, and you need to be able to apply what you have learned.
- **Whenever possible, use study guides.** Your instructor may provide them for each class, they may be a library resource, or they may be purchased in the bookstore.
- **Read over your notes, homework, study guides, and quizzes from the class.** Don't forget to read the introductions, summary, glossaries, chapter review questions, chapter tests, and examples from the textbook.

Try to Predict Test Questions

One of the most effective test preparation techniques is to try and anticipate what will be on the test. Based on the textbook and lecture notes, try to predict the questions that your instructor might ask. Be sure to look over your notes for information that you've marked as important, and turn your chapter headings into questions. In math, make sure you practice every type of problem that was presented. If you do all of this, you will be prepared to take any test.

RULES FOR FORMING A STUDY GROUP

1. **Same goal!** Make sure everyone in your group has the same goal to succeed.
2. **Set rules!** When will you have breaks? How long will your group meet (30 min., 1 hour, etc.)?
3. **Prepare early!** Don't wait until the night before the test to form a study group.
4. **Assign responsibilities or tasks!** Make sure everyone participates and comes prepared to study.
5. **Remember varied learning styles!** Include a variety of study tools, including visuals, discussion, and organization of material because everyone has different learning preferences.

Note the Instructor's Style

Knowing what the instructor is looking for will help you know what to study. Usually s/he will be consistent with a particular type of test. Preparing for an objective test requires a different study technique than preparing for an essay exam. Talking with other students who have already taken the course can help you to know what to expect on the test.

Strategies* to Use Immediately Before a Test

1. **Before the exam, try to take a brisk walk.** Physical activity increases mental alertness by increasing oxygen flow to the brain; it also decreases tension by increasing the brain's production of emotionally, "mellowing" brain chemicals (e.g., serotronin and endorphins).

2. ***Come fully armed with all the test-taking tools* you need.** In addition to the required supplies (e.g., No, 2 pencil, pen, blue book, Scantron, calculator, etc.), bring backup equipment in case you experience equipment failure (e.g., an extra pen in case your first one runs out of ink or extra pencils in case your original one breaks).

3. **Try to get to the classroom a few minutes early.** Arriving at the test ahead of time gives you a chance to review any formulas and equations you may have struggled to remember and any memory-retrieval cues you've created (e.g., acronyms). You want to be sure that you have this information in your working memory when you receive the exam so that you can get it down on paper before you forget it. Arriving early also allows you to take a few minutes to get into a relaxed pre-test state of mind by thinking positive thought taking slow, deep breaths, and stretching your muscles. Also, avoid last-second discussions with unprepared classmates about the test just before the test is handed out; their hurried and harried questions can often cause confusion and elevate your level of test anxiety

4. **Sit in the same seat that you normally *occupy in class*.** Research indicates that memory is improved when information is recalled in the same place where it was originally received or reviewed (Sprenger, 1999). Thus, taking the test in the same seat you normally occupy during lectures should improve your test performance because it puts you in the same place where you originally heard much of the information that is going to appear on the test. Studies show that when students take a test in the same environment that they studied in, they tend to remember more of that information at test time than do students who study in one place and take the test in a different place (Smith, Glenberg, & Bjork, 1978). While it is unlikely that you'll be able to do all your studying in the same room that you will take your test in, it may be possible to do your final review in your classroom or in an empty classroom with similar features. This could strengthen your memory for the information you studied, because the features of the room in which you studied the information may become associated with the information, and seeing these features again at test time may help trigger memory of the information (Tulving, 1983).

Consuming large doses of caffeine or other stimulants before exams may increase your alertness, but may also increase your level of stress and text anxiety.

Studies have shown that if students are exposed to a distinctive or unique aroma while they are studying (e.g., the smell of chocolate) and are exposed to that same smell again during a later memory test, they display better memory for the information they studied than do students who didn't study and take the test with the same aroma present (Schab, 1990). Perhaps one practical application of this finding is to wear a distinctively smelling cologne or perfume while studying, and use it again on the day of the test. This might improve your memory for the information you studied by matching the scent of your study environment with the scent of your test environment, Although this strategy may seem silly, keep in mind that the area of the human brain where smell is perceived has connections with the brain's memory pathways (Jensen, 1998). This may account for why people commonly report that certain smells can trigger memories of past experiences (e.g., the smell of a summer breeze triggering memories of summer games played during childhood). Thus, don't underestimate the sense of smell's potential for promoting memory.

DURING (D)

The following *action* is required when taking tests:

- **Follow effective test-taking rules/tips**
- **Using strategies specific to tests**
- **Dealing with test anxiety**

Strategies to Use during the Test

1. **As soon as you receive a copy of the test, write down key information you need to remember.** In particular, write down any hard-to-remember terms, formulas, and equations and any memory-retrieval cues you may have created as soon as you start the exam to ensure that you don't forget this information after you begin answering specific test questions.

2. **Answer the easier test questions first.** As soon as you receive the test, before launching into answering the first question listed, check out the layout of the test. Note the questions that are worth the most points and the questions that you know well. You can do this by first surveying the test and putting a check-mark next to questions whose answers you're unsure of; come back to these questions later after you've answered the question you're sure of, to ensure all their points are added into your final test score.

3. **Prevent "memory block" from setting in.** If you tend to experience memory block for information that you know is stored in your brain, use the following strategies:

   - Mentally put yourself back in the environment or situation in which you studied the information. Recreate the steps in which you learned the information that you're temporarily forgotten by mentally picturing the place where you first heard or saw it and where you studied it, including sights, sounds, smells and time of day. This memory-improvement strategy is referred to as *guided retrieval*, and research supports its effectiveness for recalling information, including information recalled by eyewitness to a crime (Glenberg, 1997; Glenberg, Bradley, Kraus, & Renzaglia, 1983).

   - Think of any idea or piece of information that may be related to the information you can't remember. Studies show that when students experience temporary forgetting, they're more likely to suddenly recall that information if they first recall a piece or portion of that information that relates to it in some way (Reed, 1996). This related piece of information can trigger your memory for the forgotten information because related pieces of information are typically stored within the same neural network of cells in the brain.

- Take your mind off the question and turn to another question. This may allow your subconscious to focus on the forgotten information, which may trigger your conscious memory of it. Also, you may find some information included in other test questions that can help you remember an answer to a previous test question.
- Before turning in your test, carefully review and double-check your answers. This is the critical last step in the process of effective test taking. Sometimes the rush and anxiety of taking a test can cause test takers to overlook details, misread instructions, unintentionally skip questions, or make absentminded mistakes. When you're done, take time to look over your answers to be sure you didn't make any mindless mistakes. Avoid the temptation to immediately cut out because you're pooped out, or to take off on an ego trip by being among the first and fastest students in class to finish the test. Instead, take the full amount of test time available to you. When you think about the amount of time and effort you put into preparing for the exam, it's foolish not to take a little more time on the exam itself.

* From *Thriving in College and Beyond: Research-Based Strategies for Academic Success and Personal Development* by Jospeh B. Cuseo, Aaron Thompson, Michele Campagna, and Viki S. Fecas. Copyright © 2013 by Kendall Hunt Publishing Company. Reprinted by permission.

TEST-SPECIFIC PREPARATION

Sentence Completion or Fill-in-the Blank Questions

Fill-in-the-blank and sentence-completion statements require you to supply missing information. Read the questions carefully and decide on your answer. Look for key words to help you determine the correct answer. If you have studied the vocabulary, these questions should not be difficult.

Look for clues. The verb form of the question will tell you whether the answer is singular or plural. The number of blanks may tell you how many words make up the answer. If "an" rather than "a" precedes the blank space, your answer will begin with a vowel or an "h" instead of a consonant. If you are not sure how to interpret a question/problem, ASK!

How would you fill in the following blanks?

1. *In October, _____, the stock market "crashed" to begin the Great Depression.*
2. *An _____ person can be trusted.*
3. *The U.S. entered World War II in 1941 after _____ planes attacked American Naval ships at _____ _____.*

In the first item, you are asked to complete the date by adding the year (1929). The missing word in the second item is an adjective that begins with a vowel or a vowel sound. A logical choice would be the word honest. The third item asks for an adjective that describes planes (Japanese) and then a noun that names the location of the naval ships (Pearl Harbor).

Multiple-choice Questions

Many students and instructors prefer multiple-choice tests because they provide specific answers to each question. It is easier for the instructor to grade this type of test because students can put their answers on scantron sheets, and tests may be corrected electronically, or, the instructor may have an answer key that makes for speedier scoring. Many students prefer these kinds of tests because they have a chance of guessing correctly when they do not know the answer. However, if the instructor deducts points for wrong answers, it may not be advantageous to guess.

Multiple-choice questions consist of two parts. The **stem** is the statement, question, or part that needs to be completed. Then, there are typically four or five **possible answers or choices.** One option will be correct; the others will be distracters.

> | Absolute Words |
> | --- |
> | All |
> | Everyone |
> | None |
> | Always |
> | Only |
> | No |
> | Invariable |
> | Never |
> | No one |
> | Every |

- Watch for key words. Underline them so they stand out and help you focus on the major points. As you read the question, try to answer it without looking at the options. Then read the choices to see if any match the answer you gave. Do not make a choice without reading all the responses! Eliminate the obvious distracters to improve your chances of choosing the correct answer.

- Be on the lookout for statements with absolute words or extreme modifiers. They are almost always incorrect because they do not allow for an exception. Very few things in life are absolute.

Ex. Elderly patients experiencing dementia

a. *are always diagnosed with Alzheimer's disease.*
b. *only lose their verbal skills.*
c. *are never able to reside in their own homes.*
d. *sometimes exhibit aggressive behaviors.*

The only answer that does not contain an absolute word is "d."

- Along with absolute words, be aware of statements such as "all but one" or "except for one." This means the majority of the options are correct.
Ex. All but one of the following Americans landed safely on the moon.
a. *Neil Armstrong*
b. *Edwin Aldrin, Jr.*
c. *Jackie Robinson*
d. *Michael Collins*
In this case, the correct answer is "c." Jackie Robinson was a famous baseball player, but he never landed on the moon.

- Be attentive to double negatives that can make a statement true rather than false.
Ex. In some states it is not illegal to
a. *transport heroin*
b. *manufacture LSD*
c. *use marijuana*
d. *sell cocaine*
The answer is "c." Not illegal means it is legal. Some states allow the use of marijuana for medical reasons.

- If you can choose only one response, choose the one that provides the most complete answer.
Ex. During the Civil War, major Union victories were won at
a. *Shiloh*
b. *Gettysburg & Vicksburg*
c. *Bull Run*
d. *Gettysburg, Vicksburg, and Shiloh*
The correct answer is "d." Although "a," and "b," are true, "d" is more complete.

- When two options are the same, you will know that neither is correct.
  Ex. A polar bear can run up to
  a. 1.5 miles per hour
  b. 5 miles per hour
  c. 15 miles per hour
  d. 1 1/2 miles per hour
  The correct answer will be selected between "b" and "c." "A" and "d" are the same.

- When alternatives seem equally correct, select the one that is longest and contains the most information.
  Ex. Down's Syndrome in infants is most often caused by
  a. Heredity
  b. Smoking
  c. Genetic and environmental factors
  d. Alcohol

- When statements contain digits, the answer usually is not the extreme, but rather a middle number.
  Ex. A pound is equal to
  a. 1.6 oz.
  b. 6 oz.
  c. 16 oz.
  d. 66 oz.
  "A" and "d" are definitely out of the ballpark. The answer is "c." An exception to this rule occurs when the real answer is actually lower or higher than most people would expect.

  When responses are similar, one is likely to be correct. When the choices are opposites, one of them is always wrong. The other is often, but not always, correct.

  Ex. The Caribbean Islands are located in

  a. The Pacific Ocean
  b. The Atlantic Ocean
  c. The Mediterranean Sea
  d. The Panama Canal

  In the above example, the Caribbean Islands are located in the Atlantic Ocean.

- The correct answer should agree with the stem in number, gender, and person. It will also match grammatically.
- Carefully read those test items that use two or three combined options as a possible response. Sometimes this is the correct answer. If you know for sure that more than one of the choices are correct, it is likely that "all of the above" are true. Be cautious, however, when you see "all of the above" or "none of the above." These could be trick questions, or the examiner may have used it only because s/he couldn't think of another choice.
- Unless there is a penalty for wrong answers, if you cannot figure out the answer—GUESS. If you have studied, choose the answer that sounds right. If you guess randomly, choose "b" or "c." The odds are higher that the answer is one of the middle choices. *Go over your test when you are finished to make sure you have answered all of the questions.*

Common Qualifiers

Many
Seldom
Almost
Sometimes
Frequently
Can
Most
Usually
Rarely
Ordinarily
Occasionally
Few
Some
Likely
Often
Possibly
Generally
Might

True/False Tests

These are one of the most common types of examination questions. When answering, be careful not to overanalyze the questions. Do not be consumed with the fear that these are trick questions. Assume that the instructor is asking straightforward questions. Here are some things to watch for when answering true/false questions.

> | **Negative Words and Prefixes** |
> | :--- |
> | Not |
> | Un |
> | In |
> | Dis |
> | Cannot |
> | Il |
> | Ir |
> | Im |
> | Mis |

- For a statement to be true, every part of it must be true. If any word or phrase is false, the statement is false.
  Ex. Columbus tried to find a western route to the Orient in 1492 when he set sail with three ships, the Nina, the Pinta, and the Santa Clara.

  The name of Columbus' third ship was the Santa Maria, not the Santa Clara.

- Statements that have reasons in them are often false. Words such as "because," "therefore," "consequently," "the cause of," or "as a result of" are all words used to indicate reasons.
  Ex. Obesity results from overeating.

  This is a false statement because everyone who overeats is not obese. Likewise, obesity can be the result of a medical problem.

- Statements that contain qualifiers leave open the chance for more "true" answers.
  Ex. An instructor's personal preference generally determines which type of tests s/he gives.

  This statement is true. Preferences often, but not always, influence tests.

- Some of the same rules that apply to multiple choice tests will also apply to true/ false exams. Remember what we said about absolutes.
  Ex. All candy contains sugar.

  With so many substitutes today, sugarless candy is readily available. However, be careful, because some absolute statements can be true.

  Ex. Communication is always a two-way process.

- Watch out for negative statements. Your mind is more likely to "read over" negative words, causing you to miss them. If you are allowed to write on your test paper, underline negative words as you read to draw attention to them. In the English language, a double negative makes the statement positive. This is one of those grammar rules that you may ignore in conversations with your friends, but ignoring it on a test will cost you valuable points.
  Ex. Different cultures must not be studied in an unbiased fashion.

  This statement is false. An easy way to avoid the double negative trap is to cross out both of the negatives and read the sentence without them. The above example would then read: *Different cultures must be studied in a biased fashion.* Reading the sentence this way makes it clear that this is a false statement.

- Once again, if you do not know the answer—GUESS.

  Do not leave unanswered questions on a test. If you've followed the above strategies and still don't know which answer to guess, mark the answer true. It is generally easier for instructors to write true statements when making up a test, as they usually want to accentuate the positive.

Matching Tests

Here are a few pointers for being able to logically match items on the test.

- Check to see if there are an exact number of matches. Also, check to see if any of the matches may be used more than once.
- Look for a pattern. Start with either column—whichever is easiest—and continue to work with that column.
- Read through the list of choices. Select the ones you know, and use them first to match with words in the other column.
- Use clues from other parts of the test.
- Apply all grammar rules—"a," "an," "subject/verb agreement," "singular/plurals," etc.

Strategies* to Answering Essay Questions

Along with multiple-choice questions, essay questions are among the most commonly used forms on college exams. Following are strategies that will help you achieve peak levels of performance on essay questions.

1. **Focus on main ideas first.** Before you begin answering the question by writing full sentences, make a brief outline or list of bullet points to represent the main ideas you will include in your answers. Outlines are effective for several reasons:

   - **An outline helps you remember the major points.** It prevents you from becoming so wrapped up in the details of constructing sentences and choosing words for your answers that you lose the big picture and forget the most important points you need to make.
   - **An outline improves your answer's organization.** In addition to reminding you of the points you intend to make, an outline gives you a plan for sequencing your ideas in an order that ensures they flow smoothly. One factor that instructors consider when awarding points for an answer to an essay question is how well that answer is organized An outline makes your answer's organization clearer by calling your attention to its major categories and subcategories.
   - **Having an advanced idea of what you will write reduces your test anxiety.** An outline takes care of the answers organization beforehand so you don't have the added stress of worrying about how to organize your answer at the same time you're writing and explaining your answer.
   - **An outline can add points to an incomplete answer's score.** If you run out of test time before writing out your full answer to an essay question, an outline allows your instructor to see what you planned to include in your written answer. Your outline itself is likely to earn you points because it demonstrates your knowledge of the major points called for by the question, In contrast, if you skip an outline and just start writing answers to test questions one at a time, you run the risk of not getting to questions you know well before your time is up; you'll then have nothing on your test to show what you know about those unfinished questions.

Written answers to two short essay questions given by a college sophomore, which demonstrate effective use of bulleted lists or short outlines (in the side margin) to ensure recall of most important points.

EXHIBIT 1

1. There are several different studies that scientists conduct, but one study that they conduct is to find out how genetics can influence human behavior in <u>identical twins.</u> Since they are identical they will most likely end up very similar in behavior because of their identical genetic makeup Although environment has some impact genetics are still a huge factor and they will. more likely than not. behave similarly. Another type of study is with <u>parents and their family trees.</u> Looking at a subjects family tree will explain why a certain person is bipolar or depressed. It is most likely caused by a gene in the family tree, even if it was last seen decades ago. Lastly. another study is with adopted children. If an <u>adopted child</u> acts a certain way that is unique to that child and researchers find the parents' family <u>tree. they will most likely see similar behavior in the parents and siblings as well.</u>	Identical twins Adoption Parents/family tree 6/6
2. The monistic view of the mind brain relationship is so strongly opposed and criticized because there is a belief or assumption <u>that free will is taken</u> away from people. For example, if a person commits a horrendous crime, if can be argued "monistically" that the chemicals in the brain were the reason, and that a person cannot think for themselves to act otherwise. This view limits responsibility. Another reason that this view is opposed is because <u>it</u> has been said that <u>there is no afterlife.</u> If the mind and brain are one and, the same, and there is <u>NO</u> difference, then once the brain is dead and <u>is</u> no longer functioning so is the mind. Thus, it cannot continue to live beyond what we know today as life. <u>And</u> this goes against many religions. which is why this reason, in particular, is heavily opposed.	No freewill No afterlife 6/6

2. **Get directly to the point on each essay question.** Avoid elaborate introductions that take up your test time (and your instructor's grading time) but don't earn you any points. For example, an answer that begins with the statement "This is an interesting question that we had a great discussion on in class ..." is pointless because it will not add points to your test score. The time available to you on essay tests is often limited, so you can't afford flowery introductions that waste valuable test time and don't contribute anything to your overall test score.

   One effective way to get directly to the point on essay questions is to include part of the question in the first sentence of your answer. For example, suppose the test question asks you to; "Argue for or against capital punishment by explaining how it will or will not reduce the nation's murder rate." Your first sentence could be, "Capital punishment will not reduce the murder rate for the following reasons ..." Thus, your first sentence becomes your thesis statement, which immediately points you directly to the major points you're going to make in your answer and earns immediate points for your answer.

3. **Answer all essay questions with as much detail as possible.** Don't assume that your instructor already knows what you're talking about or will be bored by details. Instead, take the approach that you're writing to someone who knows little or nothing about the subject—as if you're an expert teacher and the reader is a clueless student.

Remember

As a rule, it's better to over explain than under explain your answers to essay questions.

4. **Support your points with evidence—facts, statistics, quotes, or examples.** When taking essay tests, take on the role of a lawyer making a case by presenting concrete evidence (exhibit A, exhibit B, etc.). Since timed essay tests can often press you for time, be sure to prioritize and cite your most powerful points and persuasive evidence. If you have time later, you can return to add other points worth mentioning.

5. **Leave space between your answers to each essay question.** This strategy will enable you to easily add information to your original answer if you have time or if you recall something later in the test that you forgot initially.

6. **Proofread your test for spelling and grammar.** Before turning in your test, proofread what you've written and correct any obvious spelling or grammatical errors you find. Eliminating them is likely to improve your test score. Even if your instructor doesn't explicitly state that grammar and spelling will be counted in determining your grade, these mechanical mistakes are still likely to influence your professor's overall evaluation of your written work.

7. **Neatness counts.** Many years of research indicates that neatly written essays tend to be scored higher than sloppy ones, even if the answers are essentially the same (Huck & Bounds, 1972; Klen & Hart, 1968; Hughes, Keeling, & Tuck, 1983; Pai, Sanji, Pai, & Kotian, 2010). These findings are understandable when you consider that grading essay answers is a time-consuming task that requires your instructor to plod through multiple styles of handwriting whose readability may range from crystal-clear to cryptic. Make an earnest attempt to write as clearly as possible, and if you finish the test with time to spare, clean up your work by rewriting any sloppy written words or sentences.

* From *Thriving in College and Beyond: Research-Based Strategies for Academic Success and Personal Development* by Jospeh B. Cuseo, Aaron Thompson, Michele Campagna, and Viki S. Fecas. Copyright © 2013 by Kendall Hunt Publishing Company. Reprinted by permission.

Direction Words

When writing an essay or short answer, your response should answer the question. Failure to follow the directions can drastically lower your grade. It is important that you understand the meaning of these common direction words so you can state your answer correctly.

Special Testing Situations

Open-book Tests

Many students feel that these are the easiest tests to take, but do not be led astray. Open-book tests are probably more difficult. They may have to be completed in a certain amount of time. Not only must you study and know where to find the material quickly for your answers, you must also learn to think critically. Questions are never verbatim. Always practice making up and answering test questions that you think the instructor might choose.

Take-home Tests

Every student's dream! But, once again, don't be misled. Take-home tests are usually more difficult and ask for lengthier answers. You will still need to study and know the material. The biggest danger is waiting too long before preparing for the test. You do not want to wait until it is in your hand before learning the material. Critical thinking is also an integral part of take-home tests.

Direction	Definition
Analyze	To break or separate the whole into its parts. To determine the nature, function, qualities, characteristics, relationships, and effects of the parts to the whole. In English, you may do this with a sentence; in science, with a substance; in math, with an equation. *Ex. Analyze the properties of water.*
Argue or	To give reasons for or against something. A discussion or debate that supports or refutes
Defend	a position. In preparing an argument, you try to defend a point or persuade others to a cause. *Ex. Argue whether or not courtroom proceedings should be televised.*
Comment	To present a pro or con opinion or viewpoint on a subject. *Ex. Comment on the choice of Beijing as a Winter Olympics site.*
Compare	To identify similarities and differences on a given topic. *Ex. Compare "Buddhism" with "Hinduism."*
Contrast	To stress the differences or dissimilarities among things; to show how things are "unlike" one another. *Ex. Contrast "assertive" and "aggressive" communication styles.*
Critique or	To express your own views or the views of an "expert." You need to include positive and
Evaluate	negative points/opinions. *Ex. Critique The Raven by Edgar Allan Poe.*
Define or	To provide a clear and concise meaning, a comprehensive description, or the identifying
Identify	characteristics. Do not use the term to define itself. *Ex. Define the term Existentialism. / Identify the major stressors for college students.*
Describe,	Give a detailed account or picture, frequently in narrative form, to make something
Discuss,	understandable. Include positive and negative points or cause and effect relationships for
Explain, or	clarification. *Ex. Describe a balanced lifestyle. / Explain personality development from a*
State	Psychodynamic perspective.
Diagram or	To use a sketch, chart, graph, outline, labels, or examples to explain and clarify a point.
Illustrate	Ex. Diagram the anatomy of a heart. / Illustrate the human body's nervous system.
Justify	Demonstrate or prove what is right, just, or valid by providing reasons or evidence for a decision or act. *Ex. Justify the use of pesticides in twenty-first century orchards.*
Label	To classify, designate, identify, and attach a name to some specific group or theory. *Ex. Label the primary classes in the animal kingdom.*
List or enumerate	To provide an itemized list or to make points one by one in order. Ex. List the qualities of a good public speaker. / Enumerate the steps involved in good decision-making.

(Continued)

Direction	Definition
Narrate	To provide an accounting of something or to tell a series of events in story form. *Ex. Narrate the events that led to the economic blockade of Cuba.*
Outline	To summarize the main points or provide an organized listing of the main topics. *Ex. Outline the main events that led to the Civil Rights Movement.*
Paraphrase	To express an idea in your own words. *Ex. Paraphrase Howard Gardner's Theory of Multiple Intelligences.*
Prove	To present factual evidence and give logical reasons to support something. Frequently used in the sciences (tests or experiments) to establish something as true or valid. *Ex. Prove that Uranium 235 degrades to lead. Include all 17 steps.*
Relate	To show how things are connected with each other, to give cause and effect, or to explore relationships and correlations. This is usually done in narrative form. *Ex. Relate the importance of values, interests, and personality on career choice.*
Review or	To discuss the main points in a clear and concise manner. You may be required to give a
Summarize	critical analysis, as in a review of a book or play. *Ex. Review the study systems discussed in class. Summarize effective listening techniques.*
Trace	To narrate the development or process of something in a historical fashion, showing the sequence of events through time. *Ex. Trace the events that led to the exploration of Mars in the latter half of the twentieth century.*

*Online Tests***

More instructors are using technology to enhance their courses. It is very possible that you could have to take an online test even when you are not taking an online course. When taking a test online, you should always read the instructions carefully. Below are some things you should consider when taking online tests.

1. **Online tests are often timed.** Because you are taking these tests outside of class, you are able to use your notes and books. For this reason, many instructors will place a time limit on the test. If you do not complete the test in time, it will shut off when your time is up and you won't be able to do the rest of the test. Be sure to study for online timed tests. You will not have enough time to look up all of the answers, and if you don't study, you won't do well.

2. **Backtracking might be prohibited.** Sometimes you have to answer a question before you can move on to the next question, and once you move on, you cannot go back and change an answer. If this is a timed test, be sure to use your time wisely and don't spend too much time on any one question.

When taking online tests, be sure you are using a reliable computer and you are free from anything that could take your focus away from the test (i.e., cell phone, children, etc.). If something does go wrong during the test, be sure to contact instructor immediately.

Standardized Tests

Tests such as the ACT, SAT, COMPASS, and ASVAB are standardized tests. They are prepared by a testing service and administered under prescribed conditions. Although there are often different versions of the tests, the questions test the same content and require the same kinds of knowledge. Many times these tests are mandatory entrance or placement tests at colleges and universities, or they may be required for scholarships or enlisting in the military. There are several things to remember about standardized testing.

- *Prepare* sufficiently in *advance* for these tests.
- *Use study guides.* These resources are available in most libraries and bookstores. Preparatory classes may also be available in your area. These may be expensive; however, they will provide you with review and practice for the tests.
- Before taking the test, always *check to see if you will be penalized for guessing.* On the SAT test, a percentage is deducted for incorrect answers to discourage guessing.

Math Tests

Use all of the strategies that you use for other tests when taking math tests. Note the following special considerations:

- Break down complex problems, and work the steps one at a time.
- Show all your work in an organized fashion.
- Draw pictures or diagrams to help you visualize problems.
- Check your computations. Be sure you are using the right formulas, have the correct order of functions, and sined numbers are correct.
- Ask yourself if your answer makes common sense!

Preparing for Finals Week

- Know your schedule at least a week before finals begin. Finals week can sometimes sneak up on you, so it's a good idea to write it down in your daily planner well in advance.
- Determine how much and when you will study for each class.
- Know whether or not the final exam is comprehensive. Don't wait until the night before the exam to find this out.
- If the instructor allows you to take the final at a time other than the scheduled time for your class period, take that into consideration during your preparation. It is usually best to get the toughest finals out of the way first because fatigue sets in as the week goes on.

What Are the Causes of Poor Test Performance?

Even though the most obvious answer as to why students might not perform well on a test would be **INADEQUATE KNOWLEDGE**, this is certainly not the only answer. Part of the purpose of this chapter is to help you to analyze your typical test behavior and sort out the hindrances to your success. It is true that many students do not perform well on a test simply due to the fact that they did not study enough—or in the proper way. It is vital that you understand that it is not how **MANY** hours you study for a test that makes the difference. It is the **QUALITY** of those hours and the way they are **DISTRIBUTED** that spell out your success rate. Weekly reviews based on questions and recited answers over thorough lecture and text notes are the secrets to mastery. Intense cramming sessions the night before the test will not assure you that the information will be there when needed.

LANGUAGE-RELATED PROBLEMS can also affect your performance on tests. If you read the textbook but do not comprehend it, you will not perform to the best of your ability. If you have trouble understanding the test items, or knowing specifically what the question is asking for, your answer cannot be top-notch. Therefore, reading problems do influence many students' test grades.

Also, many students simply do not know how to take a test. Even though they may have taken hundreds in their lifetime, **INEFFECTIVE EXAM-TAKING SKILLS** may still be hindering their performance. Test-taking is a game one must learn to play—a skill that can be learned with practice. Certain rules must be learned and adhered to or the results will not please you. We will cover these "rules" in the next several sections.

Finally, **TEST ANXIETY** can cripple your test scores. You may have studied adequately, and you may feel you really do know the information, but if you panic during the test, your memory will not cooperate.

** From *Thriving in the Community College & Beyond: Strategies for Academic Success and Personal Development* by Joseph Cuseo, Aaron Thompson, Julie McLaughlin, and Steady Moono. Copyright © 2013 by Kendall Hunt Publishing Company. Reprinted by permission.

TEST ANXIETY

Before we take a close look at the symptoms and signs associated with test anxiety, complete the following assessment by checking the statements you tend to agree with. Do you ever

_____ *wish that tests did not bother you as much as they do?*

_____ *go blank during a test and not remember what you just studied?*

_____ *think that the more you study, the less you know?*

_____ *experience difficulty falling asleep the night before a test?*

_____ *find yourself feeling tense before, during, or after a test?*

_____ *worry about tests days or weeks in advance?*

_____ *find it difficult to stay focused while taking a test?*

_____ *feel your heart beating fast or experience difficulty breathing during a test?*

_____ *feel overly critical of your test performance?*

_____ *feel like running away from a testing situation?*

If you put a check by many of these questions, you may have test anxiety. Students talk about feeling anxious about upcoming tests, being unable to sleep, worrying for days about tests, and feeling pressure. Test anxiety can be debilitating. Learn to recognize the signs and symptoms early on to prevent anxious feelings from snowballing into the feeling of being utterly overwhelmed. Listed below are some specific ways that anxiety manifests itself physically, cognitively, and behaviorally.

Physical symptoms can include an accelerated heartbeat, difficulty breathing, profuse sweating, nausea, dry mouth, loss of appetite, insomnia, stomachache, headache, muscle tension, cold hands and feet, shaky hands, and an overall feeling of nervousness.

Cognitive symptoms include all the irrational, exaggerated, self-defeating thoughts and worries experienced in conjunction with test-taking. We know that thoughts influence behavior. Be aware of your thoughts. They can be powerful. Look at the list of irrational, self-defeating thoughts below, and think of how they might affect someone's performance while taking a test.

Behavioral symptoms can include procrastination, impulsive behavior, compulsive behavior, an inability to focus or concentrate, and avoidance behavior. When someone is anxious about taking a test, that person might avoid studying, decide to change majors impulsively, or engage in compulsive behaviors (e.g., checking again and again to make sure the door is locked, the oven is turned off, or their cell phone is on).

What can you do about physical, behavioral, and cognitive symptoms related to performance anxiety? The following section of this chapter focuses on how to manage test anxiety.

COMMON NEGATIVE THOUGHTS EXPERIENCED WHILE TAKING A TEST

This test is too hard. How will I ever pass?
My mind just went blank. I am doomed for sure.
I just want to finish and get out of here as soon as possible.
Everyone else is smarter than I am.
I just can't do multiple-choice questions.
I will never finish in time.
I am the only one doing poorly.
I will lose my scholarship.
It doesn't matter how hard I try, I still do poorly.
I think I'm going to throw up.
Have you ever had any of these thoughts? Below list some thoughts you have had that were associated with test taking (or another type of performance).

1. _____

2. _____

3. _____

4. _____

Strategies for Reducing Test Anxiety**

1. **Understand what test anxiety is and what it's not.** Don't confuse anxiety with stress. Stress is a physical reaction that prepares your body for action by arousing and energizing in this heightened arousal and energy can be used productively to strengthen your performance. In fact, if you're totally stress-free during an exam, it may mean that you're too "laid back" and couldn't care less about how well you're doing. Stress is something that cannot and should not be completely eliminated when you're trying to reach peak levels of performance, whether academic or athletic. Instead of trying to block, out stress altogether, your goal should be to control it, contain it, and maintain <u>it at a</u> level that maximizes the quality of your performance. The key is to keep stress at a moderate level, thereby capitalizing on its capacity to help you get psyched up or pumped up, but preventing it from reaching such a high level that you become psyched out or stressed out.

If you experience the following symptoms during tests, your stress level may be at a level high enough to be accurately called test anxiety

- You feel physical symptoms of tension during the test, such as a pounding heartbeat, a rapid pulse, muscle tension, sweating, or an upset stomach.
- Negative thoughts and feelings rush through your head—for example, fear of failure or self-defeating putdowns such as "I always mess up on exams."
- You rush through the test just to get it over with (probably because you want to get rid of the anxiety you're experiencing).
- You have difficulty concentrating or focusing your attention while answering test questions.
- Even though you studied and know the material, you go blank during the exam and forget what you studied. (However, you're able to remember the information after you turn in your test and leave the test situation.)

To minimize test anxiety, consider the following practices and strategies:

2. **Avoid cramming for exams.** Research indicates that college students who display greater amounts of procrastination experience higher levels of test anxiety (Rothblum, Solomon, & Murakami, 1986). High levels of pre-test tension associated with rushing and late-night cramming are likely to carry over to the test itself, resulting in higher levels of test-taking tension. Furthermore, loss of sleep caused by previous-night cramming results in lost dream (REM) sleep, which, in turn, elevates anxiety levels the following day—test day.

3. **Use effective test-preparation strategies prior to the exam.** Test-anxiety research indicates that college students who prepare well for exams not only achieve higher test scores, but also experience lower levels of test anxiety (Zohar, 1998). Other research findings demonstrate that using effective study strategies prior to the exam—such as those discussed in Chapter 5—reduces test anxiety during the exam (Benjamin, McKeachie, Lin, & Holinger, 1981; Jones & Petruzzi, 1995; Zeidner, 1995).

4. **During the exam, concentrate on the here and now.** Devote your attention fully to answering the test question that you're currently working on; don't spend time thinking (and worrying) about the tests outcome and what your grade will be.

5. **Stay focused on the test in front of you, not the students around you.** Don't spend valuable test time looking at what others are doing and wondering whether they're doing better than you are. If you came to the test well prepared and still find the test difficult, it's very likely that other students are finding it difficult too. If you happen to notice that other students are finishing before you do, don't assume they breezed through the test or that they're smarter than you, Their faster finish may simply reflect the fact that they didn't know many of the answers and decided to give up and get out, rather than prolong the agony.

6. **Don't spend a lot of time focusing on the amount of time left in the exam.** Repeatedly checking the time during the rest can disrupt the flow of your thought process and increase your stress level. Although it's important that you remain aware of how much time remain to complete the exam, only check the time periodically and do your time-checking after you've completed answering a question so you don't disrupt or derail your train of thought.

7. **Control your thought** by focusing on what you're getting right, rather than worrying about what answer you don't know and how many points you're losing. Our thoughts influence our emotions (Ellis, 1995), and positive emotions, such as those associated. with optimism and a sense of accomplishment, can improve mental performance by enhancing the brain's ability to process, store, and retrieve information (Rosenfield, 1988).Keep in mind that college exams are

often designed to be more difficult than high school tests, so it's less likely that student get 90 to 100 percent of the total points. You can still achieve a good grade on a college exam without having to achieve a near-perfect test score.

8. Remember that **if you're experiencing a *moderate* amount of stress during the exam, this isn't abnormal** or an indication that you're suffering from test anxiety. If you're experiencing moderate levels of tension, it indicates that you're motivated and want to do well, In fact, research shows that experiencing *moderate* levels of tension during tests and other performance-evaluation situations serves to maximize alertness, concentration, and memory (Sapolsky, 2004).

9. **Don't forget that it's just a test: it's not a measure of your ability or character.** An exam is not a measure of your overall intelligence, your overall academic ability, or your quality as a person. In fact, a test grade may be less of an indication of your effort or ability than of the complexity of the particular content covered by the test material or the nature of the test itself. Furthermore, one low grade on one particular test doesn't mean you're not capable of doing good work and are going to end up with a poor grade in the course, particularly if you use the results as feedback to improve your next test performance (See p. 151.)

10. One final note on the topic of test anxiety: if you continue to experience test anxiety after implementing the above strategies, **don't hesitate to seek assistance from a professional in your Learning (Academic Support) Center or Personal Counseling Office**.

** From *Thriving in the Community College & Beyond: Strategies for Academic Success and Personal Development* by Joseph Cuseo, Aaron Thompson, Julie McLaughlin, and Steady Moono. Copyright © 2013 by Kendall Hunt Publishing Company. Reprinted by permission.

AFTER (A)

Continue to *review, revise,* and *self-modify* your test taking style and strategies as needed.

Test Results

What do you do when the tests are returned to you? This is a great opportunity to learn from your mistakes and to help you prepare for the next exam. Go over all the errors that you made. If the instructor wants the tests returned, jot down the kinds of mistakes you made in order to develop new and better strategies for the next test. Analyze the instructor's style of testing. Was the test objective or subjective? Were the questions taken directly from the book, from lecture notes, or from both? Was there a pattern in the answers that would help you guess in the future? What kind of mistakes did you make?

Never throw away a returned test until after the final exam. You may use these tests to review for that final and improve your grades. See if you need to further develop any of the following:

- **More effective time management for studying and taking tests**
- **Better note taking techniques**
- **Reviewing throughout the semester**
- **Better study and test-taking strategies**
- **Reading and following directions accurately**
- **Providing more details for your answers**
- **Getting a full night's rest before the exam**
- **Eating a healthy breakfast the day of a test**

SUMMARY

Good test results require extra effort. Proper preparation for test taking includes class attendance, effective use of your textbook and notes, good study habits, getting information about the test beforehand, and practicing test taking. These are important components for good grades. If you learn to use the strategies suggested in this chapter you can improve your scores on exams and in your classes.

You can also learn from your mistakes by reviewing the test after it has been graded. In the future, do not repeat your errors. Set goals for improving your skills.

SUGGESTED READING

Pauk, Walter. *How to Study in College.* 7th ed. New York: Houghton Mifflin Co., 2001.

EXERCISE 9.1: CONDUCTING RESEARCH ABOUT TEST-TAKING

For each assignment below, write a paragraph summarizing what you learn from your research.

1. Using your college library and the Internet, search for information about taking essay tests. Summarize in a paragraph strategies you learned about taking essay tests. Make sure to include the web address for the site you used. (Remember to evaluate your site based on information you learned in Chapter 2)

2. Go to your College's web page and find the **Student Code of Conduct**. Write a paragraph including the following information:

    *   **The College's definition of "cheating"**

    *   **The academic sanctions that may be levied against a student who is found guilty of cheating**

    *   **The consequences for a student found guilty of a second academic violation**

EXERCISE 9.2: RECOGNIZING AND REDUCING TEST ANXIETY

Being anxious about a test is normal. Some anxiety is actually helpful as it keeps you on alert and reflects that you care about the outcome. However, for some students it can also hinder their performance.

1. Identify 3 different types of symptoms of test anxiety (1 physical, 1 cognitive and 1 behavioral) that either you or someone you know may have experienced prior to or during a test. List the symptom in the first column and then identify the type of symptom it is in the second column below.

2. Now use your critical thinking skills and apply information you learned about reducing test anxiety to develop a response plan for each of these symptoms. How could you prevent them or respond appropriately when you are experiencing the symptom? BE SPECIFIC.

Symptom	Type of Symptom (Physical, Cognitive or Behavioral)	Prevention or Response Plan

EXERCISE 9.3: SELF-REFLECTION JOURNAL – EXAMINING YOUR TEST-TAKING ERRORS

Review a test you have taken recently, on which you did not receive a satisfactory grade. Make a list of the reasons you did not do well on this test. Consider the quantity and quality of your preparation. Examine your errors. What went wrong? Using self-reflection and information learned from this chapter, summarize what you believe were the primary causes of your test-taking errors and explain how you plan to revise/apply test-preparation and test-taking skills learned to improve in the future.

_____

_____

_____

_____

_____

_____

_____

_____

_____

_____

_____

_____

_____

_____

_____

_____

_____

_____

_____

_____

_____

_____

Chapter 10

Academic and Career Planning – Where Do I Go from Here?

INTRODUCTION

We know what you might be thinking: "Have I decided on a career? Give me a break; I've barely begun college!" This is probably the way most college seniors felt when they were first-year students. However, if you ask these seniors how they feel now, they would probably say something like: "I can't believe I'm about to graduate. How did time fly by so fast?" For these seniors and other students who will be graduating in this century, they are likely to continue working until age 75 (Herman, 2000). Also, consider the fact that once you begin full-time work, you will spend the majority of your waking hours at work. The fact is, the only other single activity that you will spend more time doing in your lifetime is sleeping. When you consider that such a sizable amount of our lifetime is spent working, plus the fact that work can influence our sense of self-esteem and personal identity, it is never too early to start thinking about your career choices.

Remember

When you are doing career planning, you're also doing life planning; you are planning how to spend your future life doing what you want to do.

It is true that college graduation and career entry are years away, but the process of investigating, planning, and preparing for career success should begin during your first year of college. If you are undecided about a career, or have not even begun to think about what you'll be doing after college, don't be discouraged. In fact, you can join the club, because research indicates that the majority of college students are in the same boat. Three of every four beginning students are uncertain or have doubt about their career choice (Frost, 1991; Cuseo, 2005).

Even* if you may have already decided on a career that you've been dreaming about since you were a preschooler, you will still need to make decisions about what specific type of specialization within that career you will pursue. For example, if you are interested in pursuing a career in law, you will eventually need to decide what branch of law you wish to practice (for example, criminal law, corporate law, or family law). You will also need to decide about what employment sector or type of industry you'd like to work in, such as: for profit, non-profit, education, or government. Each of these sectors will provide you with different options relating to the same career. For example, a student who is interested in an advertising career may work for an advertising agency (for profit) to encourage the purchase of a certain product, or may work in the non-profit sector to create a campaign for increasing public awareness of safety issues (e.g., persuade the public not to drink and drive). This student could also decide to create an effective advertisement designed to increase reading (education sector), or attempt to persuade people to enter public service positions (government). As these examples illustrate, there are still many options to consider and decisions to be made, even if you have decided on a particular career path.

Thus, no matter how certain or uncertain you are about your career path at this point in time, you will need to begin exploring different career options and start taking your first steps toward formulating a career development plan.

BEFORE (B)

Preparation, self-awareness, and *planning* are all important in the academic and career planning process, and you should …

- **Complete a self-assessment**
- **Explore potential careers**

STEP ONE: SELF-ASSESSMENT

The more you know about yourself, the better your choices and decisions will be. Self-awareness is a particularly important step to take when making career decisions because the career you choose to pursue says a lot about who you are and what you want from life. Your personal identity and life goals should not be based on or built around your career choice; instead, it should be the other way around: **Your personal identity and life goals should be considered first and should provide the foundation on which you build your career choice**.

One way to gain greater self-awareness of your career interests, abilities, and values is by taking psychological tests or assessments. These assessments allow you to see how your interest in certain career fields compares with other students who have taken the same assessment, and how your interests compare with people working in different career fields who have experienced career satisfaction and success. These *comparative perspectives* can give you important reference points for assessing whether your level of interest in different careers is high, average, or low, relative to other students and working professionals. By seeing how your results compare with others, you may become aware of your distinctive or unique interests. Your Career Development Center is the place on campus where you can find these career-interest tests, as well as other instruments that may allow you to assess your career-related abilities and values.

In addition to career assessments, the learning styles instruments may sharpen self-awareness of your personal interests and preferences, and may provide useful information for making career choices. Also, self-assessment questions about your personal interests, abilities, and values to help you select a college major may also be used to help you select a career path.

Lastly, when making choices about a career, you may also have to consider one other important aspect of yourself: your personal needs. A personal "need" may be best understood as something stronger than an interest. When you satisfy a personal need, you are doing something that makes your life more satisfying or fulfilling. Psychologists have identified a number of important human needs that vary in strength or intensity from one individual to another. Listed in Box 1 are personal needs that we feel are the most relevant or important ones to consider when making decisions about careers.

Pierce Howard, author of *The Owner's Manual for the Brain*, puts it this way: "It is stressful to attempt to be someone different from who we are, to try to be solitary when our nature is to be gregarious. Being true to our nature is, in some ways, the ultimate goal. Attempting to be something different is an obstacle to that goal. Don't

---

PERSONAL NEEDS TO CONSIDER WHEN MAKING CAREER CHOICES

As you read the needs listed in the box below, make a note after each one, indicating how strong the need is for you (high, moderate, or low).

When exploring career options, keep in mind how different careers may or may not satisfy your level of need for autonomy, affiliation, competence, and sensory stimulation, each of which is described below.

1. **Autonomy:** Need to work independently, without close supervision or control.

   Individuals high in this need may experience greater satisfaction working in careers that allow them to be their own boss, make their own decisions, and control their own work schedule. Individuals low in this need may be more satisfied working in careers that are more structured and involve a supervisor who provides direction, assistance, and frequent feedback.

2. **Affiliation:** Need for social interaction, a sense of belongingness, and the opportunity to collaborate with others.

   Individuals high in this need may be more satisfied working in careers that involve frequent interpersonal interaction and teamwork with colleagues or co-workers. Individuals low in this need may be more satisfied working alone, or in competition with others, rather than careers that emphasize interpersonal interaction or collaboration.

3. **Achievement:** Need to experience challenge and achieve a sense of personal accomplishment.

   Individuals high in this need may be more satisfied working in careers that push them to solve problems, generate creative ideas, and continually learn new information or master new skills. Individuals low in this need may be more satisfied with careers that do not continually test their abilities, and do not repeatedly challenge them to stretch their skills by taking on new tasks or different responsibilities.

4. **Sensory Stimulation:** Need to experience variety, change, and risk.

   Individuals high in this need may be more satisfied working in careers that involve frequent changes of pace and place (e.g., frequent travel), unpredictable events (e.g., work tasks that vary considerably from day to day), and moderate stress (e.g., working under pressure of competition or deadlines). Individuals with a low need for sensory stimulation may feel more comfortable working in careers that involve regular routines, predictable situations, and minimal levels of risk or stress.

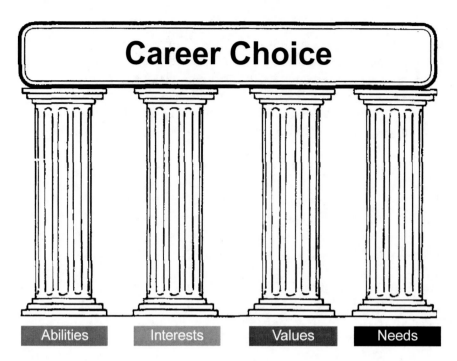

Figure 10.1 Personal Characteristics Providing the Foundation for Effective Career Choice.

expect a recluse to be motivated to sell, a creative thinker to be motivated to be a good proofreader day in and day out, or a sow's ear to be happy in the role of a silk purse" (2000, pp. 386–387).

Taken altogether, there are four key aspects of yourself that should be considered when exploring careers: your personal *abilities, interests, values,* and *needs*. As illustrated in Figure 10.1, these are the four pillars that provide a solid foundation for effective career choices and decisions. You want to choose a career that you're good at, interested in, passionate about, and that fulfills your personal needs.

Lastly, since a career decision is a long-range decision that will involve your life beyond college, self-awareness should not only involve personal reflection about who you are now, it also involves *self-projection*—reflecting on how you see yourself in the more distant future. When you engage in the process of self-projection, you begin to see a connection between where you are now and where you want to be.

Ideally, your choice of a career would be one that leads to a future career scenario in which your typical workday goes something like this: You wake up in the morning and hop out of bed enthusiastically—eagerly looking forward to what you'll be doing at work that day. When you're at work, time flies by, and before you know it, the day's over. When you return to bed that night and look back on your day, you feel good about what you did and how well you did it. For this ideal scenario to have any chance of really happening or even coming close to happening, you have to select a career path that is true to yourself—that closely matches your abilities (what you do well), your interests (what you like to do), your values (what you feel good about doing), and your needs (what brings you satisfaction and fulfillment in life).

STEP TWO: CAREER EXPLORATION

The Importance of Career Planning

College graduates in the 21st century are likely to continue working until age 75 (Herman, 2000). Once you enter the workforce full time, most of the remaining waking hours of your life will be spent working. The only other single activity you'll spend more time on in your entire life is sleeping. When you consider that such a sizable portion of life is spent working, it's understandable how you career can have such a strong influence on your personal identity and self esteem. Give the importance of career choice, the process of career exploration and planning should begin now—during the first year of your college experience.

Even if you've decided on a career that you were dreaming about since you were a preschooler, you still need to engage in the process of career exploration and planning because you still need to decide on what specialization within that career you'll pursue. For example, if you're interested in pursuing a career in law, you'll need to eventually decide what branch of law you wish to practice (e.g., criminal law, corporate law, or family law). You'll also need to decide what employment sector or type of industry you would like to work in, such as nonprofit, for-profit, education, or government. Thus, no matter how certain or uncertain you are about your career path, you still need to explore career options and start taking your first steps toward formulating a career development plan.

Remember

When you're doing career planning, you're doing life planning because you're planning how you will spend most of the waking hours of your future life

Becoming a 21st-Century Graduate

Although graduation seems to be in the far and distant future, it's never too soon to plan for the demands that will await you once you have your degree in hand. What will those

1. **App developer:** When you hear "there's an app for that," that's because a career track emerged for program developers who expanded their professional knowledge and skills into the world of mobile devices.
2. **Mark Research data miner:** Ever wonder how retailers know how to market to you? Market research data miners collect data on consumer behaviors and predict trends for advertisers to use to develop marketing strategies.
3. **Educational or admissions consultant:** Some parents take extra steps to make sure their children are accepted into the "right" schools (from) preschool to college). Educational or admissions consultants are hired to guide families through the application and interview process.
4. **Millennial generation expert**. It's very common to find members of different generations who are working together in the same organization. Millennial generation experts help employers maximize the potential of their staff by providing advice on working with their youngest employees and how to mentor them for future success.
5. **Social media manager:** The business world has made great use of social media to market and advertise their products and services. Social media managers target their marketing to the users of the various social media sites.
6. **Chief listening officer:** Similar to a social media manager, a chief listening officer uses social media to monitor consumer discussions and shares this information with marketing agents so they can design strategies that appeal to various segments of the population.
7. **Cloud computing services**. Most Web sites used every day by consumers store incredibly large amounts of data. These computer engineers, who have an expertise in data management store and index tremendous volumes of bytes for companies (in the area of a quadrillion!).
8. **Elder care**. As life expectancy in the U.S. has increased, so has the need for individuals who have the knowledge, and the agencies and companies that assist them.
9. **Sustainability expert**. For environmental and economic reasons, companies are seeking ways to minimize their carbon footprints. Sustainability experts have an expertise in the science of sustainability and the know-how to develop "green" business practices that are also cost-effective.
10. **User experience designer**. User experience designers do exactly what their titles suggest—they create experiences for consumes through technology. These designers bring to life color, sound, and images using HTML, Photoshop, and CSS.

Source: Casserly (2012)

Figure 10.2 Jobs That Didn't Exist 10 Years Ago

demands be specifically? Well, that may be hard to anticipate right now when you think about how quickly our world is changing. When you consider the list of jobs in Figure 10.2 that didn't exist 10 years ago, you can see how these careers express the global changes have occurred in the past decade. While planning for the future seems to be full of uncertainties, you can work now with your advisor and the Career Development Center on identifying your abilities, interests, and values and then factor this information into your educational plan. Be sure to take full advantage of the curricular and co-curricular opportunities that align with the components of your plan. In doing so, you will prepare yourself to become a 21st-century graduate who is ready for an ever-changing world.

Another important point to consider is that it is common for Americans to change jobs throughout their working lives. In fact, studies show that Americans change jobs 10 times in the two decades following college and that such change is even more frequent for younger workers (AAC&U, 2007). So, while you might be focused on a particular career, it's also important that you widen your focus and acquire a breadth of skills and knowledge that will make you marketable for a variety of career paths. The transferability of experiences offered by your major, the liberal arts, and the co-curricular programs offered on your campus is the key to your success. Not only are employers seeking job candidates with a strong foundation in their field, they want their new hires to have the 21st-century skills that will propel their companies and organizations forward. That is, their new hires need to be adaptable, innovative problem-solvers who have strong communications skills and are culturally competent when interacting with people from diverse backgrounds.

Choosing a Career

How do people choose a career? There are many complex factors that go into your career choice. Some of the factors involved in choosing a career include

Heredity. You inherit genes from your parents that play a role in shaping who you are.

Intelligence. Every person has a unique mixture of talents and skills. You can work to develop these skills.

Experience. Your experiences can either build your self-confidence or cause you to doubt your abilities.

Environment. What careers have you observed in your environment? Maybe your father was a doctor and you grew up familiar with careers in medicine. Your parents may have encouraged you to choose a particular career. You may want to learn about other possibilities.

Social roles. Maybe you learned that men are engineers and women are teachers because your father is an engineer and your mother is a teacher. It is important to think critically about traditional roles so that your choices are not limited.

Learning. What you have learned will play a part in your career decision. You may need to learn new behaviors and establish new habits. How you learn (your learning style) influences career choice.

Relationships. We sometimes choose careers to enhance relationships. For example, you may choose a career that gives you time to spend with your family or with people who are important to you.

Stress. Our ability to cope with stress plays a part in career choice. Some enjoy challenges; others value peace of mind.

Health. Good health increases career options and enjoyment of life.

Factors in Career Choice

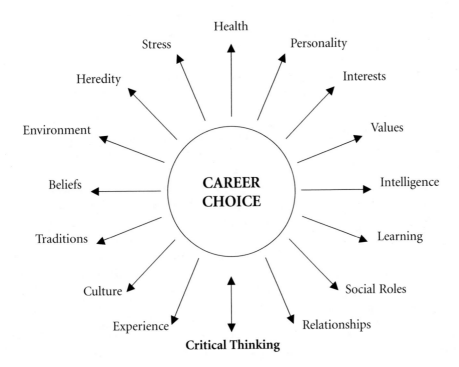

Personality. Your personality is a major factor influencing which career you might enjoy.

Values. What you value determines which career you will find satisfying.

Culture. Your culture has an influence on which careers you value.

Traditions. Traditions often guide career choice.

Beliefs. Your beliefs about yourself and the world determine your behavior and career choice.

Interests. If you choose a career that matches your interests, you can find satisfaction in your career.

To learn about career possibilities, research the following:

- **What career matches my personality, interests, aptitudes and values?** Learn how to do career research to find the best career for you. Find a career that has a good outlook for the future.
- **How can I plan my education to get the career I want?** Once you have identified your area of interest, consult your college catalog or advisor to make an educational plan that matches your career goals.

By following the above steps, you can find the major that is best for you and minimize the time you spend in college. There are many resources available to you to help in this process. Career Centers, Counselors, and Academic Advisors are great resources to help you research career and academic possibilities. However, it is up to you to take advantage of these resources. Most campus resources are free and have hours that match your school schedule. Call and set up an appointment to help you get started.

Remember

It is highly unlikely that your first career choice after college is what you will be doing for the remainder of your working life. Instead, your first career choice is likely to be a temporary choice, not a permanent choice that determines how you will make a living until the day you die (or retire).

CAREER MYTHS

When considering your career options, do not be misinformed and mislead by popular myths about careers. The following myths can lead students to make poor career choices or decisions.

Myth #1. Once you have decided on a career, you have decided on what you'll be doing for the rest of your life.

This is simply and totally false. The term "career" derives from the same root word as "racecourse," and like a racecourse, a career involves movement that typically takes different turns and twists. Like any race on any course, it's not how fast you start, but where you finish that matters most. This ability to move and change direction is what distinguishes a professional career from a dead-end job. According to the United States Bureau of Labor, Americans average four different careers in a lifetime; it also predicts that today's college graduates will change jobs 12 to 15 times, and these jobs will span across 3 to 5 different career fields (United States Bureau of Labor Statistics, 2005). You might find these statistics hard to believe because one of the reasons you are going to college is to prepare for a particular career. However, don't forget that the liberal arts component of your college education provides you with general, transferable skills that can be applied to many different jobs and careers.

Myth #2. I need to pick a career that's in demand, which will get me a job with a good starting salary right after graduation.

Looking only at careers that are "hot" now and have high starting salaries can distract students from also looking at themselves, causing them to overlook the most important question of whether or not these careers are truly compatible with their personal abilities, interests, needs, and values.

Starting salaries and available job openings are factors that are external to us that can be easily "seen" and "counted," so they may get more attention and be given more weight in the decision-making process than things that are harder to see or put a number on, such as our inner qualities and whether they are really compatible with the choices we're considering. In the case of career decision-making, this tendency can result in college students choosing careers based exclusively on external factors (salaries and openings) without giving equal consideration to internal factors such as personal abilities, interests, and values. This, in turn, can lead some college graduates to choose and enter careers that eventually leave them bored, frustrated, or dissatisfied.

Also, keep in mind that careers which may be in high demand now may not be in such high demand by the time you graduate, nor may they remain in high demand for many years after you graduate. On the other hand, there will always be at least some demand for employees in almost all careers, because there will always be natural attrition (loss) of workers due to retirement or death.

The number of job offers you receive immediately after graduation and the number of dollars you earn as your first (starting) salary are very short-term and short-sighted standards for judging whether you've made a good career choice. Keep in mind the distinction between career *entry* and career *advancement*. Some college graduates may not bolt out of the starting gate and begin their career path with a well-paying first position, but they will steadily work their way up and get promoted to more advanced positions. Beware of advice from others who may tell you that you need to pick a career that's in demand. All this means is that you may be able to enter the field immediately and easily after graduation; it does not necessarily mean you will advance in that field just as quickly and easily. In other words, what is good in the short run (career entry) may not necessarily be good in the long run (career advancement).

Career Resources*

In order to make effective decisions about your career path, you need to have accurate knowledge about the nature of different careers and the realities of the work world. The Career Development Center is the first place to go for this information, as well as for help with career exploration and planning. In addition to helping you explore your personal career interests and abilities, the Career Development Center is also your key campus resource for learning about the nature of different careers and for strategies on how to locate career-related work experiences.

The federal government lists more than 30,000 different career fields, many of which you may have never heard of, but which may represent good career options for you. You can learn about careers through nine major routes or avenues:

1. Reading about careers,
2. Becoming involved in co-curricular programs on campus relating to career development,
3. Taking career development courses,
4. Interviewing people in different career fields,
5. Observing people at work in different careers,
6. Internships,
7. Co-op programs,
8. Volunteer service, and
9. Part-time work.

Strategies for using each of these routes to acquire accurate information about careers are discussed below.

Your Career Development Center and your College Library are key campus resources where you can find a wealth of reading material on careers, either in print or online. Here are some of the most useful sources of written information on careers:

- *Dictionary of Occupational Titles (DOT)* (http://www.occupationalinfo.org)

  This is the largest printed resource on careers; it contains concise definitions of over 17,000 jobs. It also includes such information as:
  - specific work tasks that people in the career typically perform on a regular basis;
  - type of knowledge, skills, and abilities that are required for different careers;
  - the interests, values, and needs of individuals who find working in their careers to be personally rewarding; and
  - background experiences of people working in different careers that qualified them for their positions.
- *Occupational Outlook Handbook (OOH)* (http://www.bls.gov/oco)

  This is one of the most widely available and frequently used resources on careers. It contains descriptions of approximately 250 positions, including information on the nature of work, work conditions, places of employment, training/education required for career entry and advancement, salaries, careers in related fields, and sources of additional information about particular careers (e.g., professional organizations and governmental agencies). A distinctive feature of this resource is that it contains information about the future employment outlook for different careers.

- *Encyclopedia of Careers and Vocational Guidance* (Chicago: Ferguson Press)

  As the name suggests, this is an encyclopedia of information on qualifications, salaries, and advancement opportunities for a wide variety of careers.

- *Occupational Information Network (O*NET)* Online (http://online.onetcenter.org)

  This is America's most comprehensive source of online information about careers. It contains an up-to-date set of descriptions for almost 1,000 different careers, plus lots of other information similar to that found in the *Dictionary of Occupational Titles (DOT)*.

In addition to these general sources of information, the Career Development Center or College Library should have books and other published materials relating to specific careers or occupations (e.g., careers for English majors). You can also learn a lot about careers by simply reading advertisements for position openings. You can find them in your local newspaper or at online sites, such as careerbuilder.com and monstertrak.com. When reading job descriptions, note the particular tasks, duties, or responsibilities that they involve, and ask yourself if these positions fit your profile of abilities, interests, needs, and values.

You can find information about career outlooks in the sources listed above, current periodicals, and materials from the Bureau of Labor Statistics. The table below, for example, lists the fastest growing occupations, occupations with the highest salaries, and occupations with the largest job growth. Information from the Bureau of Labor Statistics is also available online.

EMPLOYMENT PROJECTIONS, 2006–2016

TEN FASTEST-GROWING OCCUPATIONS	TEN INDUSTRIES WITH THE FASTEST WAGE AND SALARY EMPLOYMENT GROWTH	TEN OCCUPATIONS WITH THE LARGEST JOB GROWTH
Network systems and data communications	Management, scientific, and technical consulting services	Registered nurses
Personal and home care aides	Employment services	Retail salespersons
Home health aides	General medical and surgical hospitals, public and private	Customer service representatives
Computer software engineers	Elementary and secondary school, public and private	Combined food preparation and serving workers
Veterinary technologists and technicians	Local government, excluding education and hospitals	Office clerks, general
Personal financial advisors	Offices of physicians	Personal and home care aides
Makeup artists, theatrical and performance	Limited-service eating places	Home health aides
Medical assistants	Colleges, universities, and professional schools, public and private	Postsecondary teachers
Veterinarians	Computer systems design and related services	Janitor and cleaners, except maids
Substance abuse and behavioral disorder counselors	Home health care services	Nursing aides, orderlies, and attendants

Career Planning and Development Programs

Periodically during the academic year, co-curricular programs devoted to career exploration and career preparation are likely to be offered on your campus. For example, the Career Development Center may sponsor career exploration or career planning workshops that you can attend for free. Research conducted on career development workshops indicate that they're effective in helping students plan for and choose careers (Brown & Krane 2000; Hildenband & Gore, 2005). Your Career Center may also, organize career fairs, at which professionals working in different career fields are given booths on campus where you can visit with them and ask questions about their carrers.

Career Development Courses

Many colleges offer career development course for elective credits. These courses typically include self-assessment of your career interests, information about different careers, and strategies for career preparation. You need to do career planning while you're enrolled in college, so why not do it by enrolling in a career development course that rewards you with college credit for doing it? Studies show that students who participate in career development courses benefit significantly from them (Pascarella & Terenzini, 2005).

It might also be possible for you; to take an independent study course that will give you the opportunity to investigate issues in a career field you're considering. An independent study is a project that you work out with a faculty member, which usually involves writing a paper or detailed report. It allow you to receive academic credit for an in-depth study of a topic of you choice without having to enroll with other students in a traditional course that has regular scheduled classroom meetings, You could use this independent study option to choose a project related to a career. To see whether this independent study option is available at your campus, check the college catalog or consult with an academic advisor.

You may be able to explore a career of interest to you in a writing or speech course that allows you to choose the topic that you'll write or speak about. If you can choose to research any topic, consider researching a career that interests you and make that the topic of your paper or presentation.

Information Interviews

One of the best and most overlooked ways to get accurate information about a career is to interview professionals working in that career. Career development specialists refer to this strategy as information interviewing. Don't assume that working professionals aren't interested in taking time to speak with a student; most are open to being interviewed and many report that they enjoy it (Crosby, 2002).

Information interviews provide you inside, realistic information about what careers are like because you're getting that information directly from the horse's mouth. The interview process also helps you gain experience and confidence in interview situations, which may help you prepare for future job interviews. Furthermore, if you make a good impression during information interviews, the people you interview may suggest that you contact them again after graduation to see if there are position openings. If there is an opening, you might find yourself being the interviewee instead of the interviewer (and you might find yourself a job).

Because interviews are a valuable source of information about careers and provide possible contacts for future employment, we strongly recommend that you complete the information interview assignment included at the end of this chapter.

Career Observation (Shadowing)

In addition to learning about careers from reading and interviews, you can experience careers more directly by placing yourself in workplace situations and work environments that allow you to observe workers performing their daily duties. Two college-sponsored programs may be available on your campus that will allow you to observe working professionals:

- **Job shadowing programs.** These programs enable you to follow (shadow) and observe a professional during a typical workday.
- **Externship programs**. *These* programs are basically an extended version of job shadowing that lasts for a longer time period (e.g., two or three days).

Visit your Career Development Center to learn about what job shadowing to externship programs may be available on your college campus. If you're unable to find any in career field that interests you, consider finding on your own by using strategies similar to those we recommend for information interviews at the end of this chapter. It's basically the same process; the only difference is that instead of asking the person for an interview, you're asking if you can observe that person at work. In fact, the same person who granted you an information interview may also be willing to be observed at work. Just one or two days of observation can give you some great information about a career.

Information interviewing, job shadowing, and externship can supply great information about a career. However, information is not experience. To get career-relate work *experience*, you have four major option:

- Internship
- Cooperative education programs
- Volunteer work or service learning
- Part-time work

Each of these options for gaining work experience is discussed on the following page.

Internships

In contrast to job shadowing or externships, where you observe someone at work, an internship actively involves you in the work itself and gives you the opportunity to perform career-related work duties. A distinguishing feature of internships is that you can receive academic credit and sometimes financial compensation for the work you do. An internship usually totals 120 to 150 work hours, which may be completed at the same time you're enrolled in a full schedule of classes or when you're not taking classes (e.g., during summer term). A major advantage of internships is that they enable college students to avoid the classic catch-22 situation they often run into when interviewing for their first career position after graduation. The interview scenario usually goes something like this: The potential employer asks the college graduate, "What work experience have you had in this field?" The recent graduate replies, "I haven't had any work experience because I've been a full-time student." You can avoid this scenario by completing an internship during your college experience. We strongly encourage you to participate in at least one internship while you're enrolled in college because it will enable you to beat the "no experience" rap after graduation and distinguish yourself from many other college graduates. Surveys show that more than 75 percent of employers prefer candidates with internships (National Association of Colleges & Employers; 2010), and students who have internships while in college are more likely to develop career-relevant work skills and find employment immediately after college graduation (Pascarella & Terenzini, 2005; Peter D. Hart Research Associates, 2006).

Internships are typically available to college students during their junior or senior year; however, some campuses offer internships for first- and second-year students. Check with you Career Center if this option may be available to you. You can also purse internships on your own by consulting published guides that describe various career-related internship along with information on how to apply for them (e.g., Peterson's Internships and the Vault Guide to Tap Internships). Consider searching for internships on the Web as well (for example, go to www.internshio.com or www.vaultreport .com).Information on internships may also be available from the local chamber of commerce in the town or city where your colleg is located or in your hometown.

Cooperative Education (Co-op) Programs

A co-op program is similar to an internship but involves work experience that lasts longer than one academic term and *often requires students to* stop their coursework temporarily to participate in the program. However, some co-op programs allow you to continue to take classes while working part-time at a co-op position; these are sometimes referred to as "parallel co-ops." Students are paid for participating in co-op programs but don't receive academic credit; however, their co-op experience is officially noted on their college transcript (Smith, 2005)

Typically, co-op are only available to juniors or seniors, but you can begin now to explore co-op programs by reviewing your college catalog and visiting your Career Development Center to see whether your school offers co-op programs in career areas that may interest you. If you find one, build it into your long-range educational plan because it can provide you with authentic and extensive career-related work experience.

The value of co-ops and internship is strongly supported by research, which indicates that students who have these experiences during college:

- Are more likely to report that their college education was relevant to their career
- Receive higher evaluations from employers who recruit them on campus
- Have less difficulty finding an initial position after graduation
- Are more satisfied with their first career position after college
- Obtain more prestigious positions after graduation
- Report greater job satisfaction (Gardner, 1991; Knouse, Tanner, & Harris, 1999; Pascarella & Terenzini, 1991; 2005).

In surveys that ask employers to rank various factors they considered important when hiring new college graduates, internships or cooperative education programs receive the highest ranking (National Association of Colleges & Employers, 2012a). Furthermore, employers report that when full-time positions open up in their organization or company, they usually turn first to their own interns and co-op students (National Association of Colleges & Employers, 2003).

Volunteer Work or Service Learning

Volunteering not only provides a service to your community, it also serves you by giving you the opportunity to explore different work environments and gain work experience in career fields that relate to your area of service. For example, volunteer work performed for different age groups (e.g., children, adolescents, or the elderly) and in different work environments (e.g., hospital, school, or laboratory, you with firsthand work experience and simultaneously allows you to test your interest in careers related to these age groups and work environments.

Volunteer work also enables you to network with professionals outside of college who may serve as excellent references and resources for letters of recommendation for you. Furthermore, if these professionals are impressed with your volunteer work, they may become interested in hiring you part-time while you're still in college or full time when you graduate.

It may be possible to do volunteer work on campus by serving as an informal teaching assistant or research assistant to a faculty member. Such experiences are particularly valuable for students intending to go to graduate school. If you have a good relationship with any faculty members who are working in an academic field that interests you, consider asking them whether they would like some assistance with their teaching or research responsibilities. You might also check out your professors' Web pages to find out what type of research projects they're working on; if any of these projects interest you or relate to a career path you're considering, contact the professor and offer your help. Volunteer work for a college professor could lead to making a presentation with your professor at a professional conference or even result in your name being included as a coauthor on an article published by the professor.

Volunteer work may also be available to you through college courses. Some courses may integrate volunteer service into the course as a required or optional assignment, where you participate in the volunteer experience and then reflect on it in a written paper or class presentation. When volunteer work is integrated into an academic course and involves reflection on the volunteer experience through writing or speaking, it's referred to as *service learning.*

Another course-integrated option for gaining work experience that may be available to you is to enroll in courses that include a *practicum* or *field work.* For instance, if you're interested in working with children, courses in child psychology or early childhood education may offer experiential learning opportunities in a preschool or daycare center on campus. Similarly, you could take a course in a field you may want to pursue as a career to enable you to get work experience in that field. For instance, taking a class in child psychology may help you to get a part-time or summer job that involves working with children.

Reflection

Have you done volunteer work? If you have, did you learn anything about yourself or anything from your volunteer work that might help you identify careers that best match your interests, talents, and values?

Part-Time Work

Jobs that you hold during the academic year or during summer break should not be overlooked as potential s0urces of career information and as resume-building experience. Part-time work-in provide opportunities to learn or develop skills that may be relevant to your future career such as organizational skills, communication skills, and ability to work effectively with an workers from diverse backgrounds and cultures.

It's also possible that work in a part-time position may eventually turn into a full-time career. The following personal story illustrates How this can happen.

It might also be possible for you to obtain part-time work experience on campus through your schools work-study program. Work-study jobs can be done in a variety of campus settings (e.g., Financial Aid Office, Library, Public Relations Office, or Computer Services Center) and they typically allow you to build your employment schedule around your course schedule. On-campus work can provide you with valuable career-exploration and resume-building experiences, and the professionals for whom you work can also serve as excellent references for letters of recommendation to future employers. To see whether you are eligible for your schools work-study program, visit the Financial Aid Office on your campus. If you're not eligible for work-study jobs, ask about other campus jobs that are not funded through the work-study program.

Learning about careers through firsthand experience in actual work settings (e.g., shadowing, internships, volunteer services, and part-time work) is critical to successful career exploration and preparation. You can take a career-interest test, or you can test your career interest through actual work experiences. There is simply no substitute for direct, hands-on experience for gaining knowledge about careers. These firsthand experiences represent the ultimate career reality test. They allow you direct access to information about what careers are like, as opposed to how they are portrayed on TV or in the movies, which often paint an inaccurate or unrealistic picture of careers them appear more exciting or glamorous than they are.

In summary, firsthand and experiences in actual work setting equip you with five powerful career advantages:

- Learn about what work is like in ad particular field
- Test your interest and stalls for certain types of work.
- Strengthen your resume by adding experiential learning to academic (classroom) learning.
- Acquire contacts who may serve as personal references and sources for letters of recommendation.
- Network with employers who may hire you or refer you for a position after graduation.

Furthermore, gaining firsthand work experience early in college not only promotes your job prospects after graduation, but also makes you a more competitive candidate for internships and part-time positions that you may apply for during college.

Be sure to use your campus resources (e.g., the Career Development Center and Financial Aid Office), local resources (e.g., Chamber of Commerce), and your personal contacts (e.g., family and friends) to locate and participate in work experiences that relate to your career interests. When you land a work experience, work hard at it, learn as much as you can from it, and build relationships with as many people, there as possible, because these are the people who can provide you with future contacts, references, and referrals. Research indicates that as many as 75 percent of all jobs are obtained through interpersonal relationships, i.e., "networking" (Brooks, 2009).

Work Skills for the Twenty-First Century

Because of rapid changes in technology, college students of today may be preparing for jobs that do not exist right now. After graduation, many college students find employment that is not even related to their college major. One researcher found that 48 percent of college graduates find employment in fields not related to their college major. More important than college major, however, are the general skills learned in college that prepare students for the future.

To define skills needed in the future workplace, the U.S. Secretary of Labor created the Secretary's Commission on Achieving Necessary Skills (SCANS). Based on

Remember

One key characteristic of effective goal setting is to create goals that are realistic. In the case of careers, getting firsthand experience in actual work settings (e.g., shadowing, internships, volunteer services, and part-time work) allows you to get a much more realistic view of what work is like in certain careers, as opposed to the idealized or fantasized way they are portrayed on TV and in the movies.

interviews with employers and educators, the members of the commission outlined foundation skills and workplace competencies needed to succeed in the workplace in the twenty-first century. The following skills apply to all occupations in all fields and will help you to become a successful employee, regardless of your major. As you read through these skills, think about your competency in these areas.

Foundation Skills
Basic Skills

- Reading
- Writing
- Basic arithmetic
- Higher-level mathematics
- Listening
- Speaking

Thinking Skills

- Creative thinking
- Decision making
- Problem solving
- Mental visualization
- Knowing how to learn
- Reasoning

Personal Qualities

- Responsibility
- Self-esteem
- Sociability
- Self-management
- Integrity/honesty

Workplace Competencies
Resources

- Time—Selects relevant goals, sets priorities, follows schedules
- Money—Uses budgets, keeps records, and makes adjustments
- Materials and facilities—Acquires, stores, and distributes materials, supplies, parts, equipment, space, or final products
- Human resources—Assesses knowledge and skills, distributes work, evaluates performance, and provides feedback

Interpersonal

- Participates as a member of a team-—Works cooperatively with others and contributes to group efforts
- Teaches others—Helps others learn needed skills
- Serves clients/customers—Works and communicates with clients and customers to satisfy their expectations

- Exercises leadership—Communicates, encourages, persuades, and convinces others; responsibly challenges procedures, policies, or authority
- Negotiates to arrive at a decision—Works toward an agreement involving resources or diverging interests
- Works with cultural diversity—Works well with men and women and with people from a variety of ethnic, social, or educational backgrounds

Information

- Acquires and evaluates information—Identifies the need for information, obtains information, and evaluates it
- Organizes and maintains information—Organizes, processes, and maintains written or computerized records
- Uses computers to process information—Employs computers to acquire, organize, analyze, and communicate information

Systems

- Understands systems-—Knows how social, organizational, and technological systems work and operates efficiently within them
- Monitors and corrects performance—Distinguishes trends, predicts impacts of actions on systems operations, takes action to correct performance
- Improves and designs systems—Develops new systems to improve products or services

Technology

- Selects technology—Judges which procedures, tools, or machines, including computers, will produce the desired results
- Applies technology to tasks—Understands the proper procedures for using machines and computers
- Maintains and troubleshoots technology—Prevents, identifies, or solves problems with machines, computers, and other technologies

Because the workplace is changing, these skills may be more important than the background acquired through a college major. Work to develop these skills and you will be prepared for whatever lies ahead.

DURING (D)

Academic and career planning involves taking the following actions:

- **Choosing a major**
- **Developing an academic plan**
- **Completing the advising and registration process**

STEP THREE: CHOOSING A MAJOR

Choosing a major is a decision all college students must make. For some it can be a relatively easy decision. However, for many it is a difficult and often frustrating process. It is important to realize that having difficulty choosing a major is a very common concern for many college students. There are several factors that contribute to the indecision. First, students entering their freshman year in college do not always know what their strengths and interests encompass. Second, there are peer and parental influences. Some parents place unintentional pressure on their children by making suggestions such as "you would make a great doctor," or "you should be a lawyer." These may not be the professions which the student is interested in pursuing. Peer influences may also play a role. For example, a student may pursue a major just because many friends have decided on that major. A third factor making choosing a major difficult is if you are uncertain about your future plans; it is perhaps the most significant dilemma students have in choosing a major. As you enter college, your future plans may change several times before graduation. Initially some students may have graduate school in mind, others may want to pursue a particular career immediately following graduation, but these plans may change several times. Despite the high frequency of indecision, students still let these future plans have a significant impact on how they determine their major. Far too often students limit their options by seeking a major that will be directly related to what they may want to do in the future. This may cause some students to choose a major that they do not have much interest in over one that they may enjoy. It is essential to understand that although choosing a major is an important decision, it will not necessarily determine the course that the rest of your life will follow.

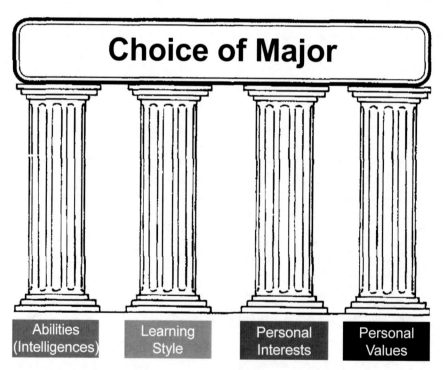

Figure 10.3 Personal Characteristics That Provide an Effective Foundation for Choice of a College Major.

Myths about the Relationship between Majors and Careers*

Good decisions are based on accurate or valid information, rather than misconceptions or myths. Good decisions about a college major are built on accurate or valid information about the relationship between majors and careers. Unfortunately, numerous misconceptions exist about the relationship between majors and careers that often lead students to make uninformed or unrealistic choices of a college major. Following are four common myths about the major-career relationship that you should be aware of and factor into your decisions about a college major.

Myth 1. When you choose your major, you're choosing your career. While some majors lead directly to a particular career, most do not. Majors leading directly to specific careers are called pre-professional or pre-vocational majors; they include such fields as accounting, engineering, and nursing. However, the vast majority of college majors don't channel you straight to one particular career: instead, they leave you with a variety of career options. All physics majors don't become physicists, all philosophy majors don't become philosophers, all history majors don't become historians, and all English majors don't become Englishmen (or Englishwomen).

For example, an English major typically leads to careers that involve use of the written language, such as editing, journalism, and publishing, while a major in art leads to careers that involve use of visual media, such as illustration, graphic design, and art therapy (The Web site mymajors.com provides useful and free information on groups or families of jobs that tend to be related to different majors.)

Furthermore, different majors can also lead to the same career. For instance, a variety of majors can lead a student to law school and to an eventual career as a lawyer ; there really isn't a law of pre-law major. Similarly, pre-med really isn't a major. Although most students interested in going into medical school graduate with a four-year degree in some field in the natural sciences (e.g., biology or chemistry), it's possible for students to go to medical school with majors in other fields, particularly if they take and do well in a cluster of science courses that are emphasized in medical school (e.g., general biology, general chemistry, organic and inorganic chemistry).

So, don't assume that your major *is* your career, or that your major automatically turns into your career field. It's this belief that can result in some students procrastinating about choosing a major; they think they're making a lifelong decision and fear that if they make the "wrong" choice, they'll be stuck doing something they hate for the rest of lives. The belief that your major becomes your career may also account for the fact that 58 percent of college graduates major in a pre-professional or pre-vocational field—e.g., nursing, accounting, and engineering (Association of American Colleges and Universities, 2007). These majors have a career that's obviously connected to them, which reassures students (and their family members) that they will have a job after graduation. However, the truth is that students in pre-professional majors may be more likely to be hired *immediately* after graduation, but within six months after graduation, college graduates with other college majors are just as likely to have jobs and aren't any more likely to be unemployed (Pascarella & Terenzini, 2005).

Additional research on college graduates indicates that they change careers numerous times, and the further they continue along their career paths, the more likely they are to work in field unrelated to their college majors (Millards, 2004). Remember that the general education curriculum is an important and influential part of a college education. It allows students to acquire knowledge in diverse subjects and to develop durable, transferable skills (e.g., writing, speaking, organizing) that qualify them for a diversity of careers, regardless of what their particular majors happened to be. Thus, for the vast majority of college majors, students first make decisions about majors, and later, make decisions about careers. Although it's important to think about the relationship between your choice of major and your initial career choice, for most college students these are different choices made at different times. Both choices relate to your future goals, but they involve different timeframes: choosing your major is a more immediate or short-range goal, whereas choosing your career is an intermediate or long-range goal.

Remember

Don't assume that when you choose your college major, you're choosing what you'll be doing for the remainder of your working life.

Remember

Deciding on a major and deciding on a career are not identical decisions: they're often different decisions made at different times.

Myth 2. If you wan to continue your education after a bachelor's degree, you must continue in the same field as your college major. After college graduation, you have two main options or alternative paths available to you:

1. You can enter a career immediately or
2. You can continue your education in graduate school or professional school. See Figure 10.4 for a visual map of the signposts or stages in the college experience and the primary paths available to you after college graduation.)

Once you complete a bachelor's degree, it's possible to continue your education in a field that's not directly related to your college major. This is particularly true for students who are majoring in pre-professional careers that funnel them directly into a particular career after graduation (Pascarella & Terenzini, 2005). For example, if you major in English, you call still go to graduate school in a subject other than English or go to law school, or get a master's degree in business administration. In fact, it's common to find that the majority of graduate student in master's of business administration (MBA) programs were not business majors in college (Dupuy & Vance, 1996).

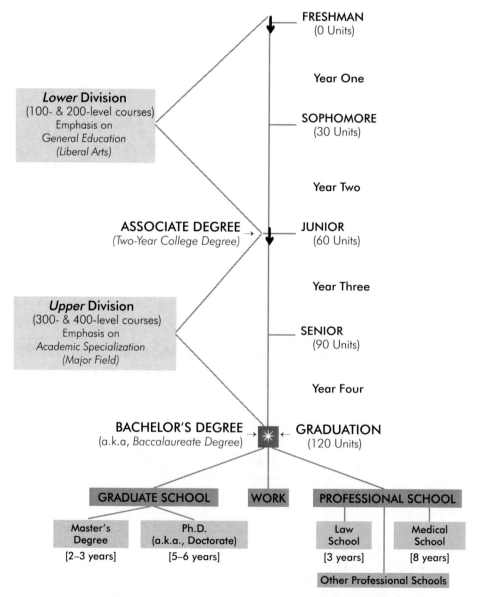

Figure 10.4 Timeline to the Future: A Snapshot of the College Experience and Beyond.

Notes

1. The total number of *general education* units and the total numbers of units needed to graduate with a bachelor's degree may vary somewhat from school in school. Also, the total number of units required for a *major* will vary somewhat from major to major and from school to school.

2. It often takes college students longer than four years to graduate due to a variety of reasons, such as working part-time and taking fewer courses per term, needing to repeat courses that were failed or dropped, or making a late change to a different major and needing to fulfill additional requirements for the new major.

3. *Graduate* and *professional* schools are options for continuing to higher levels of education after completion of an undergraduate (college) education.

4. Compared to graduate school, *professional* school involves advanced education in more "applied" professions (e.g., pharmacy or public administration).

Myth 3. You should major in business because most college graduates work in business setting. Studies show that college graduates with a variety of majors end up working in business settings for instance, engineering majors are likely to work in accounting, production, and finance. Liberal arts majors are likely to move on to positions in business settings that involve marketing, human resources, or public affairs (Bok, 2006; Useem, 1989). So don't restrict your choices of a major to business by believing in the myth that you must major in business to work for a business to work for a business after graduation. Research shows that in the long run, the career mobility and career advancement of non-business majors in the business world are equal to those attained by business majors (Pascarella & Terenzini, 1991: 2005).

Myth 4. If you major in a liberal arts field, the only career available to you is teaching. Liberal arts majors are not restricted to teaching careers. Many college graduates with majors in liberal arts fields have proceeded to, and succeeded in, careers other than teaching. Among these graduates are such notable people as:

- Jill Barad (English major), CEO, Mattel Toys
- Steve Case (political science major), CEO, America Online
- Brian Lamb (speech major), CEO, C-Span
- Willie Brown (liberal studies major), mayor, San Francisco*Source:* Indiana University (2004).

In fact, studies show that college graduates with liberal arts majors are just as likely to advance to the highest levels of corporate leadership as graduates majoring in pre-professional fields, such as business and engineering (Pascarella & Terenzini, 2005). If you are considering a major in a liberal arts field, you shouldn't e dismayed or discouraged by those who may question your choice by asking, "What are you going to do with a degree in *that* major?" (Brooks, 2009).

SELECTING THE MAJOR THAT FITS YOU

One of the first steps in choosing a major is finding one which coincides with certain interests and strengths. For example, if working with numbers and problem solving is a particular strength, a major such as math or the sciences should be explored further. Moreover, if reading and writing are preferred, majors such as English, political science, or history could be more of a match. It may help to write out some of your strengths and interests:

STRENGTHS: **INTERESTS:**

1. _____   1. _____

2. _____   2. _____

3. _____   3. _____

4. _____   4. _____

5. _____   5. _____

Another way to determine your strengths and interests is to take a personality inventory. There are several different types of personality tests. After completing the personality inventory, it is a good idea to explore the majors that match your personality as determined by the test. The majors listed may be ones that have not yet been considered or the test may simply reinforce what you were already aware of.

If you're undecided about a major, there's no need to feel anxious or embarrassed, because you're just beginning your college experience. Although you haven't officially declared a major, this doesn't mean you're a clueless procrastinator. Just be sure that you don't put all thoughts about your major on the back burner and simply drift along until you have no choice but to make a choice. Now is the time to start exploring and developing a game plan for narrowing down your options that will eventually lead to a well-informed choice of a college major.

Similarly, if you've already chosen a major, this doesn't mean that you'll never have to give any more through to that decision or that you can just shift into cruise control and motor along a mindless ride in the major you've selected. Instead, you should continue the exploration process by carefully testing your first choice, making sure it's a choice that's compatible with your abilities, interests, and values. In other words take the approach that this is your *current* choice. Whether it becomes your firm and *find* choice will depend on how well you perform (and how interested you are) in the first course you take in the field.

The next step is to determine if any majors can be linked to these strengths and interests. One method of learning about majors at a college/university is to review the school catalog. Using the results from the personality inventory, look over the majors that interest you in the catalog. Take a closer look at some of the courses offered within that major. Read the course descriptions and requirements for the major and become familiar with any possible prerequisites. Some majors are "impacted" and therefore require a certain GPA and that certain courses are passed before entering the major. Also pay particular attention to sequential courses. Some majors have sequential courses; course 1A must be completed before 1B can be attempted. Some students may prefer more flexibility in their courses. Furthermore, examine the flexibility of the major; the amount and type of courses required to complete the major. If a particular major has many course requirements, it will be difficult to take courses outside the major. All of the above steps can be labeled as preliminary research. Hopefully the aforementioned steps will assist in narrowing potential majors.

Following are specific strategies to exploring and identifying majors that may be most compatible with your personal strengths and interests.

Reflect on successful and enjoyable learning experiences you've had in the past. Think about your high school course and out of class learning experiences. If you have done well and continue to do well in a certain field of study, this may indicate that your natural abilities and learning style correspond well with the academic skills required by that particular field. This could translate into future success and satisfaction in the field if you decide to pursue it as a college major. As the old saying goes, "Nothing succeeds like success itself."

You can enter information about your academic performance in high school courses at mymajors.com, which will analyze it and provide you with college majors that may be a good match for you based on your experiences in high school.

Use your elective courses to test your interests and abilities in subjects that you might consider as a major. As its name implies, "elective" courses are those that you elect or choose to take. Your college electives come in two forms: free electives and restricted electives. *Free electives* are courses that you may elect (choose) to enroll in; they count toward your college degree but are not required for general education or your major. *Restricted electives* are courses that you must take, but you choose them from a restricted list of possible courses that have been specified by your college as fulfilling a requirement in general education or your major. For example, your campus may have a general education requirement in social or behavioral sciences that requires you to take two courses in this field, but you're allowed to choose what those two courses are from a menu of options in the field, such as anthropology, economics, political science, psychology, or sociology. If you're considering one of these subjects as a possible major, you can take an introductory course in that subject to test your interest in it while simultaneously fulfilling a general education requirement needed for graduation. This strategy will allow you to use general education as the main highway for travel toward your final destination (a college degree) while using your electives to explore side roads (potential majors) along the way If you find one that's compatible with your talents and interests, you may have found yourself a major.

Naturally, you don't have to use all your electives for the purpose of exploring majors. Depending on your major, as many as one-third of your courses in college may be electives; this leaves you with a significant amount of freedom to shape your college experience that best meets your educational and personal goals. For suggestions on how to make the best use of your free electives, see Figure 10.5

Your elective courses give you some academic freedom and sense of personal control over your college coursework. Exercise this freedom responsibility and strategically by selecting electives in a way that enables you to make the most of your college experience and college degree.

Listed below are 10 recommendations for making effective use of your college electives. As you read them, identify three strategies that appeal most to you and that you'd most likely put into practice.

Electives may be used strategically for the following purposes.

1. **To complete a minor or build an area of concentration.** Your electives can complement and strengthen your major or allow you to pursue a field of interest other than your major.
2. **To help you choose a career path.** Just as you can use electives to test your interest in a college major, you can use them to test your interest in a career. For instance, you could enroll in:
   - career planning or career development courses; and
   - courses that include internships or service learning experiences in a field that you're considering as a possible career (e.g., health, education, or business).
3. **To strengthen your skills in areas that may appeal to future employers.** For example, courses in foreign language, leadership development, and argumentation or debate can develop skills that are attractive to future employers.
4. **To develop practical life skills that you can use now or in the near future.** Courses in managing personal finances, marriage and family, or child development can help you manage your money and your future family.
5. **To seek balance in your life and develop yourself as a whole person.** You can use your electives strategically to cover all key dimensions of self-development. For instance, you could take courses that promote your emotional development. (e.g., stress management),

(Continued)

social development (e.g., interpersonal relationships), mental development (e.g., critical thinking), physical development (e.g., nutrition, self-defense); and spiritual development (e.g., world religions or death and dying).

Remember

Choose courses that contribute not only to your particular major and career, but also to your overall quality of life.

6. **To make connections across different academic disciplines (subject areas)**. Courses designed specifically to integrate two or more academic disciplines are referred to as interdisciplinary courses. For example, psychobiology is an interdisciplinary course that integrates the fields of psychology (focusing on the mind) and biology (focusing on the body), thus helping you see how the mind influences the body and vice versa. Making connections across subjects and seeing how they can be combined to create a more complete understanding of a personal or societal issue can be stimulating mental experience. Furthermore, the presence of interdisciplinary courses on your college transcript may be attractive to future employers because responsibilities and issues in the work world are not neatly packaged into separate majors: they require the ability to combine skills acquired from different fields of study.

7. **To help you develop broader perspectives on the human condition and the world around you**. You can take courses that progressively widen your perspectives. For example, you could select courses that provide you with a societal perspective (e.g., sociology), a national perspective (e.g., political science), an international perspective (e.g., cultural geography), a global perspective (e.g., ecology), and a cosmological perspective (e.g., astronomy). These broadening perspectives widen your scope of knowledge and deepen your understanding of the world.

8. **To appreciate different cultural view points and improve your ability to communicate with people from diverse cultural backgrounds**. You could take courses related to differences across nations (international diversity), such as international relations, and courses related to ethnic and racial differences in America (domestic diversity).

9. **To stretch beyond your familiar or customary learning style to experience different ways of learning and acquire new skills**. Your college curriculum is likely to include courses that were never previously available to you and that focus on skills you've never had the opportunity to test or develop. These courses can stretch your mind and allow you to explore new ideas and add to your repertoire of skills.

10. **To learn something you were always curious about or know little about**. For instance, if you've always been curious about how members of the other sex think and feel, you could take a course on the psychology of men and women. Or if you've always been fascinated by movies and how they are made, you might elect to take a course in filmmaking or cinematography.

Figure 10.5 Top 10 Suggestions for Making the Most of Your College Electives

Be sure you know what courses are required for the major you're considering. In college, students are expected to know the requirements for the majors they've chosen. These requirements vary considerably from one field to the next. Review your college catalog carefully to determine what courses are required for the major you're considering. College catalogs are often written in a technical and legalistic manner that can sometimes be hard to interpret. If you're having some trouble identifying and understanding the requirements for a major that you are considering, don't be embarrassed about seeking assistance from a professional in your school's Academic Advising Center.

Keep in mind that college majors often require courses in fields outside of the major that are designed to support the major. For instance psychology majors are often required to take at least one course in biology and business majors are often required to take calculus. If you're interested in majoring in a particular field, be sure you are fully aware of such outside requirements and are comfortable with them.

Once you've accurately identified courses required for the major you're considering, ask yourself the following two questions:

1. Do the course titles and descriptions appeal to my interests and values?
2. Do I have the abilities or skills needed to do well in these courses?

Take a look at introductory textbooks in the field you're considering a major. You can find introductory textbooks for all courses in your college bookstore, in the college library, or with a faculty member in that field. Review that tables of contents and read a few pages each text to get some sense of the writing style used in the field and whether the topics are compatible with your educational interests and talents.

Speak with students majoring in the field you're considering and ask them about their experiences. Talk to several students in the field you're considering to get a different and balanced perspective on what the field is like. A good way to find students in the major you're considering is to visit student clubs on campus related to the major (e.g., psychology club or history club). You could also check the class schedule to see when and where classes in your major are meeting and then go to the rooms where these classes meet and speak with students about the major, either before or after class. The following questions may be good ones to ask students in a major that you're considering:

- What first attracted you to this major?
- What would you say are the advantages and disadvantages of majoring in this Held?
- Knowing what you know now, would you choose the same major again?

Also, ask students about the quality of teaching and advising in the department. Studies show that different departments within the same college or university can vary greatly in terms of the quality of teaching, as well as their educational philosophy and attitude toward students (Pascarella & Terenzini, 1991; 2005).

Sit in on some classes in the field you're considering as a major. If the class you want to visit is large, you probably could just slip into the back row and listen. However, if the class is small, you should ask the instructors permission. When visiting a class, focus on the content or ideas being covered rather than the instructor's personality or teaching style. Don't forget that you're trying to decide whether you'll major in the subject, not the teacher.

Discuss the major you're considering with an academic advisor. To get unbiased feedback about the pros and cons of majoring in that field, its probably best to speak with an academic advisor who advises students in various majors, rather than someone who advises only students in that particular academic department or field.

Speak with faculty members in the department. Consider asking the following questions:

- What academic skills or qualities are needed for a student to be successful in your field?
- What are the greatest challenges faced by students majoring in your field?
- What do students seem to like most and least about majoring in your field?
- What can students do with a major in your field after graduation?
- What types of graduate programs of professional schools would a student in your major be well prepared to enter?

Surf the Web site of the professional organization associated with the field you're considering as a major. The Web site of a professional organization often contains useful information for students who are considering that field as a major. For example, if you're thinking about becoming an anthropology major, check out the Web site of the America Anthropological Association. If you're considering history as a major, look at the Web site o the American Historical Association. The Web site of the American Philosophical Association contains information about nonacademic careers for philosophy majors and the American Sociological Association's Web site identifies various careers that sociology majors are qualified to pursue after college graduation. To locate the professional Web site of the field that you might want to explore as a possible major, ask a faculty member in that field or complete a search on the Web by simply entering the name of the field followed by the word "association."

Be sure you know whether the major you're considering is impacted or over-subscribed and whether it requires certain academic standards to be met before you can be admitted. Certain college majors may be "impacted" or "oversubscribed," meaning that more students are interested in majoring these in fields than there are openings for them. Some majors that are often oversubscribed are pre-professional fields that lead directly to a particular career (e.g., engineering, pre-med, nursing, or physical therapy). On some campuses, these majors are called "restricted" majors, meaning that departments control their enrollment by restricting the number of students they let into the major. For example, departments may restrict entry to their major by admitting only students who have achieved an overall GPA of 3.0 or higher in certain introductory courses required by the majors, or they may take all students who apply for the major, rank them by GPA, and then count down until they have filled their maximum number of available spaces.

If you intend to major in a restricted field of study, be sure to check whether you're meeting the acceptance standards of the major as you continue to complete courses and earn grades. If you And yourself failing to meet these standards, you may need to increase the amount of time and effort you devote to your studies and seek assistance from your campus Learning Center. If you're working at your maximum level of effort and are regularly using the learning assistance services available on your campus but are still not meeting the academic standards of your intended major, consult with an academic advisor to help you identify an alternative field that may be closely related to the restricted major you were hoping to enter.

Reflection

Do you think that the major you're considering is likely to be oversubscribed or restricted—i.e., a major in which there are more students trying to enter it than there are available openings?

Consider the possibility of a college minor in a field that complements your major. A college minor usually requires about half the number of credits (units) required for a major. Most campuses allow you the option of completing a minor with your major. Check the course catalog or consult with an academic advisor to see if your school offers a minor that interests you and what courses are required to complete it.

If you have strong interests in two different fields, a minor will allow you to major in one of these fields while minoring in the other. Thus, you can pursue two fields that interest you without having to sacrifice one for the other. Furthermore, a minor can usually be completed along with a major without delaying your time to graduation. In contrast, a double major is likely to lengthen, your time to graduation because you must completed the separate requirements for both majors.

You can also pursue a second field of study in addition to your major without increasing your time to graduation by completing a "concentration" of "cognate area"— an academic specialization that requires fewer courses to complete than a minor (e.g., three to five courses vs. seven to eight courses). A concentration area may have ever fewer requirements (only two to three courses).

Taking a cluster of courses in a field outside your major can be an effective way to strengthen your resume and increase your employment prospects; it demonstrates your versatility and enables you to develop skills and acquire knowledge in areas that may be missing or underemphasized in your major. For example, students majoring in the fine arts (e.g., music or theater) or humanities (e.g., English or history) may take a cluster of courses in the fields of mathematics (e.g., statistics), technology (e.g., computer science), or business (e.g., economics)—none of which are strongly emphasized by their majors and all of which are very likely to increase their prospects for employment after graduation.

Visit your Career Development Center. Ask if there's information available on college graduates who've majored in the field you're considering and what they've gone on to do with that major after graduation. This will give you an idea about the types of careers the major can lead to and what graduate or professional school programs students often enter after completing the major.

*From *Thriving in College and Beyond: Research-Based Strategies for Academic Success and Personal Development* by Jospeh B. Cuseo, Aaron Thompson, Michele Campagna, and Viki S. Fecas. Copyright © 2013 by Kendall Hunt Publishing Company. Reprinted by permission.

The final step is active research. After studying the catalog, a few upper and lower division courses from possible majors should be noted. One method of actively researching a major is to take a course in that major. This can accomplish two important objectives. First, it can help you to gain exposure to the types of courses in that major. Second, if applicable, you can utilize the course to fulfill General Education (G.E.) requirements. Another method of active research is utilizing one of the largest resources on a college campus, other students. More often than not students are willing to share opinions regarding certain courses and certain professors, which may be helpful in determining what aspects of a major fit with your personality. Another step is to approach the department advisors of the majors you are interested in. Advisors can provide more detailed information about the prerequisites of a major, and can also recommend a professor or a course.

After you have completed the above steps, hopefully your list of possible majors will be a reasonable one. Ideally, this step should come sometime around the end of the second year of school, particularly for those who wish to complete their undergraduate education in four years. In addition to the above steps, students should closely monitor their academic progress with a Degree Progress Report (DPR). The DPR should be obtained at least once a semester. It explains courses and units remaining in order to graduate, as well as courses already taken and your GPA. One useful tool of the DPR is that it can be obtained with any major. If you have completed several courses in two different subjects, you may obtain a DPR for each major. If you have taken many courses in two different areas of interest, it is possible to double major or to have a minor or specialization. Students may find that they enjoy and excel in two different majors and wish to attain a degree in both. A student wishing to double major must receive approval from both major departments. For those students who wish to graduate in four years, a double major may be difficult, but can be done.

There are always students who can't avoid the "practical" major. If this is the case, an alternative is to major in a subject where the student's strengths and interests lie, and specialize or minor in what may satisfy a practical desire. For example, you may feel that you can best use your talents as an English major, but at the same time may not feel that it is "practical" enough. A specialization or minor may be a solution. You can pursue English as a major and seek out a "practical" minor such as business administration or accounting. Alternatively, if you feel this may not allow you to graduate in four years, you can take "practical" courses outside the English major. Both options will give you an opportunity to major in something you enjoy, enabling you to perform well academically, while at the same time minoring or taking other courses that will help prepare you for future plans.

In summary, there are several important things to remember:

1. **It is okay to be undecided.**
2. **A particular major does NOT limit future plans.**
3. **It is important to take the time to explore different majors and narrow the choices down through informed decisions.**
4. **Remember to find a major that is enjoyable because the amount of interest in the subject matter will probably be reflected by the GPA.**
5. **Although GPA is important, it is not the only factor that employers and graduate schools consider; they prefer students who have shown initiative by working, taking relevant courses, interning, or by participating in extracurricular activities.**
6. **Double majoring or minoring/specializing are feasible options.**
7. **Consider if graduating in four years is a priority.**

Choosing a major is not an easy decision, but it doesn't need to be a painful one either. Take the time to do the research and make the effort and the result will be worth it!

STEP FOUR: DEVELOPING AN ACADEMIC PLAN

The next step in the career planning process is to develop an **academic plan** for your education, which consists of identifying the type of degree you are seeking; determining the transfer requirements; obtaining a curriculum guide for your major; and identifying the courses you will take each semester to fulfill the requirements for graduation.

Type of Degree

First, you must decide what type of degree you are seeking: At the community college level, you can get an Associate of Arts degree, Associate of Science degree, or Associate of Applied Science degree.

Associate of Arts—awarded to students who complete a minimum of 60 hours, including the specified general education requirements, and wish to **transfer** to a 4-year college or university to continue their studies.

Associate of Science—awarded to students who complete a minimum of 60 hours, including the specified general education requirements, and wish to **transfer** to a 4-year college or university to continue their studies.

Associate of Applied Science—awarded to students who complete a minimum of 60 hours (depending on major) and prepares students for employment in their selected field.

At the university level, you can get a bachelor's degree, a master's degree, or a doctorate degree.

Bachelor's (or baccalaureate) degree—the "Bachelor of Arts" or "Bachelor of Science" is awarded to students who complete a minimum of 120 hours (depending on major), including the specified general education requirements and the specific core curriculum defined by the field of study.

Master's degree—follows the bachelor's degree; earned after completing 1–2 years of graduate level coursework (typically a minimum of 30 credit hours); types include Master of Arts, Master of Science, Master of Business Administration (MBA), etc.

Doctoral degree—follows the master's degree; earned after completion of highest level of graduate coursework; dissertation (a formal writing requirement that offers an original contribution of knowledge); and defense of dissertation to a committee; types include Ph.D. (Doctor of Philosophy), Ed.D. (Doctor of Education), etc.

Curriculum Guide

Once you have declared a major, you will need a curriculum guide which specifies the courses you must take to meet the requirements for your degree. You can obtain curriculum guides from various sources, including the college catalog, college website, the school/division/department which houses the major, or the Advising Center.

Academic Plan

Your academic plan is your map of ALL the courses you will need beginning with your first semester and ending with the final semester which leads you to obtaining a degree in your chosen field of study.

Transfer Requirements

If you plan to transfer, you must familiarize yourself with the transfer guidelines at your chosen institution by obtaining the school's transfer guide (school website) or meeting/discussing with transfer advisor(s). General transfer guidelines are as follows:

Application Process

1. Complete the application process (fill out an application form and payment of application fees) at the new school.
2. Send an official copy of your **transcript** (courses you have taken and the grades you received in them).

Transfer Frameworks and Transfer Terminology

Familiarize yourself with transfer frameworks and transfer terminology.

Research Transfer Options

It is important for you to research your transfer options.

1. Check with student services to see if any of the programs at your school offer assistance with transfer.
2. Check with your new school to see if they have set up programs which make it easier for students to transfer.

STEP FIVE: COMPLETING THE ADVISING AND REGISTRATION PROCESS

The final step in the academic and career planning process is to get advised and registered.

Academic Advising

What is academic advising? For most students, the first thing that pops into their minds is scheduling classes. While academic advisors do help students choose classes, academic advisors aren't just (or scheduling. An academic advisor plays an important role in a student's educational experience. Advisors can be effective in helping students understand the purpose of a university education, explore the expectations and demands of their chosen career path, and initiate a plan in order to graduate and utilize resources for a path in their chosen career.

From *Success Strategies for College & Life*, 4E by Kimberly Cunningham and Ashley Chance Fox. Copyright © 2012. Reprinted by permissions of Kendall Hunt Publishing Company.

Schedule of Classes

Class schedules are available online at the school's website. This schedule contains invaluable information such as the advising and registration process, advising notes, directory of services, academic calendar, payment information, and a schedule key.

When looking at the schedule, determine which type of courses best fit your individual needs based on your learning style/personality, your work schedule, your family commitments and other responsibilities. Examples of types of courses include:

- **Traditional courses**—These courses meet in a traditional classroom setting on a regular basis.
- **Internet courses**—These courses are in the category of distance learning (or e-learning) and are designed for students who need flexibility in scheduling. Internet courses require Internet access and a student login and password. Students are required to complete all readings, assignments, and tests by the posted deadlines. Students should be self-starters, have good reading and time management skills.

College Catalog

The College Catalog provides course descriptions and any prerequisites required to enroll in a particular course. The College Catalog also provides information about the general education curriculum, such as definition of categories and listings of general education courses in the specific category.

> ## AFTER (A)

After you have completed the advising and registration process, and finished the current semester, there are a few other things to *review, revise*, and *self-modify*:

- **Check financial aid requirements and deadlines**
- **Check your grades in Student Self-Service (PeopleSoft).** *Note: If you do not pass a course after you have been advised and registered to advance to the next level, you will have to adjust your schedule.*
- **Review your schedule**
- **Make payment by the posted deadline**
- **If you plan to sell your textbooks, return them to the bookstore prior to the deadline**

- **Reevaluate your study skills and strategies to prepare for the next semester and make adjustments** (use campus resources such as tutoring—early and for the entire semester, utilize time management skills by planning and completing assignments on time, form study groups, don't cram, etc.)

STEP SIX: CONDUCTING THE JOB SEARCH

After investing your time in achieving a college education, you will need some additional skills to get a job. Having a good resume and knowing how to successfully interview for a job will help you to obtain your dream job.

Your Resume

A resume is a snapshot of your education and experience. It is generally 1–2 pages in length. You will need a resume to apply for scholarships, part-time jobs, or find a position after you graduate. Start with a file of information you can use to create your resume. Keep your resume on file in your computer or on a disk so that you can revise it as needed. A resume includes the following:

- **Contact information: your name, address, telephone number, and e-mail address**
- **A brief statement of your career objective**
- **A summary of your education:**
  - **Names and locations of schools**
  - **Dates of attendance**
  - **Diplomas or degrees received**

- **A summary of your work and/or volunteer experience**
- **If you have little directly related work experience, a list of courses you have taken that would help the employer understand your skills for employment**
- **Special skills, honors, awards, or achievements**
- **References (people who can recommend you for a job or scholarship)**

Your resume is important in establishing a good first impression. There is no one best way to write a resume. Whatever form you choose, write clearly and be brief, neat, and honest. If your resume is too lengthy or difficult to read, it may wind up in the trash can. Adjust your resume to match the job for which you are applying. This is easy to do if you have your resume stored on your computer. Update your resume regularly.

Resume Tips

- **Keep the resume within 1–2 pages.** Employers spend about 30-60 seconds initially "scanning" your resume looking for a good match between you and the job they have available.
- **Highlight your background that most closely relates to the skills and experience the employer needs.** Consider the type of job you are seeking and the skills and type of personality characteristics that will be needed on the job to be successful.
- **Lead with your strongest "selling points,"** which are the background, training or skills that you have that are most closely related to the job requirements. The higher in the resume the information appears, the more likely it will be read. If you have no related work experience, you might want to lead with your education and the courses that show the skills you're learning that are related to the job.

- **When talking about your experience, be sure to use short statements with numbers, facts, and figures** that help the employer see the size and scope of activities in which you've been involved (how many customers did you serve, how much inventory did you stock, how many other people did you train, how large was the store, what type of products did you sell, what specific skills did you learn). You want the employer to understand what you were involved in so they can accurately assess your work capabilities.
- **When describing your experience, use action verbs.** These words should come directly from the job description or announcement or from the list provided below.
- **Use 10–12 pt. type.** White paper is preferred for scanning, copying, and faxing. If you have more than one page, do not staple the pages together, but do include your name and page numbers on each page to make sure your resume stays together in a stack of other resumes.
- **Always list the most recent information first and work backwards to the least recent.**
- **Use a consistent format and be ERROR FREE!**
- **Be prepared with 2–4 names of individuals who are willing to provide a reference for you.** It's best to provide professional references- Be sure to get permission from and help prepare each of your references (copy of resume, job descriptions, company names, etc.).

Strong Verbs

These words may represent skill areas you possess that would be beneficial to the prospective employer.

accomplished	developed	implemented	participated
accelerated	directed	improved	performed
achieved	discovered	increased	planned
budgeted	distributed	initiated	presented
built	earned	instituted	processed
calculated	eliminated	launched	produced
charted	established	maintained	programmed
compiled	evaluated	managed	proposed
completed	exhibited	mastered	recommended
composed	expanded	mediated	reinforced
conducted	expedited	motivated	researched
consolidated	explained	negotiated	reviewed
created	facilitated	observed	scheduled
delegated	formulated	obtained	supervised
delivered	generated	operated	strengthened

SAMPLE RESUMES

John Doe

1493 College Road • Anytown, KY 12345
(270) 234-5678 • john.doe@email.com

OBJECTIVE: To obtain the position of Sales Specialist; allowing me to utilize my education and experience in a team-oriented environment.

EDUCATION:

Western Kentucky University, Bowling Green, KY   *Anticipated May 2015*
- Bachelor of Arts in Marketing, minor in Entrepreneurship
- Cumulative GPA of 3.3; Major GPA of 3.5

RELEVANT EXPERIENCE:

Main Sales Company, Inc. – Bowling Green, KY
Sales Intern   *Summer 2011*
- Observed the style and techniques of experienced sales professionals in the company
- Conducted cold calls and utilized other direct contacting styles to interact with customers
- Created written correspondence via email and mail for current and prospective customers

RELEVANT SKILLS:

Communication Skills
- Communicated with restaurant patrons to provide customer service and a great dining experience
- Utilized verbal, nonverbal, and written skills in class assignments for written reports and presentations. Presented to groups ranging in size from 20 in class to 100 in my fraternity

Critical Thinking & Analytical Skills
- Participated in Career Services Student Advisory Committee in which I identified needs of students and provided ideas and solutions that would meet those needs
- Implemented solutions and assessed programs to see improvement

Leadership & Teamwork Skills
- Served as president of ABC Fraternity; led 45 active members and an executive board of 10 members
- Interacted with alumni, school administrators, and other fraternity presidents to represent ABC and WKU at school functions and state and national conferences

Administrative & Planning Skills
- Planned and implemented large-scale philanthropic event, "Run for WKU," which raised over $3,000 for a local charity
- Delegated, prioritized, and solicited donations from approximately 20 local business resulting in over $1,500 in prizes

ACTIVITIES:

President, Alpha Beta Chi Fraternity	*August 2011 – present*
Member, Management Club	*January 2010 – present*
Participant, WKU Intramurals	*August 2010 – present*

ADDITIONAL WORK HISTORY:

Student Office Worker, WKU Career Services, Bowling Green, KY	*January 2011 – present*
Server, O'Charley's Restaurant, Bowling Green, KY	*September 2009 – December 2010*
Ride Operator, KY Kingdom, Louisville, KY	*August 2007 – August 2009*

References Available Upon Request

SAMPLE RESUMES

Katherine Curry

1234 Oak Drive
Bowling Green, Kentucky 42101
(270) 555-1245
katherine.curry145@topper.wku.edu

OBJECTIVE: To obtain an entry level management position with ABC Technologies, allowing me to utilize my education and management experience in a team-oriented environment.

SUMMARY OF QUALIFICATIONS:
- Detail-oriented and capable of independent decision-making
- Exercise high level of confidentiality
- Experience in training, supervising, and leading a productive team
- Proficient in MS Office

EDUCATION: **Western Kentucky University – Bowling Green, Kentucky**
Associate of Science Degree – Business, Management Concentration
GPA: 3.5   *Anticipated May 2015*

RELEVANT COURSEWORK:
- Supervisory Management
- Business Entrepreneurship
- Selling & Sales Management
- Labor Relations Management
- Management of Human Resources
- Introduction to Accounting

RELEVANT WORK EXPERIENCE:
XYZ Apparel – Bowling Green., Kentucky
Assistant Manager   *April 2011 – Present*
- Train and supervise up to 15 store employees
- Achieve yearly sales quotas and ensure stole sales meet and exceed plan of $5,000
- Design store window displays and maintain clothing racks and accessory shelves

---

National Credit Union – Bowling Green, Kentucky
Teller   *June 2009 – April 2011*

- Greeted visitors with a friendly attitude
- Performed cash transactions
- Maintained a balanced cash drawer
- Assisted customers with lock box entry

References Available Upon Request

Letter Writing

During the job search process, there are many times when it is appropriate to write a letter to an employer. The following are just a few of the letters you may send to an employer.

Cover Letter

A cover letter (or letter of application) accompanies your resume. It should market your qualifications and communicate your skills, accomplishments, and potential to the employer. It should also highlight experiences most relevant to the job/employer.

Thank-You Letter

A thank-you letter should be sent to an employer immediately after an interview, Thank the employer for taking the time to interview you and reinforce your interest in the employer and in that position. Mention some of the key assets you have that were covered during the interview. If you forgot to mention something important about yourself at the interview, you can mention it in the thank-you letter.

Acceptance Letter

If an employer offers you a position and you accept it, send a letter of acceptance expressing your appreciation of joining the organization. Confirm your date of hire. If you received an offer letter from the employer, you may briefly confirm the terms of employment.

Rejection Letter

If you are hot planning on accepting an offer of employment, you should send the employer a letter letting them know that you are declining their offer. Express your appreciation for the offer, and above all, don't burn any bridges!

SAMPLE COVER LETTER

Your Address
City, State Zip Code
Date

Contact's Name
Title
Company Name
Address
City, State, Zip Code

Dear Mr./Ms. (Contact's Last name):

Your opening paragraph should arouse interest ort the part of the reader. Tell why you are writing the letter. Give information to show your specific interest in this company.

Your middle paragraph should create desire. Give details of your background that will show the reader why you should be considered as a candidate. Be as specific as possible about the kind of job you want. Don't make the reader try to guess what you would be interested in.

Refer the reader to your genera! qualifications on your enclosed resume or other material. Use as much space as needed to tell your story, but keep it brief and to the point.

In your closing paragraph, ask for action. Ask for an appointment, suggesting a time when you will be available. A positive request is harder to ignore than a vague hope.

Sincerely yours,

Your Handwritten Signature

Your typed name

Enclosure

Your Address
City, State Zip Code

Date

Mr. Michael Alexander
Director of Human Resources
ABC Retailing
123 Main Street
Townsville, IN 55555

Dear Mr. Alexander:

I learned about your company through the Job Search Manual that! received through the Career Services Center at Western Kentucky University and would like to inquire about employment opportunities in your management training program, I want to work in retail management and am willing to relocate throughout the eastern United States.

I will receive my Bachelor of Science in Management this May. My interest in business started in Junior Achievement while in high school and developed further through a variety of sates and retail positions during college. My internship with a large department store convinced me to pursue a career in retail. The enclosed resume summarizes my other qualifications. When I researched (he top retailers in the east, ABC Retailing emerged as having a strong market position, an excellent training program, and a reputation tor excellent customer service. In short, you provide the kind of professional retail environment I seek.

Realizing how busy you are. I would appreciate a few minutes of your time. I shall call you during the week of April 2! to discuss employment possibilities. In the meantime, if you need to contact me, my number is 555-555-5355. Please leave a message if I'm not in, and I will return your call as soon as possible. Thank you very much for considering my request.

Sincerely yours,

Your Handwritten Signature

Your Typed Name

Enclosure

SAMPLE THANK-YOU LETTER

Your Address
City, State, Zip Code
Date

Name of Interviewer
Title of Interviewer
Company Name
Address
City, State Zip Code

Dear Mr./Ms. (interviewer's last name):

In the first paragraph, state when and where you had your interview and thank the interviewer for his or her time. Reaffirm your interest in the organization.

In the second paragraph, mention something that particularly appeals to you about working for them, and reinforce a point or two in support of your application.

If after the interview you thought of something you wish you had said, the third paragraph of the letter is a good place to bring that up. You can also restate your understanding of the next steps in the hiring process.

In the last paragraph, thank the employer for considering your application and ask for further communication.

Sincerely yours,

Your Handwritten Signature

Your typed name

Your Address
City, State Zip Code
Date

Ms. Angela Chastain
Director of Human Resources
Modern Advertising
343 Center Drive
Centertown, PA 55555

Dear Ms. Chastain:

Thank you for meeting with me last Thursday, August 8, to discuss the position of: copywriter at Modem Advertising Inc. I was quite impressed with the enthusiasm you displayed for your company's future and tile helpfulness of your office personnel. Learning about Modern's present media campaign for the Pennsylvania Sausage Company was exciting and demonstrated your creative approach to adverting, Modern Advertising is a company with which I want to be associated.

Your description of the special qualifications needed for this position was especially interesting. My ability to work under pressure and meet tight deadlines has already been proven in the advertising position I held with the Slippery Rock Rocket. As I stated at our meeting, I enjoyed the challenge of a competitive environment in which success is based on achievement.

I would also like to mention that since our meeting, I have received the College Reporter's Award for an article of mine published in the Rocket. This is my first national award, and I am quite encouraged by this approval of my work.

Again, thank you for considering me for me position of copywriter. I look forward to hearing from you soon.

Sincerely,

Your Handwritten Signature

Your Typed Name

FORMULATE INTELLIGENT QUESTIONS TO ASK THE INTERVIEWER

- Please describe a typical day on the job.
- What do you see as the greatest challenge in this position?
- What personal qualities, skills, or experience would help someone do well in this position?
- What are the company's plans for future growth?
- How do you view this organization as a place to work?
- What are the typical career paths? What, are realistic time frames for advancement?
- How are employees evaluated and promoted?

INTERVIEW DRESS

Women

- Suit or tailored dress in a solid, conservative color
- No perfume or lotion with a scent
- Polished, sensible closed-toe shoes.
  - Your heel should not be higher than two inches
- Clean nails with a conservative polish
- Make-up should be minimal
- Clutch or small shoulder bag
- Simple, conservative jewelry

Men

- Black, navy, gray, or pinstriped suit
- Shined shoes; tassel loafers, wingtips, or lace-up shoes preferred
- Clean nails
- Conservative tie
- Solid-colored, long-sleeved, button-down shirt
- Undershirt
- Belt
- Avoid flashy accessories
- Over-the-calf dark dress socks
- No strongly fragrant cologne
- Trimmed hair and facial hair

DURING THE INTERVIEW

Do

- Give the interviewer a Arm ha.ndshake.
- Be enthusiastic, conAdent, cottcpus and honest.
- Be aware of your nonverbal behavior.
- Convey interest and knowledge hi the position and company

- Stress willingness, ability, and compatibility.
- Avoid the use of non-sentences such as "urn," "uh," "ya know," "well," "like," and "yeah."
- Always present the best of your background or qualifications.
- Listen to the questions carefully and give clear, concise, and thoughtful answers.
- At the close of the interview establish a date for your next communication.
- Always remember to thank the interviewer for their time

Don't
- Address the interviewer by his/her first name unless invited to do so.
- Let the employer casual approach fool you—always maintain a professional image.
- Dominate the interview or appear arrogant.
- Criticize yourself or discuss your personal problems.
- Speak or act in a nervous manner.
- Ask questions about pay or benefits or that the interviewer has already answered.
- Interrupt when the interviewer is talking.
- Bring' up negative information about past jobs, co-workers, or former employers.
- Smoke or chew gum.

SAMPLE INTERVIEW QUESTIONS

General Questions

1. Tell me a bout yourself.
2. What are your short-term and long-term career goals?
3. What are the most important rewards you expect in your career?
4. What are three of your greatest strengths? Weaknesses?
5. How has your college experience prepared you for a career?
6. What motivates you to put forth your greatest effort?
7. In what ways do you. think, you can make a contribution to our organization?
8. What do you know about our organization?
9. Why do you want to obtain a position at our organization?
10. Why did you choose the career for which you are preparing?
11. Why should I hire you?
12. What qualifications do you have that make you think you will be successful?
13. What do you think it takes to be successful in an organization like ours?
14. How would you define the word "success"?
15. What qualities should a successful manager possess?
16. Do you have a geographical preference? Are you willing to relocate? Travel?

Example Behavioral Interview Questions

1. How have you demonstrated initiative?
2. How have you motivated yourself to complete an assignment or task that you did not want to do?

3. Think about a difficult boss, professor, or other person. What made him or her difficult? How did you successfully interact with this person?
4. Think about a complex project or assignment you have been given. What approach did you take to complete it?
5. Tell me about the riskiest decision that you have made.
6. Can you tell me about an occasion where you needed to work with a group to get a job done?
7. Describe when you or a group that you were a part of were in danger of missing a deadline. What did you do?
8. Describe your greatest accomplishment.
9. Tell me about a situation when you had to learn something new in a short time. How did you proceed?
10. Can you tell me about a complex problem that you solved? Describe the process you utilized.
11. Tell me about a challenge that you successfully met.
12. Walk me through a situation where you had to do research and analyze the results for one of your classes.
13. What leadership positions have you held? Describe your leadership style.

SUMMARY

So where do you go from here? And how do you determine if you are there yet? Well, the answers to these questions begin and end with you. You can go anywhere you want to go, do whatever you want to do. You started off with a dream. Then you did some self-assessment. You've done your research. You've chosen a major. You've completed your academic plan. You've even been advised and registered for the next term. You're well on your way to accomplishing your educational and career goals. Just remember that your learning doesn't end when you get your degree. You will be a lifelong learner, continuously enhancing your skills and developing new ones. Don't be afraid to take risks, make changes, adjust your plans. You'll know when you're there! That place will be a good fit for you, a place where your talents and skills, and your education will match your career goals. We've given you a lift—now it's time for you to take off and soar! Accept the challenge! Go ahead, we dare you!

SUGGESTED READINGS

Fortgang, Laura Berman. *Living Your Best Life: Fortgang's insights will help you reach the success and fulfillment you are destined for.* New York: Penguin Putnam Co., 2002.

Tieger, Paul and Barbara Barron-Tieger. *Do What You Are: Discover the Perfect Career for you Through the Secrets of Personality Type.* 3rd ed. New York: Little, Brown & Co., 2001.

Any book where the major character is working in a career field you are interested in pursuing.

Where Do I Go From Here?

Western Kentucky University

Who Is My Advisor?***

If you have a declared major, your advisor is typically a professor or full-time staff advisor within your department or college. If you are Exploratory within a certain college—you know what area you want to work in but not the major—your advisor is probably a staff advisor within the college. If you are a general Exploratory student at WKU, you will probably be working with a staff advisor from the Academic Advising and Retention Center (AARC), Regardless of who your advisor is, they are a dedicated faculty or staff member who wants to see you be successful! However, whether you are successful is ultimately up to you.

Can't Remember Your Advisor? You Can Find Your Advisor's information on TopNet:

1. Log in to TopNet
2. Click on "Student Services"
3. Click on "Registration"
4. Click on "View Advisor Information"
5. You should find your advisor's name listed there, along with their phone number, email address, and office location.

If an advisor is not listed, please contact the AARC at 270-745-5065.

The Advisor-Student Relationship

In order to benefit the student at the highest level, the advisor-student relationship must be one of shared responsibilities. You as the student should not be merely a. recipient of advice but rather a participating member of the advising session. When both patties in an advising session are prepared and focused on the session, maximum learning and development of the student can occur for their overall academic success.

Advising includes more than helping students with course selection and removing die advising hold for them to register. The following areas should be considered in preparation for the advising session.

- Explore and define the student's educational and career goals at the Career Services Center.
- Explain and review degree requirements. You can do this through iCAP
- Review how the current semester is progressing.
- Learn about academic support services: The Learning Center (TLC), Student Disabilities Service (SDS), Counseling and Testing, etc.
- Encourage students to engage in campus and community activities.

All WKU associate-degree-seeking students are required to meet with their academic advisor until they have earned at least 48 hours AND filed an Application for Graduation with the Office of the Registrar. All WKU baccalaureate-degree-seeking students are required to meet with their academic advisors at least once each semester before registering for classes. A student is not required, to meet with their academic advisor if the student has achieved Senior status (90 hours) AND has filed an Application for Graduation with the Office of the Registrar.

Another tool that your advisor might use is an Academic Advising Syllabus. The syllabus is a contract between you and your advisor about what is expected of you during the academic year and the services that the advisor will provide.

What Your Advisor Will Expect from You

1. Initiate contact with your advisor during his/her office hours, by telephone, or by email.
2. Arrive at appointments on time (with your cell phone turned off) and cancel appointments in advance if you can't come.
3. Talk to your advisor if you are concerned about any aspect of your university experience.
4. Discuss important decisions or questions about your education (e.g., choice of major, change of major, change of college) well before die registration period.
5. Come prepared for appointments. Review your degree requirements. Bring a List of courses, course sections, alternate course choices, and the meeting times of these courses. Make sure any holds are lifted (e.g., parking tickets paid, library fines paid) before your date to register.
6. Ask questions regarding internships and career plans (http:Avww.wku.edu/Career/).
7. Ask questions about study abroad programs through the WK.U Office of International Programs (http://www.wim.edu/studyabroad/).
8. Follow through on referrals made by your advisor (e.g., a visit to the Career Services Center) and discuss suggestions made by your advisor.
9. After talking to your advisor, register for the classes you discussed.

What You Can Expect from Your Advisor

1. Availability during office hours and the opportunity for individual appointments.
2. Assistance in helping you to find academic information, including information on majors, minors, general education requirements, and other academic policies, procedures, and deadlines.
3. Referrals to appropriate people and offices if your ad visor cannot provide the necessary assistance.
4. A meeting to discuss grades and recommendations for academic improvement, if appropriate.
5. A meeting each semester before the registration period to help with course selection and academic planning and to approve your academic schedule for the next term.
6. Assistance in specific and correct course choices that are needed to prepare students for the particular major.
7. Assistance in understanding the purposes of academic requirements and their relationship to a major and career plan.
8. Assistance in helping you learn how to make academic decisions, how to discover the range of options available to you, and how to think through the consequences of choices.

Please take the time to research the academic program of your choice. Refer to the WKU Undergraduate Catalog for this information and use TopNet or iCAP (beginning freshmen and transfers who entered WKU in fall 2005 and after may use iCAP) to monitor your progress toward the completion of your degree requirements.

After seeking help from your major advisor, you are welcome to visit the Academic Advising and Retention Center located in DUC A330 or contact them at 270-745-5065 or acadetnic.advising@wku.edu with any unanswered advising questions.

Academic Advising Syllabus

The prior section should give you a general overview of the advisee and advisor relationship. However, your assigned academic advisor might have other expectations. Typically, they will convey their expectations of you by using an Academic Advising Syllabus.

SAMPLE

Academic Advising Syllabus Academic Advising and Retention Center Western Kentucky University

Academic Advising and Retention Center Mission Statement
The Academic Advising and Retention Center serves the diverse population of WKU students, faculty, and staff as a campus-wide leader in advising, retention services, and supplemental education. The mission of the Academic Advising and Retention Center is to help students clarify their academic direction and develop meaningful success strategies. AARC is committed to encouraging academic growth and producing informed and engaged students.

Advising Information for Western Kentucky University Students

Who is my advisor? Students with a declared major work closely with an advisor from the academic department that administers their particular program of study. Beginning freshmen and transfer students who enter the University with selected programs of study are assigned academic advisors in their chosen disciplines. A beginning freshman who enrolls as a full-time student and has not selected a major (an Exploratory/Generally Undeclared student) is advised by AARC staff.

All degree-seeking students at WKU are assigned an academic advisor (go to TopNet under "Student Services," then "Registration," then "View Advisor Information"). If you don't have an advisor listed, email Stephanie.hooker@wku.edu.

When should I meet with my advisor? In the fall semester, attempt to schedule a time with your advisor in mid-October. During the spring semester, attempt to schedule a time with your advisor during mid-March. Your advisor should contact yon throughout the semester to remind you of upcoming important dates or events.

How can I run an iCAP report?
1. Login to your TopNet Account
2. Once you're logged in, click on "Student Services"
3. Click on "iCAP (Interactive Degree Audit)"
4. Click on "Submit an Audit"
5. Click "Run Audit"
6. Click "View Submitted Audits"
7. Click "Refresh" until audit appears
8. Click on major to view audit

For more specific information on how to read an iCAP report, please visit die iCAP tutorial site.

How do I register for my classes after meeting with my advisor?
1. Login to your TopNet Account
2. Once you're logged in, click on "Student Services"
3. Click on "Registration"
4. Click on "Register/Add/Drop Courses"—the screen will ask you to select a semester term
5. Scroll down to "Add Classes Worksheet" and enter-the CRNs of die classes for which you would like to register
6. Click "Submit Changes"
7. Go back to Student Services
8. Click o "Registration"
9. Click on Student Summary Schedule"

How do I know what courses ate available for me to take?
1. Login to your TopNet Account
2. Once you're logged in, dick on "Student Services"
3. Click on "Registration"

4. Click on "Schedule of Classes" and "Look Up Classes to Add"—the screen will ask you to select a semester term.
5. Use the drop-down menu 'under "Search by Team" to select the term in which you would like to search; click "Submit"
6. On this page you can select by subject, instructor, day or evening courses, and campus, to do this, just highlight the important items you would like to search by
7. Once you have highlighted everything you need, click "Class Search"
8. When you find the class you would like to take, jot down the CRN, the course name, and the days and times it meets

How do I know if I have holds on my account?
1. Login to your TopNet Account
2. Once logged in, click on "Student Services"
3. Click on "Student Records"
4. Click on "View Holds"
5. There could be three different types of information from this screen: no holds exist; an advising hold exists on your account—contact your advisor for an appointment; or holds will be listed with a phone number to contact regarding specifics to that hold

Selecting Classes

Bringing a list of possible classes for the upcoming semester to your advising appointment is easy to do using your iCAP and the online schedule of classes. Once you have looked at what courses fulfill requirements for either your major or general education and decided on a list of classes you may be interested in, you will want to check and see if and when those classes are being offered.

Some classes, particularly 300- and 400-level classes, may only be offered in the Spring or Fall. Checking on this ahead of time ensures you don't miss out on taking the classes you need to when you need to. To know what classes are being offered each semester, and at what time, you will need to check die course schedule. You can access the course schedule through TopNet, the WKU portal, or the Office of the Registrar webpage, or get a paper copy from the Registrar Office. Once you are able to register for classes, you can also search on TopNet using the Registration/Add/Drop link. This link is where you will actually create your schedule.

To build your potential, schedule, take the list of classes you are interested in from iCAP and see which, of them are being offered next semester. From that list you will want to see what times the classes are offered to see which classes fit together. Taking this information to your advising appointment gives you and your advisor time to talk about the strategy of your schedule, how the current semester is going, and any other personal or academic issues you may be having or are curious about.

iCAP is an acronym for Interactive Curriculum and Academic Progress. Students can obtain personalized, interactive audits displaying progress toward a selected degree. An audit shows all the requirements needed to fulfill a major, minor, or concentration and displays the transfer and WKU courses that have been used to satisfy those requirements. Students can run "What-if' audits to compare their coursework against other majors.

A Step-by-Step Guide for Running and Viewing the iCAP Audit for Students

- Go to Topnet.wku.edu.
- Enter your Net ID and Password.
- Click on Student Records and Account Information.
- Click on the iCAP link.
- Select "Submit Audit."
- Select your desired options. For a full audit listing, run a default audit.
- Select "Run Audit."
- Select " View Submitted Audits."
- Select "Refresh" until your audit appears.
- Select your audit.

Running a "What-If" Audit

- Go to Topnet.wlni.edu.
- Enter your Net ID and Password.
- Click on Student Records and Account Information.
- Click on the iCAP link.
- Select "Submit Audit."
- Select your desired options. For a full audit listing, run a default audit.
- Select "What-If."
- Choose your selected minor.
- Select "Run Audit."
- Select "View Submitted Audits."
- Select "Refresh" until your "What-If" audit appears.
- Select your "What-If" audit.

(Please note that: when it asks for a term, you should enter when you started as a degree-seeking student.)

For additional assistance, please view the iCAP Tutorial at http://www.wku.edu/registrar/icap/index.php (the tutorial link is on the right-hand side).

Transferring from South to Main Campus

If A student wishes to transfer to main campus, the student must have completed 24 hours, not including developmental courses, and maintain a GPA of 2.0 or higher. If a student meets the aforementioned requirements, the student will need to complete a Change of Major Form on TopNet.

Class Standing

Your iCAP can also tell you your class standing. This is determined by the number of successful credit hours you have completed, NOT attempted. The following standings are based off earned credit hours.

0–29 Earned Credits (Freshman Standing)
30–59 Earned Credits (Sophomore Standing
60–89 Earned Credits (Junior Standing)
90 Earned Credits or More (Senior Standing)

GENERAL EDUCATION REQUIREMENTS—BACHELOR'S DEGREE GENERAL EDUCATION

Category	Subject, Course Number		Hours
A. Organization & Communication of ideas (12 hrs)	ENG 100	(A–I)	3
	ENG 300	(A–I)	3
	Foreign Language (second semester level)	(A–II)	3
	Public Speaking: COMM 145 to 161	(A–III)	3
B. Humanities (9 hrs)	Literature *ENG 200	(B–I)	3
Representing 3 fields		(B–II)	3
		(B–II)	3
C. Social & Behavioral Sciences (9 hrs)	Western Civ: HIST 119 or HIST 120	(C)	3
Representing 3 fields		(C)	3
		(C)	3
D. Natural Sciences (6 hrs) & Math (3 hrs)	MATH	(D–II)	3
Representing 2 fields in science		(D–II)	3
	Lecture/Lab (DL)	(D–DL)	3
E. World Cultures (3 hrs)		(E)	3
F. Health/Wellness (2 hrs)		(F)	2–3
		(F)	

44 total minimum hours are required in General Education, to be completed by the end of the student's college career.

* Most students complete ENG 200 to fulfill the Literature requirement in General Education Category B.

GENERAL EDUCATION REQUMEMENTS—ASSOCIATE'S DEGREE GENERAL EDUCATION

Category	Subject, Course Number	Hours
A. Organization & Communication of ideas (3 hrs)	ENG 100 / ENG 100C Freshman English	3
B. Humanities (3 hrs)	Any class from Section I or Section II (Electives)	3
C. Social & Behavioral Sciences (6 hrs)	Any two classes	3
D. Natural Sciences—Mathematics (3 hrs)	Any class from Section ! (Science) or Section II (Mathematics)	3

Developmental Courses

Developmental courses (DRDG 080, 055, DMA 096, and DENG 055) are determined based on the student ACT or SAT score. It is possible for a student to test into three developmental course areas (English, Mathematics, and Reading) with multiple developmental courses available in. Mathematics. *Students who are in a developmental course must successfully complete the course with a "C" grade or higher to advance to the college-credit-bearing course.*

Developmental courses are not college-credit-bearing, nor do they count toward the student grade point average (GPA). Developmental courses do count toward the financial aid and housing requirements of being a full-time student. **Developmental courses also count toward the student's Academic Standing at WKU.**

http://www.wku.edu/advising/glossary_terms.php Retrieved March 21, 2012.

Financial Aid and Academic Success

A student's academic success directly impacts financial aid eligibility. Specifically, Western Kentucky University is required by federal regulations to adhere to minimum standards of Satisfactory Academic Progress (SAP) that relate to a student eligibility for financial aid. Academic progress for those students who receive the following types of financial aid will be monitored at the end of *every* semester:

Federal Pell. Grants

Federal Supplemental Educational Opportunity Grant (FSEOG)

Federal and Institutional Work-Study

Federal Perkins Loans

Federal Subsidized and Unsubsidized Loans

Federal PLUS Loans

KHEAA College Access Program (CAP)

However, KEES, Incentive Scholarship, Alumni Scholarship, and the Waiver Programs arc not included in this policy.

The University's Academic Progress policy (administered through the Academic Advising and Retention Center) is separate from the Department of Student Financial Assistance's Satisfactory Academic Progress Policy. A student may be placed on probation and/or be required to appeal by both the Academic Advising and Retention Center and the Department of Student Financial Assistance.

Satisfactory Academic Progress is determined both qualitatively (GPA) and quantitatively (hours earned/pace).

Qualitative Progress (GPA):

Total HiED or WKU Quality Hours	Cumulative GPA/WKU GPA
1–17	1.7
17–33	1.8
34–50	1.9
51 or greater	2.0

Quantitative Requirements (hours earned/pace):

A student awarded financial aid must earn at least 75% of the number of hours for which they were awarded aid. Also, a student's overall GPA hours must be at least 75% of their overall hours attempted.

For example, Bill has earned 40 GPA hours. However, Bill has failed three classes and has withdrawn from two classes during his academic career (for a total of 55 hours attempted).

$$\frac{\text{Earned Hours}}{\text{Attempted Hours}} = \frac{40 \text{ hour scompleted}}{55 \text{ hours attempted}} = 72\%$$

Thus, Bill is not in compliance with Western Kentucky University's Satisfactory Academic Progress guidelines.

***Students who fail to meet either the grade point average or hours earned components of the S AP policy are placed on warning status for the next subsequent semester in which they apply for assistance. In addition, students admitted to the University on probation are likewise placed on warning status with the Department of Student Financial Assistance.

In order to receive aid on a warning status, the following criteria must be met:

- Students must complete a SAP counseling session at http://www.wku.edu/financialaid/sapoc.htm
- South Campus students on Academic Probation must meet with the Coordinator of Advising & Student Services at WKU South Campus (call 270-745-0113) to develop an **Academic Plan**.
  - Students on SAP warning must attend one of the group advising sessions offered by the Department of Student Financial Assistance (call 270-745-2755 for session dates)
- Students that are placed on warning status for a particular term and have completed SAP Counseling and established an Academic Plan must meet the following requirements to continue to receive assistance beyond the warning period:

  Satisfactory Academic Achievement (GPA): Must earn a minimum 2.0 undergraduate or 3.0 graduate grade point average for the semester

  Satisfactory Academic Progress (Home Earned): Must earn 100% or the credit hours for which aid was awarded for the semester

  Academic Plan: Must adhere to the establishment Academic Plan.

Sap Appeal Procedures

Eligibility to Appeal:

Only certain conditions allow a student to appeal:

1. If a student withdrew (officially or unofficially) after receiving federal aid (and was not already on a warning/probation status), they are eligible to submit an appeal for the term in which aid is being sought.
2. If a student has earned excessive hours without completing a degree (pursuing an associate's degree and attempted 90 or more hours; pursuing a bachelor's degree and attempted 180 or more hours), they are eligible to submit an appeal for the term in which aid is being sought.
3. If a student was on a warning status and did not meet the terms of that status and has documentable extenuating circumstances (e.g., illness, death of immediate family member, divorce) they are eligible to submit an appeal for the term in which aid is being sought. If a student was on a warning status and did not meet the terms of that status and did not have extenuating circumstances, they are not eligible to appeal and therefore not. eligible for aid until the conditions for reinstatement of aid (refer to Section VII) are met.

Students are limited to two SAP appeals per academic career level (i.e., undergraduate or graduate).

However, utilizing academic resources such as tutoring and meeting with your academic advisor regularly can help prevent this situation from occurring.

http://wku.edu/financialaid/sap.php. Retrieved March 21, 2012

Resources for Academic Success

South Campus

Alice Rowe
Learning Assistance Center

Mission Statement

The staff and tutors of the Learning Assistance Center (LAC) are dedicated to the success of the students taking courses at WKU's South Campus. We offer assistance in a variety of academic areas including Math, English, and Chemistry.

Student and Faculty Services

- Tutoring multiple subjects
- Technology Support
  - Blackboard
  - NetId
  - TopNet
  - Topper Mail
  - Textbook library
  - Calculator check-out and rentals
  - Computer lab and printers
  - Scanner
  - Copier
  - Administer Accuplacers daily

Tutors Are Available for the Following Courses

- Chemistry 109
- English 050/055/100/200
- Math 055/096/109/116
- Microsoft Office
- Select other classes

Computer Usage in the Learning Assistance Center

The computers in the Learning Assistance Center have a variety of tutorial and assistive interactive programs on them to supplement class information. Students may use the computers to do research on the Internet, type a paper for class, or access Blackboard or TopNet. We highly recommend that students bring a Rash drive with them in order to save their work. Student IDs are required for all print services.

Main Campus

At TLC, WKU undergraduate students provide free peer-to-peer course-specific tutoring. Currently enrolled WKU students should make appointments for one-on-one tutoring via our online scheduling system, TutorTrac (www.wku.edu/tlc/tutortrac.php) or call (270) 745-6254 and we will make a tutoring appointment for you. In addition to tutoring course-specific content, TLC offers assistance with academic skill areas such, as note taking, time management, test-taking skills, etc. TLC is also host to A number of other programs and services, including' the Academic Advantage Series: Workshops for Success, Peer Assisted Study Sessions (PASS), a 32-machine Dell computer lab for academic projects only, and black and white printing.

Mission

The mission of TLC is to promote student success, enhance student performance, and increase student retention at Western Kentucky University. TLC helps students enhance their academic performance and sharpen their skills to be successful Western Kentucky University graduates.

Peer Tutoring

TLC provides face-to-face tutoring in over 200 WKU courses. Studying at a distance and need a tutor? No problem! TLC offers online tutoring as well. In addition to specific WKU courses, TLC also provides tutoring in many academic skid areas including time management, note-taking strategies, and test-taking strategies. A. current list of courses for which, we offer tutoring can be found at www.wku.edu/tlc.

Peer Assisted Study Sessions (PASS)

PASS is an academic assistance program that targets traditionally difficult, high-enrollment courses. This program utilizes undergraduate students as PASS Leaders to facilitate group study sessions. PASS Leaders have successfully completed the course they lead with a grade of A, attend class lectures, take notes, and hold two-weekly group study sessions. Please visit the PASS website at www.wku.edu/tlc/pass.php for a list of PASS courses and group study session information.

Academic Advantage Series: Workshops for Success

Each semester, The Learning Center creates, schedules, and facilitates the Academic Advantage Series: Workshops for Success. These workshops are a series of presentations designed to help students succeed academically. Presentations focus on skills students are expected to know but might not have learned over the course of their academic career. Each session provide hands-on, expert instruction from professionals at WKU who are dedicated to student success. Please visit www.wku.edu/tlc/workshops.php for workshop topics, dates, times, and locations.

About TLC

All services of TLC are free to WKU students. Students may utilize TLC's study space for individual study needs, use the 32-machine computer lab to complete academic coursework, or request a tutoring appointment for assistance with difficult course concepts and academic skill areas.

Locations

TLC has four locations. Our main location (TLC@DUC) is located on the top floor of the Student Success Center (DUC A330). The remaining three locations are housed in residence halls: Douglas Keen Hall (red awning entrance), McCormack Hall (tan awning entrance), and Pearce Ford Tower (PFT) * (27th floor).

* PFF is for use by residents and their guests only.

Career Services

About the WKU Career Services Center

Out Services Include:

WALK-IN SERVICE: No appointment? No problem! Visit the Career Services Center with your questions every Monday-Friday between 8-4:30. One of our helpful staff members will be happy to assist you.

    CAREER ADVISING: We offer career counseling for students and alumni to review majors and occupations that match interests and abilities. *FOCUS and MyPlan* are web-based career planning systems with links to research careers and majors.

    JOB SEARCH COUNSELING: Counselors are available to assist students and alumni with the preparation and review of resumes, cover letters, and job application materials. We assist individuals in locating company/employer information and can provide valuable information regarding job search techniques and strategies.

    JOB VACANCY INFORMATION: Job vacancies and other opportunities are posted and updated daily on our online career and employment management system, **TopJobs**. Access listings for full-time, part-time, interns hip, volunteer, and other opportunities.

    INTERNSHIPS: These are formalized opportunities to explore and/or validate major and career choices by working in various career fields. Earn college credit and be paid for working in a position related to your career and academic interests.

    MOCK INTERVIEWS: Let us assist you. with interview preparation. We can "mock interview" you to help you prepare for your professional interviews.

    CAREER FAIRS: The Career Services Center is involved with several career and job fairs each year. These events are opportunities for students to talk with employers and explore their career and. major options.

Using TopJobs

What Is TopJobs?

An online career and employment database for WKU students & alumni that allows you to:

- search for jobs, internships, and volunteer opportunities
- receive emails about internship and job opportunities in your held of study
- submit your resume electronically to potential employers
- keep up-to-date with events at the WKU Career Services Center

Log in to TopJobs

- Visit us on1 in eat: www.wku.edu/topjobs
- Use your WKU net ID and password, to get logged in
- Click on "Search Jobs" to get started

NAME: _____ DATE: _____

EXERCISE 10.1: CAREER RESEARCH

Your career area (e.g., nursing):

1. Identify a book on career information or career decision-making.

   Book Title:_____

2. Identify a job title you are interested in researching.

   Job Title: _____

3. Use the *Occupational Outlook Handbook* (www.bls.gov/oco) to answer the following:

   a. **Nature of the work** _____

   _____

   _____

   b. **Working conditions** _____

   _____

   _____

   c. **Current employment level** _____

   _____

   d. **Training, Other Qualifications and Advancement** _____

   _____

   _____

   e. **Job Outlook**_____

   _____

   f. **Earnings** _____

   _____

4. According to the *Kentuckiana Occupational Outlook*, will employment in your career field grow or decline? By how much? (http://www.kentuckianaworks.org/outlook/)

_____

_____

_____

5. Identify a professional association related to your job title: See "Sources of Additional Information" at the bottom of the articles in the *Occupational Outlook Handbook*, consult the *Encyclopedia of Associations* or use a search engine.

_____

_____

6. Visit a professional association's website and describe what you find out about the association or your profession.

_____

_____

_____

7. Find a current job ad and determine essential qualifications:

_____

8. What is something new that you learned about your career or about research?

_____

_____

_____

_____

_____

_____

EXERCISE 10.2: CAREER RESEARCH PROJECT

The career exploration project is designed to help you learn more about a career you are interested in. This information will be helpful in choosing your major and the courses you need to take to reach your goals. This project is about researching a major that may lead you to the career you desire, and will assist you in developing your academic plan.

Please review the following guidelines:

Format: 5 typed pages (minimum), double spaced, font: Times New Roman (size 12), (should **NOT** be handwritten), works cited page, MLA format

Introduction

Introduction/Description of Career. In this section, state your major and the specific degree you plan to obtain; describe what you want to do in your career after finishing your education; and what your salary expectations are for this particular field. Be specific.

Research of College/University

Overview of Selected School or Schools. In this section, describe the college(s) you plan to attend that offers the major you have chosen for the topic of this paper. Include demographic information, location, facts about the campus, and describe a minimum of 5 aspects or characteristics about the college(s) that interest you (college catalog or college Web site). [1 paragraph]

Course of Study. In this section, identify the prerequisites you must take prior to entering the program. Also include the minimum GPA requirement for acceptance into the program and whether it is an open or selective admission program. Attach a copy of the curriculum guide for your major to your paper (include a sentence that states: *Please see attached curriculum guide for program of study*). [1 paragraph]

Educational Expenses. In this section, answer the following: What will be the total cost of your degree? What is your plan for paying for your education? How long do you think it will take to achieve your educational goal? How closely does this match the target date listed on your timeline? [1 paragraph]

Attach a copy of the timeline showing the dates you would like to have your educational and personal goals obtained (i.e., When would you graduate? When would you start and graduate from graduate school? When would you start a family? When would you retire?)

Career Research

Career Research/Job Outlook. Using various campus resources (Library, Career Center), and Internet sources (such as the *Occupational Outlook Handbook* website: http://www.bls.gov/oco/), research the following:

- *Expected availability of jobs in your career* (1 paragraph)

- From research you have done, discuss the occupational outlook for your chosen career. Give actual statistics, number of new jobs, etc. Also, discuss why this particular career field is growing or shrinking.

- *Nature of work/working conditions* (1 paragraph)

- Discuss the day-to-day job tasks of your chosen career. Also, discuss things like work environment, hours, travel involved, etc.

- *Training/education* (1 paragraph)

- Discuss what kinds of training/education would be required beyond college (once you are working in your career choice). Discuss things like certifications, training, licenses, etc. that may be required. Remember, technology and innovation is constantly changing. We are life-long learners. Training does not stop once you graduate.

- *Earnings/salary* (1 paragraph)

- From research you have done, discuss the expected salary for your chosen career. Consider discussing ways that you could earn more money and compare salary ranges for similar careers or various areas of the country.

- *Other information you found interesting* (1 paragraph)

- From your research you should have obtained lots of information about your career. Use this paragraph to discuss additional information not already explained in the above sections. You could discuss likes/dislikes about the career, related occupations, additional opportunities for advancement, etc.

Research of Individual in Your Field

Make an appointment with someone in your chosen field and interview this person by phone or in person. Include contact information (name, job title, address, telephone, e-mail address). First, start with relatives, friends, and co-workers, or referrals from people you know. If you feel comfortable, identify people in positions of interest in your community and formally contact them for an Informational Interview. If you are contacting strangers, you might begin by introducing yourself as a college student doing research on (your career of interest). Most people are willing to talk about what they do; just be sure to respect their time and busy schedule. Therefore, always have your questions prepared in advance (see below) and arrive on time.

  Once you begin the interview, record the responses for processing later.

Tips for Conducting Information Interviews

- Thank the person for taking the time to speak with you. This should be the first thing you do after meeting the person—before you officially begin the interview.

- **Prepare your interview questions in advance.** Here are some questions that you might consider asking:
  1. During a typical day's work, what do you spend most of your time doing?
  2. What do you like most about your career?
  3. What are the most difficult or frustrating aspects of your career?
  4. What personal skills or qualities do you see as being critical for success in your career?
  5. How did you decide on your career?
  6. What personal qualifications or prior experiences enabled you to enter your career?
  7. How does someone find out about openings in your field?
  8. What steps did you take to find your current position?
  9. What advice would you give first-year students about what they might do at this stage of their college experience to help prepare them to enter your career?
  10. How does someone advance in your career?
  11. Are there any moral issues or ethical challenges that tend to arise in your career?
  12. Are members of diverse groups likely to be found in your career? (This is an especially important question to ask if you're a member of an ethnic, racial, or gender group that is underrepresented in the career field.)

13. What impact does you career have on your home life or personal life outside of work?
14. If you had to do it all over again, would you choose the same career?
15. Would you recommend that I speak with anyone else to obtain additional information or a different perspectives on this career field? (If the answer is "Yes," you may follow up by asking, "May I mention that you refereed me?") It's always a good idea to obtain more than one person's perspective before making an important choice, especially one that can have a major influence on your life, such as your career choice.

Feel free to add new questions to this sample list.

- **Take notes during the interview.** This not only benefits you by helping you remember what was said, but also sends a positive message to the persons you interview because it shows them that their ideas are important and worth writing down.

   Final Note: If the interview goes well, you might ask whether you could observe or shadow your interviewee during a day at work.

Interview Summary
What did you learn that might help you in planning for your career? In a summary paragraph, discuss your interview. Identify who you interviewed and discuss what you learned from your interview that might help you in planning for your career. (Include your interview questions/answers with your paper.)

Self-Assessment Questions
After completing your interview, take a moment to reflect on it and answer the following questions:

1. What information did you receive that impressed you about this career?

2. What information did you receive that distressed (or depressed) you about this career?

3. What was the most useful thing you learned from conducting this interview?

4. Knowing what you know now, would you still be interested in pursuing this career? (If yes, why) (If no, why not)

Summary
Summary. In this section, summarize what you learned about your field. Explain how your choice of career and major matches you (your values, interests, abilities, personality, learning style and multiple intelligences). Discuss the impact this paper had on your choice of major/career, including any thoughts about changing your major/career. (1 paragraph)

EXERCISE 10.3: CHOOSING A MAJOR

Instructions: Research the general majors below until you are comfortable with the meaning of each one. Choose between the majors in the first column and write your selection in the next column blank to the right. Keep narrowing down the choices until you have only one major. If the major is not a good choice, start over and reconsider your choices until you have identified a major you want to explore.

Agriculture and Horticulture

Architecture, Construction, and Technology

Business

Culinary Arts, Food Service and Recreation

Engineering

Fine and Performing Arts

Government, Public Service, and Related Areas

Health Care, Medicine, and Nursing

Language Arts

Life Sciences

Physical Sciences

Social Sciences

NAME: _____ DATE: _____

EXERCISE 10.4: ACADEMIC PLAN RESEARCH EXERCISE

Find an academic program at three different colleges/universities and make a comparison of the higher education institution and the program for each. Print out a copy of the program description or a list of courses.

	WESTERN KENTUCKY UNIVERSITY	STATE COLLEGE OR UNIVERSITY	REGIONAL, NATIONAL OR INTERNATIONAL UNIVERSITY	WRITE A BRIEF COMMENT ON YOUR PREFERENCE AMONG THE THREE PROGRAMS
Name of school	WKU			
Admission requirements for school or program				
Number of students				
Distance from your home				
Full-time cost				
Quarter or semester system?				
Academic division under which your program is listed				
Name of program				
Number of faculty for program				
Number of general education, including elective, courses required				
Number of core or major courses required				

NAME: _____ **DATE:** _____

EXERCISE 10.5: ACADEMIC PLANNING/SCHEDULING

Using the forms provided, your task is to complete your personal academic plan; complete the Schedule Planner for next term; meet with an advisor to review Schedule and complete registration form; and register for the next term. You must submit a copy to your instructor. The steps to complete this task are as follows:

- Obtain a curriculum guide and/or Academic Program Plan (APP) for your chosen major

- Complete the Academic Profile

- Complete the Educational Planning Form (Semester System) using your curriculum guide or Academic Program Plan (APP)

- Obtain recommendation forms with signatures from your reading, math, and English instructors

- Complete your Schedule Planner for the next term (consider your work and personal commitments when choosing course load and class times)

- Meet with Academic Advisor to review Schedule Planner

- Once approved, transfer information from Schedule Planner to official registration form

- Register for class (i.e., online; meet with advisor)

- Submit completed copies of all forms to your instructor

ACADEMIC PROFILE

Name _____   Emplid _____

Major _____   **Curriculum Guide: ATTACH**

Degree: Bachelor   Major: _____
_____ Bachelor of Arts
_____ Bachelor of Science

1. What is your level of commitment to your chosen major?

    _____
    _____
    _____

2. How long do you see yourself being in college? _____

3. What are your academic strengths and weaknesses?

    _____
    _____
    _____

4. What is the career path you have chosen?

    _____
    _____

5. What were the biggest challenges you faced this semester?

    _____
    _____
    _____
    _____
    _____
    _____
    _____
    _____
    _____
    _____

(Continued)

6. What is your student status?
   _____ Full-time (12 or more credit hours)
   _____ Part-time (11 or less credit hours)

7. What campus clubs and organizations are you a member of?

   _____

   _____

   _____

   _____

8. What campus resources have you used?

   _____

   _____

   _____

   _____

9. Do you work?   Yes _____ (Number of hours per week? _____)   No _____

10. Do you have children?   Yes (How many?)   No

11. How do you plan to finance your education?

    _____

    _____

Supplemental materials: College catalog/web site
                                    Schedule of courses

EDUCATIONAL PLANNING FORM (SEMESTER SYSTEM)

Student ID or SSN _____

Fall	Spring	Summer
Total units	Total units	Total units
Fall	Spring	Summer
Total units	Total units	Total units
Fall	Spring	Summer
Total units	Total units	Total units
Fall	Spring	Summer
Total units	Total units	Total units

Total units _____ Date of graduation _____

Academic Advisor signature _____

Comments _____

SCHEDULE PLANNER

TIME	MONDAY	TUESDAY	WEDNESDAY	THURSDAY	FRIDAY	SATURDAY	SUNDAY
7:45–9:00							
9:10–10:25							
10:35–11:50							
12:00–1:15							
1:25–2:40							
2:50–4:05							
4:15–5:30							
5:45–7:00							
7:10–8:25							

SAMPLE REGISTRATION FORM AND ACTUAL FORM

NAME: _____   Semester: _____

Student ID # : _____

Class #	Course	Section #	Description	Day/Times	Credits
1.					
2.					
3.					
4.					
5.					
6.					
7.					

Alternative Schedule   Total Hours: _____

Class #	Course	Section #	Description	Day/Times	Credits
1.					
2.					
3.					
4.					
5.					

Student's Signature (required): _____   Date: _____

NAME: _____ DATE: _____

Read each statement relating to skills needed for success in the workplace. Use the following scale to rate your competencies:

5 = Excellent 4 = Very good 3 = Average 2 = Needs improvement 1 = Need to develop

_____ 1. I have good reading skills. I can locate information I need to read and understand and interpret it. I can pick out the main idea and judge the accuracy of the information.

_____ 2. I have good writing skills. I can communicate thoughts, ideas, and information in writing. I know how to edit and revise my writing and use correct spelling, punctuation, and grammar.

_____ 3. I am good at arithmetic. I can perform basic computations using whole numbers and percentages. I can make reasonable estimates without a calculator and can read tables, graphs, and charts.

_____ 4. I am good at mathematics. I can use a variety of mathematical techniques including statistics to predict the occurrence of events.

_____ 5. I am good at speaking. I can organize my ideas and participate in discussions, and group presentations. I speak clearly and am a good listener. I ask questions to obtain feedback when needed.

_____ 6. I am a creative thinker. I can come up with new ideas and unusual connections. I can imagine new possibilities and combine ideas in new ways.

_____ 7. I make good decisions. I can specify goals and constraints, generate alternatives, consider risks, and evaluate alternatives.

_____ 8. I am good at solving problems. I can see when a problem exists, identify the reasons for the problem, and devise a plan of action for solving the problem.

_____ 9. I am good at mental visualization. I can see things in my mind's eye. Examples include building a project from a blueprint or imagining the taste of a recipe from reading it.

_____ 10. I know how to learn. I am aware of my learning style and can use learning strategies to obtain new knowledge.

_____ 11. I am good at reasoning. I can use logic to draw conclusions and apply rules and principles to new situations.

_____ 12. I am a responsible person. I work toward accomplishing goals, set high standards, and pay attention to details. I usually accomplish tasks on time.

_____ 13. I have high self-esteem. I believe in my self-worth and maintain a positive view of myself.

_____ 14. I am sociable, understanding, friendly, adaptable, polite, and relate well to others.

_____ 15. I am good at self-management. I know my background, skills, and abilities and set realistic goals for myself. I monitor my progress toward completing my goals and complete them.

_____ 16. I practice integrity and honesty. I recognize when I am faced with a decision that involves ethics and choose ethical behavior.

_____ 17. I am good at managing my time. I set goals, prioritize, and follow schedules to complete tasks on time.

_____ 18. I manage money well. I know how to use and prepare a budget and keep records, making adjustments when necessary.

(Continued)

_____ 19. I can manage material and resources. I can store and distribute materials, supplies, parts, equipment, space, or products.

_____ 20. I can participate as a member of a team. I can work cooperatively with others and contribute to group efforts.

_____ 21. I can teach others. I can help others to learn needed knowledge and skills.

_____ 22. I can exercise leadership. I know how to communicate, encourage, persuade, and motivate individuals.

_____ 23. I am a good negotiator. I can work toward an agreement and resolve divergent interests.

_____ 24. I can work with men and women from a variety of ethnic, social, or educational backgrounds.

_____ 25. I can acquire and evaluate information. I can identify a need for information and find the information I need.

_____ 26. I can organize and maintain information. I can find written or computerized information.

_____ 27. I can use computers to process information.

_____ 28. I have an understanding of social, organizational, and technological systems and can operate effectively in these systems.

_____ 29. I can monitor and correct performance in a system. I can use trends to figure out how to achieve the best performance.

_____ 30. I can improve the design of a system to improve the quality of products and services.

_____ 31. I can select the appropriate tool, procedure, machine, or computer to do the desired task.

_____ 32. I can use machines and computers to accomplish the desired task.

_____ 33. I can maintain and troubleshoot machines and computers.

_____ **Total**

Score your skills for success in the workplace

165–133	Excellent
132–100	Very good
99–67	Average
66–34	Need improvement
Below 34	Need to develop skills

EXERCISE 10.7: DEVELOPING YOUR OWN RESUME

Use the sample resume and your resume worksheet to develop your own resume. Use one of the following resources: CREW Center, resume wizard in Microsoft Word, and/or library materials. *Note: Resume must be typed.*

1. What is the specific job title of your ideal job?

2. What are two or three qualifications you possess that would especially qualify you for this job? These qualifications can be listed under Highlights on your resume.

3. List your degree or degrees, major, and dates of completion.

4. List five courses you will take to prepare for your ideal career. For each course, list some key components that would catch the interest of your potential employer. Use a college catalog to complete this section.

(Continued)

5. List the skills you would need in each of these areas.

   Computer skills:

   Technical or other job-related skills:

   Personal skills related to your job objective:

6. List employment that would prepare you for your ideal job. Consider internships or part-time employment.

7. What are your interests?

8. What special achievements or awards do you have?

NAME: _____ **DATE:** _____

EXERCISE 10.8: CREATING A COVER LETTER

Use the sample cover letter and your cover letter worksheet to develop your own cover letter. Use one of the following resources: CREW Center, cover letter wizard in Microsoft Word, and/or library materials. *Note: Cover letter must be typed.*

1. What job are you interested in?

2. How did you learn about this job?

3. How will your education and experience be assets to the company?

4. How can you be contacted for an interview?

5. Did you check the cover letter for any errors?

EXERCISE 10.9: CASE STUDY

Whose Choice Is It Anyway?

Ursula, a first-year student, was in tears when she showed up at the Career Center. She had just returned from a weekend visit home, during which she informed her parents that she was planning to major in art or theater. When Ursula's father heard about her plans, he exploded and insisted that she major in something "practical," like business or accounting, so that she could earn a living after she graduates. Ursula replied that she had no interest in these majors, nor did she feel she had the skills needed to complete the level of math required by them, which included calculus. Her father shot back that he had no intention of "paying four years of college tuition for her to end up as an unemployed artist or actress!" He went on to say that if she wanted to major in art or theater, she'd "have to figure out a way to pay for college herself."

Reflection and Discussion Questions

1. What options (if any) do you think Ursula has at this point in her college experience?

2. If Ursula were your friend, what would you recommend she do?

3. Do you see any way(s) in which Ursula might pursue a major that she's interested in and, at the same time, ease her father's concern that he'll end up jobless after college graduation?

Chapter 11

"Financial Literacy – Where Did My Money Go?"

INTRODUCTION

Just as time management is a key life-management skill, so is money management. In fact, managing time and managing money have a lot in common. You may be familiar with the expressions, "Time is money," "A day late and a dollar short," and "I lost track of my time (or money)." Also, when people commit a crime, they pay their "debt" to society by doing time (jail or doing community service) and/or paying a fine. Both time management and money management require self-awareness of how they're "spent"; both can be saved or wasted, and since both come in limited quantities, they need to be budgeted for and saved or else we'll "run out" of them. Lastly, and perhaps most importantly, how we spend our time and money can tell us a lot about what really matters to us or what we truly value.

"Don't tell me where your priorities are. Show me where you spend your money and I'll tell you what they are."

—*James W. Frick*

For new college students, greater personal independence often brings with it greater demands for economic self-sufficiency, critical thinking about consumerism, and effective management of personal finances. The importance of money management for college students is growing for two major reasons. One is the rising cost of a college education, which is leading more students to work while in college and to work more hours per week (Levine & Cureton, 1998). The rising cost of a college education is also requiring students to make more complex decisions about what options (or combination of options) they will use to finance their college education. Unfortunately, research indicates that many students today are not choosing financial strategies that contribute most effectively to their educational success in college and their long-term financial success after college (King, 2005).

A second reason why money management is growing in importance for college students is the availability and convenience of credit cards. For students today, credit cards are easy to get, easy to use, and easy to abuse. College students can do everything right, such as getting solid grades, getting involved on campus, and getting work experience while in college, but a poor credit history due to irresponsible use of credit cards in college can reduce students' chances of obtaining credit after college and their chances of being hired immediately after graduation. Research also indicates that accumulating high levels of debt while in college is also associated with higher levels of stress (Kiecolt, et al., 1986), lower academic performance (Susswein, 1995), and greater risk of withdrawing from college (Ring, 1997).

On the positive side of the ledger, studies show that when students learn to use effective money-management strategies, they can decrease unnecessary spending, prevent accumulation of significant debt, and reduce personal stress (Health & Soll, 1996; Walker, 1996).

HOW DOES THE BDA STRATEGY RELATE TO FINANCIAL LITERACY?

BEFORE (B)

Remember, the Before (B) section of the strategy focuses on *preparation, self-awareness, and planning.* When it comes to financial literacy, this includes...

- Completing a self-analysis of your goals (recognizing the power of human capital)
- Completing a self-analysis of your lifestyle and spending habits
- Developing a plan (strategies) to manage your money more effectively

DURING (D)

These are your **Action** items. These include developing personal money-saving strategies and habits such as...

- Preparing a personal budget
- Paying bills on time
- Living within your means
- Economizing (spending wisely)
- Evaluating your spending, living situation, gifts, etc.
- Creating your own money-saving strategies
- Always thinking in terms of the future (long-range financial planning)

AFTER (A)

This is the section of **review, revision**, and **self-modification** as it relates to your finances. Ask yourself these questions after you have implemented new practices in regards to your finances:

- Am I consistently following my budget and spending plan?
- Do I need to set or revise some of my financial plans or goals?
- What changes are needed to ensure that I am reaching my goals?
- Are there campus or community resources that I need to contact to help me regarding my financial situation?

BEFORE (B)

Investing in Yourself: Human Capital

Congratulations!! By making the choice to come to college, you are already making a wise financial decision. The Federal Reserve Bank of St. Louis defines **Human Capital** as the knowledge and skills that people obtain through education, training, and experience. People invest in human capital (acquiring more education, training, and experience) to increase opportunities in the future. College students can look at this in terms of reaching their goals. You invest in the expense of college now, for the opportunities it will provide in the future. In financial terms, this is like receiving a return on your investment.

There are many benefits to investing in you, but here are a few big ones:

1. **Increase in job opportunities for those with more education.** According to the Federal Reserve Bank of St. Louis, the unemployment rate for those with a bachelor's degree is 4.1 percentage points lower than those with only a high school diploma.

2. **Increase in income.** Recent research suggests that the percent increase in earnings of those with a bachelor's degree compared to those with only a high school diploma has grown from 40 percent in the late 1970s to 84 percent in 2012. See Table 11.1 The average weekly earnings of a high school graduate in 2009 were $626, which was $135 less than the weekly wages of professionals who held an Associate's degree, $399 less than those who had a Bachelor's degree, and a whopping $631 less than those who had a Master's degree. (Bls. gov/emp/ep_chart_001.htm). Think about how much money this is over your lifetime…

3. **Increase in opportunities for advancement.** While you may be able to get entry-level positions without a college degree, the opportunities for promotions may not be there. Many supervisors claim that when considering candidates for promotion, often the deciding factor as to who gets the promotion will come down to education. Those with college degrees are promoted faster and more often than those who do not have a college degree. Education is something that employers like to see. When employees have obtained higher degrees, they typically feel more pride and job satisfaction. This reflects in their job performance. It benefits the employer to have knowledgeable, trained employees. (www .sixsigmaonline.org/six-sigma-training-certification-information/higher-education-leads-to-career-advancement-opportunities)

"If money is your hope for independence you will never have it. The only real security that a man will have in this world is a reserve of knowledge, experience and ability."

—*Henry Ford*

Table 11.1 Education Pays

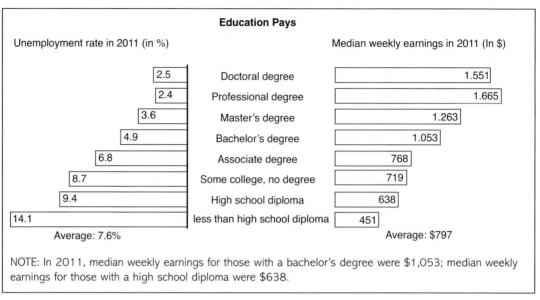

Unemployment rate in 2011 (in %)		Median weekly earnings in 2011 (In $)
2.5	Doctoral degree	1.551
2.4	Professional degree	1.665
3.6	Master's degree	1.263
4.9	Bachelor's degree	1.053
6.8	Associate degree	768
8.7	Some college, no degree	719
9.4	High school diploma	638
14.1	less than high school diploma	451
Average: 7.6%		Average: $797

NOTE: In 2011, median weekly earnings for those with a bachelor's degree were $1,053; median weekly earnings for those with a high school diploma were $638.

SOURCE: Bureau of Labor Statistics, Current Population Survey.

When evaluating the goals you have set for yourself, think about your plan to get there. For many students, this means making the investment now. Committing to stay in college and seek opportunities for training and experience so that these goals will become a reality rather than just a dream.

Developing Financial Self-Awareness*

Developing any good habit begins with the critical first step of self-awareness. The habit of effective money management begins with awareness of your *cash flow*—the amount of money you have flowing in and flowing out. As illustrated in Figure 11.1, you can track your cash flow by monitoring:

- The amount of money you have come in (income) versus the amount going out (express or expenditure), and
- The amount of money you've earned and not spent (savings) versus the amount you've borrowed and not yet paid back (debt).

Income ⟷ Expenses

Savings ⟷ Debt

Figure 11.1 Two Key Avenues of Cash Flow.

Income for college students typically comes from one or more of the following sources:

- Scholarship of grants, which don't have to be paid back
- Loans, which must be repaid
- Salary earned from part-time or full-time work
- Personal savings
- Gifts or other forms of monetary support from parents and other family members

Your sources of expenses or expenditures may be classified into three categories:

1. Basic needs or essential necessities—expenses that tend to be fixed because you cannot do without them (e.g., expenses for food, housing, tuition, textbooks, phone, transportation to and from school, and health-related costs)

2. Incidents or extras—expenses that tend to be flexible because spending money on them is optional or discretionary, i.e., you choose to spend at your own discretion or judgment; these expenses typically include:
   a. money spent on entertainment, enjoyment, or pleasure (e.g., music, movies, and spring-break vacations), and
   b. money spent primarily for reasons of promoting personal status or self-image (e.g., buying expensive brand-name products, fashionable clothes, jewelry, and other personal accessories)
3. Emergency expenses—unpredicted, unforeseen, or unexpected costs (e.g., money paid for doctor visits and medicine needed to treat illnesses or injuries)

Developing a Money-Management Plan

Once you're aware of the amount of money you have coming in (and from what sources) plus the amount of money you're spending (and for what reasons), the next step is to develop a plan for managing your cash flow. The bottom line is to ensure that the money coming in (income) is equal to or greater than the money going out (expenses). If the amount of money going out exceeds the amount coming in, you're "in the red" or have "negative cash flow."

Strategic Selection and Use of Financial Tools for Tracking Cash Flow

To track your cash flow and manage your money, there are a variety of tools available to you. These cash-flow tools include:

- Checking accounts
- Credit cards
- Charge cards
- Debit cards

What follows is a description of these different tools, along with specific strategies for using them effectively.

Checking Account

Long before credit cards were created, a checking account was the method most people used to keep track of their money. Many people still use checking accounts in addition to (or instead of) credit cards. A checking account may be obtained from a bank or credit union; its typical costs include a deposit ($20–$25) to open the account, a monthly service free (e.g., $10), and small fees for checks. Some banks charge customers a service fee based on the number of checks written, which is a good option if you don't plan to write many checks each month. If you maintain a high enough balance of money deposited in your account, the bank may not charge any extra fees, and if you're able to maintain an even higher balance, the bank may also pay you interest—known as an interest-bearing checking account.

In conjunction with your checking account, banks usually provide you with an automatic teller machine (ATM) card that you can use to get cash. Look for a checking account that doesn't charge a separate fee for ATM transactions, but offers it as a free service along with your checking account. Also, look for a checking account that doesn't charge you if your balance drops below a certain minimum figure.

Strategies for Using Checking Accounts Effectively

Apply the following strategies to make the best use of your checking account:

- Whenever you write a check or make an ATM withdrawal, immediately subtract its amount from your *balance* (the amount of money remaining in your account) to determine your new balance.
- Keep a running balance in your checkbook; it will ensure that you know exactly how much money you have in your account at all times. This will reduce your risk of writing a check that *bounces*—a check that you don't have enough money in the bank to cover. If you do bounce a check, you'll probably have to pay a charge to the bank and possibly to the business that attempted to cash your bounced check.
- Double-check your checkbook balance with each monthly statement you receive from the bank. Be sure to include the service charges your bank makes to your account that appear on your monthly statement. This practice will make it easier to track errors—on either your part or the bank's part. (Banks can and do occasionally make mistakes.)

Advantages of a Checking Account

A checking account has several advantages:

- You can carry checks instead of cash.
- You have access to cash at almost any time through an ATM.
- It allows you to keep a visible track record of income and expenses in your checkbook.
- A properly managed checking account can serve as a good credit reference for future loans and purchases.

Credit Card (e.g., MasterCard®, Visa®, or Discover®)

A credit card is basically money loaned to you by the credit-card company that issues you the card, which you pay back to the company monthly. You can pay the whole bill or a portion of the bill each month, as long as some minimum payment is made. However, for any remaining (unpaid) portion of your bill, you are charged a high interest rate, which is usually about 18 percent.

Strategies for Selecting a Credit Card

If you decide to use a credit card, pay attention to *its annual percentage rate (APR)*—the interest rate you pay for previously unpaid monthly balances. This rate can vary from one credit-card company to the next. Credit-card companies also vary in terms of their annual service fee. You will likely find companies that charge higher interest rates tend to charge lower annual fees, and vice versa. As a rule, if you expect to pay the Ml balance every month, you're probably better off choosing a credit card that does not charge you an annual service tee. On the other hand, if you think you'll need more time to make the full monthly payments, you may be better off with a credit-card company that offers a low interest rate.

Another feature that differentiates one credit-card company from another is whether or not you're allowed a *grace period*—a certain period after you receive your monthly statement during which you can pay back the company without paying added interest fees. Some companies may allow you a grace period of a full month, while others may provide none and begin charging interest immediately after you fail to pay on the bill's due date.

Credit cards may also differ in terms of their *credit limit* (also called a *credit line* or *line of credit*), which refers to the maximum amount of money the credit-card company will make available to you. If you're a new customer, most companies will set a credit limit beyond which no additional credit is granted.

Advantages of a Credit Card

If a credit card is used responsibly, it has some key advantages as a money-management tool, such as those listed below.

- It helps you track your spending habits because the credit card company sends you a monthly statement that provides an itemized list of all your card-related purchases. This list supplies you with a "paper trail" of what you purchased that month and when you purchased it.
- It provides the convenience of making purchases online, which can save time and money that would otherwise be spent traveling to and from stores.
- It allows access to cash whenever and wherever you need it, because any bank or ATM that displays your credit card's symbol will give you cash up to a certain limit (usually for a small transaction fee). Keep in mind that some credit card companies charge a higher interest rate for cash advances than credit card purchases.
- It enables you to establish a personal credit history. If you use a credit card responsibly, you can establish a good credit history that you can use later in life for big-ticket purchases such as a car or home. In effect, responsible use of a credit card shows others from whom you wish to seek credit (or borrow money) that you're financially responsible.

Strategies for Using Credit Cards Responsibly

While there may be advantages to using a credit card, you only reap those advantages if you use your card strategically. If not, the advantages of a credit card can be quickly and greatly outweighed by its disadvantages. Listed here are some strategies for using a credit card in a way that maximizes its advantages and minimizes its disadvantages.

1. **Use a credit card only as a convenience for making purchases and tracking the purchases you make; don't use it as a too! for obtaining a long-term loan.**
   A credit card's main money-management advantage is that it enables you to make purchases with plastic instead of cash. A credit card saves you the inconvenience of having to carry around cash and it provides you with a monthly statement of your purchases from the credit card company, which makes it easier for you to track and analyze your spending habits.

   The credit provided by a credit card should be seen simply as a short-term loan that must be paid back at the end of every month. Do not use credit cards for long-term credit or long-term loans because their interest rates are outrageously high. Paying such a high rate of interest for a loan represents an ineffective (and irresponsible) money-management strategy.

2. **Limit yourself to one credit card.** The average college student has 2.8 credit cards (United College Marketing Service, cited in Pratt, 2008). More than one credit card just means more accounts to keep track of and more opportunities to

Remember

Don't buy into the belief that the only way you can establish a good credit history is by using a credit card. It's not your only option; you can establish a good credit history through responsible use of a checking account and by paying your bills on time.

"You'll never get your credit card debt paid off if you keep charging on your card and make only the minimum monthly payment. Paying only the minimum is like using a Dixie cup to bail water from a sinking boat."

—Eric Tyson, financial counselor and national bestselling author of *Personal Finance for Dummies*

Remember

"If you keep charging on your credit card while you have an unpaid balance or debt, you no longer have a grace period to pay back your charges; instead, interest is charged immediately on all your purchases.

accumulate debt. You don't need additional credit cards from department stores, gas stations, or any other profit-making business because they duplicate what your personal credit card already does (plus they charge extremely high interest rates for late payments).

3. **Pay off your balance each month in full and on time.** If you pay the full amount of your bill each month, this means that you're using your credit card effectively to obtain an interest-free, short-term (one-month) loan. You're just paying principal—the total amount of money borrowed and nothing more. However, if your payment is late and you need to pay interest, you end up paying more for the items you purchased than their actual ticket price. For instance, if you have an unpaid balance of $500 on your monthly credit bill for merchandise purchased the previous month and you are charged the typical 18 percent credit card interest rate for late payment, you end up paying $590: $500 (merchandise) + $90 (18 percent interest to the credit card company).

Credit card companies make their profit from the interest they collect from cardholders who don't pay back their credit on time. Just as procrastinating about completing schoolwork is a poor time-management habit that can hurt your grades, procrastinating about paying your credit-card bills is a poor money-management habit that can hurt your pocketbook by forcing you to pay high interest rates.

Don't allow credit card companies to make profit at your expense. Pay your total balance on time and avoid paying exorbitantly high interest rates. If you can't pay the total amount owed at the end of the month, rather than making the minimum monthly payment, pay off as much of it as you possibly can. If you keep making only the minimum payment each month, you'll begin to pile up huge amounts of debt.

Debit Card

A debit card looks almost identical to a credit card (e.g., it has a MasterCard or Visa logo), but it works differently. When you use a debit card, money is immediately taken out or subtracted from your checking account. Thus, you're only using money that's already in your account (rather than borrowing money), and you don't receive a bill at the end of the month. If you attempt to purchase something with a debit card that costs more than the amount of money you have in your account, your card will not allow you to do so. Just like a bounced check, a debit card will not permit you to pay out any money that is not in your account. Like a check or ATM withdrawal, any purchase you make with a debit card should immediately be subtracted from your balance.

Like a credit card, a major advantage of the debit card is that it provides you with the convenience of plastic; however, unlike a credit card, it prevents you from spending beyond your means and accumulating debt. For this reason, financial advisors often recommend using a debit card rather than a credit card (Knox, 2004; Tyson, 2003).

DURING (D)

Money-Saving Strategies and Habits

The ultimate goal of money management is to save money and dodge debt. Here are some strategies for accomplishing this goal.

Prepare a personal budget. A budget is simply a plan for coordinating income and expenses to ensure that your cash flow leaves you with sufficient money to cover your

SNAPSHOT SUMMARY

Financial Literacy: Understanding the Language of Money Management

As you can tell from the number of financial terms used in this chapter, there is a fiscal vocabulary or language that we need to master in order to fully understand our financial options and transactions, to other words, we need to become *financially literate*. As you read the financial terms listed below, place a checkmark next to any term whose meaning you didn't already know.

Account. A formal business arrangement: in which a bank provides financial services to a customer (e.g., checking account or savings account).

Annual percentage rate (APR). The interest rate that must be paid when monthly credit card balances are not paid in full.

Balance. The amount of money in a person's account or the amount of unpaid debt.

Bounced check. A check written for a greater amount of money than the amount contained in a personal checking account, which typically requires the person to pay a charge to the bank and possibly to the business that attempted to cash the bounced check.

Budget. A plan for coordinating income and expenses to ensure that sufficient money is available to cover personal expenses or expenditures.

Cash flow. Amount of money flowing in (income) and flowing out (expenses). "Negative cash flow" occurs when the amount of money going out exceeds the amount coming in.

Credit. Money obtained with the understanding that it will be paid back, either with or without interest.

Credit line (a.k.a. credit limit). The maximum amount of money (credit) made available to a borrower.

Debt. Amount of money owed.

Default. Failure to meet a financial obligation (e.g., a student who fails to repay a college loan "defaults" on that loan).

Emergency student loan. Immediate, interest-free loans provided by a college or university to help financially strapped students cover short-term expenses (e.g., cost of textbooks) or deal with financial emergencies (e.g., accidents and illnesses). Emergency student loans are typically granted within 24–48 hours, sometimes even the same day, and usually need to be repaid within two months.

Deferred student payment plan. A plan that allows student borrowers to temporarily defer or postpone loan payments for some acceptable reason (e.g., to pursue an internship or to do volunteer work after college).

Estimated family contribution (EFC). The amount of money the government has determined a family can contribute to the educational costs of the family member who is attending college.

Fixed interest rate. A loan with an interest rate that with remain the same for the entire term of the loan.

Grace period. The amount of time after a monthly credit card statement has been issued during which the credit card holder can pay back the company without paying added interest fees.

Grant. Money received that doesn't have to be repaid.

Gross income. Income generated before taxes and other expenses are deducted.

Insurance premium. The amount paid in regular installments to an insurance company to remain insured.

Interest. The amount of money paid to a customer for deposited money (as in a bank account) or money paid by a customer for borrowed money (e.g., interest on a loan). Interest is usually calculated as a percentage of the total amount of money deposited or borrowed.

Interest-bearing account. A bank account that earns interest if the customer keeps a sufficiently large sum of money in the bank.

Loan consolidation. Consolidating (combining) separate student loans into one larger loan to make the process of tracking, budgeting, and repayment easier. Loan consolidation typically requires the borrower to pay slightly more interest.

Loan premium. The amount of money loaned without interest.

Merit-based scholarship. Money awarded to a student on the basis of performance or achievement that doesn't have to be repaid.

Need-based scholarship. Money awarded to a student on the basis of financial need that doesn't have to be repaid.

Net income. Money earned or remaining after all expenses and taxes have been paid.

Principal. The total amount of money borrowed or deposited, not counting interest.

Variable interest rate. An interest rate on a loan that can vary or be changed by the lender.

Yield. Revenue or profit produced by an investment beyond the original amount invested. For example, the higher lifetime income and other monetary benefits acquired from a college education that exceed the amount of money invested in or spent on a college education.

Figure 11.2 Financial Literacy Language.

expenses. A budget helps you maintain awareness of your financial state or condition, and enables you to be your own accountant who keeps an accurate account of your own money.

Just like managing and budgeting time, the first step in managing and budgeting money involves prioritizing. Money management requires identifying your most important expenses (indispensable necessities you can't live without) and distinguishing them from incidentals (dispensable luxuries you can live without). People can easily confuse essentials (what they need) and desirables (what they want). For instance, if a piece of merchandise happens to be on sale, it may be a desirable purchase at that time Because of its reduced price, but it's not an essential purchase unless the person really needs that piece of merchandise at that particular time.

Postponing immediate or impulsive satisfaction of material desires is a key element of effective college financing and long-term financial success. We need to remain aware of whether we're spending money on impulse and out of habit or put of need and after thoughtful reflection. The truth is that humans spend money for a host of psychological reasons (conscious or subconscious), many of which are unrelated to actual need. For example, some people spend money to build their self-esteem or self-image, to combat personal boredom, or to seek an emotional "high" (Dittmar, 2004; Furnham & Argyle, 1998). Furthermore, people can become obsessed with spending money, shop compulsively, and develop an addiction to purchasing products. Just as Alcoholics Anonymous (AA) exists as a support group for alcoholics, Debtors Anonymous exists as a support group for shopaholics and includes a 12-step recovery program similar to AA.

Make all your bills visible and pay them off as soon as possible. When your bills remain in your sight, they remain on your mind; you're less likely to forget to pay them or forget to pay them on time. Increase the visibility of your bill payments by keeping a financial calendar on which you record key fiscal deadlines for the academic year (e.g., due dates for tuition payments, residential bills, and financial aid applications). Also, try to get in the habit of paying a bill as soon as you open it and have it in your hands, rather than setting it aside and running the risk of forgetting to pay it (or losing it altogether).

Live within your means. To state it simply: Don't purchase what you can't afford. If you're spending more money than you're taking in, it means you're living *beyond* your means. To begin living *within* your means, you have two options:

1. Decrease your expenses (reduce your spending), or
2. Increase your income (earn more money).

Since most college students are already working while attending college (Orszag, Orszag, & Whitmore, 2001) and working so many hours that it's interfering with their academic performance or progress (King, 2005), the best option for most college students who find themselves in debt is to reduce their spending and begin living within their means.

Economize. By being intelligent consumers who use critical thinking skills when purchasing products, we can be frugal or thrifty without compromising the quality of our purchases. For example, we could pay less to see the same movie in the late afternoon than we could to see it at night. Why pay more for brand-name products that are the same as products with a different name? Why pay 33 percent more for Advil or Tylenol when the same amount of pain-relieving ingredient (ibuprofen or acetaminophen) is contained in generic brands? Often, what we're paying for when we buy brand-name products is all the advertising these companies pay to the media and to celebrities to publicly promote their products.

If you are working:

1. How many hours per week do you currently work?
2. Do you think that working is interfering with your academic performance or progress?
3. Would it be possible for you to reduce the number of weekly hours you now work and still be able to make ends meet?

Remember

Remaining consciously aware of the distinction between essentials that must be purchased and incidentals that may or may not be purchased is an important first step toward preparing an effective budget and avoiding debt.

Remember

Advertising creates product familiarity, not product quality. The more money manufacturers pay for advertising and creating a well-known brand, the more money we pay for the product—not necessarily because we're acquiring a product of higher quality, but more likely because we're covering its high cost of advertising.

Downsize. Cut down or cut out spending for products that you don't need. Don't engage in conspicuous consumption just to keep up with the "Joneses" (your neighbors or friends), and don't allow peer pressure to determine your spending habits. Let your spending habits reflect your ability to think critically rather than your tendency to conform socially.

Save money by living with others rather than living alone. Although you lose privacy when you share living quarters with others, you save money. Living with others also has the fringe social benefit of spending time with roommates or housemates whom you've chosen to live with and whose company you enjoy.

Give gifts of time rather than money. Spending money on gifts for family, friends, and romantic partners isn't the only way to show that you care. The point of gift giving isn't to show others you aren't cheap or show off by being a big-time spender; instead, show off your social sensitivity by doing something special or by making something meaningful for them. Gifts of time and kindness can often be more personal and more special than store-bought gifts.

Develop your own set of money-saving strategies and habits. You can save money by starting to develop tittle money-saving habits that eventually add: up to big savings over time. Consider the following list of habit-forming tips for saving money that were suggested by students in a first year seminar class:

- Don't carry a lot of extra money in your wallet. (It's just like food; if it's easy to get to, you'll be more likely to eat it up.)
- Shop with a list—get in, get what you need, and get out.
- Put all your extra change in a jar.
- Put extra cash in a piggy bank that requires you to smash the piggy to get at it.
- Seal your savings in an envelope.
- When you get extra money, get it immediately into the bank (and out of your hands).
- Bring (don't buy) your lunch.
- Take full advantage of your meal plan—you've already paid for it, so don't pay twice for your meals by buying food elsewhere.
- Use e-mail instead of the telephone.
- Hide your credit card or put it in the freezer so that you don't use it on impulse.
- Use cash (instead of credit cards) because you can give yourself a set amount of cash and clearly see how much of it you have at the start of a week (and how much is left at any point during the week).

When making purchases, always think in terms of their long-term total cost. It's convenient and tempting for consumers to think in the short term ("I see it; I like it; I want it; and I want it now.") However, long-term thinking is one of the essential keys to successful money management and financial planning. Those small (monthly) installment plans that businesses offer to get you to buy expensive products may make the cost of those products appear attractive and affordable in the short run. However, when you factor in the interest rates you pay on monthly installment plans, plus the length of time (number of months) you're making installment payments, you get a more accurate picture of the products total cost over the long run. This longer-range perspective can quickly alert you to the reality that a product's sticker price represents its partial and seemingly affordable short-term cost but its long-term total cost is much less affordable (and perhaps out of your league).

Furthermore, the long-term price for purchases sometimes involves additional "hidden costs" that don't relate directly to the products initial price but must be paid to keep using the product. For example, the sticker price you pay for clothes

"The safest way to double your money is to fold it over and put it in your pocket."

—Kin Hubbard, American humorist cartoonist, and journalist

doesn't include the hidden, long-term costs that may be involved if those clothes require dry cleaning. By just taking a moment to check the inside label, you can save yourself this hidden, long-term cost by purchasing clothes that are machine washable. To use an example of a big-ticket purchase, the extra money spent to buy a new car (instead of a used car) includes not only paying a higher sticker price but also paying the higher hidden costs of licensing and insuring the new car, as well as any interest fees if the new car was purchased on an installment plan. When you add in these hidden, long-term costs to a new car's total cost, buying a good used car is clearly a much more effective money-management strategy than buying a new one.

Sources of Income for Financing Your College Education

Free Application tor Federal Student Aid (FAFSA)

The Free Application for Federal Student Aid (FAFSA) is the application used by the U.S. Department of Education to determine financial aid eligibility for students. A formula is used to determine each student's *estimated family contribution (EFC)*— the amount of money the government has determined a family can contribute to the educational costs of the family member who is attending college. No fee is charged to complete the application, so you should complete one every year to determine your eligibility to receive financial aid, whether you believe you're eligible or not. See the Financial Aid Office on your campus for the FAFSA form and for help in completing it.

Scholarships

Scholarships are available from many sources besides the institution you've chosen to attend. Typically, scholarships are awarded at the time of admission to college, but some scholarships may be awarded to students at a later point in their college experience. To find out about scholarships that you may still be eligible to receive, visit your Financial Aid Office. You can also conduct an Internet search to find many sites that offer scholarship information. (However, don't enter your credit card or bank account information on any site.)

Also, keep in mind that scholarships are very competitive and deadlines are strictly enforced.

Grants

Grants are considered to be gift aid, which typically does not have to be repaid. About two-thirds of all college students receive grant aid, which, on average, reduces their tuition bills by more than half (College Board, 2009). The Federal Pell Grant is the largest grant program; it provides need-based aid to low-income undergraduate students. The amount of the grant depends on criteria such as (1) the anticipated contribution of the family to the students education (EFC), (2) the cost of the postsecondary institution that the student is attending, and (3) the enrollment status of the student (part time or full-time).

Loans

Student loans need to be repaid once a student graduates from college. Listed below are some of the more common student loan programs.

SNAPSHOT SUMMARY

Federal Loan versus Private Loan: A Critical Difference

Private loans and federal loans are different, unrelated types of loans. Here are the key differences:

Federal loans have fixed interest rates that are comparatively tow (currently less than 7 percent).

Private loans have variable interest rates that are very high (currently more than 15 percent) and can go higher at any time.

Note: Despite the high cost of private loans, they are the fastest-growing type of loans taken out by college students, largely because of aggressive, misleading, and sometimes irresponsible or unethical advertising on loan-shopping Web sites. Students sometimes think they're getting a federal loan only to find out later they have taken on a more expensive private loan.

"Apply for as much grant aid as possible before borrowing, and then seek lower-interest federal student loans before tapping private ones. There is a lot of student aid that can help make the expense [of college] more manageable."

—*Sandy Baum, senior policy analyst, College Board (Gordon, 2009)*

"Borrow money from a pessimist. He won't expect it back."

— *Steven Wright, American comedian and first inductee to the Boston Comedy Hall of Fame*

Source: Hamilton (2012); Kristof (2008).

Figure 11.3 Federal Loan versus Private Loan: A Critical Difference.

- **The Federal Perkins Loan** is a 5 percent simple-interest loan awarded to exceptionally needy students. The repayment for this loan begins nine months after a student is no longer enrolled at least half-time.
- **The Federal Subsidized Stafford Loan** is available to students enrolled at least half-time and has a fixed interest rate that's established each year on July 1. The federal government pays the interest on the loan while the student is enrolled. The repayment for this loan begins six months after a student is no longer enrolled half-time.
- **The Federal Unsubsidized Stafford Loan** is a loan that's not based on need and has the same interest rate as the Federal Subsidized Stafford Loan. Students are responsible for paying the interest on this loan while they're enrolled in college. The loan amount limits for Stafford loans are based on the classification of the student (e.g., freshman or sophomore).

Keep in mind that federal and state regulations require that if you're receiving financial aid, you must maintain "satisfactory academic progress" In most cases this means you must do the following:

1. **Maintain a satisfactory GPA.** Your entire academic record will be reviewed, even if you have paid for any of the classes with your own resources.
2. **Make satisfactory academic progress.** Your academic progress will be evaluated at least once per year, usually at the end of each spring semester.

3. **Complete a degree or certificate program within an established period of time.** Check with your institutions Financial Aid Office for details.

Salary Earnings

If you find yourself relying on your salary to pay for college tuition, check with your employer to see whether the company offers tuition reimbursement. Also, check with the Billing Office on your campus to determine whether payment plans are available for tuition costs. These plans may differ in terms of how much is due, deadlines for payments, and how any remaining debt owed to the institution is dealt with at the end of the term. You may find that the college you're attending will not allow you to register for the following term until the previous term is completely paid for.

Research shows that when students work on campus (versus off campus) they're more likely to succeed in college (Astin, 1993; Pascarella & Terenzini 1991; 2005), probably because they become more connected to the college when they work on campus (Cermak & Filkins, 2004; Tinto, 1993) and also because on campus employers are more flexible than off-campus employers in allowing students to meet their academic commitments (Leonard, 2008). For instance, camp employers are more willing to schedule students' work hours around their class schedule and allow students to modify their work schedules when their academic workload increases (e.g., at midterm an finally). Thus, if at all possible, rather than seeking work off campus, try to find work on campus and capitalize on its proven capacity to promote college success.

You may have heard the expression that "time is money." One way to interpret this expression is that the more money you spend, the more time you must spend making money. If you're going to college, spending more time on earning money to cover your spending habits often means spending less time studying, learning, completing classes, and earning good grades. You can avoid this vicious cycle by viewing academic work as work that "pays" you back in terms of completed courses and higher grades. If you put in more academic time to complete more courses in less time and with higher grades, you're paid back by graduating and earning the fulltime salary of a college graduate sooner—which will pay you about twice as much money per hour than you'll earn doing part-time work without a college degree (not to mention fringe benefits such as health insurance and paid vacation time). Furthermore, the time you put into earning higher

grades in college should pay off immediately in your first full-time position after college, because research shows that students graduating in the same field who have higher grades receive higher starting salaries (Pascarella &Terenzini, 2005).

* From *Thriving in College and Beyond: Research-Based Strategies for Academic Success and Personal Development* by Jospeh B. Cuseo, Aaron Thompson, Michele Campagna, and Viki S. Fecas. Copyright © 2013 by Kendall Hunt Publishing Company. Reprinted by permission.

AFTER (A)

This is the section of **review, revision**, and **self-modification** as it relates to your finances. Ask yourself these questions after you have implemented new practices in regards to your finances:

- Am I consistently following my budget and spending plan?
- Do I need to set or revise some of my financial plans or goals?
- What changes are needed to ensure that I am reaching my goals?
- Are there campus or community resources that I need to contact to help me regarding my financial situation?

SUMMARY

Obviously money is an important topic for everyone. However, for college students it can be critical. You need to learn to handle your money in such a way that allows you to stay in college. You also want to make sure that you are staying financially responsible and not taking on too much debt that will have to be repaid once you complete your degree.

Investing in yourself through your education is a great start. However, before you can see the return on the investment, you must develop the financial skills to be able to stay in college and complete your degree and your goals. Remember to continually review and revise your spending/budget plan as well as your goals. By putting into practice the tips presented in this chapter, you will become much wiser about your finances and financial decisions.

SUGGESTED READINGS AND INTERNET-BASED RESOURCES

Neck, Christopher, and Charles Manz. *Mastering Self-Leadership: Empowering Yourself for Personal Excellence.* New Jersey: Prentice Hall, 2006.
Baldwin, Amy. *Community College Experience Plus.* 2nd ed. New Jersey, Prentice Hall, 2010.

PAYING FOR EDUCATION

www.students.gov
www.fafsa.gov

FINANCIAL LITERACY

www.360financialliteracy.org
www.stlouisfed.org/education_resources/

ONLINE BUDGETING TOOLS

www.collegeanswer.com/tools/budget-calculator
www.studentaid.ed.gov/prepare-for-college/choosing-schools/consider/budget-calculator
www.mappingyourfuture.org/Money/budgetcalculator.htm

EXERCISE 11.1: SELF-ASSESSMENT OF FINANCIAL ATTITUDES AND HABITS

Answer the following questions as accurately and honestly as possible.

		Agree	Disagree
1.	I pay my rent or mortgage on time each month.	_____	_____
2.	I avoid maxing out or going over the limit on my credit cards.	_____	_____
3.	I balance my checkbook each month.	_____	_____
4.	I set aside money each month for savings.	_____	_____
5.	I pay my phone and utility bills on time each month.	_____	_____
6.	I pay my credit-card bills in full each month to avoid interest charges.	_____	_____
7.	I believe it is important to buy the things I want when I want them.	_____	_____
8.	Borrowing money to pay for college is a smart thing to do.	_____	_____
9.	I have a monthly or weekly budget that I follow.	_____	_____
10.	The thing I enjoy most about making money is spending money.	_____	_____
11.	I limit myself to one credit card.	_____	_____
12.	Getting a degree will get me a good job and a good income.	_____	_____

Sources: Cude et al. (2006), Niederjohn (2008).

Give yourself one point for each item that you marked "agree"—except for items 7, 9, and 10. For these items, give yourself a point if you marked "disagree."

A perfect score on this short survey would be 12.

Self-Assessment Questions

1. What was your total score?

2. Which items lowered your score?

3. Do you see any pattern across the items that lowered your score?

4. Do you see any realistic way or ways you could improve your score on this test?

EXERCISE 11.2: FINANCIAL SELF-AWARENESS: MONITORING MONEY AND TRACKING CASH FLOW

1. Use the worksheet that follows to estimate what your income and expenses are per month, and enter them in column 2. (Option: Research budgeting tools.)

2. Track your actual income and expenses for a month and enter them in column 3. (To help you do this accurately, keep a file of your cash receipts, bills paid, and checking or credit records for the month.)

3. After one month of tracking your cash flow, answer the self-assessment questions.

    a. Were your estimates generally accurate?

    b. For what specific items or areas were there the largest discrepancies between what you estimated they would be and what they actuary were?

    c. Comparing your bottom-line total for income and expenses, are you satisfied with how your monthly cash flow seems to be going?

    d. What changes could you make to create more positive cash flow—i.e., to increase your income or savings and reduce your expenses or debt?

    e. How likely is it that you would actually make the changes you mentioned in your response to question d?

Financial Self-Awareness Worksheet

	Estimate	Actual
Income Sources		
Parents/Family		
Work/Job		
Grants/Scholarships		
Loans		
Savings		
Other:		
TOTAL INCOME		
Essentials (Fixed Expenses) *Living Expenses:* Food/Groceries		
Rent/Room & Board		
Utilities (gas/electric)		
Clothing		
Laundry/Dry Cleaning		
Phone		
Computer		
Household Items (dishes, etc.)		
Medical Insurance Expenses		
Debt Payments (loans/credit cards)		
Other:		
School Expenses: Tuition		
Books		
Supplies (print cartridges, etc.)		
Special Fees (lab fees, etc.)		
Other:		
Transportation: Public Transportation (bus fees, etc.)		
Car Insurance		
Car Maintenance		
Fuel (gas)		
Car Payments		
Other:		

	Estimate	Actual
Incidentals (Variable Expenses) *Entertainment:* Movies/Concerts		
DVDs/CDs		
Restaurants (eating out)		
Other:		
*Personal Appearance/*Accessories: Haircuts/Hairstyling		
Cosmetics/Manicures		
Fashionable Clothes		
Jewelry		
Other:		
Hobbies		
Travel (trips home, vacations)		
Gifts		
Other:		
TOTAL EXPENSES		

EXERCISE 11.3: CASE STUDY – PROBLEMS PAYING FOR COLLEGE

A college student posted the following message on the internet:

I went to college for one semester, failed some my classes, and ended with 900 dollars in student loans. Now I can't even get financial aid or a loan because of some stupid thing that says if you fail a certain amount of classes you can't get aid or a loan. And now since I couldn't go to college this semester they want me to pay for my loans already, and I don't even have a job.
Any suggestions?

Rejection and Discussion Questions

1. What suggestions would you offer this student? What should the student do right now? What should the student do eventually?

2. What should the student have done to prevent this from happening?

3. Do you think that this student's situation is common or unusual? Why?

EXERCISE 11.4: COUNT THE COST

For this exercise you will research information from the Internet. Remember to use your critical thinking and information literacy skills to evaluate your sources. Print the first page from your source to include with your research information.

Choose **one** of the following situations, and make a budget or estimate expenses based on your research findings.

1. What is your career goal? Using information learned regarding your estimate for your first year's salary, determine how much you will earn each month. Make a monthly budget showing how you could live on that salary. Don't forget savings and student loan repayment if applicable. Expenses to consider include housing (rent), utilities, food, transportation, work clothing, entertainment, and childcare. Some students may also want to allocate money for charitable giving. Do you have money left over? If not, are there things you can cut back on or ways to increase your income?

2. How much does it cost to own a car? Make a budget for car ownership and compare the cost of car ownership to the cost of bus transportation. Visit wwwedmunds.com and look under **Tips and Advice** for information to consider regarding car ownership. If you currently own a car, you may use your actual information (car payment, insurance, gas, maintenance). If you do not currently own a car, use the information from Edmunds.com to make a budget for a car you would like to own. For information on bus costs, go to your city's web page and look for public transportation information.

3. You would like to plan a trip to celebrate graduation. Where would you go? Use travel websites to plan your trip. How much will it cost to fly? To drive? (use a map site like wwwmapquest.com to figure the mileage) How much do hotels cost in your destination city. What sorts of activities will you want to do, and how much do they cost. Plan a weekend trip (2 nights). If you currently work, how many hours will you have to work at your present rate of pay to finance a trip like the one you have planned?

EXERCISE 11.5: REFLECTION JOURNAL – HOW AM I INVESTING IN MY HUMAN CAPITAL?

In the beginning of the chapter you learned about Human Capital. Reflect on your current activities (school, work, volunteering, club memberships, sports, etc.). How are these activities helping build your human capital? How do you see these activities helping you in the future? Are you investing enough in yourself? If not, what will you commit to do to increase your investment in yourself. BE SPECIFIC.

Chapter 12

Life Skills – Why Does It Matter?

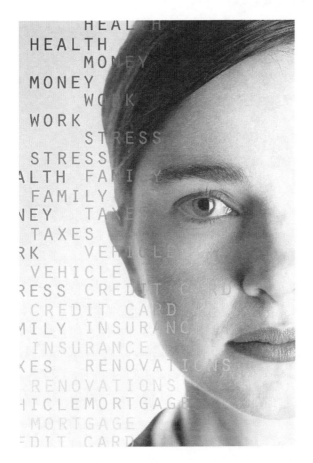

INTRODUCTION

You probably didn't expect college to be easy, but many students are unprepared for how stressful going to college can be. As a college student, you are likely to have more roles than the average person. Most students work at least part time, but many are full-time employees. If you live at home, you may have additional responsibilities. If you are married and/or a parent, you know the time and energy involved in building strong relationships and running a household. If you're just starting to live on your own, you have the pressure of paying bills, grocery shopping, etc.—things that your parents used to do for you. Many of you are also involved in extra activities either on campus or in the community. Now you've added the hours of homework and studying it takes to maintain good grades. In addition, if you were not a strong student in high school, or if it has been a few years since you were in school, you might be feeling anxious about taking tests, math classes, or writing papers. The pace of college courses goes at least twice as fast as regular high school courses. It can become overwhelming by midterm as you start thinking about all you have to do before the end of the semester.

This chapter focuses on these interpersonal or life skills, such as health and wellness, communication and relationships, diversity and leadership that impact your success as a college student and offers strategies to help you improve your skills and abilities in these areas. Life skills matter—read on and see how and why!

HOW DOES THE BDA STRATEGY RELATE TO LIFE SKILLS?

BEFORE (B)

Remember, the Before (B) section of the strategy focuses on *preparation, self-awareness*, and *planning*. When it comes to life skills, this includes

- **Completing a self-analysis of your lifestyle (i.e. habits, ways you manage)**
- **Developing a plan (strategies) to improve your life skills**

DURING (D)

The During (D) section involves taking action, such as

- **Practicing new strategies for managing life skills**
- **Researching additional strategies**

AFTER (A)

This is the section of *review, revision*, and *self-modification* as it relates to your lifestyle. Ask yourself these questions after you have practiced new strategies?

- **Have I been consistent in using the new strategies I have learned?**
- **Have I built enough time in my schedule?**
- **Have I properly assessed my health and my relationships?**
- **Make any changes as needed**

HEALTH AND WELLNESS

Maintaining good health is a key factor in being a successful college student. This section focuses on managing stress, eating properly, exercising, getting enough sleep, avoiding addictions, and protecting your body.

What does it mean? Change causes stress. The more check marks, or the more changes you have going on in your life, the higher your risk for a stress-related illness. If you have major changes taking place in all the areas of your life (check marks in each category), that can also signal the potential for trouble.

Stress

Pretest

Identify the major changes that are happening in your life right now. Check as many as apply to you within this past year.

Family changes:
- ☐ Death of spouse, parent, sibling
- ☐ Death of grandparent or other close relative
- ☐ Divorce or marital separation (you or your parents)
- ☐ Marriage
- ☐ Pregnancy
- ☐ Gaining a new family member/s (birth, adoption, stepfamily, elder moving in, etc.)
- ☐ Major changes in health or behavior of a close family member

Health changes:
- ☐ Serious personal injury or illness
- ☐ Major change in sleeping habits
- ☐ Major change in eating habits
- ☐ Quitting, starting, or major increase in smoking, drinking, or other drug use
- ☐ Major change in amount of exercise or activities

Financial changes:
- ☐ Sudden loss of income
- ☐ Major change in financial status (a lot better or a lot worse off than usual)
- ☐ Taking on a mortgage
- ☐ Foreclosure on a mortgage or loan
- ☐ Taking on a loan

Employment changes:
- ☐ Being fired from work
- ☐ Retirement from work
- ☐ Major change in responsibilities at work (promotion, demotion, transfer)
- ☐ Changing careers
- ☐ Major change in working hours or conditions
- ☐ Major conflict with your boss/supervisor, or co-workers

Personal changes:
- ☐ Detention in jail or other institution
- ☐ Death of a close friend
- ☐ "Breaking-Up" with girlfriend/boyfriend
- ☐ Conflict with spouse, in-laws, parents, or a close friend
- ☐ Beginning or ceasing formal schooling
- ☐ Moving to different residence / Major change in living conditions
- ☐ Outstanding personal achievement
- ☐ Revision of personal habits (dress, manners, associations, etc.)

Social changes:
- ☐ Changing to a new school
- ☐ Major change in usual type or amount of recreation
- ☐ Major change in church and/or social activities
- ☐ Vacation
- ☐ Major changes in holiday celebrations, and/or number of family get-togethers

What Is Stress?

Stress is the body's reaction to an occurrence or an event. You're driving to class and suddenly notice the flashing lights and siren of a police car behind you. Your body instinctively reacts. You look down at your speedometer. It shows 10 miles over the speed limit. Tension mounts. You prepare for what may follow. You don't really have time to stop and certainly can't afford a ticket. Your heart starts beating faster, and your mind is racing as you try to think of what to say. Even if the police car continues down the road, you may still feel a little shaken. Your adrenaline is high; you're stressed. A police car driving with its lights and siren turned on is not in itself a stressful event. If you were stopped at a red light on a side street or driving in the opposite direction, you would have a much different reaction to that event. The event is neutral, but your reactions can be positive or negative.

Our reactions come from a variety of sources. Some of them are the importance we place on the event, the expectation of certain consequences or results, our previous experiences, and our ability to handle a variety of situations. Our perceptions, beliefs, habits, level of self-confidence, and physical, mental, and emotional health also influence our reactions. No two people will react exactly alike. What may be a challenge for one person may be distressful for another.

We usually think of stress as always being from negative or bad events, but it can come from happy occasions as well. Starting college, planning a wedding, the birth of a child, celebrating the holidays with family, getting a new job, moving to a new house, or remodeling your current one are usually considered positive events. Yet, all of these can produce stress. Change of any kind may produce stress. That's why the pretest asked you to identify how many major changes are going on in your life right now. A little tension may be just what you need to motivate you. However, if you get too much in too short a time period, it can cause your body to become overloaded. When that happens, your body's natural immune system may be unable to defend itself against all of the germs, bacteria, and viruses that surround us. Your resistance is lowered, and you succumb to whatever illness is "going around." Being overloaded for a long period of time can be very damaging to your health. That's why it is important for you to use common sense and practice good health habits as your first line of defense.

COMMON STRESSORS OF COLLEGE STUDENTS

1. Assignments and examinations
2. Time management (including procrastination and lack of time)
3. Academic failure (grades included)
4. Friends and relationships
5. Money
6. Family

When college students were asked to list their most common stressors, they listed those above in rank order. Other areas listed less frequently were "bad habits" to change, lack of sleep, anxiety, future, and career goals. This is representative of what many students feel.

How to Reduce Stress

We cannot control all of life's stressors, but we can control how we react to them, and we can control the degree of anxiety they place on our lives. Learn how to reduce stress by identifying what is causing it and then implement your own personal stress-reduction program. If you alter your beliefs and your way of thinking, you can reduce anxiety levels. You can also condition your body to resist any ill effects that remain. Stress is manageable, providing it does not approach a life-threatening level.

Step One—Look for Stress Symptoms—Be aware of the symptoms of stress. Awareness always precedes action. Recognize the symptoms, and don't deny that you have them. Then you can start to solve the problem.

Step Two—Identify Stressful Times, Situations, and People—Identify the times and places when you feel stressed out. Did you relate to any of the typical sources of stress listed in the previous section? Think of the current causes of anxiety in your life right now. If it helps, keep a journal to pinpoint the sources of your stress. Record what happened and your reaction. Think of other possible ways you could have reacted. List the kinds of things that were helpful in relieving your anxieties.

Step Three—Eliminate Unnecessary Stress—Whenever possible, eliminate the causes of unnecessary stress. From your journal you might have noticed a pattern of things or people that always bother you. When you come to that situation/person again, think ahead. Try to anticipate what will happen. Then, avoid those stressful situations. "That's easier said than done," you say. Yes, some events and conflicts with people in our lives are unavoidable. In those cases you may have to develop a tolerance for what you cannot resolve. You cannot change someone else, but you can change yourself and your attitudes. Don't let conflict with the significant people in your life become a way of life. It's too exhausting and frustrating. Learn new skills such as assertive communication to improve and soften all your relationships.

Step Four—Reduce the Effects of Unavoidable Stress—For the stress in your life that you can't eliminate, try to control and reduce its affects. Remember to keep your perspective. Think about how important this event really is. Will you even remember it next week? Next month? If not, why get upset about it? Keep your stress at a minimum and don't over-react. People have successfully dealt with the stress in their lives by using some of the following techniques.

STUDENT STRESS CALENDAR
HTTP://WWW.UDEL.PROGMAN/

August/September

- Homesickness, especially for freshmen.
- Values crisis: students are confronted with questions of conscience over such issues as race, drugs, alcohol experimentation, morality, religion, and social expectations.
- Feelings of inadequacy and inferiority develop because of the discrepancy between high school status and grades and initial college performance.

October

- Freshmen begin to realize life at college is not as perfect as they were led to believe by parents, teachers, and counselors. Old problems seem to continue and new ones are added. An external reality they had put their hopes in has failed them.
- Grief develops because of inadequate skills for finding a group or not being selected by one.
- Mid-term workload pressures are followed by feelings of failure and loss of self-esteem.
- Pregnancies from summer relationship begin to show. Dilemma of what to do.
- Sexual conflicts and confusion result when confronting, for the first time, different heterosexual standards and homosexuality.
- Non-dating students sense a loss of esteem because so much value is placed upon dates. For people who date, the pressure to perform sexually increases feelings of rejection, loneliness, and guilt.
- Job panic for mid-year graduates.

(continued)

November
- Academic pressure is beginning to mount because of procrastination, difficulty of work, and lack of ability.
- Depression and anxiety because of feelings that one should have adjusted to the college environment by now.
- Economic anxiety: funds from parents and summer earnings begin to run out.
- Some students have ceased to make attempts at establishing new friendships beyond two or three existing relationships.

December
- Extracurricular time strain—seasonal parties, concerts, social service projects, religious activities drain student energies.
- Anxiety, fear, and guilt increase as final examinations approach and papers are due.
- Pre-Holiday/Break depression—especially for those who have concerns for fam-ily, those who have no home to visit, and for those who prefer not to go home because of family conflicts.

January
- Post Holiday/Break depression at again being away from home security and positive strokes.
- Post Holiday/break-up of high school relationships.

February
- Many students experience optimism because second semester is perceived as going "down hill."
- Vocational choice causes anxiety and depression.
- Couples begin to establish stronger ties (engagement) or experience weakening.
- Depression increases for those students who have failed to establish social relationships or achieve a moderate amount of recognition.
- Social calendar in non-active.
- Cabin fever due to weather.

March
- Drug and alcohol use increases.
- Academic pressures increase as midterms arrive.
- Existential crisis for senior—Must I leave school? Is my education worth anything? Was my major a mistake? Why go on?
- Where is God? Why am I not seeking him/her?

April
- Frustration and confusion develop because of decisions necessary for pre-registration.
- Summer job pressures.
- Selection of a major.
- Papers and exams are piling up.
- The mounting academic pressures force some students to temporarily give up.
- Social pressures: everybody is bidding for your participation in trips, banquets, and picnics.
- Job recruitment panic.
- Depression begins due to anticipation of separation from friends and loved ones at college.

May
- Anxiety develops because of the realization that the year is ending and that a deficiency exists in a number of academic areas.
- Seniors panic about jobs (or lack of jobs) and ability to finance oneself until the first paycheck.
- Depression over leaving friends and facing conflicts at home with parents.

Importance of Exercise

A primary key to establishing a healthy lifestyle is to exercise. Keep in mind that what may fit one person exercise-wise may not fit another, but do something! While balance is important (somewhere between obsessive/compulsive routines and no routine), the optimum level of exercise will vary according to age and current health level. It is always advisable to involve a professional who can help you develop a program that meets your specific needs. With that word of caution, here are several exercise tips that are known to be generally beneficial.

- **Aim to do some type of aerobic exercise, such as walking, jogging, and swimming for three 30-minutes periods per week.** (If you find it more convenient to walk or jog near your home, do not do it alone, and let others know your routine; for example, tell a roommate you are leaving to run. Human predators are sometime attracted to campuses. To be safe, expect the worse.)
- **Think about getting exercise by bicycling around campus.**
- **Walk instead of riding available campus transportation such as campus buses.** Walking up and down hills on a hilly campus is excellent exercise.
- **Instead of riding the elevator in a campus building, take the stairs.**
- **"Think exercise" by finding ways to incorporate exercise into your daily routine.** Instead of having a pizza delivered, take your class notes with you and quiz yourself as you walk to the neighborhood pizza place. Also, recognize that while handball or basketball provide more exercise than golf or bowling, these latter types of exercise are better than inactivity.
- **Reduce or eliminate consumption of substances that interfere with your ability to exercise** (e.g., cigarettes and alcohol).
- **Get enough sleep.** Being tired can interfere with your motivation to exercise.
- **Get regular medical checkups and screenings** (e.g., mammograms). Part of your exercise routine should be to hear from a medical professional concerning your current state of health and what health maintenance measures you should continue to follow or what needs to be done to correct for a detected health problem.

Getting Enough Sleep

We're well aware that when you get really busy, sleep is the first thing to go. There just aren't enough hours for classes, studying, partying, visiting with friends, and all the other interesting activities available. However, an essential self-management skill for doing well in college is to **get at least 8 hours of good, regular sleep every night**. Many college students binge and purge when it comes to sleep—getting too few hours during the week and trying to catch up on the weekend. Unfortunately, the body doesn't work that way. You can cut back a little on sleep one night and make it up the next, *if this is a rare occurrence and you are in excellent health*. Be realistic, are you?

OK, let's look at the facts about sleep. The U.S. is the most sleep-deprived country on earth, with an average of a little less than 7 hours a night—and college freshmen are one of the most deprived groups. Being out of the parental grasp is just too much for some students, and staying up late is a way of proving to yourself that you're "in control"—finally! During the first two weeks of a freshmen class, we constantly hear students bragging about how little (if any) sleep they got the night before. Interestingly, by the beginning of the third week the bragging ceases, and students are whining about lack of sleep, no energy to study (or party!), irritability, and an inability to concentrate.

We call this the "zombie period." It also marks the beginning of the "catching a cold" season for -students!

Some students find sleeping difficult because of noise around their living quarters or a fear of missing out on something exciting. Others are just trying to keep up with course work—especially as they get further behind due to poor time management and inefficient study skills. Late-teen physiology even conspires to defeat going to bed early. Although 19-year-olds (whose bodies will continue to grow for at least 2 more years) still need between 9 and 10 hours of sleep, their brains just doesn't let them get sleepy as early as they used to (e.g., Carskadon, cited in the *UC Berkeley Wellness Letter*, 1995). And then there is that 8:00 class with the professor who always takes roll.

There may be one last problem affecting your ability to sleep well—alcohol. Alcohol consumption peaks during college and, for many, during freshmen year. Consequently, many freshmen go to bed with a good dose of alcohol in their system. Unfortunately, alcohol delays the time it takes for the brain to begin having *restorative* sleep, and the only remedy for this is to sleep more than the usual amount of sleep needed (often 10 or more hours). As stress increases during the semester, don't rely on caffeine to energize you and alcohol to relax you. You may *feel* awake, but your brain will function as though it were sleep deprived! And *do not* take sleeping pills or other narcotics. They are addictive and are only effective for a couple of weeks.

So, how *do* you get enough sleep? There is no secret to getting adequate amounts of good sleep, just like there isn't about exercising. The catch is *doing it!* Keep in mind that you need to get at least 8 hours of sleep, and you need to do so every night. Here are some tactics you can use to increase your chances of sleeping soundly and long enough.

- **Go to bed and get up at the same time** *every day*—if you can only do one of these, *getting up at the same time* is more important.
- **Develop a 20- to 30-minute pre-sleep routine to get ready for bed;** do the same routine every night, and your body will be ready to sleep when you get in bed.
- **Don't do anything stimulating close to bed time**—no fights or heated discussions, no thinking about something that will stir up your emotions, and definitely no worrying.
- **Get together everything you will need for the next day** before you start your pre-sleep routine—get your books together, decide what you'll wear, etc. This habit will guarantee you one less thing to worry about once you get in bed.
- **Take a *warm* bath or shower,** if that relaxes you, but avoid really hot water within an hour of going to bed. If your body is overheated, your brain won't be able to start the sleep cycle.
- **Sleep in a "cold" room year round**—between 45 and 55 degrees is best.
- **If you are a chronically poor sleeper, don't watch TV, read, or study in your bed**—make sleeping the activity for bed, and your body will become classically conditioned to go to sleep when you go to bed.
- **Don't drink alcohol or caffeine close to bedtime,** and don't drink an excess of either anytime during the day. Some people can't handle caffeine after 5:00 or 6:00 in the evening. Although caffeine or alcohol may not keep you awake when you try to go to sleep, they will shorten the time you sleep by causing you to wake up after a few hours—and this isn't just because they are diuretics!
- **If you must eat or drink late in the evening, make it something relaxing**—remember the milk and cookies routine when you were a child? And be sure you don't overdo any eating or drinking prior to bed or your sleep will be disturbed. That 1:00 a.m. pepperoni pizza that seemed like a great idea will come back to haunt you by 4:00.

- **If you are bothered by noise, buy the highest level of noise-defeating foam earplugs you can find**. A box will last a long time, and they are also useful when you are trying to concentrate on your studies. Yes, you will still hear your alarm go off, if you aren't too sleep-deprived.
- **About that alarm**—when you get enough sleep and have a regular time to go to bed and wake up, you'll find that you will usually wake up slightly before the alarm goes off. But keep setting it because you may worry about not waking up otherwise.

Avoiding Addictions to Smoking, Alcohol, and Other Drugs

Smoking, abusing alcohol, or using illegal drugs can interfere with your success in college, on the job and in life. These addictions can cause illness and a shortened life expectancy. Knowledge in these areas will help you make the best choices to maintain your quality of life.

Smoking Tobacco: A Leading Cause of Preventable Illness and Death

Smoking is widespread in our society. One in every four adults in the United States smokes and one in every three teenagers smokes. Tobacco use is the leading cause of preventable illness and death in the United States. One out of every five deaths in the United States is related to smoking. Each year over 430,000 Americans die too young as a result of smoking related illnesses. Imagine that three jumbo jets carrying 400 people each crashes every day of the year. This is similar to the number of people who die each year from smoking-related illnesses.

Smoking is related to a variety of illnesses:

- **Smoking damages and irritates the respiratory system**. Smoking a package of cigarettes a day is like smearing a cup of tar over the respiratory tract. Smoking causes lung cancer, emphysema, and chronic bronchitis.
- **Smoking affects the heart and circulatory system**. Smoking causes premature coronary heart disease and several types of blood-vessel diseases.
- **Smoking increases the probability of having strokes**, which damage the brain and often leaves a person with permanent disabilities.
- **Smoking affects the eyes and vision**. It is speculated that smoking causes vision loss by restricting blood flow to the eyes. Recent studies have connected smoking with macular degeneration, an irreversible form of blindness. Cataracts, or clouding of the lenses of the eyes, is also associated with smoking.
- **Smoking irritates the eyes, nose, throat, and gums and can lead to cancer** of the mouth, throat, or esophagus.
- **Smoking is associated with osteoporosis**, the thinning of bones due to mineral loss.
- **During pregnancy, smoking damages the developing fetus** causing miscarriages, low birth weight, developmental problems, and impaired lung function at birth.
- **Smoking causes premature facial wrinkling** due to vasoconstriction of the capillaries of the face.

Why is smoking such a major health problem? It is because smoking is an addiction that is difficult to overcome. Only 20 percent of smokers who decide to quit smoking are successful on a long-term basis. For those who are successful in quitting, tobacco-related health risks are improved over time. Although smoking cessation is difficult, it is worth the investment in improved healthy living. Refraining from smoking, along with a healthy diet and exercise, can increase your life span by as much as ten years. For help with smoking cessation, visit your physician or college health office.

Alcohol

Each year many college students die as a result of excessive drinking. Some students drink and drive and die in car accidents. Others die from alcohol poisoning or alcohol-related accidents. Excessive drinking is a factor in poor college performance and high dropout rates. Studies have shown that heavy drinking causes brain damage and interferes with memory. Having some knowledge about alcohol use can help you to make choices to ensure your future quality of life.

Binge Drinking

Heavy drinking causes students to miss class and fall behind in schoolwork. College students who are considered binge drinkers are at risk of many alcohol-related problems. Binge drinking is simply drinking too much alcohol at one time. In men, binge drinking is defined by researchers as drinking five or more drinks in a row. In women it is drinking four or more drinks in a row. It takes about one hour to metabolize one drink, so it would take five hours to metabolize five drinks. Researchers estimate that two out of five college students (44 percent) are binge drinkers. Students who are binge drinkers are twenty-one times more likely to:

- **Be hurt or injured**
- **Drive a car after drinking**
- **Get in trouble with campus or local police**
- **Engage in unprotected sex**
- **Engage in unplanned sexual activity**
- **Damage property**
- **Fall behind in schoolwork**
- **Miss class**

It is particularly significant that there is a connection between binge drinking and driving. Among frequent binge drinkers, 62 percent of men and 49 percent of women said that they had driven a car after drinking. About half of the students in this study reported being a passenger in a car in which the driver was high or drunk. A drink is defined as

- **A 12-ounce beer**
- **A four-ounce glass of wine**
- **A shot of liquor (1.5 ounces of 80-proof distilled spirits) straight or in a mixed drink**

National studies on alcohol consumption in colleges find that students are less likely to participate in binge drinking when they put a high priority on studying, have special interests or hobbies, and participate in volunteer activities. The majority of college students (56 percent nationally) either abstains from drinking or drinks in moderation. Students least likely to be binge drinkers are African American, Asian, 24 years or older, or married. Students at highest risk for binge drinking include intercollegiate athletes and members of fraternities and sororities. Students most likely to be binge drinkers are white, male, and under 24 years of age.

Blood Alcohol Content (BAC)

The amount of alcohol in your blood is referred to as blood alcohol content (BAC). It is recorded in milligrams of alcohol per 100 milliliters of blood. For example, a BAC of .10 means that 1/10 of 1 percent or 1/1,000 of your total blood is alcohol. BAC depends on the amount of blood in your body, which varies with your weight, and the amount of alcohol consumed over time. The liver can only process one drink per hour. The rest builds up in the bloodstream. Below are listed the effects of increasing BAC:

- **.02 Mellow feeling, slight body warmth, less inhibited**
- **.05 Noticeable relaxation, less alert, less self-focused, coordination impairment begins, most people reach this level with one or two drinks**
- **.08 Drunk driving limit, definite impairment in coordination and judgment**
- **.10 Noisy, possible embarrassing behavior, mood swings, reduction in reaction times**
- **.15 Impaired balance and movement, clearly drunk**
- **.30 Many lose consciousness**
- **.40 Most lose consciousness, some die**
- **.50 Breathing stops, many die**

The above figures point out some important facts for college students. It does not take many drinks to reach the drunk driving limit. Most people reach the drunk driving limit if they have one to three drinks depending on weight and time since the last drink. BAC increases if you are lighter weight or if you have just had a drink. As the BAC increases, more serious effects occur. Tragically, each year college students die from alcohol poisoning, which occurs when large quantities of alcohol are consumed in a short period of time. This sometimes occurs during the hazing periods in college fraternities and sororities. Colleges are taking steps to stop hazing on college campuses nationwide.

Other Drugs

While alcohol is the most commonly used drug, street drugs such as *marijuana, cocaine, LSD, methamphetamines, rohypnol* (the "date rape drug"), *ecstasy, ketamine* (a PCP-like anesthetic), and *heroin* interfere with the accomplishment of life goals. Clark Carr, President of Narconon, describes the following impact of illegal drug usage:

One of the worst impacts of street drugs is their impact on ambition. Drugs have insidious yet devastating effects upon children and their ability to envision hopes and dreams. Ambition enables a person to learn to enjoy life and to pursue happiness without drugs, but it can be destroyed through drug use. When a person is intoxicated by drugs, important functions are adversely affected, including concentration, recording, and recalling. These tools are essential to learning, and without them education is impaired. Addiction becomes the all-consuming focus of activities aimed at procuring more drugs. Education, careers, relationships, and life itself take a back seat.

> # WARNING SIGNS OF ALCOHOLISM
>
> Alcoholics Anonymous has published twelve questions to determine if alcohol is a problem in your life. Answer these questions honestly:
>
> 1. *Have you ever decided to stop drinking for a week or so but could only stop for a couple of days?*
> 2. *Do you wish people would mind their own business about your drinking and stop telling you what to do?*
> 3. *Have you ever switched from one kind of drink to another in the hope that this would keep you from getting drunk?*
> 4. *Have you ever had to have a drink upon awakening during the past year? Do you need a drink to get started or to stop shaking?*
> 5. *Do you envy people who can drink without getting into trouble?*
> 6. *Have you had problems connected with drinking during the past year?*
> 7. *Has your drinking caused problems at home?*
> 8. *Do you ever try to get extra drinks at a party because you do not get enough?*
> 9. *Do you tell yourself you can stop drinking any time you want to, even though you keep getting drunk when you don't mean to?*
> 10. *Have you missed days of work or school because of drinking?*
> 11. *Do you ever have blackouts from drinking, when you cannot remember what happened?*
> 12. *Have you ever felt that your life would be better if you did not drink?*
>
> If you answered yes to four of the above questions, it is likely that you have a problem with alcohol.

People take drugs in order to feel better. The problem is that drugs can become life destroying. Anyone contemplating taking drugs should ask these four questions:

1. Are the benefits going to outweigh the liabilities?
2. Will I experience more pleasure than pain, or more pain than pleasure?
3. Will the pleasure be temporary? How will I feel tomorrow?
4. Will the drug do more harm than good?

Answering these questions honestly can help you to make the right choices. Having an addiction to smoking, alcohol, or illegal drugs can be difficult to control. If you need help with problems caused by drug or alcohol addiction, see your physician or contact your college health office.

Protecting Yourself from HIV/AIDS and Other Sexually Transmitted Diseases

Basic Facts about HIV/AIDS

HIV/AIDS has been described as the worst plague in modern history. AIDS is the fourth leading cause of death in the world. It is estimated that by 2020, the number of people dying from AIDS will be approximately equal to all people killed in wars in the twentieth century. At present, there is no cure for AIDS. Since AIDS continues to be a leading cause of death among Americans ages 25 to 44, knowing how to protect yourself from HIV/AIDS and other sexually transmitted diseases is an important survival skill. The

U.S. Centers for Disease Control and Prevention provides some helpful information to minimize your risk of infection.

What is HIV?

HIV is the human immunodeficiency virus that causes AIDS. The virus kills the "CD4" cells that help your body fight off infection.

What is AIDS?

AIDS is the acquired immunodeficiency syndrome. It is the disease you get when HIV destroys the body's immune system. Normally your immune system helps to fight off illness. When the immune system is destroyed, you can become very sick and die.

How is HIV Acquired?

HIV is acquired in the following ways:

- **It is acquired by having unprotected sex (sex without a condom) with someone who has HIV.** The virus can be in an infected person's blood, semen, or vaginal secretions. It can enter the body through tiny cuts or sores on the skin, or the lining of the vagina, penis, rectum, or mouth.
- **It is acquired by sharing a needle and syringe to inject drugs or by sharing equipment used to prepare drugs for injection with someone who has HIV.**
- **HIV can be acquired from a blood transfusion received before 1985.** Since 1985, blood is tested for HIV.
- **Babies born to women who are HIV-positive can become infected during pregnancy, birth, or breast-feeding.**

You **cannot** get HIV from the following:

- **Working with or being around someone who has HIV**
- **Sweat, tears, spit, clothes, drinking fountains, phones, or toilet seats**
- **Insect bites or stings**
- **Donating blood**
- **A closed-mouth kiss**

What are the Best Ways to Protect Yourself?

Here are some guidelines:

- **Don't share needles or syringes for injecting drugs, steroids, vitamins or for tattooing or body piercing. Germs from an infected person can stay in the needle and then be injected into the next person using the needle.**
- **Don't have sex. This is truly "safe sex."**
- **If you choose to have sex, have sex with only one partner that you know doesn't have HIV and is only having sex with you.**
- **Use a latex condom every time you have sex. This is referred to as "safer sex."**
- **Don't share razors or toothbrushes because of the possibility of contact with blood.**
- **If you are pregnant, get tested for HIV. Drug treatments are available to reduce the chances of your baby being infected with HIV.**

How Do I Know if I Have HIV or AIDS?

A person can have HIV or AIDS and feel perfectly healthy. The only way to know is to get tested. Most college health offices and your local health department offer confidential testing.

Other Sexually Transmitted Diseases (STDs)

There are more than twenty-five different diseases spread through sexual activity. There are 15 million new cases of sexually transmitted diseases (STDs) each year, and one-fourth of these new infections are in teenagers. According to the Centers for Disease Control and Prevention, these diseases can "result in severe health consequences, cancer, impaired fertility, premature birth, infant death and disability." The increase in STDs has paralleled the AIDS epidemic. The guidelines for protecting against HIV apply to other STDs as well.

The most common STDs in the United States include chlamydia, gonorrhea, syphilis, genital herpes, human papillomavirus, hepatitis B, trichomoniasis, and bacterial vaginosis. Bacterial diseases such as gonorrhea, syphilis, and chlamydia can be cured with antibiotics. Viral diseases such as herpes, hepatitis, and genital warts can be treated but not cured. A vaccine has been developed to prevent hepatitis B, and it is recommended that teenagers and college students obtain this vaccination to avoid the serious liver damage that can result from this disease.

Women suffer the most from STDs because they have more frequent and serious complications from them than men do. Chlamydia and gonorrhea can lead to pelvic inflammatory disease (PID), which can cause chronic pelvic pain, infertility, or potentially fatal ectopic pregnancies. The human papillomavirus can increase the risk of cervical cancer in women. Many STDs can be passed to the fetus, newborn, or infant before, during, or after birth.

COMMUNICATION AND RELATIONSHIPS

Our ability to succeed in life is often affected by our ability to get along with others. How we interact with family members, friends, co-workers, teachers, classmates, supervisors, and others in our environment can have a positive or negative impact on whether our needs are met or whether we are meeting the needs of others. For example, our relationship with a co-worker or supervisor can affect our satisfaction with our job, and can determine whether we are promoted, or even dismissed.

As you continue with your college education at a college/university, you may see changes in your interpersonal relationships. Some of your old friendships may weaken, especially with those who are away at different schools or with those who haven't continued their education. New supportive relationships may begin. Adjustments in family life may be required. This can be true if you are a traditional age student, gaining more independence from your parents, and it is certainly true for adult students whose families must make many adjustments when mom, dad, or spouse becomes a student again. Using effective communication skills will help you promote positive relationships with other people in your lives and can help you meet your physical, emotional, social, intellectual/educational, and economic needs.

This section focuses on the use of effective communication skills to maintain and build strong interpersonal relationships. You will explore the following:

- **Components of the communication process,**
- **Aggressive, assertive, and passive communication styles and how to distinguish among them,**

- **Developing and using specific assertive communication techniques in inter-personal relationships**.

Communication—A Two-way Process

As human beings, our lives revolve around our interpersonal relationships with others in our environment—family members, friends, co-workers, teachers, classmates, sales clerks and service personnel, supervisors, and many others with whom we interact on a daily basis. We solve problems, purchase goods and services, socialize, and work with others by using communication skills. Communication is a **two-way process** involving a "sender" and a "receiver/listener." The **sender** expresses his/her feelings, ideas, or needs (known as the message) to a **receiver or listener**, who is expected to respond in some way (feedback). The process is interactive—we act as both the sender and the receiver/listener during the course of any conversation.

The sender's message is carried both **verbally** (words) and **nonverbally** (gestures, posture, facial expressions, appearance). The receiver/listener also responds (provides feedback) both verbally and nonverbally. This interchange completes the "communica-tion loop," although both parties may change sender/receiver roles several times during their communication exchange.

We use our interpersonal skills to handle problems and conflicts in our daily lives. Disagreements with friends, the division of household responsibilities, requesting help on a work project, resisting pressure from peers or parents, work-ing on a committee, returning defective merchandise to the store, or solving differences with family members/partners, roommates/apartment-mates are all examples of situations which require the use of effective communication skills to solve the problem.

Unfortunately, many people never develop strong interpersonal skills and are thus unable to communicate effectively with others. Divorce lawyers see many couples whose relationships have fallen apart primarily due to their inability to effectively communicate with one another. Parents and children sometimes experience a "com-munication gap" when neither understands the other. At work, an employee may become isolated from co-workers or have a negative relationship with a supervisor due to an inability to "get along" with others. In the college environment, students may fail to achieve in classes that require group interaction for academic success. They may feel uncomfortable asking an instructor to explain something they didn't under-stand in the lecture or reading material, thereby decreasing their potential for success in the class.

It is apparent that developing effective communication skills can improve our rela-tionships with others—at home, in the workplace, in social or business situations, in school, and in every day interactions with the general public. Remember that the com-munication process involves both the sender and the receiver (listener). If we hope to become effective communicators, we must develop specific skills in BOTH parts of the communication process.

The Receiver/Listener

Just as good note taking requires effective listening skills, the effective communicator must also practice effective listening techniques. Listening is NOT the same as hearing. Hearing is a passive, involuntary process in which our brain receives a signal (sound) from the external environment. **Listening** requires that we pay attention to the message received and respond in some way. Use the following strategies to become an *active listener*, fully involved in the communication process:

1. *Listen—don't talk*. Allow the sender to communicate his/her message without interruption. Concentrate on the message being sent rather than on trying to plan your response to the message.

2. *Use attending skills*. Generate an attitude of interest in what the speaker has to say by using and maintaining eye contact. Keep facial expressions attentive and lean forward slightly to show your attention to the speaker.

3. *Consider your response* before beginning to speak. Do NOT interrupt.

4. *Provide feedback* by first summarizing what you've heard. "Check out" your understanding of what was said before making your response. Responses such as, "In other words …" or, "If I understand you correctly …" allow you to clarify your understanding and keep communication going.

5. *Respond in a non-judgmental manner*. Respond to the sender's feelings as well as to his/her words. Be willing to acknowledge the speaker's views and his/her right to have them, even though they may differ from your own.

The Sender

When in the role of sender, use the following strategies to increase your communication effectiveness.

1. *Take responsibility for your ideas/feelings*. Use "I" messages to get your point across without blaming, criticizing, or making personal attacks upon your listener. "You" messages such as, "You make me crazy!" or, "You're always late!" make the receiver/listener defensive. Such messages almost certainly will be "tuned out." Instead, use "I" message responses such as, "I worry/get annoyed when you're late, and I haven't heard from you." This simple technique can prevent misunderstanding and promote open, honest communication.

2. *Be aware of your nonverbal messages*. Is your tone angry and/or your body language threatening? Are you avoiding eye contact? Is there a difference between what you are saying and how you are saying it? An apology can express the words "I'm sorry," but an angry facial expression or rude tone of voice will make the listener doubt your sincerity. If a classmate is trying to start a conversation or is asking for help, and you are repeatedly glancing at your watch, you've sent a non-verbal message that you aren't interested in what s/he has to say.

3. *Clarify what you want to say* in your own mind before beginning to speak. You can't expect others to understand you if you are not sure what it is you want to say.

4. *Be aware of the tone and quality of your voice*. Refusing your friend's request to borrow your car in a firm, decisive tone will make it clear that you are not going to change your mind.

5. *Be sensitive to issue appropriateness and timing*. Trying to arrange a study time with a classmate who just had an accident on the way to class or insisting on going out to dinner when your partner just completed a twelve-hour shift shows a lack of awareness of the listener's needs. More importantly, such actions reveal a lack of care and concern for the person him/herself.

6. *Avoid making demands* and using statements such as "you should," "you need to," or "you have to." Comments such as these tend to cause resentment or anger in the listener.

BARRIERS TO COMMUNICATION

Even when people want to communicate, barriers may exist which can cause a breakdown in the communication process. These barriers are usually internal "blockers" which can prevent us from either sending or receiving a clean, undistorted message. Some common communication blocks are identified below:

1. *Preoccupation/Distractedness*—If you have something on your mind, you will not be able to listen effectively. Reading or doing something else while trying to listen, thinking about what else you need to do today, or worrying about a financial problem are just a few examples of ways in which your concentration can be lowered. Being unable to give the speaker your full attention can cause misunderstandings or a total breakdown in the communication attempt.

2. *Stereotyping*—Stereotypes are fixed ideas about people as part of a *group* rather than considering each person as an individual. Ethnic and gender differences account for many stereotypes, but other differences such as political, sexual, or religious preferences may also result in stereotyping. Persons with disabilities, people whose body size falls outside the socially accepted height/weight norms, and others who exhibit some difference are all targets for stereotypes.

3. Some stereotypes may seem positive, such as categorizing women as "naturally nurturing and caring of others," or thinking "all Asian-Americans are good students." These assumptions, however, are generalizations that may be totally false when applied to individuals. Making false assumptions always interferes with clear, accurate communication. Stereotypes are also a form of discrimination, and, as such, inhibit the communication process.

4. *Emotional blocks*—Anger/defensiveness/grief—when either the sender or the receiver is attempting to communicate while angry or defensive, the communication attempt will most likely not be successful. An angry sender often communicates that anger through facial expressions and body language or through tone of voice, even though the words s/he is saying are not necessarily argumentative.

5. *An angry or defensive listener* is likely to "tune out" much of the speaker's words or react in a hostile manner during the communication attempt. Grief, whether suffered by the sender or receiver, is also likely to cause a breakdown in the communication process. A parent who has lost a child, for example, may have very negative reactions during a classroom discussion or conversation about abortion.

6. *Past experience*—All of our past experiences also play a part in "filtering" our communication efforts with others. Students with previous negative experiences speaking in front of groups may resist their advisor's attempt to register them for Communications 181 (Basic Public Speaking), even though they know the course is required for their degree. Spouses/girlfriends/boyfriends may bring up past difficulties or problems in the relationship whenever a new disagreement arises.

These kinds of barriers can make effective communication extremely difficult, and sometimes impossible. Try to eliminate any barriers you may bring to the process. If emotional blocks are the problem, it may be necessary to wait until you or the other

(continued)

party has had a chance to calm down before you attempt your conversation. If distraction is the culprit, ask the other person to give you a few moments of undivided attention. Don't destroy your friendship with someone you care about just to win an argument. Be aware that bad communication can damage relationships just as good communication can enhance them.

Communication Styles

Previously we have stressed the importance of interpersonal communication skills. As we examine the ways in which people communicate, we can see several distinct styles in action. The following scenario illustrates the difference between the passive, aggressive, and assertive communication styles.

> *Janet is taking a psychology class this semester that requires participation in a group project. The project will count for 1/3 of her final course grade. She is the group leader, and one of the four members (Tom) has missed several meetings and has not been completing his share of the work.*

The Passive Style

If Janet takes a passive communication approach, she will hint around about how soon the project deadline is coming up but not make a direct statement. She may say something like, "Tom, March 15th is just around the corner. I sure hope we can get it together by then." This approach shows a lack of acknowledgement of Janet's own feelings (concern over the grade and annoyance with Tom) and does not clearly communicate what she wants to happen. Tom may not get the hint or may not realize why Janet is concerned. Another passive approach would be to complain to the other group members, but say nothing to Tom. Either way, a behavior change on Tom's part is not likely to take place.

Passive communication is emotionally dishonest because you're denying your own needs and feelings. The passive communicator frequently allows others to manipulate or take advantage of him/her. This may result in feelings of anger, resentment, or depression. Passive communicators may have chronic ailments such as ulcers, stress, or high blood pressure because they internalize their conflicts with others instead of bringing them out and resolving them. Passive responses have the unconscious effect of absolving one of his/her actions rather than taking responsibility for them.

The Aggressive Style

An aggressive communication approach, on the other hand, would be if Janet confronted Tom in a demanding manner with comments like, "You're ruining all of our grades! How can you be so lazy and inconsiderate, or are you just too stupid to do the assignment? If you don't get it together, I'm going to tell the professor!" This approach does not respect Tom's feelings because Janet attacked without knowing why he hasn't completed the work as scheduled. It is also unlikely that Tom will respond positively and get the work done after this kind of attack.

Aggressive responses are inappropriately directed and frequently ignore the rights and feelings of others. Those who have been hurt or angered may, in turn, avoid or take revenge against the aggressive communicator. Aggressive behavior may, therefore, get short-term results, but in the long run will hurt your relationships with others. Think about the last time you were verbally attacked by someone. Did it make you care for that person and want to please him/her? In this section we are defining aggressive communication as demanding, selfish, hostile, confrontational and/or combative. Do not get this form of aggressiveness confused with the secondary definition of being aggressive which means working energetically, taking the initiative, being enterprising, or doing your best in a sporting event.

The Assertive Style

The assertive approach allows Janet to express her specific needs in a way that respects her classmate. She might say, "Tom, I'm worried that our group project is due next week and you haven't completed your part. I had mine ready yesterday as we agreed. My grade in this course is very important to me, and I would appreciate it if you completed your part by Wednesday so we can meet again on Friday for a final review. Thanks very much for your help."

This approach tells Tom specifically what Janet wants (his part finished by Wednesday) without attacking him, and it gives Janet a much better chance of meeting her needs (cooperation from Tom resulting in a good grade). Assertive behavior is

COMPARISON OF PASSIVE, ASSERTIVE, AND AGGRESSIVE COMMUNICATION STYLES

	Passive	Assertive	Aggressive
Statements	Hints, uses indirect messages	Makes clear, concise statements	Speaks for self *and* others
Social Behavior	Denies own needs and feelings Lets others choose Puts self down Manipulates others into feeling guilty Absolves self of responsibility for own actions	Respects others Negotiates conflicts Chooses for self Accepts strengths and weaknesses or mistakes Feels good about self	Disregards the rights *and* needs of others Chooses for self and others Blocks communication May use verbal/physical abuse
Voice	Weak Quiet Child-like	Firm Strong	Loud Angry
Body Language	Poor eye contact Moves away, distances self from others Smiles are forced Uses few gestures	Uses good eye contact Relaxed—uses gestures Face matches mood Confident appearance	Moves into others' space Overreacts
Possible Consequences of Behavior	You feel hurt, angry, anxious Others feel guilty or superior Outcome—needs not met Others may take advantage of you	You respect yourself Others respect your honesty Trust Outcome—needs may/may not get met Mutual respect	You feel lonely, angry, anxious Others feel hurt or defensive Outcome—may get needs met *at the time* Others may avoid you or seek revenge

emotionally honest because it requires us to "own" our thoughts, feelings, and opinions. On the other hand, it respects the rights of others and generally allows our needs to be met.

The chart on the previous page and above provides a comparison of passive, assertive, and aggressive communication styles. Examples of statements made, behavior exhibited, voice tone and body language used, and possible consequences of each behavior are identified for each style.

Defining Assertive Communication

What is assertive communication, and why does this approach result in more open communication and better interpersonal relationships? Assertive communication allows us to express our feelings, needs, opinions, or preferences in a direct and honest manner without threatening, harming, "putting down," or manipulating others. This communication style does NOT guarantee that our needs/wishes will always be met, but simply ensures that we have expressed those needs in an appropriate manner. In other words, the rights of both parties in the communication exchange have been acknowledged and protected.

Developing assertive communication behavior is a learned skill. We are not born being assertive communicators, and we do not generally behave in an assertive manner in all situations. We may, for example, be able to communicate in an assertive way when we are with friends, but be less able to use these skills when communicating with family members, college instructors, co-workers, or supervisors.

Our ability to practice assertive communication may also change depending upon the specific situation. We may feel comfortable in expressing positive feelings—giving and receiving compliments, initiating conversations, and expressing affection/love. On the other hand, we may feel uncomfortable when we have to request help or make requests of others, when we want to express personal opinions, or when we feel annoyance or anger with others.

To increase our assertiveness levels, we need to consciously practice using assertive communication skills. One way to better our skills is to practice using the "I" message format described earlier in the chapter. "I" messages:

1. Identify the sender's feeling about the conflict/problem
2. Describe in a nonjudgmental way the specific action or behavior which took place
3. Focus on the effect or consequence that the action/behavior has on you.

The factual description of the behavior, rather than an attack on the person performing the action, reduces defensiveness in the listener and avoids judgmental evaluations by the sender/speaker. Compare the following responses in terms of their probable impact on the listener.

"You" Messages vs. "I" Messages	
"You always interrupt me!"	"I feel upset when I'm interrupted because it seems like my ideas aren't important to you."
"You're lazy!"	"I feel annoyed when you don't do your share of the work because I have to do it or live in a mess.
"You never let me know what your plans are!"	"I am upset when I don't know your plans because I've kept time free for you."

"You" messages attack the other person. They put all the control or ownership of the situation on him/her. They are not likely to make the other person feel sorry about their offenses, which is what you really want. Instead, that person will probably attack back with insults or complaints about you. An argument will likely ensue or escalate, and your relationship with that person will suffer.

"I" messages, on the other hand, are designed to increase your communication and get cooperation from the other person. Although they may sound contrived at first, with practice, you will find this a more honest way of communicating with the people in your life. When you use "I messages," you take ownership of your emotions and actions. An "I" message may also include a statement about what you plan to do about the problem situation. This approach cannot guarantee a behavior change by the other person, but it lets you control your response to the situation. In the above "I" messages, for example, the statements might continue with the following intents:

> *"The next time you interrupt me when I'm talking, I'm going to just walk away."*

> *"From now on, I won't be cleaning up after you. I will only do the chores I previously agreed to do. If you'd like to talk about a change in how we divide up the work, please let me know."*

> *"I'll keep Friday evenings open until Wednesday. If I haven't heard from you by then, I'll make other plans."*

Learning to communicate by using "I" messages requires practice. Exercise 10.3 gives you another opportunity to practice writing assertive communication responses.

Developing and Using Assertive Communication Skills

Dealing with Negative Feelings

College life is full of stress. It is inevitable that work demands, family commitments, study requirements, and the stress of personal relationships will sometimes result in anger, criticism, and/or complaints. It is important to recognize these feelings within ourselves and to learn to express justified anger or criticism in an appropriate way. Conversely, we should also team how to accept criticism or expressions of anger from others.

How do we express anger or criticize others in an "appropriate" way? The following common workplace scenario can be used to illustrate how criticism or anger can be legitimately expressed without causing injury to the listener.

> *John has been assigned responsibility for preparing a market analysis for a new client, but he failed to complete the report on time. Before leaving for the night, he tells his supervisor that he's sorry, but he just didn't get the report done. The supervisor, knowing that a client could be lost, decides to stay late himself to make sure it gets done. He is very angry with John but also recognizes that he should have checked the status of the report prior to the last day. How might the supervisor express hisanger/criticism at John without being unjust?*

FIRST—the supervisor should use an **"I" message** to take ownership of his feelings (anger). "I am angry …"

SECOND—the supervisor should describe the **action** or **behavior** that produced his anger, rather than throwing accusations at John. "… when I assign a task to you, and you don't complete it on time… ."

THIRD—the supervisor should identify what **effect** John's failure to complete the work has on him. "... **because** we might have lost this account if I had not stayed late and completed the work."

FOURTH—the supervisor should refuse to get involved in an argument or to let the situation push him into an aggressive response—threatening, using sarcasm, yelling, etc. It is better to walk away rather than to let a situation escalate beyond your control. At the same time, the supervisor should make clear what his/her expectations will be if a similar situation should occur in the future: "... I'd appreciate your letting me know in advance if you're having trouble in meeting the deadline on future assignments."

The above responses allow the supervisor to express his/her anger and frustration in a constructive way. The supervisor "vents," thus avoiding a build up in resentment, which might result in negative interactions with the employee in the future. The employee can accept the criticism because he was not humiliated or "put down" by the boss, and the communication link has been kept open to promote better working relationships in the future.

Keeping the focus on the **behavior** or **action** that caused a problem rather than on the person behind the behavior/action will help you to respond in an appropriate way whenever you need to express complaints/criticism/anger toward others. Whenever you are the recipient of a complaint/criticism, you will be more accepting of requested changes in behavior if you've been treated with respect. The criticism should be focused on your behavior or action rather than on you as a person.

Requesting Help/Service/Information from Others

How easy is it for you to ask others for help? If you left your night class and found that your car wouldn't start, who would you call—a friend, a family member, or an auto club service? Asking for "favors" or assistance from others may be relatively easy or very difficult depending upon the situation in which you find yourself.

Asking for a personal loan or for a favor which requires a serious time commitment from others will generally be more difficult than calling someone to give you a ride home from your night class. Our ease or "comfort level" in asking for help or assistance from others also varies with our relationship with our communication "partner."

If your relationship with your boss, teacher, or other authority figure is positive, then requests such as these will obviously be easier to make. As you make a request for assistance or a favor, remember that the listener has the right to refuse your request. It is then your responsibility to accept that refusal without attempting to pressure or "guilt trip" the other party into changing his/her mind. Ultimately, you may have to make some tough choices if it comes to a showdown between work and college schedules.

Another area in which assertive communications skills are helpful is when we are requesting expected service from others. Returning an item which we decided not to keep, returning a well done steak when we ordered it medium rare, or returning our car to the mechanic who failed to solve the problem are all examples of ways in which we may request satisfactory service. Would you eat the meat that was not prepared as you ordered without comment or return it to the kitchen? Would you negotiate for adjustments on car repairs or accept unsatisfactory service?

As consumers, we are entitled to receive satisfactory services. Requests for appropriate compensation or service must, however, be made in a courteous manner rather than blaming or accusing the other party. Factually describing the event or problem that occurred will bring about better results than if you attack or blame the person who provided the service. In addition, making requests for changes or accommodations must be specific—"This steak is well done, and I ordered mine medium rare. Please return this to the kitchen and bring me one which is prepared as I requested." This approach makes your service needs clear without blaming the server.

Refusing Requests and Saying "NO"

We've already learned that appropriate assertive behavior includes the right to request help, assistance, or favors from others without feeling guilty. Others have the right to refuse to grant favors or to provide the help we've requested, and we also have the right to refuse such requests and say "No" to others.

Most people are able to ask others for help without feeling too uncomfortable. On the other hand, saying "No" positively and directly is very difficult for many people. Think about these situations:

- **Your friend's car is in the shop for a week, and she needs a ride to her 8:00 a.m. class. Your first class is at 11:00, and you hate getting up any earlier than absolutely necessary.**
- **A friend who has previously borrowed money and not returned it wants to borrow $20 until next week when she gets paid.**

How would you handle the above situations? Would you be able to say "No" if you were really uncomfortable in granting the request? Would you feel guilty if you did refuse the request? If you granted the request when you really didn't want to, would you be resentful?

Our right to say "No" to requests from others is a very important right. By denying requests with which we are uncomfortable, we are taking responsibility for our own feelings and actions. Thus, we can avoid being manipulated into situations in which we might be taken advantage of or in which we might feel uncomfortable.

Once you have decided to refuse a request, you need to refuse in a firm voice without making excuses. Don't get involved in allowing the other party to try to persuade you into changing your mind. Accept the fact that you have the right to refuse any request that makes you feel uncomfortable or which you just don't feel like granting, and make your intentions clear to the other party.

Communicating Across Cultures

Human beings communicate through the use of symbols. A symbol is a word that stands for something else. Problems in communication arise when we assume that a symbol has only one meaning and that everyone understands the symbol in the same way. For example, we use the word "dog" to stand for a four-legged animal that barks. However, if I say the word "dog," the picture in my mind probably doesn't match the picture in your mind because there are many varieties of dogs. I might be picturing a Chihuahua while you are picturing a German Shepherd. Language becomes even more complex when we have multiple meanings for one symbol. Consider the ways we use the word "dog":

- **She is a dog**. (She is unattractive.)
- **He is a dog**. (He is promiscuous.)
- **He is a lucky dog**. (He is fortunate.)
- **It's a dog**. (It is worthless.)
- **Just dog it**. (Just do enough to get by.)
- **He went to the dogs**. (He was not doing well.)

- **He was in the doghouse**. (He was in trouble.)
- **Let sleeping dogs lie**. (Leave the situation alone.)
- **My dogs hurt**. (My feet hurt.)
- **He put on the dog**. (He assumed an attitude of wealth or importance.)
- **These are the dog days of summer**. (These are hot days when people feel lazy.)
- **The book is dog-eared**. (The corners of the pages are bent.)
- **He led a dog's life**. (He was not happy.)
- **May I have a doggy bag?** (May I have a bag for my leftovers?)
- **Doggone it!** (I am frustrated!)
- **I am dog-tired**. (I am very tired.)

The problem of communication becomes even more difficult for those who are learning English. People who speak a different language might not understand the word "dog" at all because they use a different symbol for the object. Even after studying the language, it is easy to misinterpret the meaning of the word "dog." A recent immigrant was horrified when he was offered a hot dog at a ball game. He thought that this was a civilized country and was surprised that we ate dogs!

Here are some ideas to help improve your communications with people who are culturally different from you or speak a different language:

- **Be sensitive to the fact that communication is difficult and that errors in understanding are likely.**
- **Remember that the message sent is not necessarily the message received.**
- **Give people time to think and respond**. You do not have to fill in the silence right away.
- **Check your understanding of the message**. Rephrase or repeat the information to make sure it is correct. Ask questions.
- **If you feel insulted by the message, remember that it is quite possible that you could be misinterpreting it**. (Remember all the meanings for "dog" listed above.)
- **If you are having problems communicating with someone who speaks a different language, speak slowly and clearly or use different words**. Talking louder will not help.
- **Remain calm and treat others with respect**. Be patient.
- **Find a translator if possible.**
- **Study a different language**. This will help in understanding other cultures and the different ways that other cultures use symbols.
- **Before traveling to a different country, read about the culture and learn some basic phrases in the language used**. This will help you to enjoy your travel and learn about other cultures. Attempting to speak the language will show others that you care about and respect the culture.
- **Sometimes nonverbal communication can help**. If you are adventurous or desperate, smile and act out the message. Be aware that nonverbal communication can be misunderstood also.
- **Don't forget your sense of humor.**

DIVERSITY

If you live and attended high school in a small, suburban or rural community, you may be encountering more diversity at your college university than you've ever seen in your life. If you are from an urban environment, you may find your campus has more, less, or about the same amount of diversity, that you are used to. Whichever the case may be, your future will include living, working, and doing business with people from all walks of life. They may be from different racial/ethnic/cultural groups, practice different religions, have different social or economic status, speak different languages, be different ages, have physical/mental disabilities, have different sexual orientations, or work/be training for jobs that are not traditionally held by people of that gender. The ability to cooperate and work effectively with all types of people is an important skill that you need to develop in order to be successful in today's world.

TERMS DEALING WITH DIVERSITY

American Values

Just as individual behavior is guided by one's value system, so is American society guided by a "Value system." It is based on the European, white Anglo Judeo-Christian ethic. Basically what this says is that we speak English and live in a society predicated on "freedom, democracy and fairness." Within freedom, democracy, and fairness, individuals are to value responsibility, productivity, community, family, and work.

Diversity

Diversity refers to differences in society. Differences include male and female; black and white; Hispanic, African, Asian, Native American; young and old; able and disabled; socioeconomic status; sexual and religious preferences.

Ethnicity

An ethnic group is a group whose members **identify** with one another because they share a common culture. Race, religion, and ethnicity are often confused with each other with unfortunate results.

In South Florida, for example, blacks are often thought of as an ethnic group, but American-born blacks are different ethnically from Bahamian-born, Jamaican-born, or Haitian-born blacks who all have distinct identities.

Likewise, people often speak of Hispanics without realizing that many Cubans, Puerto Ricans, Nicaraguans, and Argentineans would resent being lumped together in one eth-nic group just because they all happen to speak Spanish.

Jews are regarded as an ethnic group in the United States because of their common religious heritage, but in Israel, there are very distinct lines drawn among ethnic Jews from Russia, Germany, Yemen, Morocco, etc. In the United States, religion provides Jews with a source of ethnic cohesion, but the same is not true of most other religions in America. Both the Catholic and Protestant branches of Christianity contain dozens of ethnic -nationalities.

American Indians are racially distinct from white Anglos, but each major tribal group, i.e., Navaho, Hopi, Sioux, etc., is composed of different cultural traditions.

In summary, there are numerous ethnic identities in America. Only in isolated cases is an ethnic group represented exclusively by an entire race or religion.

Race

Race has traditionally referred to a group of people who share inherited characteristics of outward appearance such as skin color, hair texture, stature, and facial features. Race should not be confused with culture or ethnicity, or religion, or kinship groups.

Racism

Racism couples the false assumption that race determines psychological and cultural traits with the belief that one race is superior to another. Based on their belief in the inferiority of certain groups, racists justify

(continued)

discriminating against, segregating, and/or scapegoating these groups. Racists, in the name of protecting their race from contamination, justify the domination and sometimes even the destruction of those races they consider inferior.

Prejudice

Prejudice is a set of rigid and unfavorable attitudes which are formed in disregard of facts toward a particular group or groups. It is an unsupported judgment usually accompanied by disapproval.

Discrimination

Discrimination is differential treatment based on unfair categorization. It is denial of justice prompted by prejudice. When people act on their prejudices, they engage in discrimination. Discrimination often involves keeping people out of activities or places because of the group to which they belong.

Scapegoating

Scapegoating refers to the deliberate policy of blaming an individual or group when the fault actually lies elsewhere. It means blaming a group or individual for things they really did not do. Those who are scapegoats become objects of aggression in work and in deed. Prejudicial attitudes and discriminatory acts lead to scapegoating. Members of the disliked groups are denied employment, housing, political rights, and social privileges. Scapegoating can lead to verbal and physical violence as well as death.

Anti-semitism

Anti-semitism is prejudice or discrimination against Jews based on negative perceptions of their religious beliefs and/or on negative group stereotypes. Anti-semitism can also be a form of racism as when Nazis and others consider Jews an inferior "race."

Stereotyping

Stereotyping is the process of lumping perceptions into broad categories and processing these perceptions on the basis of what the categories are like rather than on the unique characteristics of each individual or object. This process extends into all aspects of life. Because your brain is constantly inundated with what is going on around you, you have to find a way to process this mass of information. You "tune out" or ignore perhaps 99 percent of all incoming stimuli and attempt to organize the remaining 1 percent in a manner that is meaningful to you. For example, if you see a field covered with a dense, low-growing plant with thin leaves, you probably think of grass and are prepared to act toward the grass in a customary way. You haven't the time or the inclination to analyze the individual blades of grass to determine what kind of grass it is or even if it is grass at all. If it looks like grass from a distance, that is sufficient cause for you to stereotype it by thinking that it is a suitable surface for a picnic or a game of touch football, or a place to walk the dog.

Ethnocentrism

Ethnocentrism is the belief that one's own ethnic, religious, or political group is superior to all others.

Culture

Culture is the behavior, beliefs, and values shared by a group of people. It includes language, morals, and even food preferences. Culture includes everything that we learn from the people around us in our community.

Gender, Sex

Gender refers to cultural differences that distinguish males from females. Different cultures raise men and women to act in specified ways. Sex refers to anatomical differences.

Sexism

Sexism is a negative attitude or perception based on sex.

Cultural pluralism

Each group celebrates the customs and traditions of their culture while participating in mainstream society.

Genocide

Genocide is the deliberate and systematic destruction of a racial, political, or cultural group. It can include the destruction of the language, religion, or cultural practices of a group of people.

Ableism

Prejudice or discrimination against people with mental, emotional, and physical disabilities.

Ageism

Prejudice or discrimination based on age.

Classism

Prejudice or discrimination based on economic background.

Homophobia

An irrational fear of gays, lesbians, or bisexuals.

Privilege

Unearned access to resources due to membership in a particular social group.

Attitudes can create barriers to interacting with people from diverse backgrounds. When you see someone walking toward you, what do you tend to notice? Gender? Weight? Skin color? Clothing? Hair? What kinds of assumptions do you make based on your observations? Student? Sorority girl? Nontraditional student? Professor? Athlete? Foreigner? Finally, what assumptions do you make about each kind of person? We all assume things about people. Just remember that your assumptions are often incorrect. Prejudice is a learned habit, and it takes a conscious effort to break it.

Major Forms or Type of Diversity in Today's World: Ethnic and Racial Diversity*

America is rapidly becoming a more racially and ethnically diverse nation. In 2008, the minority population in the United States reached an all-time high of 34 percent of the total population. The population of ethnic minorities is now growing at a much faster rate that the While majority. This trend is expected to continue, and by the middle of the 21st century, the minority population will have grown from one-third of the U.S. population to more than one-half (54 percent), with more than 60 percent of the nation's children expected to be members of what we now call minority groups (U.S. Census Bureau, 2008).

By 2050, the U.S. population is projected to be more than 30 percent Hispanic (up from 15 percent in 2008), 15 percent Black (up from 13 percent), 9.6 percent Asian (up from 5.3 percent), and 2 percent Native American (up from 1.6 percent). The Native Hawaiian and Pacific Islander population is expected to more than double between 2008 and 2050. During this same time period, the percentage of White Americans will drop from 66 percent (2008) to 46 percent (2050). As a result of these population trends, ethnic and racial minorities will become the new majority because they will constitute the majority of Americans by the middle of the 21st century. (See Figure 12.2)

Socioeconomic Diversity

Diversity also appears in the form of socioeconomic status or social class, which is typically stratified (divided) into lower, middle, and upper classes, based on level of education and income. Groups occupying lower social strata have significantly fewer social and economic opportunities or privileges (Feagin & Feagin, 2007).

According to U.S. Census figures, the wealthiest 20 percent of the American population controls approximately 50 percent of the country's total income, and the 20 percent of Americans with the lowest income controls only 4 percent of the nation's income. Sharp discrepancies also exist in income level among different racial, ethnic, and gender groups. In 2007, Black households had the lowest median income ($33,916), compared to a median income of $54,920 for non-Hispanic White households (Annual Social and Economic Supplement, 2008).

Poverty continues to be a problem in America. In 2007, 12.5 percent of Americans (37.3 million people) lived below the poverty line making the United States on of the most impoverished of all developed countries in the World (Shah, 2008). Although all ethnic and racial groups experience poverty, minority groups experience poverty at significantly higher rate than the White majority. In 2007, poverty rates for different ethnic and racial groups were as follows:

- Whites: 8.2 percent
- Asians: 10.2 percent
- Hispanics: 21.5 percent
- Blacks: 24.5 percent
  Source: U.S. Census Bureau, 2008.

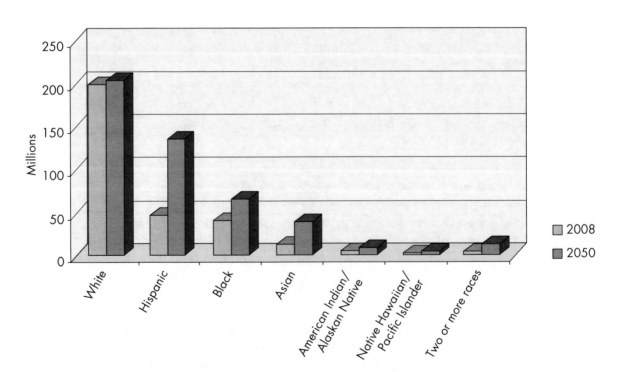

Figure 12.2 The "New Majority"

It's estimated that 600,000 families and 1.25 million children are now homeless, accounting for roughly 50 percent of the homeless population. Typically, these families are comprised of a mother and two children under the age of five (National Alliance to End Homelessness, 2007).

International Diversity

Beyond our particular countries of citizenship, humans are members of a common, international world that includes multiple nations. Communication and interaction across nations are now greater than at any other time in world history, largely because of rapid advances in electronic technology (Dryden & Vos, 1999; Friedman, 2005). Economic boundaries between nations are also breaking down due to increasing international travel, international trading, and development of multinational corporations. Todays world really is a small world after all, and success in it requires an international perspective—a 21st-century perspective. By learning from and about different nations, you become more than a citizen of your own country: you become cosmopolitan—a citizen of the world.

Taking an international perspective allows you to appreciate the diversity of humankind. If it were possible to reduce the world's population to a village of precisely 100 people, with all existing human ratios remaining the same, the demographics of this world village would look something like this:

- 61 would be Asians, 13 Africans, 12 Europeans, 9 Latin Americans, and 5 from the USA and Canada
- 50 would be male, 50 would be female
- 75 would be non-White; 25 White
- 67 would be non-Christian; 33 would be Christian
- 80 would live in substandard housings
- 16 would be unable Jo read or write
- 50 would be malnourished and *1* dying of starvation
- 33 would be without access to a safe water supply
- 39 would lack access to improved sanitation
- 24 would not have any electricity (and to the 76 that do have electricity most would only use it for light at night)
- 8 people yould have access-to the Internet
- 1 would have a college education
- 1 would have HIV
- 2 would be near birth; 1 near death
- 5 would control 32 percent of the entire world's wealth; all 5 would be US citizens
- 48 would live on less than USS2 day
- 20 would live on less than USS1 a day
  Source: Family Care Foundation (1997–2012).

GENERATIONAL DIVERSITY

Humans are also diverse with respect to the generation in which they grew up. "Generation" refers to a group of individuals born during the same historical period whose attitudes, values, and habits have been shaped by events that took place in the world during their formative years of development. Each generation experiences different historical events, so it's likely that generations will develop different attitudes and behaviors as a result.

GENERATIONAL DIVERSITY

- **The Traditional Generation, a.k.a the Silent Generation (born 1922–1945)**. This generation was influenced by events such as the Great Depression and World Wars I and II. Characteristics associated with: this generation include loyalty, partriotism, respect for authority and conservatism.
- **The Baby Boomer Generation (born 1946–1964)**. This generation was influenced by events such as the Vietnam War, Watergate, and the human rights movement. Characteristics associated with this generation include Idealism, Importance of self-fulfillment and concern for equal rights.
- **Generation X (born 1965–1980)**. This generation was influenced by Sesame Street, the creation of MTV, AIDS, and soaring divorce rates that produced the first "latchkey children"—youngsters who let themselves into their homes after school with their own keys

because their mother (or single mother) was working outside the home. Characteristics associated with this generation include self-reliance, resourcefulness, and being: comfortable with change.
- **Generation Y, a.k.a Millennials (born 1981–2002)**. This generation was influenced by the September 11, 2001, terrorist attack on the United States, the shooting of students at Columbine High.School, and the collapse of the Enron Corporation, Characteristics associated with this generation include a preference for working: and. playing in groups, being technologically savvy, and a willingness to provide volunteer service in their community (the civic generation). They are also the most ethnically divere generation, which may explain why they are more open to diversity and see it as a positive experience.

Figure 12.3 Generational Diverstiy

Figure 12.3 provides a brief summary of the major generations, the key historical events that occurred during the formative periods of the people in each generation, and the personal characteristics that have been associated with particular generations (Lancaster & Stillman, 2002).

Gender Diversity

Recent research has shown that the concept of gender is quite complex and cannot be limited to the categories of "men" and "women" Other groups, such as transgender and gender queer, have emerged as gender diversity has become more recognized and accepted. The term "gender" has been used interchangeably with the word "sex;" however, "sex" is associated with categories that are biologically determined by external genitalia, such as male, female, intersex, etc. Gender, on the other hand, refers to one's identification along a continuum of masculine and feminine traits and roles, regardless of external genitalia (Muehlenhard & Peterson, 2011). These traits and roles are reflective of social and cultural conventions, interests, and customs. Certainly, there is interplay between sex and gender as they both contribute to our individual identity. Therefore, while the characteristics associated with masculinity and femininity are socially ascribed, how rigidly we adhere to these definitions depends on the level at which we see these qualities in ourselves (Priest et al., 2012).

Gender characteristics are not exclusive to a single gender or set in stone. For example, would you consider a woman not feminine if she were a semi-professional football player? Would you consider a man not to be masculine if he were a nanny? These questions give us pause because there are certain behaviors and qualities that socially define what is masculine and feminine, but these definitions are also open to our individual interpretation. A woman can be very feminine and also enjoy playing a sport that is typically played by men, and a man can be very masculine and also enjoy fulfilling duties that are typically thought to be maternal. The characteristics we associate with gender also change over time and vary between cultures. Consider how these same two questions might have been answered 50 years ago and how the responses of different cultural groups might vary even today. In sum, our interpretation of femininity and masculinity depends on how strictly we personally adhere to the social definitions of gender (Parker, 2009).

Sexual Diversity

Sexuality is another aspect of our human identity that contributes to diversity. We all express our sexuality in our own ways and come into various aspects of our sexuality throughout our lives. "Sexual diversity" refers to the full continuum of the human sexual experience and identity, Represented in this range include lesbians, gay men, bisexuals, transgendered people, and heterosexuals. When we accept individuals who self-identify within this range of sexual diversity, we look beyond heterosexuality as the norm and recognize the variation that contributes to the human experience (Dessel, Wooford, & Warren, 2012)

Campuses are increasing their support for LGBTQIA (lesbian, gay, bisexual, transgendered, questioning, intersexed, and asexual) students and creating centers and support services to assist them with their adjustment to campus life. These offices also play an important role in helping to reduce homophobia in the campus community and promote mutual respect for all types of sexual diversity.

Diversity an the College Experience

There are more than 3,000 public and private colleges in the United States. They vary in size (small to large) and location (urban, suburban and rural), as well as in their purpose or mission (research universities, comprehensive state universities, liberal arts colleges, and community colleges). This variety makes America's higher education system the most-diverse and accessible in the world. The diversity of educational opportunities in American colleges and universities reflects the freedom of opportunity in the United States as a democratic nation (American Council on Education, 2008).

America's system of higher education is also becoming more diverse with respect to the variety of people enrolled in it. College students in the United States are growing more diverse with respect to age; almost 40 percent of all undergraduate students in America are 25 years of age or older, compared to 28 percent in 1970 (U.S. Department of Education, 2002). The ethnic and racial diversity of students in American colleges and universities is also rapidly rising. In I960, Whites made up almost 95 percent of the total college population; in 2005, that percentage had decreased to 69 percent. At the same time, the percentage of Asian, Hispanic, Black, and Native American students attending college increased *(Chronicle of Higher Education*, 2003). First-year college students are more likely than sophomores, juniors, and seniors to have contact with students from different racial and ethnic backgrounds, probably because first-year students are more likely to live on campus and in close proximity to other students (Kuh, 2005),

The Benefits of Experiencing Diversity

Diversity Promotes Self-Awareness

Learning from people with diverse backgrounds and experiences sharpens our self-knowledge and self-insight by allowing us to compare and contrast our life experiences with others whose experiences differ sharply from our own. This comparative perspective gives us a reference point for viewing our own lives, placing us in a better position to see how our unique cultural background has influenced the development of our personal beliefs, values, and lifestyle. By viewing our lives in relation to the lives of others, we see more clearly what is distinctive about ourselves and how we may be uniquely advantage or disadvantaged.

When students around the country were interviewed about their diversity experiences in college, they reported that these experience often helped them learn more about themselves and that their interactions with students from different races and ethnic groups produced unexpected or jarring self- insights (Light, 2001).

Diversity Enriches a College Education

Diversity magnifies the power of a college education by liberating students from the tunnel vision of ethnocentricity (culture-centeredness) and egocentricity (self-centeredness), enabling them to get beyond themselves and view the world from a multicultural perspective. Just as the various subjects you take in the college curriculum open your mind to multiple perspectives, so does your experience with people from varied backgrounds. A multicultural perspective helps us become aware of our "cultural blind spots" and avoid the dangers of *groupthink*—the tendency for tight-knit groups of people to think so much alike that they overlook flaws in their thinking (Baron, 2005; Janis, 1982).

Diversity Strengthens Learning and Critical Thinking

Research consistently shows that we learn more from people who are different than ourselves than we do from people similar to ourselves (Pascarella, 2001; Pascarella & Terenzini, 2005). When our brain encounters something that is unfamiliar or different from what we're accustomed to, we must stretch beyond our mental comfort zone and work harder to understand it, because doing so forces us to compare and contrast it to what we are already familiar with (Acredolo & O'Connor, 1991; Nagda, Gurin, & Johnson, 2005). Stretching our minds to understand something that's unfamiliar to us requires extra psychological effort and energy, which produces a deeper, more powerful learning experience.

Diversity Promotes Creative Thinking

Experiences with diversity supply you with a broader base of knowledge and wider range of thinking styles that better enable you to think outside your own cultural box or boundaries. In contrast, limiting your number of cultural vantage points is akin to limiting the variety of mental tools you can use to solve new problems, thereby limiting your creativity. When like-minded people only associate with other like-minded people, they're unlikely to think outside the box.

Drawing on different ideas from people with diverse backgrounds and bouncing your ideas off them is a great way to generate energy, synergy, and serendipity—unanticipated discoveries and creative solutions. People who approach problems from diverse perspectives are more likely to look for and discover multiple partial solutions" (Kelly, 1994). Diversity expands students' capacity for viewing issues or problems from multiple vantage points, equipping them with a wider variety of approaches to solving unfamilair problems they may encounter in different contexts and situations.

Furthermore, ideas acquired from diverse people and diverse cultures may combine or "cross tertilize," giving birth to new approaches for solving old problems. When ideas, are generated openly and freely in groups comprised of people from diverse back-grounds, powerful "cross-stimulation" effects can occur, whereby one group members idea can trigger different ideas from other group members (Brown, Dane, & Durham, 1998). Drawing on different ideas from people of diverse back-grounds and bouncing ideas of them serves to stimulate divergent (expansive) thinking which can lead to synergy (Idea multiplication) and serendipity (unexpected discoveries of innovative solutions).

In contrast, when different cultural perspectives are not sought out or tolerated, the variety of lenses available to students for viewing new problems is reduced, which, in turn, limits or shrinks one's capacity for creative thinking. Creativity tends to be replaced by conformity or rigidity because ideas do not flow freely and divergently (in different directions): Instead, ideas tend to converge and merge into the same cultural channel—the one shared by the homogeneous group of people doing the thinking.

Diversity Education Promotes Career Preparation for the 21st Century

Learning about and from diversity has a very practical benefit: it better prepares students for their future work roles. Whatever line of employment students may eventually pursue, the, re likely to find themselves working with employers, co-workers, customers, and clients from diverse cultural backgrounds. America's workforce is now more diverse than at any other time in the nation's history and it will grow ever more diverse throughout the 21st century. The proportion of America's working-age population comprised of workers from minority ethnic and racial groups will jump from 34 percent in 2008 to 55 percent in 2050 (U.S. Census Bureau, 2008).

A national survey revealed that policymakers, business leaders, and employers were seeking college graduates who were more than just "aware" or "tolerant" of diversity; they wanted graduates who had actual *experience* with diversity (Education Commission of the States, 1995). These findings are reinforced by a national survey of American voters, the overwhelming majority of who agreed that diversity education helps students learn practical skills that are essential for success in today's world, such as communication skills, teamwork, and problem-solving skills. Almost one-half of the surveyed voters also thought that the American school system should "put more emphasis on teaching students about others' cultures, backgrounds and life-styles" (National Survey of Voters, 1998). Thus, both employers and the American public agree that diversity education is *career preparation*. Intercultural competence is now a highly valued skill and one that is essential for success in today's work world.

The current "global economy" also requires intercultural skills relating to international diversity. Work in today's global economy is characterized by economic interdependence among nations, international trading (imports/exports), multinational corporations, international travel, and almost instantaneous worldwide communication—due to advances m the World Wide Web (Dryden & Vos, 1999; Friedman, 2005). As a result, employers now seek job candidates with the following skills and attributes; sensitivity to human difference ability to understand and relate to people from different cultural backgrounds, international knowledge, and ability to communicate in a second language (Fixman, 1990; National association of Colleges & Employers, 2007; office of Research, 1994). Thus learning about and from diversity is not only good education: It's also good career preparation.

Remember

The wealth of diversity on college campuses today represents an unprecedented educational opportunity. You may never again be a member of a community that Includes so many people from such a rich variety of background. Seize this opportunity! You're in the right place at the right time to experience the variety of people and program that will enrich breadth and depth of your learning.

Stumbling Blocks and Barriers to Experiencing Diversity

Stereotypes

The word *stereotype* derives from a combination of two roots: *stereo* (to look at in a fixed way) and *type* (to categorize or group together, as in the word *typical*). Thus, stereotyping is viewing individuals of the same type (group) in the same (fixed) way.

In effect, stereotyping ignores or disregards individuality; instead, all people sharing the same group characteristic (e.g., race or gender) are viewed as having the same personal characteristics—as in the expression, "You know what they're like: they're all the same," Stereotypes involve bias, which literally means "slant." A bias can be slanted either positively or negatively. Positive bias results in a favorable stereotype (e.g., "Italians are great lovers"); negative bias produces an unfavorable stereotype (e.g., "Italians are in the Mafia'). Snapshot Summary 10.2 lists some common stereotypes.

EXAMPLES OF COMMON STEREOTYPES

Muslims are terrorists

Whites can't jump (or dance).

Blacks are lazy.

Asians are .brilliant in math.

Irish are alcoholics.

Gay men are feminine; lesbian women are masculine

Jews are cheap.

Hispanic men are abusive to women.

Men are strong.

Women are weak.

Have you ever unintentionally perceived or treated someone in terms of a group stereotype rather than as an individual? What assumptions did you make about that person? Was that person aware of, or affected by, your stereotyping?

Prejudice

If virtually all members of a stereotyped group are judged or evaluated in a negative way, the result is prejudice. (The *word prejudice* literally means to "pre-judge.") Technically, prejudice may be either positive or negative; however, the term is most often associated with a negative prejudgment that involves *stigmatizing*—associating inferior or unfavorable traits with people who belong to the same group. Thus, prejudice may be defined as a negative judgment, attitude, or belief about another person **or** group of people that's formed before the facts are known. Stereotyping and prejudice often go hand in hand because individuals who are placed in a negatively stereotyped group are commonly prejudged in a negative way.

Someone with a prejudice toward a group typically avoids contact with individuals from that group. This enables the prejudice to continue unchallenged because there's little chance for the prejudiced person to have positive experiences with any member of the stigmatized group that could contradict or disprove the prejudice. Thus, a vicious cycle is established in which the prejudiced person continues to avoid contact with individuals from the stigmatized groups which, in turn, continues to maintain and reinforce the prejudice.

Sources of Prejudice

Where do these prejudices come from? They come from a variety of sources.

Economic Competitiveness and Scapegoating

Scapegoating is the process of displacing aggression or projecting guilt onto a group of people. When the economy is bad, accusations like "Those immigrants are taking away all our jobs" increase in frequency. Political candidates sometimes appeal to prejudices among voters. They may scapegoat immigrants, for example, in an effort to win votes from those who feel disempowered or frustrated with the economy.

Parents and Relatives

What messages did your parents send about other people? When you were young and found yourself near a person in a wheelchair, what messages did you receive about how to behave? Did you observe the adult look away or maybe address the person accompanying the person with the disability rather than communicating directly with the person who was disabled? What about when you asked a parent if a friend who was from another socioeconomic or cultural group could come home with you or if you could go to his or her house? Messages can be overt or covert. The effect is the same. When negative messages are attached to differences between people, prejudice takes root.

Institutions

Prejudice is learned through living in a society where prejudices are sustained. Who received the most privileges in your school? Did the gifted students get to engage in more creative learning situations than the other students? What about overweight children in your school? How were they treated? Who participated in sports and organizations with you? Were accommodations made for someone who was mentally or physically disabled? As a child, were you ever conscious of the fact that all U.S. presidents have been white males?

Media

What kinds of messages do you receive from magazines, movies, and television? What prejudices are perpetuated in the media? What groups of people are stereotyped? What types of misinformation about certain groups of people are broadcast? When you watch television or go to a movie, how are women depicted? How often are they depicted as sex symbols? Stereotyping is based on ignorance. Have you heard any disparaging remarks about others lately through the media? What about jokes about religion, sexual orientation, skin color, or weight?

Social Fragmentation

Levine and Cureton (1998) found that undergraduate students across the country described themselves more in terms of differences than similarities. Their study also revealed that students today are more socially isolated than previous generations; increasingly, they voluntarily segregate themselves to form small self-interest groups. Look around you. Gaps between socioeconomic groups in this country seem to be widening.

The sources that fuel prejudice come together to create a powerful, destructive force that can lead to discrimination and even violence. The number of reported incidents of prejudice and discrimination are reported to be on the rise throughout the country. The Anti-Defamation League and the National Institute Against Prejudice and Violence

(NIAPV) record and report incidents of prejudice, discrimination, and hate crimes. The brutal murders of Matthew Shepard, a gay, white man who was a student at the University of Wyoming, and James Byrd, Jr., a black man who was chained to the back of a pickup truck and dragged to his death, outraged the country. Yet *Life* magazine reported that at Matthew Shepard's funeral, a protestor appeared with a sign that read "God hates fags."

*Discrimination**

Literally translated, the term *discrimination* means "division" or "separation"; Whereas prejudice involves a belief or opinion, discrimination involves an action taken toward others. Technically, discrimination can be either negative or positive—for example, a discriminating eater may be careful about eating only healthy foods. However, the term is most often associated with a negative action that results in a prejudiced person treating another person, or group of people, in an unfair way. Thus, it could be said that discrimination is prejudice put into action. Hate crimes are examples of extreme discrimination because they are acts motivated; solely by prejudice against members of a stigmatized group.

Other forms of discrimination are more subtle and may be practiced by society's institutional systems rather than particular individuals. These forms of *institutional racism* are less flagrant or visible, and they are rooted in societal policies and practices that discriminate against members of certain ethnic groups. For instance, *redlining*, a term coined in the late 1960s, refers to the practice of banks marking a red line on a map to indicate an area where they will not invest or lend money; many of those areas are neighborhoods in which African Americans live (Shapiro, 1993). Studies also show that compared to White patients, Black patients of the same socioeconomic status are less likely to receive breast cancer screenings, eye exams if they have diabetes, and follow-up visits after hospitalization for mental illness (Schneider, Zaslavsky, & Epstein, 2002).

Thus, trying to be "race blind" and getting along with people of all colors with whom we interact on an *individual* basis is not all there is to eliminating discrimination. Racial discrimination is an issue that goes beyond individual interactions to larger institutional policies and societal systems. One goal of multicultural education is to empower students to eventually change these societal systems by 'laying a foundation for the transformation of society and the elimination of oppression and injustice" (Gorski, 2010, p. 1).

What Is Cultural Competence?

Research suggests (Thompson & Cuseo, 2012) that when we focus on differences alone, we create cultural environments in which some groups will feel excluded. Authentic appreciation of diversity takes place when remembers from different groups interact, work together, and learn from one another (Smith, 1997). Someone who merely tolerates diversity, or simply coexists with diverse groups, might say things like "Let's just get along," "Live and let live," or "To each his own" Cultural competence moves us beyond diversity tolerance to a higher level of diversity *appreciation*, which involves learning about, with, and from diverse people. It empowers us to be culturally sensitive and responsive individuals who recognize, appreciate, and capitalize on human differences (Etsy, Griffin, & Hirsch, 1995). Therefore, when we attain cultural competence, we move beyond mere acceptance or tolerance of diversity to a deeper, more authentic appreciation of diversity.

Achieving this level of diversity appreciation requires us to not only be introspective and reflective, but to regularly step out of our usual comfort zones. This is because we develop insights about ourselves and others in relation to diversity through interaction and experience. By acknowledging and accepting your own cultural identity as well as the cultural identities of others, you open yourself up to the human experience. Maintaining this level of diversity appreciation requires that you engage in *action* (Thompson & Cuseo, 2012). Examples of such action include, but are not limited to:

- Attending meetings and activities on campus or in your community to gain a deeper understanding of your peer's cultural backgrounds
- Enrolling in courses that expand your knowledge of the culture, history, and language of various ethnic and cultural groups, including your own
- Participating in a service-learning or community activity
- Meeting and interacting with students in your residence hall or in the Student Center who are from various cultural backgrounds
- Forming study groups in your classes comprised of diverse members
- Participating in a study abroad experience
- Becoming an advocate for diversity on your campus and in your community.

Strategies for Diversity Appreciation

The following practices and strategies may be used to help us open up to and appreciate individuals from other groups toward whom we may hold prejudices, stereotypes, or subtle biases that bubble beneath the surface of our conscious awareness.

1. **Consciously avoid preoccupation with physical appearance.** Go deeper and get beneath the surface of appearance to judge people not in terms of how they look, but in terms of who they are and how they act. Remember the old proverb: "It's what inside that counts." Judge others by their inner qualities, not by the familiarity of their outer features.

2. **Perceive each person with whom you interact as a unique human being.** Make a conscious effort to interact with people as individuals not group members, and form your impressions of others on a case-by-case basis, not according to some general rule of thumb. This may seem like an obvious and easy thing to do, but research shows that humans have a natural tendency to perceive individuals from unfamiliar group as being more alike (or all alike) than members of their own group (Taylor, Peplau, & Sears, 2006). Thus, we need to make a conscious effort to counteract this tendency.

3. **Make an intentional attempt to interact and collaborate with members of diverse groups.** Once we've overcome our biases and begin to perceive members of diverse groups as unique individuals, we move into a position to take the next step of interacting, collaborating, and forming friendships with members of diverse groups. Interpersonal contact between diverse people takes us beyond simple awareness and acceptance, and moves us up to a higher level of diversity appreciation that involves intercultural interaction. When we take this step to cross cultural boundaries, we transform diversity appreciation from an internal attitude or personal conviction into an observable action or interpersonal commitment.

Remember

While it's valuable to learn about different cultures and the common characteristics shared by members of the same culture, it shouldn't be done at the expense of ignoring individual differences among members of the same culture. Don't assume that all individuals who share the same cultural background share the same personal characteristics.

Your initial comfort level with interacting with people from diverse groups is likely to depend on how much experience you have had with diversity before college. If you've had little or no prior experience interacting with members of diverse groups, it may be more challenging for you to initiate interactions with diverse students on campus. However, the good news is that you have the most to gain from interacting and collaborating with those of other ethnic or racial groups. Research consistently shows that when we have social experiences that differ radically from our prior experiences, we gain the most in terms of learning and cognitive development (Acredolo & O'Connor, 1991; Piaget, 1985).

Following are specific strategies for interacting with, and learning from people of diverse backgrounds.

1. **Intentionally create opportunities for interaction and conservation with individuals from diverse groups.** Studies show tat stereotyping and prejudice can be sharply reduced if contact between members of different racial or ethnic groups is frequent enough to allow time for the development of friendships (Pettigrew, 1998). Make an intentional attempt to fight off the tendency to associate only with people who are similar to you. One way to do this is by intentionally placing yourself in situations where individuals from diverse groups are nearby so that interaction can potentially take place. Research indicates that meaningful interactions and friendships are more likely to form among people who are in physical proximity with one another (Back, Schmukle & Egloff, 2008; Latané et al., 1995). You can create this condition in the college classroom by sitting near students from different ethnic or racial groups or by joining them if you are given the choice to select whom you will work with in class discussion groups and group projects.

2. **Take advantage of the Internet to chat with students from diverse groups.** Electronic communication can be a more convenient and more comfortable way to initially interact with members of diverse groups with whom you have had little prior experience. After you've communicated successfully *online*, you may then feel more comfortable about interacting with them *in person*. Online and in-person interaction with students from other cultures deepens your understanding of your own culture and elevates your awareness of cultural customs and values that you may have overlooked or taken for granted (Bok, 2006).

3. **Seek out the views and opinions of classmates from diverse backgrounds.** During or after class discussions, ask students from different backgrounds if there was any point made or position taken in class that they would strongly question or challenge. Seeking out divergent (diverse) viewpoints has been found to be one of the best ways to develop critical thinking skills (Inoue, 2005; Kurfiss, 1988).

4. **Join or form discussion groups with students from diverse backgrounds.** You can gain exposure to diverse perspectives by joining or forming discussion groups with students who differ from you in terms of such characteristics as gender, age, race, or ethnicity. You might begin by forming study groups with students who are different than you in one way but similar to you in other ways, For instance, you can form learning teams with students who have the same major as you, but who differ from you in terms of race, ethnicity, or age. This strategy gives the diverse members of your team some common ground for discussion (your major) and can raise your team's awareness that although you may be members of different groups, you can share similar educational goals and life plans.

5. **Form collaborative learning teams.** A learning team is more than a discussion group or a study group. It moves beyond discussion to collaborate learning—its members become teammates who "co-labor" (work together) as part of a joint and mutually supportive effort to reach the same goal. Studies show that when individuals from different ethnic and racial groups work collaboratively toward the attainment of a common goal, racial prejudice is reduced and interracial friendships are promoted (Allport, 1954; Amir, 1976; Dovidio, Eller, & Flewstone, 2011). These positive developments probably take place because individuals

Remember

Including diversity in your learning groups not only provides social variety it also promotes the quality at the group's work by giving its members access to diverse perspectives and life experiences of people from different backgrounds.

from diverse groups working on the same team creates a social environment in which no one is a member of an "out" group ("them"): they're all members of the same "in" group ("us") (Pratto et al., 2000; Sidanius, Levin, Liu, & Pratto, 2000). For specific strategies on how to form diverse and effective learning teams.

*From *Thriving in College and Beyond: Research-Based Strategies for Academic Success and Personal Development* by Jospeh B. Cuseo, Aaron Thompson, Michele Campagna, and Viki S. Fecas. Copyright © 2013 by Kendall Hunt Publishing Company. Reprinted by permission.

> *It is time for us to teach young people early on that in diversity there is beauty and strength. We all should know that diversity makes for a rich tapestry, and we must understand that the threads of the tapestry are equal in value, no matter their color; equal in importance, no matter their texture.*
>
> —Maya Angelou

LEADERSHIP

In order to make a better world, we need better leaders. Citizenship requires leadership. So does professional success. If you can lead no one, your education is incomplete. True, you probably won't be President of the United States, a Four Star General, or the CEO of a major corporation. (But then, why not?) More likely, you will be a director, a teacher, or an entrepreneur. And you will almost certainly at some point chair a committee, head a project, propose an idea to neighbors or colleagues, or parent a child. Each and every one of these roles/activities requires you to lead. How do you do it, and can you learn the skills it takes?

The Components of Leadership

We believe there are at least six characteristics that make for successful leadership:

Vision

Before you can lead someone to the promised land, you must be able to see it yourself—even if you haven't been there yet. Indeed, the greatest leaders are able to create the future by vividly imagining it. John Kennedy envisioned a man on the moon. Stephen Jobs envisioned a world in which we all use personal computers. Mary Kay envisioned a network of small business women who were also saleswomen creating a business juggernaut. Why couldn't your vision be greater still?

While we encourage you to dream big, we also know that not every business prospers, nor is every dream realized. Nor is every vision about changing the world. Sometimes it's about changing a small part of it—seeing the successful child in the troubled youth you mentor, seeing a team that wins by playing together, picturing a residence hall in which students are a community of learners.

A vision is related to the goals that together will make the vision a reality, but a vision isn't a goal or even a collection of goals. A vision is a portrait of a future you wish to create. Although it comes from your imagination, it is something you can describe vividly. It is something that you can see and so you can describe it to others. A vision can sustain you in tough times. It can compel others to work together in the service of that vision. It can unite, motivate, and provide a common direction.

Ethics and Integrity

Before individuals will follow someone's lead, they must believe in that person. Leaders, therefore, must be true to their words. Their walk must match their talk. Why commit yourself to a cause to which the leader claims to be invested, but who behaves otherwise?

Ethics are important because leaders exert power. That power can be expended for good or evil. While membership in the human race carries with it the responsibility to behave honorably, leaders must bear an even heavier responsibility. When they pursue the common good, society is enriched. When they do not, others will suffer.

Ethics are important because without them organizations cannot flourish. Customers do not want to buy from a company they don't trust. Customers won't come back to a store that sells faulty products. Organizations perceived to be unethical may not last very long. Members of an organization will form a culture that is based upon the practices of its leadership. If managers, directors, vice-presidents, and CEOs lie to their employees and fail to keep their promises, the employees soon start lying to management. As deceit and petty politics rise, morale and productivity plummet. This is true whether the organization is a giant multinational corporation, a local high school, or a college fraternity.

There is inevitably an ethical component to leadership. Think of great leaders, and you think of honorable men and women. This doesn't mean our greatest leaders were saints, but they are remembered as having a firm moral center. It's not enough to have good ideas and charisma. You must have a coherent set of values. Your actions must match your words. If people don't know where you stand, they will not want to back you. If people doubt your word, why in the world would they want to follow you?

Service Orientation

You can intimidate some people into following your lead, but people follow out of fear only so long as you have some power over them. Most of us do not typically have that sort of positional power over those whom we would influence. If you want to be an effective leader of a student organization, you will be effective because you are somehow able to connect with members who volunteer their time and energy. Even in the business world, the best managers and executives know that their best staff members are, in essence, volunteers. Top employees can always get good jobs somewhere else.

The best leaders motivate people to *want* to follow them. How do you get people to want to? Communicating a compelling vision certainly helps, but others won't even consider your vision unless they're convinced you have their well-being at heart. Think about some leader whom you would gladly follow through thick or thin. Chances are, you believe this person respects you, cares about you, desires your success. The best leaders exude concern for their colleagues and constituents.

You demonstrate concern for those whom you would lead by being considerate, by understanding them, and by encouraging them. While your first image of a leader might be some take-charge person giving an inspiring speech, you must learn to listen if you want others to listen to you. Good leaders are empathic: they can see things from the other person's perspective. The very best leaders understand others deeply, grasping what events mean to their followers. Because good leaders know their followers well, they know what resources are needed in order for the followers to complete their missions. Much of a good leader's energy is devoted to preserving the well-being and morale of every member of the organization and of securing the resources to enable members to do their jobs. A true leader, then, serves the organization and its members.

Communication Skills

OK, you have a great idea—an idea that is positively visionary. It's almost certain that you will need help to make your vision a reality. How do you get others to buy into your vision? In order to lead you must communicate your vision to the people whom you want to help you. Not only must you paint a clear picture, you must persuade others to make a commitment to work with you towards the realization of your vision.

This is partly a "public speaking" issue. Can you stand up in front of a group and speak confidently and sincerely? Can you do this before a handful, a dozen, a roomful, a thousand? Speaking effectively before a group may intimidate or even terrify you, but it is a VERY useful skill. Among the activities that most executives claim to like is speaking before large groups.

In the business world, would be leaders are encouraged to master the art of the "parking lot speech." Everybody is busy, and the only time you have to sell your idea to a colleague may be in the minute or so when you meet in the parking lot on the way to or from the office. For students, the analog is the "walk to class speech." You run into somebody whose support you need, and you have just minutes together on your way to History class. Can you boil down your ideas so they are clear and simple, yet still persuasive before you reach the classroom?

If you are not sure of your persuasive abilities, work to improve them. Consider some of the following ways to improve this essential skill:

- **Take a class in public speaking**
- **Attend an assertiveness workshop**
- **Participate in a sales seminar or workshop**
- **Volunteer to give a committee's report to the group-at-large**
- **Join an organization**
- **Run for office in an organization**
- **Try out for a part in a play**

The written word is also an important tool for those who would lead. An executive with experience in both the public and private realm recently underscored the importance of writing clearly. Almost every day in the workaday world, you must write reports, memos, letters, summaries, and proposals. Your success hinges partly on how well you write. Moreover, if you write poorly, you leave a tainted track record. The only knowledge of your work that the CEO possesses might be your proposal. If it's laced with grammatical errors, misspelled words, and awkward phrasing, it is unlikely that your proposal will find favor. It is even less likely that your star will rise in the organization.

Communication is, of course, a two-way street. You must receive information from others as well as dispense it. Listening with sensitivity for the deeper meanings and emotions behind the words of others is vital for leaders. Through active listening, a leader can learn about the concerns of the members of an organization. By listening attentively, a leader demonstrates concern for those members and thereby motivates them. By listening, a leader can get ideas which will influence the very direction an organization takes.

Self Awareness.

As a leader, your biggest resource is yourself. Does it not, therefore, make sense to know as much as possible about this resource—***strengths and weaknesses, beliefs and values, skills and abilities***. If you understand your weakness in public speaking, you can work on improving that skill. You can also delegate that responsibility to another member of your team who will better express your organization's perspective.

We urge you to cultivate a clearer self-understanding while you are in college. If self awareness is valuable for every person who will be educated, it is crucial for those who will lead.

Warren Bennis, in *On Becoming a Leader*, states that to "know thyself" is to understand clearly the differences between the way you define yourself and the way others define you. Leaders create change. Since not everyone likes change, those who interact with leaders may define them quite differently than would the leaders themselves. Some will assume a woman lacks the toughness to lead. Others will assume that a person of color possesses insufficient talent for leadership. There are countless ways that constituents can dismiss someone's leadership—too new to the organization, the wrong age, from the wrong part of the world, from the wrong social class. It is the leader's firm sense of self that will enable that person to perform in the face of such resistance.

It is not just that leaders know themselves, however; it is that they constantly try to improve themselves. Leaders use their self awareness as a springboard for recreating themselves. When they discover deficiencies, they work to overcome them. They read, they train, they study successful leaders, they seek out the experiences which will enable them to grow.

Teamwork in Diverse Groups

Think back for a moment on some of your experiences as a member of a sports team, a member of a committee, or one of a team charged with completing a project. It is highly likely that you can recall some team member who was domineering, self-absorbed, inattentive, unfocused, argumentative, or irresponsible. Remember how frustrated you felt, how disheartening it was to have to cope with this character. You could have won the game, but Chris let everybody down because of poor practice habits. You could have had an outstanding organization which consistently got first-rate results, but Pat held the entire organization back because of a giant ego. Perhaps the group was able to compensate for the counter-productive member, but it made it harder for everyone else.

Managers and corporate recruiters are quite aware of the importance of teamwork. Business and management writers have covered many organizational success stories that were powered by effective teams.

Student organizations are no different. Fraternities and sororities, sports clubs, and professional societies are less successful without teamwork. No officer wants to take on new members who impede group progress. Therefore, you must be a team player in order to succeed in today's world. Team skills are crucial for your professional success. They are also necessary for your success as a student and as a developing leader.

In *The Breakthrough Team Player*, Andrew DuBrin lists skills and attitudes that make for effective teamwork including:

- **Assuming resonsibility for problems**
- **Willingness to commit to team goals**
- **Ability to see the big picture**
- **Belief in consensus**
- **Willingness to ask tough questions**
- **Helping team members do their jobs better**
- **Lending a hand during peak workloads**
- **Rarely turning down a co-worker request**

- **Openness to new ideas**
- **Recognizing the interests and achievements of others**
- **Active listening and information sharing**
- **Giving helpful criticism**
- **Receptiveness to helpful criticism**
- **Being a team player even when personally inconvenienced**

Learning to Lead

We believe that learning to lead is imperative for every college student. Yet many students are notoriously indifferent to the leadership opportunities available to them. Leadership certainly requires careful reflection. Taking classes, attending speeches, and reading books about leadership can provide students with both insight and inspiration about their own capacity to lead. We believe, however, that leadership is a "contact sport." You learn by entering the fray. If you are not a member of an organization, if you never vote, if you avoid participating in the governance of your residence hall—your commitment to learning to lead is questionable.

In order to get a college degree, you are required to take an array of courses, including core course, courses in a major, and a smattering of electives. Chances are, you are NOT required to study leadership either in the classroom or through your involvement in campus activities. You will be cheating yourself, however, and jeopardizing your career if you do not resolve to improve as a leader. Today's apathetic student is tomorrow's indifferent citizen whose very inactivity amounts to fiddling while society burns.

While we urge you to cultivate your capacity to lead, do not make the error of confusing a position or an office with true leadership. While chairing a committee, presiding over an organization, and joining campus organizations all provide excellent leadership developmental opportunities, none of these inevitably guarantees excellence. That comes from practicing the six habits we identified at the top of this section. Leadership then is about serving others and operating ethically. It is about envisioning how to make things better and communicating that vision effectively. Leadership is about understanding yourself and collaborating with all kinds of people. These are six skills which are as important as anything you will ever learn, and no matter how committed you are to cultivating them, you will never master them. Like most things in life that matter, learning to lead is a life-long process. It's time to get started!

SUMMARY

In case you haven't figured it out by now, improving the quality of your life has just as much impact on your college success as learning academic skills and strategies. Developing life skills such as health and wellness; communication and relationships; diversity and leadership really do matter, not only in your college success, but in the workforce and your personal life!

SUGGESTED READINGS

Neck, Christopher, and Charles Manz. *Mastering Self-Leadership: Empowering Yourself for Personal Excellence*. New Jersey: Prentice Hall, 2006.

Baldwin, Amy. *Community College Experience Plus*. 2nd ed. New Jersey, Prentice Hall, 2010.

NAME: _____ DATE: _____

EXERCISE 12.1: WHAT IS YOUR STRESS INDEX?

Do You Frequently   Yes   No

1. Neglect your diet?   ____   ____

2. Try to do everything yourself?   ____   ____

3. Blow up easily?   ____   ____

4. Seek unrealistic goals?   ____   ____

5. Fail to see the humor in situations others find funny?   ____   ____

6. Act rude?   ____   ____

7. Make a "big deal" of everything?   ____   ____

8. Look to other people to make things happen?   ____   ____

9. Have difficulty making decisions?   ____   ____

10. Complain you are disorganized?   ____   ____

11. Avoid people whose ideas are different from your own?   ____   ____

12. Keep everything inside?   ____   ____

13. Neglect exercise?   ____   ____

14. Have only a few supportive relationships?   ____   ____

15. Use psychoactive drugs, such as sleeping pills and tranquilizers, without physician
    approval?   ____   ____

16. Get too little rest?   ____   ____

17. Get angry when you are kept waiting?   ____   ____

18. Ignore stress symptoms?   ____   ____

19. Procrastinate?   ____   ____

20. Think there is only one right way to do something?   ____   ____

21. Fail to build in relaxation time?   ____   ____

22. Gossip?   ____   ____

23. Race through the day?   ____   ____

24. Spend a lot of time lamenting the past?   ____   ____

25. Fail to get a break from noise and crowds?   ____   ____

What Your Score Means

Score 1 for each "yes" answer, 0 for each "no." Total your score.

1–6 There are few hassles in your life. Make sure, though, that you aren't trying so hard to avoid problems that you shy away from challenges.

7–13 You've got your life in pretty good control. Work on the choices and habits that could still be causing some unnecessary stress in your life.

14–20 You're approaching the danger zone. You may well be suffering stress-related symptoms and your relationships could be strained. Think carefully about choices you've made and take relaxation breaks every day.

Above 20 Emergency! You must stop now, rethink how you are living, change your attitudes, and pay scrupulous attention to your diet, exercise, and relation programs.

NAME: _____ DATE: _____

EXERCISE 12.2: INTERCULTURAL INTERVIEW

Find a student, faculty member, or administrator on campus whose cultural background differs from your own and ask if you can interview that person about his or her culture. Use the following questions in your interview:

1. How is "family" defined in your culture, and what are the traditional roles and responsibilities of different family members?

2. What are the traditional gender (male vs. female) roles associated with your culture? Are they changing?

3. What is your culture's approach to time? Is there an emphasis on punctuality? Is moving quickly and getting things done rapidly valued more than reflection and deliberation?

4. What are your culture's staple foods and favorite beverages?

5. What cultural traditions or rituals are highly valued and commonly practiced?

6. What special holidays are celebrated?

* From *Thriving in College and Beyond: Research-Based Strategies for Academic Success and Personal Development* by Jospeh B. Cuseo, Aaron Thompson, Michele Campagna, and Viki S. Fecas. Copyright © 2013 by Kendall Hunt Publishing Company. Reprinted by permission.

EXERCISE 12.3: HIDDEN BIAS TEST

Go to www.tolerance.org/activity/test-yourself-hidden-bias and take one or more of the hidden bias tests on the Web site. These tests assess subtle bias with respect to gender, age, Native Americans, African Americans, Asian Americans, religious denominations, sexual orientations, disabilities, and body weight. The site allows you to assess whether you have a bias toward any of these groups.

Self-Assessment Questions

1. Did the results reveal any bias that you were unaware of?

2. Did you think the assessment results were accurate or valid?

3. What do you think best accounts for or explains your results?

4. If your closest family member and best friend took the test, how do you think their results would compare with yours?

EXERCISE 12.4: COMMUNICATION STYLES

DIRECTIONS: Read the situations listed below and decide whether each of the statements given is a passive, assertive, or aggressive response. Use the following codes to indicate your choice: A—Passive, B—Assertive, and C—Aggressive.

Situation 1: You're out with your friends and are trying to make a group decision on which movie to see. One person has just mentioned a movie you don't want to see. You say:

• You always pick movies I don't like and just think about what you want to see. You're really selfish!

• I don't care for movies with too much violence. How about one of those showing at the Plaza Theater?

• Well, I don't know much about that movie. If that's what everyone else wants to see, I'll go along.

Situation 2: You and two friends car-pool to classes. One friend is not very dependable and has twice failed to call on her day to drive to let you know she wasn't going to class. The first time it happened, you finally called her and managed to get to class on time, but the second time, your spouse/roommate had made plans for the car, and you ended up without a ride. You're angry at your friend's lack of responsibility and say:

• You are totally unreliable, and I refuse to be involved with you any longer. Drive yourself from now on!

• Gee, Susan, do you think you could be sure and call me next time if you're not going to be able to drive?

• Susan, I have a heavy schedule this semester and can't afford to miss any classes. Since you haven't been able to keep our ride arrangement, I prefer that you drive yourself for the rest of the semester.

NAME: _____ **DATE:** _____

EXERCISE 12.5: ASSERTIVE COMMUNICATION PRACTICE

After reading about assertive communication skills and learning to distinguish among communication styles, it is important to be able to practice using assertive communication responses. Read over the situations below and use "I" messages to write out your assertive communication responses. Remember that becoming skilled in any area requires practice!

Use the following guidelines in writing your responses:

- **TAKE OWNERSHIP OF YOUR FEELINGS** by stating: I feel/I am (specify the emotion—angry, disappointed, hurt, sorry, annoyed, scared, frustrated, concerned, etc.)

- **DESCRIBE THE SITUATION OR EVENT THAT TOOK PLACE** rather than making personal comments or blaming/attacking the other person. Be specific in your description and focus on one issue at a time.

- **DESCRIBE THE EFFECT OF THE BEHAVIOR**—what are the consequences of the behavior upon you?

If you are requesting a behavior change from another person, be specific about the change you want to see.

If you are going to change your own behavior based upon the response made by another person, be prepared to follow through.

Use the following format in writing your responses:

I feel/I am _____(specify emotion)_____ when _____(describe behavior or event)_____
because _____(describe effect upon you.)_____ .

Situation 1: One student in your history class often interrupts others who are talking and has now interrupted you. You say:

I feel/I am _____ when _____

because _____ .

Situation 2: You've stopped by your instructor's office during his/her scheduled office hours for the second time, and she/he hasn't been there. When you next see your instructor, you say:

I feel/I am _____ when _____

_____

because _____ .

Situation 3: You did not understand your doctor's explanation for why she/he has ordered a battery of blood tests. You say:

I feel/I am _____ when _____

_____

because _____ .

Situation 4: A friend borrowed a CD/tape from you over two weeks ago and hasn't returned it. You say:

I feel/I am_____ when _____

_____

because _____ .

Situation 5: You and your best friend commute to classes together. You've been trying to save money, but s/he continually wants to stop off at fast-food restaurants before going home. You say:

I feel/I am _____ when _____

_____

because _____ .

Situation 6: Your roommate/partner/sibling/ has not completed his/her agreed-upon household responsibilities. You say:

I feel/I am _____ when _____

_____

because _____ .

EXERCISE 12.6: LEADERSHIP SELF-ASSESSMENT

Vision

In order to be "visionary," you must first be well-informed. Today, that means being a continuous learner, both in school and on your own. How many of the following statements can you affirm?

_____ 1. I frequently read a daily newspaper.

_____ 2. I can name four political columnists of varying ideological points of view.

_____ 3. I frequently read a weekly news magazine.

_____ 4. I often watch a national news show on television.

_____ 5. I often read a business periodical (e.g., *Wall Street Journal, Fortune, Business Week*, etc.)

_____ 6. I follow the latest developments in science and technology.

_____ 7. I've been to a play within the past year.

_____ 8. I've seen a movie with subtitles within the past year.

_____ 9. I have read an unassigned work of literature within the past year.

_____ 10. I periodically read a professional or trade journal within my field of interest.

_____ 11. I attend meetings or conferences of a professional society.

_____ 12. I've learned some new computer skills within the past year.

_____ 13. I sometimes discuss my field of interest with others to find out more about it.

_____ 14. I have attended a serious concert/performance within the past year.

_____ 15. I occasionally watch television documentaries that cover history, science, or current affairs.

_____ 16. I have eaten the food of at least six different countries within the past year.

_____ 17. I have friends and acquaintances of a variety of ethnic and religious backgrounds.

_____ 18. I can readily identify most countries on a world globe.

_____ 19. I understand some basic features of most major cultural groups throughout the world.

_____ 20. I have read a serious nonfiction book which was not assigned within the past year.

_____ 21. I know the basic tenets of each of the world's major religions.

What other actions do you take to indicate your commitment to continuous learning?

What do your responses reveal about your commitment to continuous learning? What do you need to do differently in the future?

Ethics and Integrity

Name an individual whom you judge to be high in integrity: _____

How long have you known this individual?

_____

How long did it take before you recognized the person's integrity?

_____

_____

What characterizes this person that spells integrity?

_____

_____

What actions does this person take that suggest integrity?

_____

_____

Can you identify a situation in which this person's integrity was tested?

_____

_____

How did (s)he handle the test?

_____

_____

Name an individual whom you judge to lack integrity:

How long have you known this individual?

_____

(Continued)

How long did it take before you recognized the person lacked integrity?

_____

_____

What characterizes this person that spells weak integrity?

_____

_____

What actions does this person take that suggest weak integrity?

_____

_____

Can you identify a situation in which this person's integrity was tested?

_____

_____

How did (s)he handle the test?

_____

_____

In what related ways are you like the person with high integrity?

_____

_____

In what related ways are you like the person with weak integrity?

_____

_____

How will you increase your personal integrity?

_____

_____

Service Orientation

There are many ways you can serve others: through the political process, through philanthropic work, and through your demeanor in daily interactions. Check those items below which reflect YOUR personal behavior:

_____ 1. I'm registered to vote.

_____ 2. I vote in most elections.

_____ 3. I know who my congressman is.

_____ 4. I've worked in a political campaign.

_____ 5. I know the news well enough to be an informed voter.

_____ 6. I contribute money in support of my beliefs.

_____ 7. I contribute time in support of my beliefs.

_____ 8. I stay informed of the causes I'm committed to addressing.

_____ 9. I contribute money to the cause.

_____ 10. I contribute time and energy to the cause.

_____ 11. I'm a member of a group which serves the cause.

_____ 12. I avoid activities which harm the cause.

_____ 13. I compliment people when they succeed.

_____ 14. I congratulate people when they win an award.

_____ 15. I encourage people when they have setbacks.

_____ 16. I send notes or e-mail to encourage people.

_____ 17. I keep track of people's birthdays.

_____ 18. I send birthday cards to friends and acquaintances.

_____ 19. I give gifts or stage a surprise when a colleague achieves something big.

_____ 20. I work more for organizational goals than for personal glory.

Communication

_____ 1. I can be silent when others need to speak.

_____ 2. I can hear the feelings and meanings behind the words.

_____ 3. I can ask questions that encourage self-revelation.

_____ 4. I avoid criticizing other persons.

_____ 5. I convey my interest by eye contact and body language.

_____ 6. I ask questions in class.

_____ 7. I contribute to class discussions.

_____ 8. I offer my views during meetings.

_____ 9. If I disagree strongly during a meeting, I'll say so.

(Continued)

_____ 10. I can effectively report a committee's discussion back to the main group.

_____ 11. I can run a meeting effectively.

_____ 12. I know Robert's Rules of Order.

_____ 13. I can address a small group effectively.

_____ 14. I can hold a large group's attention when I speak.

_____ 15. I can make a strong case for my point of view.

If you're not satisfied with your persuasive skills, here are ten antidotes.

1. *Prepare a meaningful question before class. Ask it during class.*

2. *Prepare a thoughtful observation before class. State it when appropriate during class.*

3. *Think about an issue likely to come up at your next meeting. Ask for the floor, and make your point.*

4. *Think about a perspective with which you're likely to disagree at the next meeting. Prepare a rejoinder. State your rejoinder at the next meeting.*

5. *Volunteer to speak for your committee.*

6. *Volunteer to run a committee meeting. Prepare an agenda, and stick to it.*

7. *Study Robert's Rules of Order.*

8. *Volunteer to speak before a small group on something that's important to you. Prepare thoroughly, and practice your speech.*

9. *Volunteer to speak before a large group on something that's important to you. Prepare thoroughly, and practice your speech.*

10. *Try to convince a friend or acquaintance to join you in some cause.*

Self Awareness

It is difficult to assess yourself accurately. For example, answer the following question: Are you blind to your own faults? Even if you are, your blindness prevents you from knowing it. There are some habits that suggest an openness to self-examination that are worthy of cultivating, however. How many do you practice?

_____ 1. I read any critique of my work made by a professor and reflect on it.

_____ 2. I attempt to understand my personality inventory scores in this class.

_____ 3. I solicit feedback from others about my performance.

_____ 4. I am willing to take some moderate risks in order to improve as a leader.

_____ 5. When others criticize me, I honestly try to weigh the validity of their remarks.

_____ 6. I compare my own skills to those discussed in this section.

_____ 7. When I read other leadership literature, I use the ideas to look at myself.

_____ 8. I can honestly identify some areas in which I need to improve myself.

_____ 9. I can honestly identify some areas of personal strength.

_____ 10. I use experiential activities in class and workshops to learn about myself.

Teamwork

_____ 1. I contribute my fair share on group projects.

_____ 2. When I disagree with other team members, I say so.

_____ 3. When forming a team, I try to select diverse talents.

_____ 4. I understand the stages of group development.

_____ 5. I understand how my personality best contributes to team performance.

Putting It All Together

Most of us will never head up a major corporation or hold a major political office. Nonetheless, we can exert leadership in many ways—by holding an office in a smaller organization, by speaking up at organizational meetings, by volunteering to handle a problem. Here are some ways you could stretch your leadership wings.

1. Identify an issue about which you have strong, unexpressed feelings in an organization to which you belong. Think about what you could say or do to strengthen the organization's stand on this issue. Craft a statement which you could make at a meeting. Imagine what it would be like to make the statement. What would the response of your fellow members be? Can you think of effective ways of responding to them? Pick an ally within the organization that you could share your views with. How does (s)he respond? Does (s)he have any suggestions for improvements? Are you accurately understanding the opposing point of view? Select a time when you will raise the issue and state your position. Go for it!

2. Identify a concern or a problem which you have. Then identify a person in authority who could address your concern. Think of a _reasonable_ course of action which the authority could take to improve the situation. Make _sure_ that the authority has the power to effect the change you recommend, that the action is cost-effective, that it will not cause undue damage elsewhere. Craft a recommendation you could make to the authority. Practice it with an ally. Make an appointment with the authority. When you meet, explain your concern, recommend your solution, and state your willingness to help implement the solution, if that's feasible.

3. Identify an office or position you would like to hold. It should be in an organization in whose goals you believe. Declare your intention to run for office. Or, if more appropriate, speak with current officers about your desire to assume a greater leadership role. If you run for office, secure the commitment of some friends who will help you. Get organized, plan a campaign, implement it. If the more likely route to power is through appointment, discuss your desire to serve on a particular committee or as a particular office holder. Explain why you think you can do the job. Ask for feedback and a commitment to be given the opportunity to lead.

4. Read some books and articles on leadership and citizenship.

5. Attend a leadership workshop.

6. Sign up for an academic class in leadership.

EXERCISE 12.7:   CASE STUDY

Hate Crime: A Racially Motivated Murder

Jasper County, Texas, has a population of approximately 31,000 people. In this: county, 80 percent of the people are. White, 18 percent are Black, and 2 percent are of other races. The county's poverty rate is considerably higher than national average, and its average household income is significantly lower. In 1998, the mayor, the president of the chamber of commerce, and two councilmen Were Black, From the outside, jasper appeared to be a town with racial harmony, and its Black and. White leaders were quick to state that there was no racial tension in Jasper.

However, on June 7, 1996, James Byrd Jr., a 49-year-old. African American man, was walking home along a road one evening and was offered a ride by three White men, Rather than taking Byrd home, Lawrence Brewer (age 31), John King (age 23), .and Shawn Berry (age 23), three individuals linked to White supremacist groups, took Byrd to ah isolated area and began heating him. They dropped his pants to his ankles, painted his face black, chained Byrd to their truck, and dragged him for approximately three miles. The truck was driven in a zigzag fashion to inflict maximum pain on the victim. Byrd was decapitated after his body collided with a culvert in a ditch alongside the road. His skin, arms, genitalia, and other body parts were strewn along the road, while his torso was found dumped in front of a Black cemetery. Medical examiners testified that Byrd was alive for much of, the dragging incident.

While in prison awaiting trial, Brewer wrote letters to King and other inmates. In one letter, Brewer wrote: "Well, I did it and am longer a virgin. It was a rush and I'm still licking my lips for more." Once the trials were completed, Brewer and King were sentenced to death. Both Brewer and King, whose bodies were covered with racist tattoos, had been on parole before the incident, and they had previously been cellmates. King had spent an extensive amount of time in prison, where he began to associate with White males in an environment in which each race was pitted against the other.

As a result of the murder, Byrd's family created the James Byrd Foundation for Racial Healing in 1998. On January 20, 1999, a wrought iron fence that separated Black and White graves for more than 150 years in Jasper Cemetery was removed in a special unity service. Members of the racist Ku Klux Klan have since visited the gravesite of Byrd several times, leaving racist stickers and other marks that have angered the Jasper community and Byrd's family.

Sources Houston Chronicle (June 14, 1998), San Antonio Express News (September 17, 1999) Louisiana Weekly (February 3, 2003).

Reflection and Discussion Questions

1.   What factors do you think were responsible for causing this incident to take place?

2.   Could this incident have been prevented? If yes, how? If no, why not?'

3.   How likely do you think it is that an incident like this could take place in your hometown or near your college campus?

4.   If this event took place in your hometown, how would you and members of your family and community react?

Credits

Chapter 4

This chapter contains adapted material from: "Learning with Style" from *Practical Approaches for Building Study Skills and Vocabulary*, second edition by Gary Funk et al, © 1996 by Kendall Hunt Publishing Company; "Understanding the Way You Learn" from *The Community College: A New Beginning*, third edition by Linda S. Aguilar, Sandra J. Hopper, and Therese M. Kuzlik, copyright © 2001 by Kendall Hunt Publishing Company; and "Learning: The Cornerstone of Success" from *Building Success* by Bill Osher and Joann Ward, copyright © 2000 by Bill Osher and Joann Ward.

Chapter 5

This chapter contains adapted material from: "Prioritizing Your Time to Match Your Goals" from *The Community College: A New Beginning*, third edition by Linda S. Aguilar, Sandra J. Hopper, and Therese M. Kuzlik, copyright © 2003 by Kendall Hunt Publishing Company; "Learning Strategies for Academic Success" from *Your Utah State Experience: Strategies for Success*, eighth edition by Noelle A. Call and LaVell E. Saunders, copyright © 2002 by Academic Support Services, Utah State University; "Creating Time through Effective Time Management" from *Life Skills for College: A Curriculum for Life* by Earl J. Ginter and Ann Shanks Glauser, copyright © 2002 by Earl J. Ginter and Ann Shanks Glauser; and "Taming Time" from *Practical Skills for Building Study Skills and Vocabulary*, second edition by Gary Funk et al, copyright © 1996 by Kendall Hunt Publishing Company.

Chapter 6

This chapter contains adapted material from: "Your Memory at Work" from *The Community College: A New Beginning*, third edition by Linda S. Aguilar, Sandra J. Hopper, and Therese M. Kuzlik, copyright © 2003 by Kendall Hunt Publishing Company; "Remembering to Concentrate" from *Practical Approaches for Building Study Skills and Vocabulary*, second edition by Gary Funk et al, copyright © 1996 by Kendall Hunt Publishing Company; and "Learning Strategies for Academic Success" from *Your Utah State Experience: Strategies for Success*, eighth edition by Noelle A. Call and LaVell E. Saunders, copyright © 2002 by Academic Support Services, Utah State University.

Chapter 7

This chapter contains adapted material from: "Learning Strategies for Academic Success" from *Your Utah State Experience: Strategies for Success*, eighth edition by Noelle A. Call and LaVell E. Saunders, copyright © 2002 by Academic Support Services, Utah State University; "How to Study" from *The Community College: A New Beginning*, third edition by Linda S. Aguilar, Sandra J. Hopper, and Therese M. Kuzlik, copyright © 2001 by Kendall Hunt Publishing Company; and "Learning: The Cornerstone of Success" from *Building Success* by Bill Osher and Joann Ward, copyright © 2000 by Bill Osher and Joann Ward.

Chapter 8

This chapter contains adapted material from: "Becoming a Better Note Taker" from *The Community College: A New Beginning*, third edition by Linda S. Aguilar, Sandra J. Hopper, and Therese M. Kuzlik, copyright © 2001 by Kendall Hunt Publishing Company; "Learning Strategies for Academic Success" from *Your Utah State Experience: Strategies for Success*, eighth edition by Noelle A. Call and LaVell E. Saunders, copyright © 2002 by Academic Support Services, Utah State University; "Listening and Note Taking" from *Keys to Excellence*, fourth edition by Carol Cooper et al, © 1997 by Kendall Hunt Publishing Company; "Taking Notes of Lectures" from *Practical Approaches for Building Study Skills and Vocabulary*, second edition by Gary Funk et al, © 1996 by Kendall Hunt Publishing Company; "Survival Note Taking: Pencils, Books, and Teachers' Dirty Looks" from *Surviving College: A "Real World" Experience* by Connie Schick, Eileen Astor-Stetson, and Brett L. Beck, copyright © 2001 by Connie Schick, Eileen Astor-Stetson, and Brett L. Beck; and "Note Making" from *Get What You Want Out of College* by Elizabeth Boucher and John Pigg, copyright © 2003 by Elizabeth Boucher and John Pigg.

Chapter 9

This chapter contains adapted material from: "Taking Tests with Confidence" from *The Community College: A New Beginning*, third edition by Linda S. Aguilar, Sandra J. Hopper, and Therese M. Kuzlik, copyright © 2001 by Kendall Hunt Publishing Company; "The Art of Test Taking" from *Keys to Excellence*, fourth edition by Carol Cooper et al, © 1997 by Kendall Hunt

Chapter 10

Chapter 12